D1241384

A Quiet Corner of the War

A Quiet Corner of the War

The Civil War Letters of
GILBERT AND ESTHER CLAFLIN,
Oconomowoc, Wisconsin, 1862–1863

Gilbert Claflin and Esther Claflin

Edited by JUDY COOK

THE UNIVERSITY OF WISCONSIN PRESS

PUBLICATION OF THESE LETTERS
IS AIDED BY A GRANT FROM
Jewish Federation of Greater Hartford

The University of Wisconsin Press
1930 Monroe Street, 3rd Floor
Madison, Wisconsin 53711-2059
uwpress.wisc.edu

3 Henrietta Street
London WC2E 8LU, England
eurospanbookstore.com

Printed in the United States of America

Library of Congress Cataloging-in-Publication Data

Claflin, Gilbert.
A quiet corner of the war : the Civil War letters of Gilbert and Esther Claflin,
Oconomowoc, Wisconsin, 1862–1863 / Gilbert Claflin and Esther Claflin ;
edited by Judy Cook.
p. cm.
Includes bibliographical references and index.
ISBN 978-0-299-29480-9 (cloth : alk. paper) — ISBN 978-0-299-29483-0 (e-book)
1. Claflin, Gilbert—Correspondence. 2. Claflin, Esther—Correspondence.
3. Claflin family—Correspondence. 4. Soldiers—Wisconsin—Oconomowoc—
Correspondence. 5. Wisconsin—History—Civil War, 1861–1865—Personal narratives.
6. United States—History—Civil War, 1861–1865—Personal narratives.
7. Oconomowoc (Wis.)—History. I. Claflin, Esther. II. Cook, Judy. III. Title.
E601.C545 2013
973.7′8—dc23
2013010467

Contents

Illustrations

Foreword

KEITH BOHANNON

A *Quiet Corner of the War* consists of the edited Civil War correspondence of Gilbert and Esther Claflin, a farming couple from the town of Oconomowoc in southeastern Wisconsin. The Claflins wrote these letters between November 1862 and September 1863 when Gilbert Claflin served in the Thirty-Fourth Wisconsin Infantry Regiment of the Union Army. The regiment had its origins in a state draft enacted in the fall of 1862 by Governor Edward Salomon at the insistence of U.S. Secretary of War Edwin Stanton. When the Thirty-Fourth formed for nine-month service at Camp Washburn, Milwaukee, in December 1862, its ranks included large numbers of German Americans opposed to conscription, a government measure these immigrants thought they had left behind in their homelands upon migrating to the United States.

Gilbert Claflin's earliest letters describe numerous desertions from his regiment while in barracks and en route south. On January 18, 1863, he opined that "the 34th regiment of drafted men will be of little service to the government." Claflin was not alone in expressing such a pessimistic assessment. A Wisconsin newspaper correspondent characterized the Thirty-Fourth as being plagued with poor discipline, having little understanding of the use of arms, and being almost strangers to battalion drill. Army officers, likely influenced by anti-German sentiments, were "in the habit of saying that the regiment is a humbug, and many uncharitable persons are prone to believe them."[1]

Perhaps because of the Thirty-Fourth's short term of enlistment and problems with desertion and discipline, Union military authorities sent it at the end of January 1863 to Columbus, Kentucky, for garrison duty. A size-able portion of the Thirty-Fourth, including Claflin's company, remained there for the duration of its service. Columbus, located on high ground along the eastern bank of the Mississippi River, had been heavily fortified by the Confederates during their occupation of the post. The fall of Forts Henry and Donelson to Union forces in February 1862 prompted the Confederate evacuation of Columbus—poorly named the "Gibraltar of the West"—on March 2, 1862. Union troops marched in the following day.

The letters that Gilbert Claflin sent home from Columbus are note-worthy for providing details of occupation duty in a fortified town in the Upper South. Unlike many men in the Thirty-Fourth, Claflin was patriotic and at times actually took to soldiering, claiming in the fall of 1862 that he liked drilling first rate. Several months later, Gilbert told Esther that he had "but little faith in the Union sentiment of the majority of the people that I have seen in Kentucky." As Benjamin F. Cooling relates in *Fort Donelson's Legacy*, Union soldiers in garrisons like Columbus worried constantly about guerrilla raids, and Gilbert's letters describe the measures taken to guard against such incursions.

Some of the most striking passages in Gilbert Claflin's correspondence concern the ex-slaves who congregated in Columbus seeking freedom within Union lines. Claflin, a staunch abolitionist, related successful efforts to recruit freedmen into regiments of U.S. Colored Troops. Claflin person-ally encouraged ex-slaves to join the Union Army, noting that many had "such a burning hatred towards the slave master that they would not hesi-tate a moment were they in their power to strike the deadly blow."

Gilbert Claflin, a deacon in the Congregationalist Church, also took a keen interest in the spiritual activities of freedpeople. A May 25, 1863, letter offers a vivid description of two "Negro meetings," one of which included a sermon delivered by an African American preacher. The scriptural story of "Moses' passage through the Red Sea leading the children of Israel through safely; whilst the Egyptians were destroyed" had been chosen to "awaken strong feelings in the hearts of [the] colored listeners." After offer-ing details about ex-slaves shouting, clapping, and "weeping for joy," Claflin concluded that "few I believe can look upon such a scene and have a heart to ridicule or disturb them."

Claflin and other white Union soldiers in Columbus did more than just observe African Americans worshipping. The soldiers helped build a church for these people, Claflin investing a "small sum" in the endeavor. While

Gilbert unfortunately related few additional details in his correspondence home about this activity, he wrote Milwaukee Congregationalist minister and abolitionist William De Loss Love of helping organize the first freedman's Sabbath school in Columbus. Those slaves who had books brought them to the school, Claflin related, "but not one in fifty could read."[2]

Esther Claflin comes across in her letters as a religious and industrious woman who struggled periodically with depression and serious health issues. At one point she describes an ailment that caused excessive coughing and prevented her for weeks from walking farther than the family's barn. Despite such trials, she expressed self-confidence in her ability to manage the farm, claiming in the spring of 1863 that "we get along on the whole better than I ever thought we could without you." Like Gilbert, Esther expressed patriotic sentiments, writing that "I try to be very heroic and I almost always feel glad that I can suffer with my country."

The range of Esther's activities reveal a great deal about how Northern farm women dealt with economic hard times during the Civil War. She oversaw the family's budget, being extremely frugal and assuring her husband that he would "not find fault with my managing" money. By the end of March 1863, she told Gilbert that she had "repaired almost everything" she could think of, including shoes and clothing. She maintained a garden, washed wool from the family's several dozen sheep and worked it into flannel, and sold wool, wheat, and currants to contribute to the family's small savings.

Like the farm women described in Judith Giesberg's *Army at Home: Women and the Civil War on the Northern Home Front*, Esther Claflin relied on extended family to assist with the heaviest farm chores. Although Esther and her boys sowed crops in the family's farm fields, broke new land, and hoed beans and corn, the mother considered threshing wheat in the fall a chore too difficult for her or the teenage sons. Esther's older brother William, who lived nearby, instead performed this strenuous task, also helping with cutting oats and selling some of the family's wool.

Esther Claflin's correspondence, as well as a few letters from her sons, suggests some of the ways that the Civil War affected adolescents. The Claflin boys took on additional chores while their father was away, but apparently also taxed their mother's patience at times. Esther told Gilbert twice she needed him at home to deal with their sons by providing "advice and restraint." The couple's older son, Elton, lost all interest in going to school during his father's enlistment. Instead, Elton's mother related how his "whole mind is taken up" with farmwork, which included at one point cutting hay on shares for a neighbor.

Even as her husband's nine months of military service came to a close, Esther Claflin continued to worry about her country and family, especially several brothers serving in Union Army regiments that had sustained heavy casualties in battle. On August 4, 1863, she wrote Gilbert that the "great National trouble that is now upon us has, I believe, spread a shadow over my life that time will never obliterate." Readers interested in the Northern homefront and the experiences of Union soldiers in the occupied South will find much to ponder in the correspondence of Esther and Gilbert Claflin. Those same readers owe a debt to editor Judy Cook for doing a fine job of providing family background about the Claflins and identifying the people, places, and events mentioned in their letters.

NOTES

1. Frank L. Clement, *Wisconsin in the Civil War* (Madison: State Historical Society of Wisconsin, 1997), 27–30; M.D., "Our Troops in Western Kentucky," clipping from unidentified Wisconsin newspaper, Newspaper clippings, 1861–1930, vol. 4, Wisconsin Local History and Biography Articles, Wisconsin Historical Society, Madison, Wisconsin.

2. Gilbert Claflin apparently assisted Love in writing a brief sketch of the Thirty-Fourth Wisconsin. William De Loss Love, *Wisconsin in the War of the Rebellion*, 2 vols. (Chicago and New York: Church and Goodman; Sheldon & Co., 1866), 2:849–50.

Preface

This fascinating window on history opens through the correspondence of my great-great-grandparents Gilbert and Esther Claflin. Gilbert was a forty-year-old Wisconsin farmer when he was drafted to serve in the Union army in November 1862. From that December, when his regiment was mustered in, until September 1863, Gilbert was with the Thirty-Fourth Wisconsin Infantry while his wife Esther struggled with farm and family. During these ten months, they exchanged roughly one hundred twenty letters about their lives and the goings-on around them. The horrors of the battlefield and the grim realities of war hovered in the background, but they did not come to either Esther in Oconomowoc in southeast Wisconsin or Gilbert at Fort Halleck in Columbus in western Kentucky. In their quiet corners of the war, Gilbert and Esther, an intelligent, thoughtful couple, had time to observe, reflect, and question, and also support one another. The Claflins' solid marriage makes them a unit, even though they were separated by a great distance. It seems fitting to speak of this chapter of their life in the singular and to call their shared experience "A Quiet Corner of the War."

The book begins with a short prologue that takes you back to November 1862 in Oconomowoc and quickly sets the stage at the point in which the letters begin: when Gilbert is drafted. We introduce you to this delightful Wisconsin farming family and the community where they live. You will meet Gilbert and Esther, their extended family, and a few of their closest friends in the small town and the surrounding farms.

The letters are presented chronologically from the time Gilbert was drafted until he was mustered out. Relevant notes with clarifying information and interesting asides about people, things, and events that Gilbert and Esther mention follow many of the letters.

The letters themselves tell a fascinating story of a family, community, and country severely challenged—yet in some ways strengthened—by America's great Civil War. As we read Gilbert and Esther's correspondence, we get to know the couple much better through the words they use, their observations, and the way they react to each of the events of their ten months of separation. Because we have nearly all the letters from both Gilbert and Esther during this time, we do not have much need of a twenty-first-century voice to fill in what is missing. We explore what life was like in a community where many of the men left to be in harm's way and in the army camps where Gilbert was inducted, stationed, and mustered out.

Both general readers and researchers should be pleased to find how articulate and insightful the Claflins are in their letters. Gilbert was forty years old when he was drafted—twice the age of many in his regiment. His maturity and his calm, cheerful temperament are evident in his letters. Esther shares her own thoughts and experiences as she keeps farm and family together, and provides an outsider's perspective to what Gilbert says about the war and military life. In addition, she is the one who encourages Gilbert to share more details. In one letter she writes, "I have a sort of aching desire to know *just exactly* how you are situated. Can't you write the little minutia? That is what interests us most, and what we never get anywhere else." Gilbert, to our delight, obliges.

Readers who may be interested in social history will find insights into how women and adolescents were affected by the extended absence of husbands and fathers. Esther writes not only about herself but about friends and other family members in the community. There is information about how they dealt with farming, child care, financial matters, emotions, and health issues. Readers can watch as Esther gains confidence in her abilities to run things while Gilbert is away.

Those interested in Union army life in the Civil War will also gain understanding from Gilbert's letters. He shares his observations on the state draft, desertion, bonuses, and substitutes. He writes of conversations with Confederate prisoners, ex-slaves, and other soldiers. His letters describe artillery practice, discipline, food, and both manmade and natural surroundings. Sometimes Gilbert's duties change, and he views situations from different perspectives. For example, while at the fort, Gilbert was at different times a company cook, a prison guard, or the person in charge of the hospital. His descriptions of Negro camp meetings and of funerals and his reactions to emancipation are particularly fascinating.

The epilogue then brings us back to the present and to me, Gilbert and Esther's great-great-granddaughter, and my discovery of the letters. The epilogue also tells some of what happened to Gilbert and Esther and their family after Gilbert returned home and the letters ended.

At the end of the book are extensive appendixes that give clarifying information in much greater detail. The appendixes also includes generals' correspondence corroborating military actions mentioned in the book and details of my transcribing and editing process.

Transcribing the letters was a delight. The physical letters and the handwriting of Gilbert and Esther, as well as that of their sons Elton and Price, were a personal invitation to the past. As I read the letters, their lives opened, and through their accounts and their language, I glimpsed their worlds in 1862 and 1863: the small, new town of Oconomowoc and the raw outpost of the Union army.

It was difficult to decide how much to edit the letters to make them more readable. These are letters from another age and were not meant to be read by folks who did not know the writer well. Changes are detailed in Appendix E.

On my first pass through the letters, I was eager and fearful. The stories excited me; I needed to learn what happened next. The pages were fragile, the ink faded, pencil fainter still. It took time to get used to the hand, the spelling, the language of each of the participants. Gilbert's "first rate," "prospects," "line," "enjoy each other's society" were words and phrases he used repeatedly. I smiled to see some of those same phrases echoed in the letters his sons wrote to him.

I didn't want to handle the pages too much, so I did not shuffle them to find the right order. Someone else had put many of them in order years ago. A number of undated scraps of paper were pinned together with a straight pin from an earlier time.

Wearing two pairs of reading glasses at the same time was an effective magnifier for reading some of the difficult words.

A conversation with the archivist at Oberlin, Ohio, after I had done the first pass, convinced me that it would not harm the letters to photocopy them with our flatbed scanner. Once that was done, difficult words could be enlarged, the darkness and contrast adjusted, and parts of different letters compared without further handling of the documents. It was, as Gilbert would have said, "first rate." I wish I had scanned them before transcribing.

Some words gave me a feeling of how the Claflins spoke. Gilbert bought himself some "overhalls," Price said he was "a-going to answer his letter." Then there was a mysterious phrase in Gilbert's May 5 letter when he was talking about how much the boys from the Twenty-Fifth Regiment resented their captain's treatment of them. Gilbert wrote, "some of them would as lief as not try a bayonet on him if he did not walk the mark exactly." What was "lief"? I had heard the phrase "as *like* as not," or "as *likely* as not," but I could not make the word in question look anything like "like." It looks like "livs" or "lins." The *Dictionary of American Regional English* gave me the answer: "Lief," it explained, is sometimes pronounced "liv."

It is very satisfying to see the Claflins' actual handwriting and to read the letters in their original form. I have included a few partial scans and urge the reader to take a look at more of them online at judycook.net/Letters.php.

Special thanks go to my husband Dennis Cook for his help and unfailing support. Thanks, too, to Kristen Travis for superb illustrations and editing. Finally, thanks to the fine folks at the Wisconsin Historical Society and the historical societies and public libraries of Oconomowoc and Waukesha County, Wisconsin.

I hope you will enjoy reading the letters of Gilbert and Esther Claflin as much as I have. I also hope my additions will give you a sense of my own excitement over this amazing little window into a personal history and the background necessary for a fuller understanding of the people, places, and events the Claflins wrote about.

Time Line

September 19, 1822—Gilbert Claflin born, Sandisfield, Berkshire County, Massachusetts.

November 9, 1823—Joshua Claflin (Gilbert's father) dies.

April 20, 1830—Esther Patience Colby born, LeRoy, Geauga County, Ohio.

1830s—Esther's family moves to Freedom, Cattaraugus County, New York.

1837—John S. Rockwell buys land for Oconomowoc, Wisconsin.

June 1844—Gilbert and his mother move to Waukesha County, Wisconsin.

September 1844—John Metcalf (Esther's uncle) buys land in Summit Township.

November 27, 1845—Gilbert and Esther marry in Oconomowoc.

July 1846—Gilbert buys land in Summit Township.

July 1846—James Colby (Esther's father) buys land in Oconomowoc Township.

January 3, 1847—Elton Abijah Claflin born to Gilbert and Esther Claflin.

1848—Esther's parents and siblings move to Wisconsin.

October 17, 1849—Price Colby Claflin born to Gilbert and Esther Claflin.

November 3, 1862—Gilbert drafted.

November 20, 1862—Gilbert's regiment sent from Waukesha, Wisconsin, to Camp Randall in Madison, Wisconsin.

December 31, 1862—Gilbert's regiment mustered in at Camp Randall.

January 9, 1863—Gilbert's regiment sent from Camp Randall to Camp Washburn in Milwaukee, Wisconsin.

January 31, 1863—Gilbert's regiment leaves Milwaukee for Kentucky.

February 2, 1863—Gilbert's regiment arrives in Columbus, Kentucky.

August 13, 1863—Gilbert's regiment leaves Columbus for Milwaukee by way of Cairo and Chicago, Illinois.

August 16, 1863—Gilbert's regiment arrives at Camp Washburn in Milwaukee.

September 8, 1863—Gilbert's regiment mustered out at Camp Washburn.

May 15, 1864—Esther's brother Asa Call Colby killed at the Battle of Resaca, Georgia.

March 8, 1866—Alice Marion Claflin born to Gilbert and Esther Claflin.

January 24, 1871—James Colby (Esther's father) dies.

October 8, 1872—Price Colby Claflin marries Elizabeth Hooker Montague.

October 16, 1878—Achsah Maria Kibbie Claflin (Gilbert's mother) dies.

February 13, 1879—Gilbert Elton Claflin dies.

1884—Esther Claflin moves to Stevens Point, Wisconsin.

August 10, 1887—Abigail Metcalf Colby (Esther's mother) dies at her son J.P.'s home in Iowa.

October 14, 1887—Alice Marion Claflin marries Niels Eugh Reton.

1888—Price and Elizabeth Claflin move to Washington, DC.

September 6, 1891—Marguerite Esther Claflin born to Price and Elizabeth Claflin.

December 13, 1900—Esther Patience Claflin dies.

December 28, 1914—Price Colby Claflin dies.

January 1923—Elton Abijah Claflin dies.

September 21, 1947—Alice Marion Claflin dies.

A Quiet Corner of the War

Prologue

It is now November 1862.

Oconomowoc, Wisconsin, a flourishing town of a thousand people, has grown around a depot of the Chicago, Milwaukee, and St. Paul Railroad. About a mile from the railroad depot in Summit Township, Gilbert and Esther Claflin live with their two sons and Gilbert's mother on a forty-acre farm, and Esther has both parents and numerous siblings nearby. In addition, most of Gilbert and Esther's friends are from farming families in the area, a number having moved from New York State.

Oconomowoc is like many small towns along the railroad. It has a number of businesses: insurance agencies, tailor shops, pharmacies, lumberyards, meat markets, livery stables, footwear establishments, and, of course, places that sell "goods." The railroad cars stop here twice a day carrying passengers and mail, and twice more carrying freight: eastbound in the morning, westbound in the evening.[1]

Recent issues of the local paper, the *Free Press*, give a flavor of Oconomowoc. A reader might see in the latest edition the following: train and post office schedules; a list of letters remaining at the post office; notices of local meetings in churches and halls, including serious war meetings to encourage enlistment and temperance meetings to promote abstinence; and reports of the meetings after they have happened. In addition, articles on matters from across the state and around the world, like the full text of a lengthy address by Governor Salomon, war news, and news from Europe— with opinions from the editors strongly put forth, yet thinly disguised as news articles—would be featured. Someone might also find a poem or two ("The Home of My Heart," "A Mountain Stream," "Advance of Our Army into Virginia"), a column of short news items in no particular order, and advertisements. In August, however, the paper stopped publishing when the editor and publisher left to join the army.

Because the bustling town of Oconomowoc serves a larger farming community that includes both Summit and Oconomowoc Townships, the newspaper also features ads focusing on farmers' needs, such as ads for "Farmers Utensils & Harvesting Tools" and others that promise "The highest price paid for WHEAT in exchange for Goods." In addition there are articles giving the formula for a "Wash for Fruit Trees" or the current market prices for wheat (five different kinds), barley, corn, oats, rye, beans, potatoes, pork, butter, eggs, hides (green and dry), sheep pelts, timothy, clover, salt, as well as mink, raccoon, and muskrat furs.

Both Gilbert and Esther Claflin come from very old New England families. All four of their parents had ancestors from England who moved to Massachusetts in the mid-seventeenth century and, with the exception of a couple of short sojourns to Ohio, stayed in New England for the next two hundred years.

Gilbert Claflin has been a farmer for as long as he can remember. Just past his fortieth birthday, he now lives with his wife, thirty-two-year-old Esther, and their two sons, fifteen-year-old Elton and thirteen-year-old Price. Gilbert was born in Sandisfield in southwestern Massachusetts. He was the only child of Joshua and Achsah Claflin. Esther was born in LeRoy, Ohio, the fifth of ten children born to James and Abigail Colby. In the middle of 1844, both the Colby and Claflin families moved to Summit Township in Wisconsin. Gilbert Claflin and Esther's father, James Colby, each bought forty-acre farms in adjacent sections in far northern Summit. The Colbys' eldest daughter, Emily, was nineteen to Gilbert's twenty-two years, but it was fourteen-year-old Esther who stole Gilbert's heart. A year and a half later, Gilbert and Esther were married.

An important member of the family is Gilbert's widowed mother, Achsah Maria Kibbie Claflin; her husband Joshua died at the age of twenty-five when Gilbert, their only child, was just a year old. She moved to Wisconsin with him when they left her brother's farm in Massachusetts. At sixty-one she is a quiet and productive presence.

About a year ago, Esther's parents, James and Abigail, sold their farm and separated. Both live nearby and help their children as much as they can.

Esther is one of eight surviving adult children. They are all based in Wisconsin, though four of her five brothers are now serving in the Union army.

James Colby (64 years old in 1862)
+ Abigail Metcalf (59 years old)
   Jonas Parmenter Colby (39 years old)
   + Margaret Sommerville (27 years old)
      Cordelia Minona Colby (3 years old)
      Elmer E. Colby (1 year old)
   Emily Colby (37 years old)
   + Evelou Crosby (47 years old)
      Ellen Crosby (12 years old)
      George Crosby (11 years old)
      James Crosby (9 years old)
      Arabelle Crosby (8 years old)
      Florence Crosby (6 years old)
      Anna Crosby (4 years old)
   William Milton Colby (34 years old)
   Esther Patience Colby (32 years old)
   + Gilbert Elton Claflin (40 years old)
      Elton Abijah Claflin (15 years old)
      Price Colby Claflin (13 years old)
   Wealthy Asenette Colby (30 years old)
   + George N. Doty (29 years old)
   James Metcalf Colby (29 years old)
   + Anna Maria Jacques (21 years old)
      Milton J. Colby (4 months old)
   Asa Call Colby (22 years old)
   John Barrus Colby (21 years old)

Jonas Parmenter Colby is the oldest of the Colby siblings, seven years older than Esther and just a year younger than Gilbert. Sometimes folks call him Parmenter, but most often he is "J.P." He has a farm and family of his own in Ixonia, Wisconsin, ten miles northwest of Summit. Back in 1858, he married Margaret Sommerville, one of the many first-generation Americans who moved with her family from New York to Wisconsin. They have a sunny three-year-old daughter, Cordelia Minona (often called "Minnie"), and a year-old son, Elmer. Last October, J.P. joined the Thirteenth

Wisconsin Infantry. Since the beginning of June, J.P.'s regiment has been in western Kentucky guarding railroads and supply steamers and keeping surveillance over guerrillas. They are stationed now at Fort Henry, Kentucky.

Esther's oldest sister, Emily Colby Crosby, has a hard life as a single mother. Two years after Esther married Gilbert, Emily married Evelou Crosby, and they had six children in quick succession. In 1860 Emily and her six children, but not Evelou, were living with Emily's father James Colby in Oconomowoc. Evelou and the three oldest children are not mentioned in any of Gilbert's and Esther's letters. Emily is working for Elijah and Washington Perrin, farmers who raise sheep and cattle in Oconomowoc, and her three little girls are shuttled about, living with Esther, Emily, or Abigail. Eight-year-old Arabelle is a bit of a problem. Esther describes her as full of scowls and snarls, and no one finds her easy to live with. Six-year-old Florence and four-year-old Anna are easier.

William Milton Colby is between Emily and Esther in age. If Esther has a favorite brother, it is probably William. He teaches from time to time at the Summit school where school terms are usually three or four months in summer and four in winter. In the spring and fall so many of the children are needed to help on the farms, that it is not appropriate to hold school. When school is not in session, William often comes to live with the Claflins and help with the farmwork.

Wealthy Colby is never mentioned in the letters, though she is Esther's sister, two years younger. Last year she married George N. Doty, a maker of Daguerreotypes in Stevens Point, Wisconsin, one hundred miles northwest of Summit.

James Metcalf Colby is sixth of the eight siblings. He teaches school in Delafield, five miles away. Two years ago, at the age of twenty-six, James married nineteen-year-old Anna Maria Jacques from Nova Scotia, Canada. Their first child, Milton, was born earlier this year. Three months ago James joined the Twenty-Fourth Wisconsin Infantry. They trained briefly and then headed for Kentucky. James's regiment has marched more than three hundred miles in forty-two days, and he is ill.

Abigail Metcalf Colby named her two youngest children after her sisters' husbands: Asa Call and John Barrus. Asa Call Colby is ten years younger than Esther, and John Barrus Colby, a year younger still.

Asa joined the Union army in June 1861. He serves in Wisconsin's Third Infantry Regiment and has been fighting and marching in Virginia and

Maryland. Three and a half months ago, Asa was wounded in the foot at the Battle of Cedar Mountain. He was still in the hospital on September 17 when his regiment took part in the Battle of Antietam. Out of the 345 members of the Third who commenced the action that day, less than 50 men were left. The rest were killed or wounded.

John Barrus Colby, Esther's youngest sibling, was nineteen when he became the first of the family to join the army. He is now serving with Wisconsin's Sixteenth Infantry Regiment. In their first fight, the Battle of Shiloh, 225 members of John's regiment were killed or wounded. John was wounded a few weeks later at Corinth. By November 3, less than a year after they were mustered in, the Sixteenth Regiment was so reduced by battles and sickness that the ten companies of the regiment were consolidated into five, and half of the company officers were discharged. John is now home on furlough, awaiting orders to return to the war.

Gilbert and Esther work hard to make ends meet. Cash flow is always a problem for the small farmer. Occasionally they borrow a bit from Esther's father or a friend, but careful accounts are kept and debts paid as quickly as possible. They have a few cattle and sheep, but most of their livelihood is from selling grain. The orchard of plums and apples—that Gilbert planted, grafted, and tended—gives them joy and brings in a bit more cash in the fall.

The farmers in Summit and Oconomowoc help each other out, especially now when many of the men have been called to serve in the war. The Eastmans, the Goodells, and the Newnhams are all near enough to be a help and a comfort to Esther.

Amasa Eastman is Gilbert's closest neighbor. He lives with his wife and three young children, as well as his seventy-five-year-old father, Ira Eastman. Amasa is several years older than Gilbert, and Gilbert and Esther usually refer to him as "Mr. Eastman." Esther often turns to him for advice in financial and farming matters, or even for loans of money and equipment.

Amasa's brother Cooledge Eastman has a farm about two miles southeast of Gilbert in Summit Township with his wife and two children, twenty-four-year-old Leander and twelve-year-old Albert. The Claflins sometimes consult Cooledge about farm animal matters.

Prescott Watson Goodell is also a farmer in Oconomowoc. Like Gilbert, he is now forty years old and came to Wisconsin from New York State. He and his wife, Lovilla, attend the same church as the Claflins.

Just across the road from Gilbert and Esther is the Newnham farm. James and Eliza came from England originally, but have lived in Wisconsin

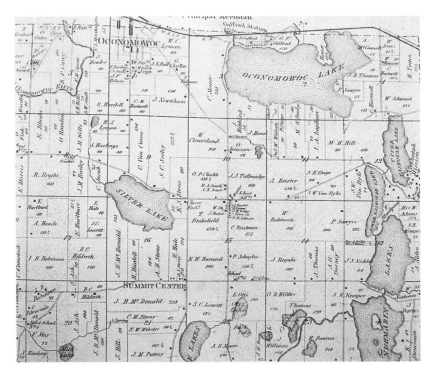

Map of Summit Township. Claflin's forty-acre farm, marked "G. Claflin," is just southeast of the village of Oconomowoc: the southeast quarter of the northeast quarter of Section 4. This map also shows the farms of many of the neighbors mentioned in the letters. (*Atlas of Waukesha Co., Wisconsin*, 27)

twenty-five years. James is sixty years old; Eliza is fifty-three. Their boys, Howard and Henry, are now twenty-two and eighteen.

The war has been escalating for more than a year with the end nowhere in sight. Losses from battles and disease are already staggering on both sides. The enthusiasm for volunteering is waning. In mid-July the Federal government passed a law that required a quota of soldiers from each state. The law outlined draft procedures for states that did not already have them, but the actual process was left up to each state's governor.

In Wisconsin, newly installed Governor Salomon worked hard to develop a fair system for the draft. He credited counties for volunteers who had already enlisted and compiled accurate lists of eligible men. More than forty-five thousand additional Wisconsin men were needed. Most of the counties filled their quotas soon after harvest was completed.

Even so, there is evidence of strong resistance to the draft in Wisconsin, one example being a riot that took place in Port Washington, about fifty miles from Oconomowoc on the shores of Lake Michigan. Much of the resistance is taking place in the counties of Manitowoc, Milwaukee, Ozaukee, Sheboygan, and Washington, because there are many recent German and Irish immigrants who find it especially hard to have the head of the household gone for long periods of time. The Germans are particularly opposed to the draft since many left Germany to avoid mandatory war service. Objections are also raised on the basis of fairness. More than a third of the men who are drafted simply do not report. Then there is the matter of substitutes; a drafted man may pay someone to serve in his place, but this option is out of reach for men without much ready cash.

In November, Governor Salomon scheduled drafting to begin in the counties with insufficient volunteers. Gilbert is among the first to be drafted from Summit. He is one of 181 men drafted from Waukesha County. The drafted men go first to the town of Waukesha, twenty miles east of Oconomowoc, before being moved to Camp Randall in the state capital of Madison, fifty miles west of Oconomowoc.

NOTE

1. Much of the local historical information in this prologue is drawn from the *Oconomowoc Free Press*, November 4, 1858, to August 16, 1862. Much of the biographical information is drawn from the letters of Esther and Gilbert Claflin, the federal censuses of 1850, 1860, and 1870, and Vezzetti, *Index to Waukesha County, Wisconsin, Marriages, 1846–1907*.

The Letters

Gilbert and Esther Claflin,
April 10, 1874.
(family collection)

[Probably November 19, 1862]

Waukesha

Dear Esther,

We are still here; shall probably go to Madison tomorrow. We have had thus far first rate fare. There are a good many long faces here, and some cases are truly pitiable.

I have learned from the commissioner that we have got to furnish our blankets for the present. You will have to send me one by express to Madison.

I am better.
Love to all,

Gilbert Claflin

⁓

[Probably November 19, 1862]

Dear Gilbert,

William has just brought in your letter. I was a little surprised that you were still at Waukesha. I had supposed you were in camp having soldier's fare. I finished my washing and cleaning today, and when I sat down tonight I went *to sleep as usual.*

Elton has made him a whip stalk this evening, but he is minus a lash. He sold a bushel of little apples today and brought me the quarter. The boys have drawn two wagonloads of chips and got them in today. Everything has went on smoothly. I could not ask for any better children than they have been so far.

Your mother is very quiet, knitting your socks. I read your letter to her. She says you can have her blue and white coverlid and I shall send you the one we have had on the lounge. I shall send them out tomorrow morning so they will get to Madison as soon as you do.

Gilbert, I always thought if you were called from my side life would be nothing but a dark blank; but there has come a change in my feelings. It seems as though I could bear the separation with a cheerful resignation and put my whole trust in God.

Now Gilbert, if by making this great sacrifice we can help the cause of truth and liberty is it not better than living merely for ourselves?

Price is very careful of my health. He said tonight, "Mother you had better go to bed. You can't stand it to work so."

If you can't come home this week please let us know.

Yours affectionately,

Esther Claflin

⌒◡

[In pencil]

Madison

Dear Esther,

I am enjoying camp life[1] much better than I expected I should, but when I shall come home is a matter of uncertainty as it is now next to impossible to get a pass. I have just been to the quartermaster's and got all the bread I could carry. You would be surprised to see [the] quantity that our boys, 115 in number, consume in a day.

I suppose you got the letter that I sent, and have sent the blanket.

I got my blanket today.

Love to all,

G. Claflin

NOTE
1. Camp Randall, where Gilbert was posted, was on ten acres of gently sloping, well-drained land that was previously the state fairgrounds a mile and a half west of Madison, Wisconsin. When Gilbert arrived a year and a half after the first soldiers came, animal sheds had been transformed into barracks, and the "Temple of Art" (where fair-goers had admired the works of Wisconsin artists) had become an indoor drill room (Mattern, *Soldiers When They Go*, 4).

⌒◡

Camp Randall
November 21, 1862

Dear Esther,

I sent you a line out of camp yesterday by William Campbell,[1] which you will doubtless get before this. I had but a short time to write in, and could say but little. But today I got a pass down town to get some things which I need. When I was in Waukesha I bought me some overhalls, and they do not come amiss.

It will be some time, doubtless, before we get a furlough. The pressure on the drafted men is very great, and every inducement that can be offered is offered to induce them to enlist or procure substitutes as most of the substitutes enlist, and a good many are enlisting in order to get home on furlough.

So far as the hardship and the disagreeableness of camp life is concerned, I can stand it first rate, but the privileges of a social and religious nature which we are, to a great degree, deprived of is the hardest of all. But on the whole it is much better than I expected.

I wish you could see the boys when meals are ready. A pack of hungry dogs would not be more voracious. But things will soon be arranged and then there will be more order. We draw plenty of rations, and if well cooked, can live first rate.

We are not organized yet and when we shall be is a question. We have to answer to our names 3 times a day. The rest of the time we are employed in fixing up our quarters. The drafted men will doubtless stay here this winter.

Substitutes are being contracted for here for 200 dollars,[2] and I think they can be got soon for 150 and perhaps less.

One of the 16th regiment boys said to me that John had got the position of first Sergeant.

It is next to impossible to get anything outside unless you have friends outside or plenty of money. There is but one case of favoritism among the Waukesha boys and that is Mr. Potter who has friends in Madison. He is fisting for the office of captain, but it will be a hard berth for him if he gets it, judging by what the boys say.

I guess you will have hard work to make this out as I have to write in a place that is not as comfortable as might be, and [there is] noise on every side.[3]

The boys will have to get some boxes to feed the horses in, or make some. That big box of [illegible] would answer for one. They had better fix up the ox stable so that they can feed the cattle.

Give my love to all the folks. Let Mother see this.

Direct Gilbert Claflin drafted Militia Camp Randall Madison Wisconsin Your Husband,

G Claflin

Answer soon and send some stamps from my pocketbook.[4]

NOTES

1. In 1862, William Campbell lived in Oconomowoc with his wife and two young children. Like Gilbert, he was a forty-year-old farmer; however, Campbell was born in New York ("1860 United States Federal Census," hereafter 1860 census). For more about the Campbells, see Appendix B.

2. Gilbert's $200 in 1862 would translate to roughly $4,000 in the early twenty-first century.

3. At about the same time Gilbert was writing his first letters, several other recruits described the difficulties of writing letters at Camp Randall. One soldier wrote, "One by a block, another by a box, others seated around paper placed in a portfolio, or a strip of board with eyes nearly blinded by the smoke of the nearby fire or seated in our bunks shivering." Another sent home, "such are the inconveniences, I wonder that any letters are written in camp. For it is first that there are no places except on my knees and now it is twilight and the soldiers are having great fun and in the midst of bedlam I am writing." A sixteen-year-old wrote to his sister, "I can count more than 40 of the boys writing letters to their Mothers and their girls. Mostly to their girls. It's easy to tell if a fellow is writing to his Mother. He don't squirm and cover his paper when some guy looks over his shoulder. There is a lot of such teasing. The only way is to get away up in the top bunks out of reach and hold their portfolios on their laps for a desk" (Mattern, *Soldiers When They Go*, 87–88).

4. A pocketbook can be a wallet or any flat, folding container.

⁓

November 23, 1862

Dear Gilbert,

I received both of your letters from Madison last night and I got your letter from Waukesha the same day it was written and answered it that night and directed to Madison. William said you would get it by inquiring at the P[ost]. Office.

Your blankets, three in number, were sent out Wednesday morning. You spoke of getting your blanket. I should like to know if you have not got those we sent you. Mr. Stone called here yesterday.[1] He said the state had furnished you with one.

We heard from you through Mr. Vroman the same day you left Waukesha.[2]

John starts for Milwaukee in the morning. I had hoped he was going Madison so that I could send you some things. Do you think I had better send you some under clothes by express?

Anna came over Wednesday to see you before you went away, and she is here yet. She has not had any letters from James in three weeks but her brother-in-law has written that he is sick with the ague.[3] His regiment is in Nashville.

The boys get along very pleasant with their work. School does not commence until a week from Monday. Elton has ploughed some and they have got up quite a pile of wood.

We went to church today. It seemed very strange not to have you sit with me. The Governor's proclamation was read and the services are to be held in the Methodist Church (that is Thanksgiving services).[4]

I have been to the village once with Anna to get her baby's picture taken. But Gilbert, I feel so widowed to go out I shall stay at home mostly, though I shall go to prayer meeting when the weather and my health will permit. I should like to know if you have been to meeting today, and if you have prayer meetings in camp, and if you meet with any congenial spirits among the drafted men.

I hope you won't work yourself poor on those barracks. I wish you would tell me if your cold has settled on your lungs, and just how your health is. I know you must suffer with the cold these nights. My cough is no worse.

Your Mother appears just as she always does. She went out twice last week.

You don't say whether you think of procuring a substitute.

I did hope we might be together next Thursday, but it is all right. Let us be thankful that we were permitted to live together so long.

Elton said tonight he was going to shoot a duck for Thanksgiving.

Perhaps if you can send at the post office you can get the letter we sent you.

Gilbert from your Wife Esther

[Marginal note]

Had the boys ought to go on the ice skating now?

NOTES

1. Eli Stone was a farmer originally from New York. His eighty-acre farm was about two miles south of Gilbert's in Summit Township (*Atlas of Waukesha Co.*, 27; 1860 census). For more about him, see Appendix B.

2. The Mr. Vroman of this letter could have been one of four farmers originally from New York (1860 census). Details of their families are in Appendix B.

3. *Ague* is a fever that is marked by periods of chills, fever, and sweating. It is a symptom of several diseases, including dysentery. Dysentery was a major killer of soldiers during the Civil War, and was often contracted by drinking polluted water.

4. In 1862 there was no national Thanksgiving holiday, but many states celebrated it individually. The governor would proclaim a given day as a statewide Thanksgiving Day. In October 1863, Abraham Lincoln, looking for ways to unite the nation, proclaimed the last Thursday in November as a national day of thanksgiving. Every president after Lincoln proclaimed a Thanksgiving Day sometime in November. It was not until 1941 that Congress finally made Thanksgiving Day a permanent national holiday on the fourth Thursday in November.

Camp Randall
November 27, 1862

Dear Esther,

I received your letter this forenoon and was glad to hear that you were getting along so finely, [and] that the boys were doing so well. I hope they will not go on the ice until it is safe. You must be judge of that matter, and they must abide your judgment.

So far as my health is concerned, I am as well as usually I am, and the great trouble is I do not have enough to do.

I like drilling first rate. We are now under a temporary organization. A drillmaster has been appointed by the governor. We have an officer drill twice a day, in the morning and early in the afternoon, then these officers drill the men in squads of 5 to 8. I have a squad and am getting along quite well, all things considered.

You must not worry about me. I do not suffer at all with the cold as yet. I got the blankets all right, and have enough to keep me warm. I guess you had better send me some under clothes, vest and pantaloons, by express.[1] Do not work nights to fix anything nor be so afraid I shall suffer. My situation is better than a majority of the men here. Many do actually suffer for sufficient to cover them during the night.

I have a partner in my bunk by the name of Peter.[2] He is an earnest Christian man.

Last Sunday the chaplain of the 30th regiment preached on the grounds. Some three hundred were there. In the evening I attended a German prayer meeting.[3] A good degree of earnestness was manifest.

I do not spend my evenings in barracks, but in the tent of the chaplain or at the quartermaster department, Lieutenant Curtice of the 30th having charge. We are going to start a prayer meeting if we can get a room.

I am sorry I could not be at home today and have a Thanksgiving dinner with you, but I trust I am thankful that God's mercy and care has been towards us thus far and I can trust Him still.

I have been appointed to draw rations for the Waukesha Militia. All I have to do is to get and present the order and detail the men to get that which I order in the provision line.

I hope you will not shut yourself up at home because I am gone, but improve every opportunity you can visiting.

You must tell Anna not to get the blues because James is sick, as it will not help him a great deal. I should have been very glad to have seen her.

So far as a substitute is concerned I do not care but little about one on my part. There are plenty of them here in camp, and if the draft that is ordered is made, there will be more substitutes than there is [those] that want them. $200 is the highest that is offered. Then it is a question, if I got a substitute, whether I would not be liable to another draft,[4] which will probably be soon. Captain Stone said if I wanted any money, he would let me have all I wanted to get a substitute.

Perhaps you had better get some money of Mr. Eastman or speak to him about it so as to be sure of it. If I do not get back before the taxes are called for, get him to pay them. I guess we shall want 15 or 20 dollars.

The boys had better take some boards and fix up the shed so that the cattle cannot get under the shed where the sheep go, leaving a place for them to go out.

[On an undated scrap of paper that may have been part of this letter]

They had better take some of boards and make a place for the sheep to eat out of. Take that long 2 by 4. Cut it 4 pieces about 3 feet long. Nail on a

wide board at the bottom and a narrow one at the top, leaving a space wide
enough to let the sheep eat without getting in. The end boards should be
2½ ft long. They will have to nail it strong. They had better make it under
the shed, and then the sheep can eat out of the storm.

You must answer soon.

Yours Truly,

G. Claflin

NOTES

1. Camp Randall was very crowded. Each company was assigned two long halves of
a fifty-by-eighteen-foot barrack—about ten square feet of living space per man. A bunk,
shared by two men, was a wooden shelf with a load of straw and a blanket.

Both the Federal government and the state scrambled to provide supplies for the
enormous number of recruits who continued to pour in to the training camps. At the
opening of Camp Randall, blankets had been donated by the citizens of Wisconsin, but
the men of the Thirty-Fourth Regiment were asked to furnish their own. By late 1862,
manufacturers of soldiers' clothing were catching up, but the regiments still had to
be supplied in chronological order. The Twenty-Ninth Regiment was finally issued its
uniform shirts, pants, and coats on October 12, 1862. Gilbert was in the Thirty-Fourth
Regiment; his supplies came later (Mattern, *Soldiers When They Go*, 4, 75).

2. Gilbert's bunkmate was most likely Peter Olson from Coon, Wisconsin; a Nor-
wegian carpenter four years younger than Gilbert ("Roster of Wisconsin Volunteers";
1860 census). For more about Peter Olson, see Appendix D.

3. Germany experienced repeated crop failures and political unrest from 1845 to
1855, and many Germans fled to America. This was also a period when settlers were
flooding into Wisconsin. By 1850, one-third of Wisconsin's population was foreign
born. Fewer than half of these were English speakers. Of the non-English-speaking
immigrants, the Germans were by far the most numerous. There was intensive German
settlement in Waukesha and the surrounding counties ("19th-Century Immigration").

4. On July 21, 1863, following the passage of the Federal Enrollment Act, the *Waukesha Freeman* reported from the provost marshal: "That men who, on the 3d of March
1863, were in the military service of the United States as substitutes under the draft of
1862, and whose terms of service have since expired, are not liable to the present draft;
but the persons for which they were substituted are liable for draft, the same as if they
had not been drafted and furnished substitutes."

∽

November 30, 1862

My Dear Gilbert,

Price brought home your letter last night about ten o'clock and I need
not say that it was most welcome, but if you had brought yourself along it
would have been more acceptable.

I had the griddle hot and the pancakes ready to bake but no Gilbert came. I listen involuntarily for his footsteps when the house is still at night and once I thought (I don't believe I dreamed it) that he came in at the door so still and came to the bed and kissed me, and another time I heard his name called away in the distance and yet so plain. But these are dream thoughts.

I don't want you to think I am melancholy for I am not. I feel as though it was a wise Providence that called you away from home, and I know it is my duty to submit cheerfully and trust wholly to Him. And I do trust to Him Gilbert, I am a wonder to myself when I think how I am sustained. At first it was for these dear children that I must not wear a "long face" and now it is easy not to. I have cast my burden on the Lord and He has sustained me.

Your mother's health seems good. I have not heard any complaints on that scene. I don't see any difference in her appearance. She goes about the house just as she always has. She talks with the boys about you, not in a mournful tone but as she would if you were about.

I am glad you like drilling. Elton was very much pleased to think Dad was an officer, and William laughed and said that was worth all the draft to think of Gilbert drilling men.

I am glad you find some Christian and intelligent companions and that you are not obliged to spend your evenings among the vulgar.

Last Monday the boys fixed up the stables and made a door to go out of the barn into the shed, and yesterday they took the shingles in the new house. School begins tomorrow but I am afraid they won't be able to go very steady it takes so much time to do the work.[1]

I get along with Arabelle just about the same as usual but there has been a swap among the girls. Florence would not stay with mother so her mother has her, and Arabelle is to stay with mother and I take Anna. I hope you will not object for I think it will be easier for me. Perrins won't have Emily if she has more than one child.

Sister Anna is now at Mother's. She has been at Margaret's the most of last week. M. had a miscarriage and she stayed to take care of her.

I think I can have your bundle ready to start Wednesday morning, perhaps Tuesday.

You wished me to tell you about myself. I don't think I shall be able to stand going out in the cold; it seems to take my breath and set me coughing but don't worry about me. I feel very well when in the house.

Abigail Colby, Esther's
mother, about 1863.
(family collection)

I am glad you did not forget the 27th. Elton did not get his duck, nor we did not any of us go to church. Jack's folks gave us our invitation to come there to dinner if you come back.

Mr. Eastman is declining rapidly so is Leander.

It is very wintry tonight. Anna has had a letter from James. He is some better but very much discouraged.

Yours in love,

Esther

[Upside down]

I want you to buy a good pair of leather gloves.

NOTE

1. School had a summer session and a winter session with long breaks in spring and fall when many students had farmwork to do. There is more about the Summit School in Appendix C.

❧

Camp Randall
December 2, 1862

Dear Esther,

Your letter was perused by me last evening, and it is a comforting thought to me that you are so resigned to the ordering of God as it respects us. I firmly believe that good will result from it. I hope you will be careful of your health, and do all that you can to remove that cough of yours, and tell me how you are and the rest of the family.

As for myself I enjoy good health and camp life agrees with me first rate so far. But Esther, no one that has not experienced the moral disease of the camp can have any idea of its fearful results. I would sooner lay our 2 dear boys in the grave than have them become so morally debased as hundreds are by whom I am surrounded. I tremble at the prospect before me, and am led to feel how weak and dependent I am on grace divine for support and assistance to carry me through the dangers that beset my pathway which now I tread. But I do not murmur or complain. The days are short; the nights are not wearisome because I see an overruling hand in it all.

I hope you will not be over anxious about my return: I shall come as soon as I can get a chance. I wish you would in your next give me your *views* as it respects a substitute. The work that I do now is not one quarter as hard as it was at home.

Yesterday we moved to new barracks. I have fixed up a comfortable bunk and sleep warm, though many of the boys complain of the cold.

A new order of things begins to appear. You have doubtless seen or heard the new order of the government respecting drafted men. Some of the drafted men are availing themselves of it for the sake of office but I shall not enlist under any circumstances. The drafted men that are left are now being organized into companies. Permanent officers will be chosen. To give you some idea how things are moving: we came here with 115 men; yesterday I drew rations only for 48. Some have been discharged and a good many have enlisted, or got substitutes which have enlisted.

I have not asked for a pass out of camp but once since I have been here and that was to get my blankets. I have got a wash dish and 2 towels, and can wash when I please.

So far as rations are concerned, we draw enough and can live first rate. But Esther, we do not get such bread as you make. I can assure you, I think, when I get home I shall know better how to appreciate the dear relation of husband and father than I ever did before.

I hope the boys will continue to be good boys and take good care of the stock. The sheep will need some grain every day. Perhaps they had better pull some oats out of the snow by the big door. I want they should be careful of the fodder; feed enough but not waste it.

As to the change you have made, I have no objection to it and think it is the best thing that could be done.

I should like to know how you disposed of the apples that were in the barn, and how you are getting along drying them.

Mr. Meigs, one of the drafted men from Waukesha County, will probably call and see you soon. He got his discharge. You will have to make some allowance for his story as he sees through different glasses from what I do. He claimed the office of first sergeant on the ground that the town which he came from had not commissioned officers and was entitled to one. But such claims are of no avail here.

I am sorry that the boys will be hindered from going to school. I was in hopes that they could go every day and improve a great deal this winter. I hope I shall be able to get a furlough and come home and help them a little before long.

Give my love to all.

Answer soon.

Yours Truly,

Gilbert

[Written upside down at the top of page 1]

I guess you will have to study some to make this out as I write on a shingle and am in a hurry to get it in the office so as to go this afternoon.

❧

December 4, 1862

My Dear Husband,

I received your letter last evening. You wish to know what I think about your getting a substitute. I will tell you. I think unless you feel that it is clearly your duty to go in person as a soldier, that *if* you can loan the money, which you say you can, of Mr. Stone, that you had better do it. I think we shall be helped some and I think under the circumstances we may accept it, and I believe we can make a turn to pay the rest. Mother says she will give you her land north if you can make any use of it.

Everyone that speaks of it seems anxious you should return. I saw Mr. Eastman today he told me that Mr. Stone said to him the people here ought never to allow you to go away and leave your family. Mr. Meigs called yesterday. He says you had better go to Madison to a physician and have your lungs examined, and if they are not strong you may get a discharge on that score. Mr. Meigs seemed very anxious that you should get out some way nd if there is so much fraud and corruption among the officers how can you serve under them

I have been down to Mother's and Mr. Montague's today.[1] He says if you are willing, he will see what can be done for you. Miss Montague says you don't know how much they all miss you. But Gilbert, I know how much you are missed at home.

It is very cold tonight and I hope you have got your clothes. They were sent out Tuesday morning.

You say you don't have to work very hard. Don't you think when you come to do the marching you would say quite another thing?

My health is just about as it has been. Last week I suffered a good deal from soreness and itching but am better now.

Price got hurt quite badly today; he drove down as far as the school house, and when he got out he fell his whole weight on his knees. I tried to have him go over to Mother's and be doctored but he thought not. He says it pained him all day when he moved it, and he came home crying. I took care of it as well as I knew how and he has slept quiet all the evening. His left knee is considerably swollen.

And now I must tell you how lazy I have been. We have not dried any apples since you went away. The boys have been so busy through the day I had not a heart to ask them to work nights, but I think we shall cut some next week. The boys have sold a number of bushels out of the barn and the rest are there yet. I thought they would keep as well there as in the house.

Mr. and Mrs. Goodell spent the evening here so my letter writing is quite late, but I don't care. It is for my Gilbert.

Yours ever the same,

Esther

NOTE

1. Enos James Montague was the pastor of Gilbert and Esther's church. He lived in Oconomowoc with his wife and two daughters. There is more about Enos James Montague in Appendix B, and more about the Oconomowoc Congregational Church in Appendix C.

Camp Randall
December 8, 1862

Dear Esther,

Your letter was received, and so were the things—all safe.

I am well; never better. I was sorry to learn that you had not been as well and that Price had got hurt.

I wrote a letter to Rev. Mr. Montague this morning but did not get it done in time to go out by mail but sent it to Madison to be put in the Office, and fearing that there might be some mistake in its being forwarding, I will give you something of its contents.

I told him that I thought I could get a substitute for 135 dollars and probably for less but how it will be I cannot tell as yet. Perhaps one of the boys, when you get this, had better go and see him if you do not hear from him. I wished the money to be so arranged that it could be drawn from the Bank of Madison if he gets the money or any other way that may be thought best to get it to me.

Love to all.

Yours truly,

Gilbert Claflin

∾

Friday, December 12, 1862

Dear Gilbert,

When I received your last letter I thought it would not be best to write again, but I am troubled in both my waking and sleeping hours. I have a vague impression that you are being led from what I have said to act differently from what you would if you acted according to your own inclination.

But my dear Gilbert, if ever I prayed for divine guidance it has been in this affair and I have been sustained in your absence beyond measure. I can sometimes almost make these words my own, "I can do all things through Christ who strengheneth me." But when I have thought of the tyranny of petty officers and the thousand wrongs to which a private is subjected, I felt as though we could not let you go if it could be prevented. But I don't mean to let my hopes be so high that I shall be crushed if you are not successful in getting a substitute. There seems to be a movement on foot among our

Southern brethren for peace. If it should be successful you may not be gone long if you have to go.

Price's leg did not prove as bad as I feared it would. It has not kept him out of school, but he is lame yet.

Elton has lost three days and Price one since school commenced. They are very faithful so far as I know about their work, and very pleasant. I don't hear any complaints. Elton keeps wood ahead and Price got a wagonload of shavings at the cooper's shop. They took a grist of provender Monday and filled our bag with some buckwheat flour.

Don't give yourself uneasiness on my account. I am quite as well as usual.

When you come home you had better make a bag of your sheet (sew it stout) to put your things in.

Yours truly,

Esther Claflin

⌒

Camp Randall
December 15, 1862

Dear Esther,

Your letter came to hand Saturday evening. I was glad to hear that you were so reconciled to the ordering of Providence as it respects our separation. I have looked upon it from the first as my destiny to be a soldier. You speak of the tyranny of petty officers, but Esther I have no fears on that ground. I shall endeavor to find the path of duty and walk in it, discharging all the duties of a soldier with promptness and efficiency. I know it is hard for friends to part when they look from the social standpoint merely, but when the standpoint which Providence places us on, it should not be hard.

I was afraid that Price would have a serious time with his leg, but was glad to learn that it was not serious. I hope the boys will endeavor to improve all they can this winter and learn to be good and faithful in all that they undertake.

It has been quite wet and muddy here and for several days we did not drill. A good many of the boys took cold. I have had for a day or two a cold but am better now. I have given myself a regular cold water dressing off and think I shall be all sound in a few days. I hope you will not worry about it for it will not ease me.

I suppose you will make the application to me. I am surprised when I think how little my business affairs at home occupy my thoughts. It seems to me that all is going on well.

I am in hopes to get a furlough for a few days soon but when I cannot tell. There are so many who want them whose families are suffering that I shall have to take my turn I suppose. I hope you will rest contented 'til I appear in the door and then it will be all right.

I heard by Rev. Mr. Montague that you was to the prayer meeting last Wednesday evening. I hope you will improve all these privileges you are able to and endeavor to bear all the trials which you may be called to pass through with Christian meekness.

I want you when you write to tell me how Mother gets along and all the rest of the folks.

I suppose I must close as I am going down town to get some soap to wash in, as the soap in camp is more than half tallow I should think.[1]

Yours Truly,

Gilbert

[Upside down underneath it says]

Gilbert Claflin
Camp Randall
Rendezvous of the
Waukesha Militia
Madison
Wisconsin

NOTE

1. Soap is made of three basic ingredients: fat, alkali, and water. Many folks think the best fat for homemade soap is tallow, which is beef fat. The alkali used is often lye, which can be bought in cans or made by boiling down water that has been filtered through wood ashes. Soap made with too great a proportion of fat will be soft and mild. Even the strongest lye/tallow soaps will be more than half tallow. The proportion in most recipes seems to be about seven or eight parts tallow to one of lye.

December 16, 1862

My Dear Gilbert,

Your letter came to hand tonight and I know by the tone of it you felt low spirited, but I am glad you don't feel troubled about home matters, for that would not help the matter any.

I think the boys get along with the stock pretty well, excepting the sheep. I think they did not understand how to make the feeding boxes. Elton says it don't work well. Some of the men tell him to feed on the frozen ground, and what they leave the cattle will eat, and he says it works well. He got a buck of Cooledge Eastman last week. He says he will take a ewe or he will lend it to him.

You must [have] thought it very strange when you got my last, for I did not then suppose there was any doubt about your getting the money, and I should like to know if the time is past for getting a substitute. If it is not, maybe your Uncle would lend you the money if you thought it was best to ask him. It seems as though this burden was greater than I could bear and yet I bear it not alone. There is almost always a sweet Presence with me which seems to say, "Have I not borne infinitely more than this for you who are so undeserving?"

Emily Little made us a short call today and I should not [have] known her if I had been with her a week. Her eyes have that peculiar wild look that opium eaters have.

Mr. Newnham's boys are delivering straw for twelve shillings a load.[1] Do you think we had better get a load?

We have seven dollars in bills. I spoke to Mr. Sawyer about the committee refunding that ten dollars and he has seen them and says we shall have it in a short time.[2] Mr. Sawyer said if he could do anything for us anytime he would be glad to. People seem very kind to me. Mr. and Mrs. Goodell were over again last night. Don't you think it is very kind in them not to forget me when you are gone?

December 18th:

Leander Eastman died last night. There have been a number of deaths since you left and diphtheria and typhoid fevers are quite prevalent. Mrs. Lieutenant Whitaker, John Comstock, a sister of D. R. Thompson, and Ed McCuell's wife have died recently. Mrs. Brainard and Lew Alvord's wife are sick with typhoid fever.

Your Mother seems quite well, and composed for her, though she is getting very anxious to have you come home. When the boys come home from the post office she comes in to hear your letters read. It may seem strange but I almost dread to have you come home to stay a little while and then go. I have given her a dollar since you went away. She is out of work now, but she reads and acts perfectly contented. I could furnish her with work if she wished.

You must [think] that I was a dolt not to send you some soap. I thought of that and other things after the package was gone.

Little Anna is as quiet and happy as any child I ever saw. It does seem strange here not to see scowls or hear snarls. It is more than I can conjecture what will become of Arabelle. It does not seem as though I could ever have her again. I don't think Mother ought to keep her long.

Sister Anna has not gone back. She has been staying with Mother and she is here now. Her baby is not very well. It worries a great deal.

When you write, tell me if you have a cough and how you are and take as good care of yourself as you can. And O Gilbert, my prayer is that the Lord will protect your health and your life and return you to us in safety.

Yours affectionately,

Esther

[Upside down at top of page 2]

William says you don't notice his letters.

NOTES

1. A shilling, twelve and a half cents, was a denomination of money left over from the British. There was no American coin for this denomination, though some states accepted certain foreign coins to be worth a shilling. The *American Dictionary* of 1828 said of the shilling, "This denomination of money still subsists in the United States, although there is no coin of that value current, except the Spanish coin of 12½ cents, which is a shilling in the money of the state of New York" (cited in *Dictionary of American Regional English*).The Claflins and many of their neighbors in Oconomowoc and Summit came from New York State. It seems from the letters that shillings were still in common use.

2. Parker Sawyer was a Vermonter and an abolitionist with enough money to help him work for his beliefs (Johnson, *Illustrious Oconomowoc*, 51–52; Barquist and Barquist, *Oconomowoc: Barons to Bootleggers*, 22). For more about Parker Sawyer, see Appendix B.

Camp Randall
December 17, 1862

Dear Esther,

You will doubtless hear of the great fire in camp last night before the receipt of this, and to relieve your mind from anxiety about me I write.[1]

Between 11 & 12 o'clock the fearful cry of "Fire! Fire! Fire!" sounded through the camp. In a moment hundreds of men jumped from their bunks in wild confusion, each endeavoring to find and secure his all of camp equipage. The orderly man had decidedly the advantage. (I think I am improving in this respect under camp discipline.) I dressed myself in short order, got all my things together, then went out to see where the fire was and at once saw that our barracks were safe. But what to us was merely excitement was to others a fearful reality.

Some barely escaped with their underclothes; some saved a part, others all they had. The captain of Company K, 30th Regiment lost all his company papers; all that he saved was his sword.

The fire commenced near the end of the barracks, and took from a stovepipe. It was but a few minutes before nearly 20 rods of the barracks was all in flames.[2] The fire was stopped by tearing down a part of the barracks and throwing water on the straw. About 25 rods of barracks was destroyed. 11 government rifles were burnt. The fire was stopped about 15 rods from our establishment.

I never had such a chance in my life to see the workings of human nature, and the acts as called to mind during that short time of 15 or 20 [minutes] will furnish amusement for many an hour. One man in our squad room slept through the whole of the excitement in the center of the room and knew nothing of it 'til morning when some of the time a man was yelling, "Fire! Fire!" within 10 feet of him.

My cough is better than when I sent my last to you. I hope you will all prosper be cheerful and happy.

I must close.

Your Husband,

Gilbert

NOTES

1. The *Janesville Daily Gazette* ran the following short article on December 18, 1862: "FIRE AT CAMP RANDALL—The old barracks on the south side of Camp Randall

caught fire last night from a sheet iron stove, and several rods were burned down before the flames could be arrested. The barracks burned and destroyed contained accommodations for about 300 men.—*Madison Journal.*"

2. A rod is a linear measure of sixteen and a half feet; so twenty rods is 330 feet or 110 yards.

∞

Camp Randall
December 21, 1862

Dear Esther,

Your letter was received this morning and found me in good spirits and enjoying usual health. I was somewhat disappointed last evening when I went to the post office in not finding a letter, but the lieutenant of our company took it out for me and I did not see him 'til morning.

I have been to church today. The text was in Hebrews 2nd chapter, 1st & 3rd verses: "How shall we escape if we neglect so great salvation." It was an interesting and profitable discourse, and well calculated to impress upon the mind the importance of availing our selves of the only salvation offered.

You said you knew by the tone of my letter that I was low-spirited. I suppose that I had a slight touch of diphtheria and it would probably have been quite serious had I not commenced in time to doctor.[1] There has been quite a number of cases in camp and one man has died with it.

This may in part account for it, but that which occupied my thoughts most was how will you bear the disappointment of my not getting a substitute. You speak of its being a great burden thus to be separated; I hope not greater than you will be able to bear. If I could feel that you were reconciled to my destiny I would pass through the 9 months with a light heart, for it will soon pass away.

I am very glad the people are so kind to you and that you get along so well, but Esther we are not alone. I am surrounded by men who, like myself, have left home with all its endearments; and who sigh for its quiet resting place. Some of them have small children with little for their families to depend upon but charity. I have seen more anxiety depicted upon the faces of men during my short stay in camp than I ever saw in all my life before. This may be partly accounted for by the fact that most of the drafted men came here with the impression that they would soon return home and have time to arrange their business, but in this respect they were disappointed.

But all the drafted men are to have furloughs of a few days. I shall probably get a furlough of 5 or 6 days about New Years. I want you to make up your mind to be reconciled to this short visit and be thankful for the favor that those in authority confer upon us.

Last Thursday the 25th Regiment from the Indian war engagement came into camp.[2] On Friday the whole regiment with the exception of one company got furloughs, and [a] more jolly set of fellows I never saw.

You wished to have me write what I thought of getting a load of straw. Perhaps you had if it is good.

I am writing and cannot see the line very well.

I want you to give brother Goodell & wife my best respects. I often think of them and am truly thankful for their kindness to you.

I was somewhat disappointed at what you said about your getting back that 10 dollars.

I see by your letter that others who go not to the army are deprived of friends. This is truly a world of separations, but by faith I see a brighter happier world where friends will never part.

I should like an answer soon.

Yours Truly,

Gilbert

NOTES

1. Diphtheria is a highly infectious bacterial disease that begins with a sore throat and fever. The bacteria attack the mucous membranes of the throat. This can result in the production of systemic toxins and the formation of a tough, grey membrane, which can spread to the larynx and cause suffocation. In 1863, diphtheria was still quite common and dangerous. Antitoxins for diphtheria were not developed until the 1890s, and effective vaccines not until after World War II.

2. The Indian War was an armed conflict in southern Minnesota; now it is sometimes called the Sioux Uprising or the Dakota War. The fighting was between the United States and several eastern bands of the Dakota people, often referred to as the Santee Sioux. Broken treaties, dishonest agents, famine, and large numbers of new white settlers who stripped and farmed Dakota lands and decimated wild game populations led to rising discontent among the Dakota.

The uprising began on August 17, 1862, and lasted until September 26, 1862, when most of the Dakota fighters surrendered. The estimated number of settlers who died ranged from 300 to 800. There was no accurate accounting of Dakota deaths. In December of that year, the Federal government hanged 38 Dakota men, imprisoned 300, and eventually forced the Dakota to leave Minnesota.

The Twenty-Fifth Wisconsin Regiment was mustered in on September 14, 1862. On September 19, they were sent to St. Paul, Minnesota, to help police the Dakota uprising. The regiment were divided and dispersed around south central Minnesota to help monitor Native American activity. Finally on December 19, 1862, the regiment reunited and marched about 250 miles to Winona. From there they were sent to Camp Randall in Madison ("U.S.–Dakota War of 1862"; Quiner, *Military History of Wisconsin*, 734–35; Fortney, "Participation of the Twenty-Fifth Regiment," 3–4; Dyer, *Compendium of the War of the Rebellion*, vol. 1, pt. 3, 1684).

❧

December 25, 1862

Dear Gilbert,

Your letter of the 21 is before me. I also received the one which contained the intelligence of the fire. I had not heard anything of it before. I know less than ever since you went away. I think I realize, in part at least, the meaning of these words, "It is not good that man should be alone." I suppose it is just as applicable to woman.

I felt a little guilty that you did not get my last earlier, but it is hard work for the boys to get their work done in time to mail a letter and I make as few errands for evening as possible.

I wish you would let me know if you have bought some gloves. If you have not, I will make arrangements to have you have some when you come back.

Mr. Eastman has paid your taxes $68.16.

Jack Woodruff wants Billy.[1] Mr. Eastman told Elton he ought to bring $65.

I meant to have written you a long letter, but it is impossible.

Yours ever,

Esther

NOTE
1. Billy was one of the Claflins' horses. He was mentioned in nine of the letters.

❧

Sunday, December 28, 1862

My Dear Gilbert,

The boys and myself have been to Church today and Mr. Montague preached a most sublime sermon from Matthew 16, last half of the 3rd verse.[1] He made it appear a thing to be sought for to become a sufferer, or even a martyr, in the cause of truth and justice. But my dear Gilbert, I think it needs the faith of a prophet to see the good resulting from so much suffering and bloodshed. And yet I have faith to believe that God rules, and all this strife will result in man's good. But I sometimes think our nation must, as a nation, be destroyed when corruption and dishonesty run riot in high places. I feel that there is no hope but in God alone, and I don't know but our day of grace is past.

The sun has just set and all is clear and serene and beautiful, and now I think, "Where is Gilbert? How is he employed? And what a privilege it would be for him to have a quiet home Sabbath."

William says you rather hurry off about a substitute. I want you to do just what you think is for the best. You, of course, have thought of it in all its bearings.

William said one of the men told him that you got a letter from your wife that made you feel pretty bad. I did not mean to write anything to give you the impression that my health was worse. The second week after you went away I was not as well; but I got better immediately. I think I am better now than I have been for a long time. We get along very well; much better than I should think we could without a Pa.

There is no school between Christmas and New Year; and Elton is trying to split rails and do considerable large work. Price milks.

If you can, I wish you would get your picture taken in Madison.

Anna is here yet. She and the boys are singing now. I think if they had someone to sing with them they would be quite singers. The first singing school term has just expired.[2]

My old disease (getting sleepy) is coming on, and I will say good night.

Esther Claflin

P.S. When I finished this I expected Homer would call for it, but he has probably changed his mind.

It is Monday night and the rest are eating supper.

Next Saturday is preparatory lecture.[3] I do hope that there will be nothing to prevent your being here.

NOTES

1. Matthew 16:3: "O ye hypocrites, ye can discern the face of the sky; but can ye not discern the signs of the times?"

2. The American singing schools were started in New England in about 1720 by Harvard-trained ministers who wanted to improve the singing of their congregations. Singing schools taught sight singing and a bit of music theory. By the 1860s in the West,

singing schools were often taught by traveling singing masters who stayed in town for just a few weeks. Often singing schools were important social events for a small town (Justin Thomas, "The American Singing School Movement," Smith Creek Music, 2011, http://www.smithcreekmusic.com/Hymnology/American.Hymnody/Singing.Schools/Singing.School.movement.html).

3. Preparatory lectures were held on the Saturday afternoon preceding each Communion service, the latter being held the first Sunday of each alternate month, beginning with January. These meetings were for the purpose of preparing members for this most sacred and solemn service. A meeting for the transaction of business of the church was held after each preparatory lecture ("History of the First Congregational Church," *Oconomowoc Enterprise*, June 21, 1929). For more about the Oconomowoc Congregational Church, see Appendix C.

◠◡

Madison
January 2, 1863

Dear Esther,

I expected before this to have been home; but I am still here and am doing all I can to get a substitute. I shall ascertain whether I can get one in 3 or 4 hours. If I do not succeed I shall probably be home tomorrow.

I am well. Should I be able to get one, I cannot tell for certain whether I shall be home this week or not as it takes some time to get matters fixed in proper shape.

I hope you will not be over anxious about the matter, for I am satisfied that in case I do not succeed in getting one it will be all for the best.

In haste Yours Truly,

Gilbert

◠◡

Camp Washburn[1]
January 11, 1863

Dear Esther,

I went into camp a little before dusk Friday and found the barracks much more convenient and comfortable than in Camp Randall. We also have better bread.

You will remember that I was in Company A 35th regiment. Our company is Company A, 34th regiment now. We were the first company mustered in among the drafted men, and the captain claimed it as a right that we should be Company A 34.[2]

Our regiment left Camp Randall on last Monday, and were on the train that was so badly smashed up, but none of the boys were hurt. The wife of the 1st lieutenant came very near being killed and yet she was not hurt much; they had to tear away the seat behind her to get her out. Four cars were smashed to pieces, and a number of passengers were seriously hurt. The car that had our rick was flung off, but those in which the soldiers were in was left on.

I think I shall like this place better, when I get acquainted, than I did our camp in Madison. We do not have to go outdoors to eat but have good tables to eat on. We do not have to go out at roll call to answer to our names, only when we drill. We have roll call at 6:00, 10:00, 2:00, and 9:00 at night.

Yesterday we got our guns. They are old muskets.[3] I saw one that was made in 1818 and is now 44 years old. The latest one that I have seen was 1843. They are good for nothing but to drill with and guard camp with.

I did not go to meeting today as it was nearly 10 o'clock before we could get ready to go, and it is 3 miles to meeting. It is a great deal more quiet here on Sunday, as we have more room, and I do not suffer one quarter as much from tobacco as I did in Camp Randall.

This morning a young man came into camp with a lot of tracts. I got one and read it aloud. The caption was, "Harken, Oh, Harken, Unto the Words of Him who Spake as Never Man Spake!" I felt strengthened and comforted by its perusal. Since I have been in camp here I have not seen a pack of cards, and the boys do not swear so much. One reason for it is they do not get so much intoxicating drink as they did in Camp Randall.

The 27th regiment is here. Four men were burnt to death when their barracks were burnt.[4] They were drunk as I am informed. Quite a large amount of government stores were burnt. All the barracks here have a guard in them every night now to prevent a like scene here.

The drafted men and substitutes are deserting all the while & have deserted since I left camp from our camp. There are about 800 drafted men here, and they are growing less every day. Of 33 substitutes in one company, 30 have deserted as I am informed.

It is 2 o'clock at night, and I am on guard and although not an officer I, for the time, have charge of the guardhouse. Three men are in irons and four are not, making seven in all. 8 or 10 men are here with me.

I saw Mr. Mann and he said the boys might have a load of straw and would take nothing for it.[5] If John does not go away, I wish he would help the boys get it. If he cannot, they will have to get someone else.

Gilbert Claflin

[Upside down at top]

Direct to Co A 34 Regiment Camp Washburn Milwaukee

NOTES

1. After January 2, there was no further discussion of Gilbert's getting a substitute. Within a week after his final letter from Camp Randall, Gilbert's regiment moved to Camp Washburn on the outskirts of Milwaukee. The camp had been established as a Civil War reception center and trading post in October 1861 and was located on the old Cold Spring Racetrack west of Twenty-Seventh Street.

2. At Camp Washburn, the men completed their organization under the direction of Colonel Fritz Anneke. Gilbert's regiment, Wisconsin's Thirty-Fourth Infantry, was the only organization from Wisconsin whose term of service was less than "three years . . . during the war." Instead, they were mustered in for nine months, from December 31, 1862, until September 8, 1863. A soldier's term of service is counted from the date he is "mustered in." In the case of Gilbert's regiment, that was nearly six weeks after they were drafted.

3. It has been said that no army, with the exception of the Confederate forces, ever went to war with such a variety of firearms as the Federal volunteer in the Civil War. This statement rings so true because the mid-19th century was a period of dramatic development of numerous firearms and firearms systems. . . .

Two generations before the Civil War, slow flintlock firing mechanisms and smoothbore musket barrels insured that a soldier could get off only one shot every couple of minutes, and that, when he did, the bullet would not go far, nor would it be likely to hit its target. The development of the percussion system, in which a copper cap could be quickly placed over a nipple at the breech, sending a spark into the powder charge when struck by the hammer, meant that three or more shots per minute could be fired. Moreover, the use of rifling grooves inside the barrel, imparting gyroscopic "spin" to the bullet as it exited, increased both the range and accuracy of the projectile, especially once the French Minie bullet was introduced. Its hollow base expanded upon firing, gripping the rifling effectively, while its cylindroconoidal shape kept it steady in flight. (Pritchard, *Civil War Weapons and Equipment*, 43)

4. *Janesville Weekly Gazette* and *Oconomowoc Free Press* ran the following article on the front page of their January 9, 1863, issue. The story was about the fire at Camp Sigel (another induction camp in Milwaukee) where the Twenty-Seventh Wisconsin Regiment was stationed:

CAMP SIGEL BARRACKS BURNED. Three Privates Lose Their Lives. About 12½ o'clock last night, a fire caught in the extensive barracks at Camp Sigel on North Point, resulting before it was extinguished in the entire destruction of all the old barracks and the loss of three lives, privates in the regiment. One other soldier was badly burned, but is expected to recover. The barracks consisted of four or five very large frame structures, all standing close to each other, and occupied as mess and sleeping quarters, and by some of the offices that are connected with the regiment. Close to the barracks on the east were four or five small structures, occupied by the commissioned officers, which were all saved. There was also a small building on the south, occupied by the field and staff officers, which was also saved. The barracks were occupied by the 27th regiment, Col. Krez, who have since removed to Camp Washburn, and will remain there till they leave the state. The value of the structures that were burned was not very great, perhaps not over $2,000, but the loss of life was of course of more consideration than any amount of material loss.

It is unknown how the fire caught. It first started in the sleeping quarters occupied by Capt. Marscener's company. It spread so suddenly that it was but a few moments before the entire barracks were wrapped in a general sheet of flame. The men who were waked had not time, generally, to save anything more than themselves and the clothes they had on them, and the muskets in a great many cases. There was a large number of muskets lost, however, and this morning the ground was thickly strewn with gun barrels, everything else belonging to the guns having been consumed. The men were almost universally sleeping in their uniforms, or else there would unquestionably have been a great destruction of uniforms. Several of the soldiers had trunks and valises with them which were mostly lost. The poor fellows who were burned were probably in a deep sleep, from which they were not waked until it was too late to escape that other sleep which knows no waking.

There was great confusion among the soldiers as they came running, jumping, and tumbling out of the buildings. Some rushed out half dressed, others crawled out on all fours and there was the wildest kind of a scene for a few moments. They soon rallied, however, and began to exert themselves in an attempt to save the officers' quarters. There were a few on the sick list in the hospital, but they were not in a serious condition, and were all saved. The regiment numbers about 800 men. They are now in comfortable quarters at Camp Washburn.

One of those who lost their lives lived quite a length of time after the fire, but was shockingly burned. His hair was all burned off, he could not see, and his skin fairly dropped off from him. He begged of his comrades, as they were rescuing him, for them to kill him, and put him out of misery. It was a heart-rending spectacle.—Milwaukee Wisconsin.

5. The Mann farm was 335 acres immediately east of the Claflins', Amasa Eastman's, and Newnhams' farms (*Atlas of Waukesha Co.*, 27). For more about Curtis Mann and his family, see Appendix B.

January 10, 1863

My Dear Husband,

As I returned to our home Friday it did not seem so desolate as you might suppose. Elton came back with me and there is nearly always a pervading spirit of faith and love, which calms these outward troubles and says, "The time is very short; be faithful to the end and then a crown of life is yours."

Elton's knees are better but his throat is quite bad. He has just been taking a hot sweat. He and Price threshed yesterday, and I think it hurt him for he was better Friday night. They threshed 70 bundles and when it was cleared they had seven and three-fourths bushels.

Price and I attended church today. The sermon was on prayer; a most excellent one, like all of our pastor's. While I was listening the thought came that perhaps you were listening to Mr. Clapp or Mr. Love.

January 12:

I was somewhat disappointed in not getting a letter last evening. I slept upstairs last night to let Elton sleep in our bed, and was awakened quite often by the wind and rain and the clothes flying, but we got them in all safe this morning. But Gilbert was not here to help me. How much you are missed no one can tell but a wife who has had such a husband.

It is a dark and stormy day today and I am wishing that I could have you home in all the cold and stormy weather.

January 14:

I attended prayer meeting last evening. It was rather a dull one. Mr. Montague was at the convention, Mr. Rockwell was not there, Gilbert was not there.[1] Old Mr. Wood was there, but did not say anything. Mr. Montague preached his farewell sermon at Summit last Sunday.

We received your letter Tuesday evening and you may know that I am really glad you are in more comfortable quarters and now, Gilbert, tell me truly if you sleep warm *every* night. You may not suppose that I go to bed in my warm bed without thinking of *you*. Does your lieutenant's wife stay in Milwaukee? Mrs. Danforth said to me you are so near I could visit you.[2] Do you think it would be entirely impracticable?

I have been thinking if you should stay there long, and should get the privilege of going out often, that perhaps you could go to some cabinet shop and fix a handle on my Eagle fan, but if you think it would bother you, I would not like to send it. You know how much I should prize it in your absence if *you* could fix it.

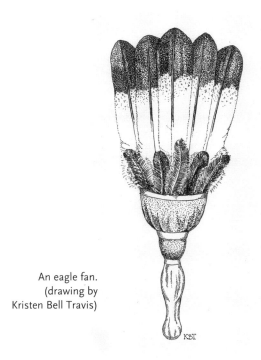

An eagle fan.
(drawing by
Kristen Bell Travis)

I have not heard from any of the absent friends since you left. John has not gone to Madison.

There was a man here yesterday to look at Billy, but I did not see him after he saw the colt. Do you think we had better sell him if we have a chance? I think our fright before you left was nothing but a fright. I have seen no indication of scratching.

Since writing the above, Elton has seen Mr. Eastman and he talks some as though he would like to buy the mare. How much shall we ask for her?

Elton has been too unwell to go to school this week, but today he seems to be nearly well.

The boys shut up a wether to fat the day you went away. How long will they want to keep it up, and do you think they can kill it?

Your roll call comes so often I am afraid you can't go to church.

Price is a most excellent boy to do shopping. He gets the right things and remembers them all, and brings back the right change.

This rubber cord is to sew on the earpieces to your cap.

It is 9 o'clock and very cold and windy.

Good night my love,

Esther Claflin

NOTES

1. John S. Rockwell founded Oconomowoc and then worked hard to establish the town. He helped to build its first sawmill, first flour mill, first school, and first hotel and to start the first bank and first newspaper. He also was influential in getting both the Watertown Plank Road and the Milwaukee & Watertown Railroad to come to Oconomowoc (Johnson, *Illustrious Oconomowoc*; Potter, Punko, and Leitzke, *Historic Oconomowoc*; Behling, *The Story of the Founder of Oconomowoc*, 1–14). For more about the Rockwells, see Appendix B.

2. In 1862, the Danforths were a farming family in Summit. Both Edward and his wife Nancy were in their thirties and were born in New York State, but their three children were born in Wisconsin (1860 census). For more about the Danforth family, see Appendix B.

∽

Camp Washburn
January 18, 1863

Dear Esther,

Your letter was perused by me last evening. I was glad to hear that you were getting along so well and that Elton was getting better. I was afraid that he would have a serious time of it.

As for myself, I am getting along well. I never had a better appetite in my life and can eat anything which is on the table with a relish. There is quite a number of our boys that have been on the sick list but mostly hard colds.

You asked me to tell you truly if I sleep warm every night. I can say that I do and wish you could sleep as warm. There are 2 stoves in our barracks, and fire is kept in them day and night. Four are detailed every day to cut wood, and two every night to keep fire; each having to watch 2 hours.

I went to church today, attended the Reverend Mr. Helmers, and listened to an excellent discourse from Proverbs, 12th chapter, 14th verse.[1] I trust it will be a means under God of strengthening and encouraging me in the Christian journey. The church is the one that the Sunday School Convention was held in that I attended 3 years ago. I am the only one in our company that attends the Congregational Church. I have a pass of my own and can come back when I please inside of the time specified in the pass.

When several go out together they have to wait one for another, as it is a difficult matter for all to agree when to go.

You wished to know if the lieutenant's wife was in Milwaukee. She is. You wished to know what I thought about your coming to see me. I hardly know what to say about it. If you should come it is doubtful whether I could see you for any length of time unless you came into camp. Our captain has had a considerable trouble about his men leaving; some 12 have deserted and failed to return on furlough. The result is that he is more strict with the rest of us. I think the result will be that more will follow their example as he now refuses to grant any more furloughs 'til they return.

I am satisfied that the 34th regiment of drafted men will be of little service to the government. There is a growing feeling of discontent among the men; not so much on account of their treatment, but on the account of the slackness of government in bringing in those who failed to report. And I do not believe if the drafted men here were at home and were called to report to the com's that 1 in 20 would go.

We have got the best company in the regiment; the boys agree first rate.[2] I have not heard an angry word among them since I have been in camp; and if any of them get in the guardhouse, when ration time comes he gets a big one.

January 19:

There has been but two of our men in the guardhouse here.

Our chaplain is a German. I have not had an interview with him yet; he was appointed last week. I am inclined to think from what I have heard that he will be of little service to any but his own countrymen. Perhaps I am mistaken. I think that the chaplain ought to be a German as a large majority of the regiment are Germans, but if he is a good man and is laboring for the good of those around him I shall be satisfied.

Yours Truly,

Gilbert

[Upside down on the top]

These pieces that you fixed on my cap have been a great comfort to my ears. I am very glad you sent that rubber as it was what I needed.

NOTES

1. Proverbs 12:14: "A man shall be satisfied with good by the fruit of his mouth: and the recompense of a man's hands shall be rendered unto him." You will be satisfied if you say good things; and will be rewarded if you do good things.

2. Company A, Thirty-Fourth Wisconsin Regiment, officers and staff: Colonel—Fritz Anneke; Lieutenant Colonel—Henry Orff; Major—George H. Walther; Adjutant—Herman Hasse; Quartermaster—J. A. Becher; Surgeon—J. W. Weinern; First Assistant Surgeon—James S. Kelso; Chaplain—Rev. F. A. Beckel; Captain—W. Eugene Ferslew; First Lieutenant—Henry T. Calkins; Second Lieutenant—Michael A. Leahy (Quiner, *Military History of Wisconsin*, 820).

∽

Camp Washburn
January 19, 1863

Dear Boys,

I am glad to hear that you are doing so well and are getting along so finely and shall ever rejoice in my absence to hear that you are good boys and doing all that you can to make home comfortable and happy.

I am getting along in drill exercise first rate and can execute all the movements in the gun exercise without any trouble now.

Your mother wished me to write about the horses. I think that you had better sell one of them. If Mr. Eastman wants the mare, you had better let him have her. I do not know what she is worth; ask him what he will give. I think he will do what is right in the matter, or if you have to sell one of the colts for what they are worth, allowing Mr. Eastman to be the judge, let it go.

I did not, in your mother's letter, inform her about the fan. I will see what I can do when I go down town and then I will let her know.

I think that you had better give your sheep which you have got a falling ground feed for the grain that you give. Do not give too much at first.

I want you to write me a letter and tell me how you are getting along at school and at home. I hope you will improve all your time at school in the best manner possible, and at home do all that you can to make your mother and grandmother comfortable and happy.

From Your Father,

Gilbert Claflin

∽

January 19, 1863

Dear Gilbert,

Another week has passed and we are all in good health.

Yesterday the boys went to church, and we all went to concert in the evening. We are to have preaching evenings after this. There is to be three lectures this week in the hall on Ancient Egypt, and Uncle John lets the soldiers' families in free, and I think we shall go if it is not too cold.[1]

I guess you did not think—I did not until after you were gone—that the day you returned from Madison Elton was 16 years old.

John and the boys got their straw Saturday. They found Mr. Mann at home. He told them to get as large a load as they could carry.

Anna tells me that there is a case in Brookfield [a town twenty miles east of Oconomowoc] of a young man being drafted whose only brother had enlisted, and he had an aged mother whose name is Humbert. I thought perhaps it was the same one you told me of. She and James knew them and said they were fine people.

I got my washing out today by noon, and your Mother is carding and spinning.

Gilbert, don't wear your stockings more than a week. If you do, you will have cold feet.

Potter has sent you a patent office report. Would you not like to have me send it to you? And where shall we send things? I hear Mr. Emery is not at the depot.

January 22:

Your letter was received Monday evening, and next to hearing the footsteps of my dear husband is a letter from him. I was glad you wrote to your mother and the boys. I also received a letter from Parmenter Monday night and one from William Tuesday night.

J.P. writes a full letter but no particular news. They are still near Ft. Henry; have done no marching since he wrote to William. He says the *rainy season* has seemed to forget its annual visit and he says they have skies which he should think rivaled Italy in beauty. Their food is meager in variety, being limited to the *everlasting* hard bread, a little baker's bread, ham, coffee, and a few beans. He says his health is fair.

William writes a letter glowing with brotherly love and full of high and noble sentiments. I think I shall send it to you, but I don't want you to think I endorse all that he says about me.

Anna has gone to her mother's but she is to return Monday and stay the rest of the winter with Mother.

The bell has rung, the engine whistled and John has gone; gone back again to the War. The youngest of four, all gone to the War; and for what? To suffer and die for *Liberty*! I would it were so, but I almost hate the word. It seems as though it meant Oppression. Liberty to those that have the power to oppress whom they can, if they can get gain thereby. They tell us about the dark days of the Revolution. Think you *they* were as dark as the darkness of this *our* day: *not* because of the physical suffering which we at home are called upon to endure. For we are not called to suffer in that way; but it seems as though God had forsaken this nation. We are being tried so as by fire and if there is gold enough in this nation to save it, it will be saved. But if not, it ought to be among the nations that were.

Gilbert, I want you should buy fruit sometimes to eat. I think it will be for your health.

Your picture has been a real comfort.

I have spent some truly happy hours since you went away last. Surely all of the happiness here is not worldly happiness, and I will say to you now that since you first went away I have endeavored to sustain the family altar in my poor way. O, I could not bear to see it broken down because you were gone while these dear children were left to be injured or benefited by it.

From your wife,

Esther Claflin

[Upside down at the top of page 2]

If you have anything to say particularly to me, write it separate for your mother comes in every time I get a letter and I have to read it aloud the first thing.

E.

NOTE

1. Esther's uncle John Metcalf was her mother's brother. He was the owner of a shoe store in Oconomowoc. Uncle John and his wife Mahala Mead Metcalf had twin daughters who died in infancy in 1862 and were expecting a child in early April 1863. They often found themselves caring for other people's children. In 1862, Franciss (Frank) Lockwood, the sixteen-year-old daughter of John's former business partner, was living with them. Occasionally Esther's sister Emily and her children lived with them as well. For more about John Metcalf, see Appendix A.

☙

Thursday evening, January 29, 1863

My Dear Husband,

Old time and us are jogging along very pleasantly together. The children seem to do their chores very easily, but Elton can't stand going to school. He came home Tuesday before noon and has not been able to go since. His trouble seems to be his throat and lungs. He says he feels the best outdoors. He is able to do his chores and more, but he can't get along with the impure air of the schoolroom.

I am better than when I last wrote. My cough is much better. I read a letter last evening from J.P. to Marg. He thinks they may leave soon. He wrote quite a long poem entitled "The Dead" and he wrote some sweet words to Minnie.

John has been here today and he looks as solemn as the grave, and he barely spoke unless asked a question.

And now I feel incapable of being cheerful and imparting cheerfulness to others when they are cast down. It is a gift; yes a "talent," which you possess and I pray you may use it aright, as I believe you will.

Last Sunday Price and I went to church, and as we neared home I felt and told him it never seemed better to get home than it does now. Here are my children and here whichever way I turn my eyes, I see the fruit of the labor of him I love better than my life. And Gilbert, I sometimes feel when we are using what you have wrought out with so many years hard labor, as if it were almost a sin for us to enjoy these things when you are placed out of the reach of the most of the privileges of civilized life.

I went to prayer meeting last evening. There were seven men and eleven women there, and so it is wherever I go: so many more women; sad-looking women with husbands, brothers, and sons gone.

I think Price is doing well at school. He seems interested and is not willing to lose a day. And I believe he has not lost but two days this winter.

I understand that drafted men's families are to receive pay from the state the same as volunteers. How is it, and are you getting out of money? We have the three-dollar bill besides the change, and I think we shan't have to buy much for a good while.[1]

Yours affectionately,

Esther Claflin

[Upside down at top]

What about our box at the post office? Are we to pay for it before long for this year? I feel very much like giving you a scolding for not sending home your washing, but you see I haven't the room. Now don't you forget to tell me which of these you read first.

Your Esther

NOTE

1. The Bureau of Engraving and Printing has never been authorized to print a three-dollar note. During the early nineteenth century, however, banks operating under Federal or state charters issued notes of that denomination. These notes were printed by private contractors and were not obligations of the Federal government ("Do $3 Notes Exist?" US Department of the Treasury, Bureau of Engraving and Printing, http://www.moneyfactory.gov/faqlibrary.html, accessed May 25, 2013).

January 30, 1863

Dear Esther,

You wished me to inform you about my health when I wrote you. I think that I must be gaining in flesh as my pants have got to be so tight that I have to put a string in the button hole at the top in order to button them and my coat is a getting so that it fits rather snugger than I like when buttoned.

I think the camp is more healthy than Camp Randall. There has not been a death in camp since we have been here.

Last night a dispatch came into camp that the 34th Regiment was under marching orders and that we were to leave the state soon. I expect that we shall soon leave this camp, but whether we leave the state or go to some other camp is all a matter of uncertainty so far as the soldiers are concerned. We have our outfit with the exception of our rubber blankets. We shall, if we leave, go to guard someplace where prisoners are confined, probably, as we are not fit for active service, having never drilled only in company drill.

The 34th Regiment cannot muster more than 500 men, although they have 750 enrolled. They are leaving continually. Last night an extra guard was detailed, and one company had 3 guards at each door of the barracks. Some 80 had got things ready to start, but notwithstanding all the precaution 6 men deserted. It is the officers that are urging the removal of the regiment out of the state. They know that their shoulder straps will be worthless if they remain in the state as the regiment would soon be composed of officers and no privates the way things are now going. 100 men were on guard last night; all of them had loaded guns. But notwithstanding all the array, this morning report of 6 companies shows that 13 have deserted. Four companies had not reported when our report was sent in.

I hope you will not be concerned about me although I stand in the contending elements. I never was more cool and composed in my life. I believe I shall have divine guidance and direction day by day.

Last Sunday I attended Reverend Mr. Clapp's church. He had exchanged with a minister from Waukesha. The text was from Genesis, 22nd chapter, part of the 13th verse, "And Abraham called the name of that place Jehovah jireh."[1] He said that the meaning of Jehovah jireh is "The Lord will provide." He referred in the first place to Abraham's faith and of the wonderful deliverance which saved His only son upon whom the promise rested. He cited other instances to prove that God was always faithful concerning His promises, and that to believe in Him and act accordingly was all that is necessary to render man happy under any and every emergency. I felt that it was meant for my good, and trust that I shall profit by it.

So far as money is concerned, I have got 19 dollars and expect my pay soon. You wished to know about the 5 dollars from the state. Arrangements are being made so that you can draw the money. How soon before you will get it I do not know.

All sorts of stories are going the rounds about our leaving. I hope you will be reconciled to any movement I shall be called to make. I am prepared for it. I shall send home my things that Price does not take by express. He will tell you about things. I was glad to see him and should be glad to see you all, but it is all for the best.

The wife of one of our men came to see him yesterday; they could not get out of camp last night and she was allowed to stay in the barracks along with the men.

Whilst I am writing they are a going out the gate. I was glad to get a letter from Elton. I hope He will write often.

Yours truly,

Gilbert

NOTE

1. In this Bible story, God asked Abraham to sacrifice his only son Isaac as a burnt offering. Abraham, ready to obey God, took Isaac to the appointed mountaintop, bound

him on top of the wood laid for the fire, and had the knife ready to kill his son. At the last moment, God told Abraham not to sacrifice Isaac, but instead to sacrifice a ram caught in a bush nearby. Because Abraham was prepared to obey God even to the point of killing his only beloved son, God sent great blessings on Abraham and all his descendants.

⌒⌣

Columbus, Kentucky[1]
February 3, 1863

Dear Esther,

I am the first one in our company to write to dear ones left behind. I am well and stood the trip quite well.

The day Price left camp we left. At 12 o'clock we were ordered to be ready; at half past 12 we were ordered to march. Instead of going direct to the Lake Shore Depot by the way of Milwaukee which is about 4 miles, we were marched back into the country and clear round to the second station on the railroad arriving there at dark. We must have gone 8 or 10 miles. The reason was the officers knew that a good many would desert if they got into the city. The 27th regiment guarded us to the cars and saw us all aboard, but some did not stay on long but left.

We arrived at Chicago about 12 at night, and during that day we lost over 100 men by desertion; 21 from our company left the cars on the way to Chicago. We were marched to the Illinois Central and got on the cars and left for Cairo about 2 o'clock. I did not get much sleep during the night as there was too much excitement for that. As the day dawned we saw a beautiful sight: the prairie on fire. The first hundred miles the land that I saw was very low and wet, (The boys have just had a time with a rat—the biggest one I ever saw. He came right into the box on which I am writing— right by the candle where I am writing—as confused as if he was at home. 4 of the boys made a dive at him, and after some stomping killed him) then it is better for 40 or 50 miles but on the whole it is a hard section of country all the way to Cairo that I saw.

We arrived in Cairo about 10 o'clock Monday morning. It is all that it has been represented to be: a low sunken hole.[2] We expected to stop there, but no preparation had been made for us. We stood a couple of hours in the streets; got some rations; then went on one of the river steamers and went down to Columbus, arriving about 4 o'clock; found that no preparation had been made for us here, but we being cold got into barracks and some of the other companies. The rest got tents. It commenced snowing about dark,

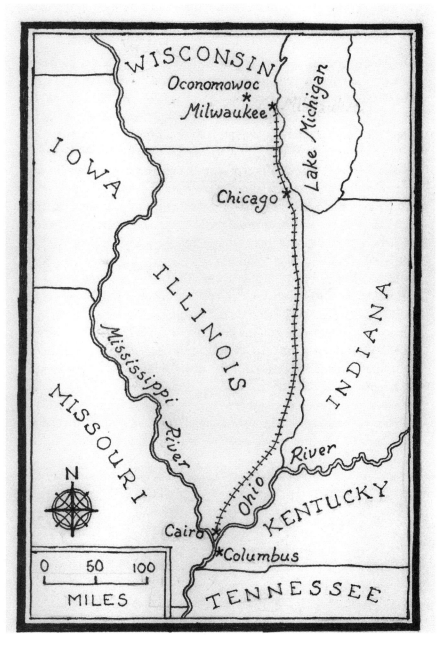

Gilbert's route shown here was only one of many rail lines in that section of the country.
(drawing by Kristen Bell Travis based on 1862 rail and political maps)

and this morning it is as cold as almost any day I have seen in Wisconsin this winter. I slept warm and comfortable during the night for the first night in camp, which is always the worst.

Columbus you will remember was one of the strongholds of the Rebels. We are encamped on the bluff about 200 ft above the river right across the river. The battle of Belmont was fought and from this position.[3] The Rebels fired a hundred and twenty pounder 'til it burst doing considerable damage to our men during the engagement.[4] I went down this morning and saw the great chain that General Pillow had stretched across the river and the great anchor used to anchor it to prevent the gun-boats passing.[5] The links are made of 2-inch diameter iron bar and are about 10 inch long and 6 inches broad. There are hundreds of torpedoes which our men have raked from the river. They are in shape of the balls that John brought back. They are most of them about 18 inches long and about 5 inch diameter.

It is a beautiful pleasant morning and I guess will be warmer before night.

How long we shall stay here I cannot say. You had not better write before I write again which will be as soon as I ascertain what we are going to do. I am standing and writing on my knapsack and it is rather a hard place to write. I hope this will find you all well and reconciled to my situation for I am contented and am doing all I can to make those around me cheerful and happy.

Give my love to all the folks that enquire as to my welfare. I hope that we shall be prospered spiritually and temporally as shall be for our good and that we shall all be brought together again and be permitted to enjoy each other's society again.

Yours truly,

Gilbert Claflin

NOTES

1. Kentucky was a carefully neutral state for the first four and a half months of the war. It was sandwiched between the conflicts in the eastern states and those in western Missouri and Kansas. On orders of General Polk, Confederate General Gideon Johnson Pillow left Confederate strongholds in Northern Tennessee about ninety miles southeast of Columbus, Kentucky. General Pillow entered Kentucky on September 3, 1861, and moved to Columbus where his troops began setting up and strengthening their position. The next day General Grant arrived at Cairo, Illinois, where he established Union headquarters. These actions were the final links in an unbroken front between North and South from the Atlantic west to Kansas. Abraham Lincoln wrote to the Republican senator from Illinois on September 22, 1861: "I think to lose Kentucky is nearly the same

as to lose the whole game. Kentucky gone, we can not hold Missouri, nor, as I think, Maryland. These all against us, and the job on our hands is too large for us" (Basler, *Collected Works of Abraham Lincoln*, 4:532).

In early February 1862, Grant's forces captured two Confederate posts, Fort Henry and Fort Donelson, just over the Kentucky border in Tennessee. This left Columbus an isolated Confederate outpost. On March 2, 1862, without a battle, the final units of Confederate troops left Columbus. Of the 140 Confederate guns, only two were left behind. The next day, March 3, Federal troops occupied the town and the forts on the bluff. When Gilbert arrived in early 1863, the Federals held Columbus. Here they collected and guarded prisoners, sheltered and enlisted runaway slaves, and sent out occasional minor expeditions. It was a quiet corner of the war (Long, *Civil War Day by Day*, 114, 136, 177–78; Boatner, *Civil War Dictionary*, 57–58, 394–96). For more about Columbus, Kentucky, before Gilbert's arrival, see Appendix D.

2. Cairo, Illinois, is about forty miles up the Mississippi River from Columbus. It had been the subject of a wildly optimistic town development scheme in the late 1830s. The company that marketed bonds for the Cairo City and Canal Company in London went bankrupt in 1840, and both British and American investors lost their holdings. Whether or not the great Victorian novelist Charles Dickens had been one of those investors, he certainly knew of the fiasco when he visited Cairo in 1842, twenty years before Gilbert's arrival. Dickens wrote of the town in his book *American Notes*:

> At length, upon the morning of the third day, we arrived at a spot so much more desolate than any we had yet beheld, that the forlornest places we had passed, were, in comparison with it, full of interest. At the junction of the two rivers, on ground so flat and low and marshy, that at certain seasons of the year it is inundated to the house-tops, lies a breeding-place of fever, ague, and death; vaunted in England as a mine of Golden Hope, and speculated in, on the faith of monstrous reputations, to many people's ruin. A dismal swamp, on which the half-built houses rot away . . . teeming . . . with rank unwholesome vegetation, in whose baleful shade the wretched wanderers who are tempted hither, droop, and die, and lay their bones; . . . a hotbed of disease, an ugly sepulchre, a grave uncheered by any gleam of promise: a place without one single quality, in earth or air or water to commend it: such is this dismal Cairo.

Apparently it had not improved much by 1863 (Hall and Wood, *Big Muddy*, 104; Channick, "Boz in Egypt").

3. The Battle of Belmont, November 7, 1861, took place in the hamlet of Belmont, Missouri, just across the river from Columbus. The greatest significance of the battle was that it provided battle experience to General Grant and his troops (Boatner, *Civil War Dictionary*, 57–58; Long, *Civil War Day by Day*, 136). For more about the Battle of Belmont, see appendix D.

4. On November 11, 1861, four days after the Battle of Belmont, one of the large 128-pound guns on the bluff exploded accidentally, killing seven men and wounding Confederate Major General Leonidas Polk (Long, *Civil War Day by Day*, 139). There is a description of this incident under "Columbus, Kentucky, before Gilbert's Arrival" in Appendix D.

5. Part of Confederate General Pillow's strategy to keep Union forces from using the Mississippi River was stretching a large chain across the river, just below the surface, with torpedoes suspended from the chain. This part of the river defense did not work quite as well as General Pillow had hoped. They had to use barges instead of rafts of logs

to buoy the chain because it was so heavy, which made it pretty obvious where the torpedoes were.

Union General U.S. Grant wrote, on January 6, 1862, "The rebels have a chain across the river about 1 mile above Columbus. It is sustained by flats at intervals, the chain passing through staples placed about the water's edge, the chain passing under the boats. Between each pair of the boats a torpedo is attached to the chain, which is expected to explode by concussion. An experiment was made with one of these machines about ten days ago by directing a coal-boat against it. The experiment resulted satisfactorily to the enemy. The position of them being so distinctly marked cannot be regarded as much of an obstacle. Others are supposed to be planted in the river above these, not so distinctly located. From information received through a gentleman up from Memphis there are about 600 torpedoes in the river from Columbus to that city" (Scott, *War of the Rebellion*, vol. 7, pt. 2, 534; vol. 52, pt. 2, 194).

∽

[Probably February 7, 1963] ⇒ 1863

Dear Esther,

In my last to you I said that I would inform you whether we were to stay here. The prospect is that we shall stay here for some time.

I am well and am getting along first rate. We have not drilled any as yet and the prospect is that we shall have to do guard duty which will occupy most of our time.

I suppose there are about 6,000 men here in camp. There was, a few weeks since, 16,000 here.

I was detailed yesterday morning to go on guard to guard secesh prisoners and deserters.[1] I had a good time as I did not have to stand guard. I had to work during the 24 hours about 2½ hours.

There are some advantages in my favor here which were not in Wisconsin. Tobacco is worth, the best kind, $1.50 a pound; whiskey is $4.00 a gallon; and a man that sells a soldier a drink of whiskey, if found out, goes into the guardhouse. Beer is 5 cents a drink.

Last night one of the 111th Illinois boys got a bottle of whiskey and brought it to the guardhouse in the morning.[2] He got to fooling with one of the boys. His bottle fell on the floor and smashed it, spilling all the whiskey. The boys felt the loss.

I do not expect to go to meeting again very soon; and as to Christian association, I expect it will be limited. Perhaps I shall find more congenial associates than I expect; but the thought that I have Christian friends, though far away, brings comfort and contentment to my heart. And then there is a never failing source to which I can at all times look and find joy and peace.

I have had but little time as yet to look around but have seen a good many sights that have interested me much. I got a look at one of the gunboats. It carries 14 guns and looks as if would do terrible work. The heaviest guns they have mounted here are 168 pounders.

The fortifications extend about 4 miles. The number of guns that are mounted here I do not know. I wish the boys could see the splendid steamers that pass here. I had but little idea of the size of them before I saw them. There is one called the Ruth which for size and beauty exceeds anything I ever saw in the sailing line by a good deal.

I mentioned in my last that I saw the torpedoes that the rebels sunk in the river; but they were small to those I saw afterwards. They were cast iron, 20 inches in diameter and 26 inches long, and would hold 75 or 100 lbs of powder I should judge.

I mentioned about the anchors. I mentioned one was 10 inches. They are now loading the anchors and chains on a boat with the other fixings which the Rebels had prepared for defense. There is enough to load 2 or 3 boats I should judge.

I have had a little insight into the glorious institution, and am satisfied that to perpetuate slavery is to degrade those who perpetuate it.[3] There are a great many blacks here, and I should judge from what I see and hear that there is a good deal of suffering among them here.

I send home to the boys a few kernels of corn. It came from an ear that had 18 rows on the cob.

I have not time to write more. I shall expect that the boys will write to me in your next.

Columbus, Kentucky, from the Mississippi River, March 4, 1862. (Frank Leslie, *Famous Leaders and Battle Scenes of the Civil War* [New York: Mrs. Frank Leslie, 1896])

I must tell Elton about the cavalry horses within a short distance of our barracks. Some 75 horses stand picketed day and night without shelter and they look first rate. The cavalry go a-scouting through the country around the camp.

You must direct your letters to Columbus Kentucky Company A 34th Regiment Wisconsin Militia.

Yours Truly,

Gilbert Claflin

NOTES

1. *Secesh* is short for secessionist, i.e., Confederate.

2. Columbus was the first post of the 111th Illinois Infantry Regiment after its two weeks of training at Camp Marshall in Salem, Illinois. The regiment had been at Columbus since November 1, 1862, about three months, and had not seen any action yet (Dyer, *Compendium of the War of the Rebellion*, 1093). There is more about the 111th Illinois Regiment in Appendix D.

3. Gilbert may have been quoting this or something similar: "Verily, it is the opinion of these men, that this free government was established on purpose to extend the blessings of the glorious institution of slavery" (Howard, "Report of the Decision of the Supreme Court of the United States," 407).

⌒

February 11, 1863

Dear Esther,

I have not had a letter from home as yet but shall look for one now 'til it comes.

I am well and never enjoyed better health in my life.

Since my last to you I have looked around the fortifications here and am astonished at the extent and strength of the works here. Last Monday I went to the stockade fort. There are 3 large guns mounted and are so arranged that they can reach all points of the compass. In the stockade (which is built of timber standing on end sunk in the ground sufficient to hold them in an upright position and rising above the surface about 10 ft) are cut loop holes for sharp shooters. Two sides are built in this manner the other 2 are earth works with a wide ditch in front. In about 40 rods of where I am sitting is a battery mounting 6 large guns. Two of them are 120-pounders. Within 20 rods are 4 more the largest 120. About 60 rods is another battery which has 3 guns, the smallest 32-pounders. This is said to be the strongest national position on the river.

The bank rises over 200 ft above the river. They are gradually caving off and are being swept away by the current.

Today I went to see the water batteries which the Rebels erected at an enormous expense. One of them is built of sandbags and is 20 rods long and 2 rods wide. The whole extent of the works is nearly 50 rods long. All the cannon that were mounted on these works are now in the bottom of the river.

All the water which is used here is taken from the river. It is raised to the top of the bluff by a powerful steam engine and runs in to a tank that will hold 300 hundred barrels and runs from this to various places in the fortifications. I saw one cistern, the top of which had fallen in, which would hold 500–600 barrels.

I have visited only the fortifications right in this vicinity. They extend as I am informed some 2 or 3 miles.

I have been cooking for several days past. Two of us do the cooking for the company. I do not know whether I shall cook longer than this week or not. The man that is with me has got to go on duty next week. The captain told me to cook 'til further orders. I do not have to do any duty aside from the cooking and do not have to answer to roll call. I get along first rate and can cook beans, rice, and *hog* as good as the best of them. And can make good coffee. We draw our bread and crackers.

Yesterday we moved into our cook tent, and last night I slept in a tent for the first time in my life.

February 12:

It is now about half past 4 and I am sitting on my bed with the top of my book for a candle stand. My bedstead is 2 canvas tents folded so as to accommodate 2 of us. We have a good lot of hay on top, and 3 blankets, and our overcoats.[1] When I got up this morning the stars were shining.

Now it is about 6 o'clock and it is raining and the wind is blowing to a terrible rate: a regular summer shower. It seems like spring. Bluebirds and larks are singing around here, and the grass looks green although they have had more snow here than in Wisconsin.

We have not as yet got any money and when we shall get any is all a matter of uncertainty.[2] I have got a plenty and you need not feel anxious about me in this respect, but I am afraid you will run short before I get it.

I have got some of the apples Price fetched me to Milwaukee and have not tasted of the honey as yet. I have stewed some of the dried fruit once, and gave one of the boys who was sick some twice. Such things are hard to get here and are valuable and I shall use them accordingly.

I was informed last Sunday that our Chaplain would preach in English at 2 o'clock. I went, stayed about an hour but saw no preacher. Work goes on here Sunday the same as any other day, and I feel to some extent its blighting influence. But notwithstanding all the obstacles that present themselves, there is a guiding Spirit within me that gives me peace.

Yours Truly,

Gilbert

[Upside down at top of first page]

I hope the boys will let me know how they are getting along, and how the fodder holds out, and what is going on in Oconomowoc. If you are like to be short of fodder perhaps Mr. Mann will let you have some more straw. He said he would if he had any to spare.

[Upside down at top of third page]

Direct your letters to Fort Halleck Columbus Kentucky Company A 34 Regiment Wisconsin Infantry

NOTES

1. The overcoats issued to enlisted foot soldiers were made of blue-grey wool cloth. They were single-breasted, with brass buttons, a stand-up collar, and a cape that fell to the elbow (Pritchard, *Civil War Weapons and Equipment*, 22).

2. As a private, Gilbert earned thirteen dollars per month with two dollars withheld until the end of his term and a shilling a month taken out to support the Soldiers' Home (Varhola, *Everyday Life during the Civil War*, 37).

༑

February 12, 1863

My Dear Gilbert,

I hardly know where to begin or what to say.

I was so astonished when Price returned and told me you had left for southern climes. But the next Monday and Tuesday and Wednesday were so *very cold* I was glad that you was where it was warmer. Tuesday it was so cold that it seemed as though I should freeze, and it is still snug winter weather, but pleasant. Now that I have thought it all over, I had rather you would go south now than in the spring.

You must [have] had an awful time going; so cold and windy on those prairies, and the men running away. I should like to know who guarded, and if they got off the cars while they were running, and did your bunkey desert?

Don't you find it awful dirty down there? Are you kept pretty close there? Of course you have not been across the river to view the battle ground. Is Columbus a business town, or is it turned into a military depot?

Gilbert, don't you sometimes feel bewildered; or have you got so thoroughly initiated into camp life that you feel at home? I hope you will not get stronger love for it than for your own quiet home.

I received your first letter the next Friday and Gilbert, the days and nights were anxious ones until I got it. Your second was received last night so you see it takes four days for the mail to come through.

Margaret got a letter from J.P. last night. He said they were sent up to Donelson but got there too late for the fight.[1] An Illinois regiment defended the fort—not Ft. Donelson, that is not considered worth holding, but another a few miles from there whose name I've forgot. It was defended against great odds. I will not attempt to tell the figures but he said it reflected great honor on the defenders. He has been in one skirmish. They were sent with provisions to Corinth and were attacked by the Rebels, but no lives were lost. But he is now back at Ft. Henry, only about 60 miles from you, almost in the same latitude, a little south and if you have time I would write to him. He is Company H, Wisconsin 13th.

And now I would like to know if you have written to anybody since you left home but us? And did you ever get a letter from me with one enclosed from William? I thought you never did, or you would [have] sent William's back. I was sorry to lose it.

You may be sure if I had thought of your leaving the state so soon, I should [have] sent you some things. I intended to make you a portfolio. What do you carry your paper in? Price said you had not got much. I think by writing fine, I can send enough in my letters . . .

(Just at this juncture Mr. and Mrs. Montague and Mr. Danforth called. They send their love to you and inquire your address. I think Mr. Danforth will send you some papers.)

I attended prayer meeting last night. There seemed to be more life in the meeting than any I have attended this winter. I think Mr. Rockwell is a deep, thorough Christian. Mr. William Thompson, J. Stratten, C. Eastman and wife, and Mrs. Boyer were mentioned as subjects for prayer. They are holding a series of meetings at the Methodist Church with what result I do not know. Mr. Montague says there is quite a revival in the church at Hartland [a town eight miles east of Summit].

O Gilbert, I hope our intercourse will not always be so clogged as it is now. I cannot think of half I wish to say, and yet I am thankful that we can send and receive letters.

Anna has not heard from James since you were here. I don't know as there is anything new to write about family matters. Things move along just about the same. We are all well. I feel much better than I have for a long time.

Gilbert, we may never meet again, and I feel that I have many times been an unfaithful wife and I now ask your forgiveness for all my naughty actions. When I sit by the fire in a comfortable seat I think of you, when I sit down to my meals I think of you, when I go to church I think of you, when I go out evenings I think of you, when I go to bed at night and when I get up in the morning I think of you, and may we meet in heaven if never again on earth.

To my own dear Gilbert

From Esther

[Next page of same letter]

Dear Father,

The night before Price went into Milwaukee, Mr. Allison died. He died with the diphtheria. Mr. John S. Rockwell died a few days ago.

I think we have not fed near half the oats out. And we have not fed hardly any hay out yet. And the corn stalks are more than half gone and I think that we have fed about half of the corn.

The bucket lambs are doing finely. I was offered twelve shillings for the one that got run over.

We got a load of straw of Mr. Eastman and he told me when that was gone to come and get another.

Oats are bringing 60 cents a bushel and I think that we will have some to sell. What do you think about it? I have heard a good many say that wool would bring a dollar a pound.

Yours truly,

Elton Claflin

[In Esther's hand again]

There! Ha'nt Elton done bravely? He has wrote this in about fifteen minutes and now he is off to team Billy. Price has gone to a surprise party at Mrs. Woodruff's. I have spent nearly all day in writing to you and Parmenter.

When you can get some, will you send some cotton seeds? I guess the boys will plant the corn in a box this winter. I have not had to work very hard for the last two weeks, and everything now wears a more cheerful aspect. If you were not where you are, and the rest of our friends and finally our country, our poor riven, bleeding, suffering country! What will become of her, God only knows.

Won't you write a list of all your officers' names? It may be of service to us sometimes. Have you made out a bill so that you know how much you owe Father? If I can get state bounty I mean to pay the debts.

NOTE

1. Fort Donelson and Fort Henry were in Tennessee just over the border from Columbus, Kentucky. On February 3, 1863, Confederate forces under Generals Wheeler, Forrest, and Wharton attempted to take back Fort Donelson. They were repulsed by the Eighty-Third Illinois Regiment, with cavalry from Iowa and Minnesota, under Colonel Abner Harding. Harding's report estimated that his force numbered 750, and that of the Confederates, 900 (Scott, *War of the Rebellion*, vol. 23, pt. 1, 34–39; Dyer, *Compendium of the War of the Rebellion*, 1082).

❧

Sunday [February] 15, 1863

My own Dear Gilbert,

The shades of night are just closing up a most beautiful Sabbath day and it is now more than all other times that my thoughts turn to you, the husband of my *youth* and the almost sole companion of more than half the years of my life. It is at this hour I feel if I could be transported to you I quickly would be. I have a sort of aching desire to know *just exactly* how you are situated. Can't you write the little minutia? That is what interests us most, and what we never get anywhere else. I should like to know if your food is wholesome and sufficient, and if you have good straw to sleep on, and how many blankets you have, and how you get your washing done.

I saw a short extract from a letter written by your Major Walther dated the fifth stating that snow was 6 inches deep (snow fell here at the same time, but not as deep). He says too, the men are all in good spirits and dates his letter Ft. Halleck. You are not in a fort are you?

I recall a little incident yesterday which happened on board the Ruth. You spoke of seeing her and as things we have seen are always invested with more interest; I will relate it in short.

Mrs. Hodge of Chicago, Mrs. Clinton of St. Louis, and Mrs. Cold of Milwaukee who have for months been laboring in the cause of charity for the soldiers had been devoting themselves to a private in a Missouri regiment. He was very ill and their attentions could not save him. They hung over the dying man as if he had been their only son. He seemed in a stupor when suddenly he opened his eyes and recognized them, smiled, and said, "Heaven bless you my good angels, you will be rewarded for your goodness. You are making a flank movement on God Almighty." So speaking he expired amid the tears and prayers of the faithful women.

February 17, Tuesday morning:

This is a most beautiful morning and I can hardly realize that our country is involved in this fearful war and that my husband is so far away, and engaged in the conflict. When I think of the effect a bright sunlight day has on the mind and the intimate connection between the outer and inner man I do not wonder that the Ariates, without the light of the gospel, worship the sun. This morning I heard Elton say to Price while they were in the barn turning the straw cutter, "I am darn glad it is drawing nigh spring, ain't you Price?"

February 18:

Yesterday I went to Uncle John's a-visiting; the first visit we made since you went away. Frank [Franciss Lockwood, sixteen-year-old daughter of John Metcalf's former business partner Charles Lockwood] is making them a great deal of trouble. She has left Mr. Osburn's and she won't go to Uncle John's or Learnpmans [?]. She had a legacy of about three hundred fall to her a little while ago and I suppose she thinks she is an heiress.

While speaking of her, I can't help contrasting the difference between her and Elton who is about her age. She has everything provided for her which a reasonable child could ask without care or labor of hers, and Elton is just as faithful in his business at home as a man of forty and not a word of complaint have I heard this winter, but what there was enough of everything.

Their coats are getting very shabby, and I wonder they don't refuse to go to meeting. But clothing is so dear, I don't see any other way but to stay out when they get so bad they can't be worn. But I fear for the effect, especially now you are gone.

Last night I wrote to William to know if he could find out about the state bounty, but I don't rely on it very much. Summit has promised a great deal but fulfilled nothing. I have understood that Mr. Hinkley has reported to the effect that we have received the same as volunteer families. I don't want you to think that we are out of money. We have the silver and a dollar and a half besides. But you know it is getting time of year when we shall need more. There is seed wheat to be bought, and Mr. Eastman ought to be paid; but he told me not to worry; he could wait. But you know that don't pay debts. I don't think anyone we owe will distress us, and I don't want you to be troubled on our account, but you know everything in the clothing line is missing, and I should be glad if I could make some purchases now as I have time to sew, and perhaps when it gets warm they will find it pretty hard in the spring with an unruly ox and colt. And I guess some of the fences are pretty poor.

We got your 3rd letter last night. I am glad you don't forget us, and you have answered some of the questions I have asked here. But I am afraid three blankets are not enough. And can you keep dry in a tent?

February 16, 1863

Dear Father,

I am going to write a letter to you. I am well, and am going to school, and am getting along first rate in my studies. I got a grammar a little while after school commenced and am getting along first rate [in] that too.

Mr. Hendrickson the county superintendent was here a week ago Friday and visited our school and in the evening he gave a lecture to our church, to parents, and to teachers on the subject of schools; and the next day he held a kind of school in the hall. He had each teacher in the town come there with a class and show their way of teaching.

There has been two couples married since you left the state. The first was Miss C. Whipple was married to Mr. Smith, the man that went to Pikes Peak to get gold.[1] The other was Miss L. James to Mr. Tom McPherson. And I expect there will be another wedding before spring. Frank Lockwood is going with Harmon Baxter to all the dances.

When I left you that day I was in Milwaukee for the cars, and after I started and had got about two miles this side of Milwaukee, I should think, I happened to think that I had left my ticket to the house that I stopped. The next day I wrote to John to go there and see if he could find it, but he did not. I got home that night all safe with my bundles. I did not carry the . . .

[This is the bottom of page—I have not found a continuation—this is obviously from Price]

NOTE
  1. Pike's Peak articles from the *Oconomowoc Free Press*:
     A PIKE *Speaker.*—Saturday afternoon about 5 o'clock, "Charley" was around the streets, ringing the *bell* with great energy; we asked what was the matter; he said that "a feller who had been to Pike's Peak, was going to lecture at the La Belle." We did not go to hear him, but understand that he gave a glowing account of the gold diggings. We are *inclined* to think that he spoke the truth, for he was ragged and dirty *and took up a collection.* (March 17, 1859)
     PIKE'S PEAK:—Mr. John C. Trowbridge is about starting for Pike's Peak; he says he has not much confidence in the stories about the gold there, but that if he should not be able to find the dust in sufficient quantities at the Peak, he will push on to California. (April 21, 1859)
     PIKE'S PEAK:—Yesterday afternoon, Mr. E. C. Hartwell, Carl Mann and Charles Tucker left our village for Pike's Peak. (April 7, 1859)

February 18, 1863

Dear Esther,

You may be sure that I was glad to hear from home. I had looked for a letter several days, and had come to the conclusion that If I did not get a letter today to write another. It seems that you had not got my last letter when you wrote.

My health is very good; never enjoyed better in my life.

You seem to think that we must have had an awful time going on account of the cold; but we did not suffer at all.

You wished to know if the men got off the cars when running. Some of them did. One man struck on his head and shoulder, and as long as he could be seen he did not stir. Most of them jumped as they were stacking up at the stations. In our company the guards left. Some got out of the windows. My bunkey did not leave.

It is more filthy here than in the camp in Wisconsin; and as to being kept close, we have 5 times as much liberty here as we did in Wisconsin.

As to being baddened by that which is transpiring around me I can say I am not. Each day brings its changes and I find much to interest me. I do not think, however, that I shall become so much attached to soldier life that I shall be willing to follow the business more than 6 months longer.

Columbus is a low sunk hole. It is not as large as Oconomowoc. It was destroyed by the Rebels when they left, I am told, and what we now see has to a great extent [been] built since.

I have not been across the river to see the battleground but intend to go if I can get time.

I received your letter with William's enclosed, and sent it back with the letters in the satchel I am quite sure. It is possible I did not, but I intended to. I think you will find it by looking over the letters enclosed as you sent it.

I keep my paper, which you see is cut into folds, in a newspaper which answers a very good purpose. I have not written to anybody else as yet but intend to soon. I have got plenty of paper as yet, enough to last me nearly or quite through the remainder of the time I have to serve.

While in Camp Washburn we saved on our rations which we did not draw about 30 dollars which is now held as a company fund in the captain's hands to be used for the good of the company. We made a draw the other day got some things for the kitchen department, got some blacking and brushes to make our boots shine, some writing paper & stamps. Each gets his proportion of them.

I suppose you would like to know my surroundings. I am in the cook tent.[1] It is a round one about 16 ft in diameter. In the center is our fire. I am now sitting on my bed; my bunkey is asleep. Around the outside of the inside are boxes and our barrels and a bench to set things on. Under our bench stand our camp dishes which we use to cook in. I like the business of cooking quite well now, but think it will be rather hot work in summer. I think it is better for me than to stand on picket as it is rather cool nights, and sometimes wet and we have not got our rubber blankets as yet.

I was glad to learn that there was more interest in the prayer meetings, and that you attended them. I should like to enjoy similar privileges, but a wise Providence orders it otherwise and it is all right. There is no day of rest here. Things move the same as other days except for an hour when our Catholic Chaplain holds forth. A small number stop to listen. I hope and trust I shall be sustained and quickened to discharge the duties devolving upon me, and that we shall be fully prepared for the solemn duties devolving upon us, and shall have thus grace given us that shall sustain us under every threat that we may be called to pass through.

I must close as it is time to have the light put out.

Yours Truly,

Gilbert

P.S. February 19: I do not have to use my government clothes cooking. The boys rigged me out with a pair of pants and coat, and I had my over-halls. Otherwise I should have spoilt my coat and pants as we have to handle much grease. I use the grease to kindle fire and it is a good substitute for shavings. I have been careful about what I eat and do not drink but little water. The water that we use is river water and looks rather hard—about like the water in a mud hole—but they say it is healthy. It does not look so.

Gilbert

[The letter was started on the back page. Written around the perimeter of that page is the following.]

You can get your state bounty at any time now. I have been in 3 months and you are entitled to 15 dollars. You had better not pay the debt with it but keep it for use as it is not certain about my getting my pay very soon and you may need it before I do get it. I have not time to look up that account you spoke about.

NOTE

1. Each company had a "cook tent," and the cooking was done over a fire in the open. The cook fires of companies from the northern lumbering regions could always be distinguished by the "bean holes" in which the covered iron pot containing the frequent "pork and beans," the favorite and distinctive article of Yankee diet, was buried in hot embers and, barring removal by unauthorized hands, allowed to remain all night. The lumberman and the soldier declare that he who has not eaten them cooked in this manner does not really "know beans." (Johnson, *Campfire and Battlefield*, 496)

Columbus
February 19, 1863

My Dear Son,

I was glad to get a letter from you, and you may be assured that it is a great satisfaction to me that I can be so far away from home and feel so contented about home affairs under your and Price's management.

I have not been out drilling but once since I have been here and on guard once. You will understand my business by your mother's letter.

There is stationed around our camp a picket guard occupying a belt of some 4 miles, the right and left of it resting on the river. Beyond the line of pickets is a cavalry picket.

One of the boys in Company B in our regiment shot his hand; the ball went through the palm of it making a terrible hole through it. He was out on picket when he done it.

They are now taking away the cannon that are not mounted and shipping them, where I do not know. Some say down and some up the river. Yesterday they undertook to take a one hundred and twenty eight pounder; the gun weighs 15 thousand one hundred and 80 lbs. It was swung under a pair of trucks. They got it about 25 rods when smash went one of the wheels. There were 13 yoke of oxen hitched to it and it was a good load for them.

There is a rifled gun lying on the bank of the river which the Rebels left that weighs 14 thousand 8 hundred and 50 lbs. The creases in the bore of the gun are nearly ¼ of an inch deep and 2 inches wide. The balls used in this gun are about 14 inches long and 6 inches thick. There is on the big end of the ball a brass band about 12 inches wide and ribbed so as to fill the creases in the gun. Cannon balls are scattered in every direction about the camp and by the river.

I must close as it is time to get breakfast. The long roll is beating for roll call.[1] You must write again and so must Price, and I will answer.

Your Father,

Gilbert Claflin

You must show this to your Grandmother and tell her that in my next I will write to her. You must take good care of her and furnish lots of wood in this cold weather.

[Upside down at top of first page]

I am glad that you are getting along well with the school.

You had better not sell the oats 'til you are through foddering the spring.

NOTE

1. The long roll is a prolonged roll of the drums. This was the signal for troops to form ranks immediately.

[This is one of the undated letters pinned together]

Dear Son,

I was glad to get a letter from you and to learn that you were getting along so well.

You asked to know what kind of wheat to sow. It is Fife wheat.[1]

One day last week we had a very hard wind. It blew down 8 or 10 of our tents. I was in the cook tent and expected it would blow down, but it stood.

You will remember in my last letter that I spoke of moving a large cannon and the breakdown. They got a pair of trucks, and got it on them, and hitched on the 13 team of oxen. They could not draw it. The men then put some ropes, and hitched on to the trucks and around the cannon, and drew it 8 or 10 rods; and there it stands, and will stand for some time, I guess, unless they get better conveyance.

Your mother wanted to know if I was in a fort. There are fortifications all around here, but they are built of earth and timber. It is called a fort. The fortifications are all the work of the Rebels.

The boys on guard at the prison told me that there was a young man by the name of Wells there who knows me. He belonged to the 7th Battery, and it must have been Sam Wells' boy. I intended to go and see him, but did not get time. He deserted, they said. I should like to have you find out if he is in the army. You had not better say anything about it 'til you find out.

I hope you will be a good boy and do all you can for your mother.

Your Father,

G. Claflin

NOTE

1. Fife wheat was a new variety of wheat named for David Fife, the Ontario farmer who, in 1842, was the first to grow it in North America. It became famous on both sides

of the Atlantic as a wheat that is high yielding, resistant to disease, and excellent for bakers' flour (Stephan Symko, *From a Single Seed* [Ottawa: Agriculture and Agri-Food Canada, 1999]).

∽

Columbus
February 23, 1863

Dear Esther,

I received your kind letter about 3 hours since and I went out on the bluff and read it. It is on a point and is one of the most beautiful views I ever saw. You have a fine view of the river for 5 miles each way and a perpendicular elevation of over 200 ft above the river. As I stood upon the point and perused the friendly lines penned by dear ones far away; I looked, but intervening space closed from view dear ones; but thought traversed the space in a moment and in spirit I was with you. The sun was setting a most beautiful sunset, and as I read your letter your thoughts about the sun were similar to my own feelings and thoughts.

I have left the cook tent and am now doing soldier duties. Our old cook has come back from a sick furlough. He is one of the best I ever saw and is a first rate fellow. I think that it will be better for me to be out of doors than in the cook tent now it is getting warm weather. I had to be confined all the time and could not get time to go out and see what was going on, but yet I liked it—all but fetching our water. We had to carry all our water about 40 rods and it was quite a job.

Yesterday I went out on picket for the first time and I was happily disappointed; it was not as hard as I expected, and today I do not have to do any duty. When I got home I took a nap, and now I feel first rate. I slept 4 or 5 hours last night sleeping on some shucks rived out like stars, with my blanket to cover me, and my cartridge box for a pillow. We had a big fire by the side of a big whitewood log.[1] The tree was 5 ft through at the butt. I slept first rate. There were 10 of us on one post, 3 reliefs and 1 corporal to relieve the guard. My duty came in the night from 8 to 10 & from 2 to 4, giving 4 hours in the middle of the night for sleep, and a good nap after 4 o'clock. You need not worry about my sleeping. I can sleep on the floor first rate, and much better than I could on a feather bed. We do not have straw to sleep on but hay, and I intend to sleep on the boards soon and not have the hay *and then I shall not find any lumps under me.*

As to the rations we have enough to satisfy me, but some of the men complain bitterly. I cannot eat all of them. We draw good bread and the graham crackers are first rate, and agree with me first rate. We have beans, rice, and ground corn—not cracked as it was in Wisconsin. It is the same kind of corn that I sent home, and it is better than any rice I ever saw. We have bacon and salt pork and occasionally beef. I eat but little meat. Most of the pork that I eat is raw, cut very thin, and eat it on bread. I do not drink as much water here in three days as I used to drink in Wisconsin in one, on an average. I commenced in Camp Randall to eat short and now I drink by measure and think I have found about the right quantity: a cup in the morning and one at night of coffee, and about ½ a cup of tea when we get it, and occasionally 3 or 4 swallers of water. I do not think I have drinked a quart of water in 2 weeks, and it is seldom that I am dry between meals.

I have not been bothered at all with diarrhea, though most of the boys have. Some of them have been quite bad.

I have not seen any 6 inches of snow nor half of it here.

I do my washing and find no difficulty in that particular. I have, as you know 3 pair of socks. One of them wants a little mending, and I have the tools and time and I guess ingenuity enough to do it. As to taking the pants; I thought that one pair would do me with my overhalls, and my knapsack was full, and I could draw another pair if I wanted.

I am now in the barracks. They are much more comfortable than the tents in cold weather, but in warm are the best. There are 18 in this barrack.

I have got up and built a fire. The rest are all in bed and most of them asleep. I generally awake about half past 4 and get up; and it is then that I have a quiet, thoughtful time free from the confusion of voices which usually greets my ears.

There is a quietness about picket duty that I like; and as it was Sunday when I was out, I spent the happiest Sunday that I have in Kentucky. The birds were singing in the woods around me, and my heart was full of joy as with measured step I walked back and forth my deploy with loaded gun upon my shoulder; but with no expectation of using its deadly contents.

I hope you will get the bounty money. I suppose you will have to go before a justice and take oath that you are my wife and that I am in the service. He will give you a writing by which you can draw the money.

I hope you will not suffer for clothes, and I do not want the boys to stay out of meeting for the want of clothes. Sell one of the colts if you do not get half price for it. We shall be mustered for pay the first of March, but I do not expect to get my pay. If I do, I will forward it. I hope you will not trouble yourself about the debts at present.

Gilbert

NOTE

1. A whitewood tree is any of various trees with white or light-colored wood. In western Kentucky, it might well have been a tulip tree (*Liriodendron tulipifera*).

Thursday, February 26, 1863

My Dear Husband,

Your last letter came to hand Tuesday night. The boys came home from the donation about 11 o'clock with two letters and I could not help feeling and saying how rich I am: one from Gilbert and one from William.[1]

You will remember that I wrote to William about the state pay. He tells me to go to a justice and get the papers and when the regiment reports we can get it. John says they may never report. William sent me 5 dollars and said he would wait until the state paid me. Gilbert, I did not ask him for money. I told him we was not out, but you know what a brother he is. Mother told me the next day she was out of funds, and I let John have it. It will be so much towards paying the 25. John was not willing to take it, but I left it there. If I had not let them have it, I should Mr. Eastman. And I thought they needed it most. Mother has not got any weaving to do this winter.

I bought the outside for Price a coat for 12 shillings and have made it. It is poor satinette, but I thought I done very well considering the price of goods. The heavy sheeting such as we used to get is now 50 cents a yard, common calico 25.

Really Gilbert, I never thought you would come to the office of cook. It is well for you perhaps that you can do anything. Mother laughed heartily when I read that you used grease for kindle wood. I think it is a very good use to put it to. You say your fire is in the middle of your tent. Have you stove or fireplace, or is your fireplace after the Indian fashion? I suppose you are established head cook in the culinary department.

I am sorry your water is so bad. I had supposed the Mississippi water was tolerable. John says they always considered it good.

Don't you think when it grows we can send you some asparagus by express; not for luxury but as a preventative for the gravel?[2] Parmenter and all of the men where he is had it in the fall. He said it was owing to the bad water. If it gets wilted, you know you could make use of the broth.

Mr. Meigs called here yesterday to inquire after you. He wants you to remember him to the captain. He said if he and a few others had stayed that [they] would have shot the captain before now.[3]

We have had a freeze, a thaw, and a rain since I wrote. Last night it rained and today it is colder. But it is dreadful muddy (I suppose you have plenty of mud).

Tomorrow is preparatory lecture, but I am afraid the going will be so bad that I cannot go.

The Summit church is expected to join tomorrow.[4]

The Summit School has been a failure this winter. The first teacher left, and the second one, Maryann Gifford, they turned out before the term closed. And I think it is a just retribution on them for treating William as they did.

I went to church last Sunday evening; listened to a sermon preached from Romans 8th, part of the 6th, "to be spiritually minded is life and peace." He divided mankind into four classes: the spiritual, the intellectual, the worldly, and the fleshly minded. I almost felt as if I belonged to the lowest, thinking and caring more for the things of the body than anything else.

Have you heard that it is expected there will be another call of eight hundred thousand, and there has been a new law passed which exempts married men over 30?[5] But I can't tell it all for I don't know it. But it is a law that will take nearly all of the young single men. If I can get it, I will send it to you. I have often thought of a remark Uncle John made over two years ago. He said if there was Civil War, there would be such times as never was known since the destruction of Jerusalem.

Anna has come back to Mother's. Her baby is quite sick. The top of its head is a complete sore. Her anxiety and care for it is taking off her flesh.

Arabelle has got so she shows off at Mother's as she did here. Mother don't get the least bit of help from her. I am afraid she will worry Mother to death. What can we do with that child? I feel as though I had a duty to perform to her, but what I can do to benefit her I am at a loss to conjecture.

Gilbert, you did not send home any of your letters by Price from Milwaukee. They got lost somewhere of course, but never mind. I am sure anything I wrote was not worth preserving. My pen is very poor and I am afraid you will be troubled to read this.

Thursday evening: Price has brought home a letter from J.P. and I think I will send it.

Yours in the bonds of conjugal love,

Esther Claflin

[On the back of Esther's February 26 letter]

Dear Father,

We are all well but me, and I have a hard cold.

We keep plenty of wood on hand. Price cuts Grandmother's wood and I cut our wood.

Mrs. Newnham came over and made Mama a visit, and Mr. Newnham sent word that we might have all the straw that we wanted. And so we went over and got a couple of loads. And he said that when that was gone to come over and get some more.

Howard [James and Eliza Newnham's eldest son, aged twenty-two] is to work in the pinery now. He went and worked in Milwaukee and the man that he worked for had too many hands. And so he went to work in the pinery.

Mr. Clark has sold his place. Mr. Penks has sold out to Mr. Hardle and he is a-going to Illinois.

Mr. Eastman offered $15 and a cow. She is coming in next month. I have milked her last summer, and she milks easy, and she stands good, and she is in good order. Cooledge wants to give a cow and he did not say what he would give. He said that what he gave to boot he would pay right down. I think if we trade I think that I we had better trade with Mr. A. Eastman because we know what [his] cow is. What do you think about it? I told A. Eastman that I would trade if he would pay fair.

Elton Claflin

[In Esther's hand again]

Mr. Eastman values his cow at $25. It seems as though we had better trade, but I want to know just what you think of it.

NOTES

1. According to "History of the First Congregational Church" in *Oconomowoc Enterprise*, June 21, 1929: "Perhaps the greatest social event in the church life was the 'donation party' for the minister. . . . Provisions of all kinds were then bestowed upon the pastor, 'potatoes and all kinds of vegetables for the winter supply; meats of all kinds, maple sugar, all kinds of groceries, and wood to last all winter long.'"

2. *Gravel* is another name for kidney or bladder stones. Depending on the composition of the stone one gets, asparagus can be good or bad. The National Institutes of Health suggests that people at risk for uric acid stones should avoid eating too much asparagus (Medline Plus, "Kidney Stones—Self Help").

3. Richard Meigs from Ottawa, Wisconsin, was one of the men drafted at the same time as Gilbert. He was discharged in early December while the regiment was still in Wisconsin. W. Eugene Ferslew was Gilbert's captain. About the time Meigs was discharged, Captain Ferslew had considerable trouble with men deserting and failing to return from furlough. The captain became stricter with the rest of the men and refused to grant furloughs until the deserters returned (*Waukesha Freeman*, November 18, 1862; Quiner, *Military History of Wisconsin*, 820). Read more about Captain Ferslew and Richard Meigs in Appendix D.

4. Since January 1862, Reverend Enos James Montague had been serving both the Summit Presbyterian Church and the Oconomowoc Congregational Church. The two started as a single church back in 1841, and separated in 1845. Reverend Montague was minister for the Summit church from at least 1850. In 1862 the two churches wanted to reunite as a Congregational church ("History of the First Congregational Church," *Oconomowoc Enterprise*, June 21, 1929; "1850 United States Federal Census," hereafter 1850 census).

5. Abraham Lincoln signed the Enrollment Act, also known as the Conscription Law, on March 3, 1863. This was the nation's first Federal draft and required all men between the ages of twenty and forty-five to register. Those who registered were divided into two classes. The first was all men between the ages of twenty and thirty-five years as well as all unmarried men between thirty-five and forty-five. The second was the married men older than thirty-five but younger than forty-five. The older married men were not called into service until those of the first class were called.

Federal agents determined a quota for new troops from each congressional district. States were responsible for meeting the quotas by voluntary enlistment, and offered enlistment bounties in addition to the $100 offered by the Federal government. If quotas were not met in this manner by mid-July, the Federal government called registered men into service. Men were exempt from military service if they furnished $300 for a substitute or if they were shown to be physically or mentally unfit for service. Men were also exempt if they fell into certain social categories such as state governor or only son of a widow dependent on him for support. The details of this law as reported in the *Waukesha Freeman* are given in Appendix D.

❧

Columbus
March 2, 1863

Dear Esther,

I have just come off from picket guard, and as I have not any duty to do today I improve the time to write to those that are as dear to me as is my own life.

I look upon life from a different standpoint to that which I have formerly looked from, and am led to feel that I have been too selfish and too much engrossed in things of a worldly nature; and you may be sure that time passes with me in quite a different way from what it used to at home.

I will give you a sketch of the week that has just passed beginning with last Tuesday morning 24th which was the day I sent my last letter.

I was detailed that day to cut wood at the hospital. I went, taking my dinner. Arriving I found 7 or 8 sticks of cordwood. I cut them into splits and piled it; was told that some more would come about noon. I then went about the town of Columbus, came back at noon, took dinner at the hospital, but the wood did not come. I took another survey of the town after dinner, came back, but no wood came. I got back to camp to supper, and attended roll call, and the day had passed.

February 25. It commenced raining about sunrise. I done my washing in the morning, and darned the sock that had a hole in it, and put one of those pockets that I ripped off from my wrapper in my vest. It makes a good one. I fixed a place in the peak of the roof to hang my clothes.

February 26. In the morning one of the boys says, "Come and see a Wisconsin wagon!" and we all made a rush for the door, and sure enough there was the wagon and a fine pair of bay horses. It was a striking contrast to heavy, clumsy wagons used here, and the ugly mules used to draw them. It is muddy and no drill.

February 27. It is a beautiful morning and I stood on the bluff. The guards were firing at a log floating in the river. Three steam boats have just passed. The river is very high and is overflowing its banks in some places. We had a company drill of about 1 hour.

February 28. After breakfast I went to the edge of the bluff, which is about ⅔ as far as from the house to the barn. The steamer Glendale was passing loaded with cotton. The steamer Ruth is at the dock and as I read the name I called to mind the incident you related in your letter that transpired on board of her.[1] It was a pleasing view, and my imagination reached back to you then to the steamer and the scene that transpired on her; and my heart was led to rejoice that amid the turmoils of earth such heavenly scenes were enjoyed by mortals here on earth.

About 11 one of the iron-clad gunboats passed down the river. It was truly a formidable looking craft. In company was a government dispatch boat or telegraph boat—small but very fast—also a steam dredge and a government transport which had attached to her 4 mortar boats with mortars on them. They were going to Vicksburg, I believe, and may be used to take the place.

After dinner we were mustered for pay. We have to be mustered every 2 months.

March 1st. I was detailed to go on picket. It is a beautiful morning. My post is about 2 miles from here. I stood about an hour before noon from 10 to 11, went on again at 6 and off at 8, on again at 2 and off at 4. I went back in the woods—just was in the woods alone, and sat down upon the ground in the sun and had a good time reading my testament and copy of *The American Messenger* and meditating on things relating to time and the connection they have with Eternal realities.[2] I think it was a more profitable day to me than many I have spend under more favorable circumstances.

March 2. About daylight I got my breakfast. I got a stick and roasted some beef, warmed a cup of coffee from my canteen, got some crackers and cheese from my haversack and had a good breakfast. I expect you will think it is hard fare but I never had a better appetite in my life, and my health is all I could ask for.

I wish the boys could be here for a short time and gather walnuts. The woods are full of them, so to speak. I went out after breakfast about 20 rods from the post and gathered my haversack full under one small tree. They are not black walnuts, but nearly as large. You can get 3 kinds.

You wished to know how my boots are. They are the best ones I ever had, and have not got any holes in them, and do not wear out my stockings as they have done in years back.

I have given you my last week's work, and you see that I do not do much work. It is a lazy life to live.

Yours Truly,

Gilbert Claflin

[Written very small around the edges]

Whilst I am writing, the boys are trying to get each other to go and get a pack of [illegible] and they have been trying to get one of the sergeants to go and get one.

I got some lettuce seeds. The boys must plant them in good ground.

I do not expect to get any money this muster, though some do. I have got 30 cents more than I had when I landed in Columbus. I got some money selling lard that came out of the pork which belongs to the cooks. It is not half so hard to be soldier as it is to cook.

We have got our rubber blankets; fine ones.

I think that the boys had better agree about seed wheat in time to get it before it is time to sow.

I have not got a letter this week from you, but shall expect one tomorrow. I got a letter from Rev. Mr. Montague today. I wrote to brother J.P. Colby about 10 days ago but have not got an answer.

NOTES

1. Letter to Major General Grant from Jas. B. McPherson: "February 18, 1863 . . . The Ruth, which I had directed the quartermaster to stop here and carry a portion of my command, was permitted to go to Cairo for Government supplies, with a promise from the captain that he would be back by a certain day. As soon as she got to Cairo she was taken possession of for a hospital boat and ordered to Saint Louis." Letter to Major General Grant from L. B. Parsons, Colonel and Assistant Quartermaster General, Supt. Transportation: "March 16, 1863 . . . There have gone to you, in addition, of large boats, since your order, as follows: . . . Ruth, capacity 1,500 men . . . making in all, a capacity for 25,200 men" (Scott, *War of the Rebellion*, vol. 24, pt. 3, 59, 115–16).

2. The *American Messenger* was a monthly religious paper put out by the American Tract Society. It contained national news, religious commentary, and missionary news.

March 1, 1863

My Dear Gilbert,

On rising this morning we found everything white with snow. I have rarely seen the face of nature wearing a more beautiful dress. The snow being damp and the day warm it nearly all disappeared before noon.

Notwithstanding the bad walking, I did go to church today. You no doubt have thought more than once that it was communion today. The Summit church did not unite today on the account of the church property there. But Mr. Montague united with this church today. The church that he was a member of was in Connecticut. Mr. Stansbury officiated as deacon at the service.[1] You was remembered by our pastor in prayer.

Gilbert, how very strange and sad it seemed to have your seat filled by another, for it is the first time that chair was ever filled in that capacity by anyone else. But it is sweet to know the Savior is there as well as here and though you cannot have their privileges now, you have had them many years.

March 2:

We received yours of the 23 today and suppose it came in Friday or Saturday. It was so muddy no one went to the office, and we did not expect another quite yet. I believe I feel thankful that we can send and receive these messages at such regular intervals.

Anna don't hear from James only once in a great while. She has heard from him recently however. He is still in the hospital; has had another attack of diarrhea. He thinks he may get a discharge.

Gilbert, I have got over having that longing desire to die. I realize now how lonely it would make you, more than I ever did before, and think it has been selfishness on my part to desire it. And these boys need a mother as well as father. But I want to feel and do and act as my Father in Heaven desires.

The snow has fallen deeper last night and today than any we have had this winter.

It is now nearly ten, and I will bid you goodnight and take my brick and go to bed alone (not on a bed of shakes, but one of feathers).[2]

March 4:

Gilbert, don't it sometimes seem to you as if the service you are rendering your country was almost useless. When you are out on picket duty, if you should see an enemy, *could* you shoot him? I sometimes feel as if I had rather you would fall a victim than to imbue your hands in a brother's blood. Maybe this is cowardice, but it seems a fearful thing to take the life of another.

NOTES

1. Erskine Stansbury was another of the New York farmers. He and his family lived just less than a mile south of the Claflins. The 1850 census forms for the town of Delafield, five miles east, were filled out by hand with each page signed by Erskine Stansbury (or E. Stansbury), Ass't Marshall. Erskine was also active in the Congregational

church and served as deacon during Gilbert's time in the army. He was a help to Esther and able to fill out the appropriate government forms to allow her to collect the state bounty for enlisted men's families. For more about the Stansbury family, see Appendix B.

2. A brick, heated in the fire, makes a fine bed warmer.

March 4, 1863

Dear Father,

I was glad to get a letter from you and to hear that you was well. I went to school today and I wanted to go downtown tonight but Ma wanted me to stay at home and write to you so I did.

Aunt Anna came up to our house last Friday and her baby is most well. It has been getting better ever since she came here.

I took the buck home yesterday. I led him down there. He led like a horse.

You spoke about there being a Wells among the deserters in the prison. There is not any of Sam Wells's folks there as I know of, but Aunt Anna said that there was a Wells among the students at Nashotah, and perhaps he is the one.[1] Ma said that he has stopped here quite a number of times and gave her some flowers just as she was getting over the mumps.

A few nights ago I caught two rats in two nights. Ma said that it was something that you never did.

But I must stop as it is 9 o'clock.

Yours as ever,

Price C. Claflin

[The rest is in Esther's handwriting]

Mr. Stansbury says he will call here and make out those papers for me, and I shall not be obliged to go to Summit.

I am not suffering for clothes, nor any of us. But I have felt a good deal of anxiety on account of their church rig giving out. But you know I have made Price a coat, and Anna tells me they have a store of second hand clothes at Nashotah that are sent on from Eastern Cities for the benefit of the students, and can be had very cheap.[2] And I think I shall go up there and get Elton a coat.

Elton seems to be quite ailing. When he goes to school he has headache and cough. He is staying out now and I don't know as he will go any more.

He don't seem interested in his studies. His whole mind is taken up with the work at home. I had rather he would care less for the work and more for his studies, but I don't know what I can do to make him more interested in his studies.

March 5:

Emily has been here today and took Annie, she says, to make a visit. I told her I would keep one of the little girls. I don't know as I care which. She thinks she will go to Indiana and live with Uncle Sam [Samuel Metcalf was the younger brother of Emily and Esther's mother, Abigail Metcalf Colby], but I don't think he would keep her children long.

It is a rainy and windy March night, and you may be standing guard or on picket duty with nothing to shelter you from the storm.

Esther

[Upside-down postscript]

There has a discussion arose among the folks here whose letters you read first. Anna and Price say you do mine and I say you do the boys'.

Esther Claflin
Oconomowoc, Wisconsin

NOTES
   1. Samuel Wells and his family lived a mile or two south of the Claflins in Section Nine of the town of Summit (*Atlas of Waukesha Co.*, 27).
   2. Nashotah, Wisconsin, is a town about five miles northeast of Summit where there is an Episcopal seminary of the same name, founded in 1842 as a mission to the frontier and incorporated in 1847 as "a College of learning and piety."

[Probably March 10, 1863]

Dear Esther,

I received your kind letter the 3rd and although I have written one this week I must answer yours & in the first place I must inform you that Elton did not inform me what you wished to disperse of for the cow & 15 dollars but I think it must be the old mare. I do not care: do as you think best about it and I shall be satisfied. I think another cow would make you quite comfortable in the milk and butter line and be more useful to the family than so much horse flesh.

I have had the good luck to get $19.05 of my pay from government, being in full to the 1st of Jan. I think I shall send home all but 5 dollars.

One of our boys by the name of John Roberts living about 5 miles from Merton [a town about twelve miles northeast of Summit]. He has got his discharge, and as soon as arrangements here can be made he will go home. I will send the money by him in a letter directed to you, and he will put it in the P.O. where he lives, and it will then come safe.

I have been informed that they have sent here from Madison to get the new muster roll so as to find out who are in the service and who have deserted, and when it is ascertained there will be no difficulty in getting the 5 dollars from the state.

The water in the river here is considered healthy, but it looks like the water in a mud puddle after a rain. I do not think you had better send any of that you spoke of by express as I do not think I shall need any.

Our captain is liked much better than he was at first. He is the best drilled man in the regiment. His name is E. W. Ferslew.

Gilbert's letter, March 10, 1863, page 1.

I expect that our regiment is to man the guns of the fortification here. We commenced artillery drill yesterday. I did not go out drilling as I was on guard at the battery. Some of the boys like the idea and some do not. I can tell better when I have tried.

Our colonel's name is Fritz Anneke. He is an old artillery man and has, by a good deal of exertion, got the command of the guns and magazines here. I think that we shall be more likely to stay here if we work in the artillery service than if we were infantry.

Gilbert

[More from the margins]

I send you some flannel you can put it in your carpet when you make your next. It is part of a Rebel cast for a 39 pounder and was taken from the Rebels.[1]

You spoke of mud. You do not know but little about it to what they do here in Columbus. I was in the main street the other day and horses went over knee deep in mud, and now some of the houses are surrounded by water the river is so high. But in the fortifications it is dry and nice.

You speak of Arabelle. I think you have done your duty to her and that the best thing that can be done is to put her in some family that has not got any children and make her stay there if such a place can be found. If not, let her mother take the responsibility.

NOTE

1. In the 1840s, Thomas Jackson Rodman invented a new method for casting big guns that made them much less likely to explode. He brought back the older hollow casting process, but instead of a solid core, he used a hollow tube. Water circulating through the tube cooled the bore while coals were piled against the mold to keep the outer surface hot. Rodman's manufacturing method, now known as the "wet chill process," forced the impurities outward while the outer metal shrank against the hardened interior (Donald B. Webster Jr., "The Strip District: Rodman's Great Guns," *Ordnance* [July–August 1962]: 60–62, online at Carnegie Library of Pittsburgh, http://www.clpgh.org/exhibit/neighborhoods/strip/strip_n41html).

Sunday, March 8, 1863

My Dear absent Husband,

Last night after looking and waiting with a little nervous anxiety for Elton to come back from the [post] office with your letter, *I dropped asleep in my chair,* and was awakened by his opening the door and saying he had got a letter from Pa.

And it was one of your best: a history of the week seemed to be just the thing to take our minds to you and some of the days I remembered what I was doing at the same time.

The day you went to cut wood for the hospital I was sewing on Price's new coat so that he could go to the donation that night.

And the day you washed and repaired your clothes I done my washing but *not* any mending, and that evening I went to prayer meeting.

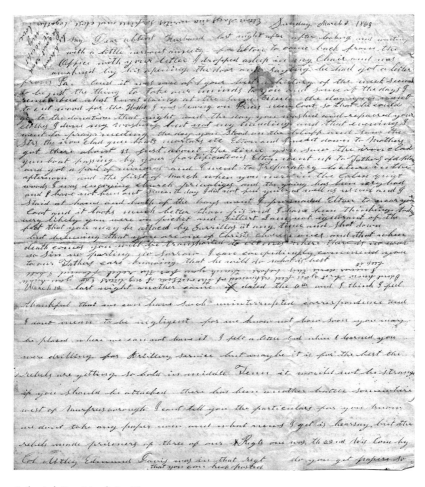

Esther's letter, March 8, 1863, page 1.

The day you stood on the bluff and saw the steamers, the iron clad gun-boats, mortars, etc. Elton and I went down to Mother's, got there about 11—just about the time you saw the ironclad gunboat passing by your fortifications. Elton went up to Father's old place and got a pail of minnows, and I went to preparatory lecture in the afternoon.

And the first of March, when you were in the calm quiet woods, I was enjoying church privileges. And the going has been very bad, and I have not been out since.

Today I did not feel quite as well as usual; and I stayed at home and both of the boys went. I persuaded Elton to wear your coat and it looks much better than his.

And I have been thinking today, very likely, you were on picket.

And *Gilbert* I am not ignorant of the fact that you may be attacked by guerrillas at any time and shot down; but believing that you are one of Christ's chosen ones, and that when death comes you will be transported to climes where there is no war, no sin, no parting, no sorrow, I can confidingly commend you to our Father's care knowing that he will do what is best.

March 12:

Last night another came dated the 6th and I think I feel thankful that we can have such uninterrupted correspondence, and I don't mean to be negligent for we know not how soon you may be placed where we cannot have it.

I felt a little bad when I learned you were drilling for artillery service, but maybe it is for the best. The Rebels are getting so bold in middle Tennessee; it would not be strange if you should be attacked. There has been another battle somewhere west of Murfreesboro.[1] I can't tell you the particulars for you know we don't take any paper now and what news I get is hearsay. But the Rebels made prisoners of three of our regiments. One was the 22nd Wisconsin, Commanded by Colonel Utley. Edmund Davis was in that regiment. Do you get papers so that you can keep posted?

The trade that was in prospect has gone up. They all seem to think the mare is not going to have a colt this spring; and of course nobody wants her. But Cooledge E. is now talking of buying Billy. Amasa E. says he is worth 10 or 15, and if we do sell him we can pay up everything and get a cow, and I hope have enough for our spring expenses without taking your wages. I want they should go, as I told you last fall, towards building the house. If your life and health is spared and you return at the end of 9 months, perhaps you can finish it enough so that we can live in it.

Mr. Sawyer has just called here and asked if that money had not been refunded. He said he would see Mr. Reed and give him a jug. He wished to be remembered to you.

Yesterday I went down cellar for the first time in several weeks and found that full half of our early seed potatoes were frozen. The ground had been caving off from the old cellar so the cold came in that side. We are now having another cold spell. I was afraid that the frost was all coming out of the ground the forepart of this month, but it don't act much like it now. There has been a regular March wind yesterday and today.

I wish you would send home Father's bill and the account due him. You know if we have enough and more too, it would be better to pay him; but that will be the last debt to pay. Mr. Stansbury called last Friday and made out the rate papers for me, and I sent them to William.

Now if we should get all this money that is in prospect, what had we better do with what we don't use? Put it in the bank, or let Uncle John have it for safe keeping?

You know I can't waste but little in the house. I had thought of getting a parlor stove; such a one as we should want for the new house so that we can have the use of it here this summer. Do you think we had better?

If you are caring less for the world, I am afraid I am getting more worldly. It seems necessary for me to think a good deal about these things.

Do you think the boys had better try and have the mare raise another colt?

I feel better than I did Sunday.

Esther Claflin

[Written upside down over parts of the letter are the following]

Elton says Ma writes so fine and close together he knows Pa can't read it. Accept my love.

I don't know but you feel ashamed of the outside of my letters. *I do.*

You know I never done this before.

[Written in very tiny handwriting upside down over other parts of the letter]

Thank you for the rebel flannel. I shall keep it.

Have you ever paid double postage on anything I have sent?[2]

Hadn't we better take a paper, and what one would you prefer, when we get the means?

NOTES

1. The battle west of Murfreesboro, where the Twenty-Second Wisconsin Regiment was captured, happened on March 5, 1863, at Thompson's Station, Tennessee. Coburn's Union brigade was surrounded and captured by a much larger Confederate force. Coburn's brigade comprised the Eighty-Fifth Indiana, Thirty-Third Indiana, Nineteenth Michigan, and Twenty-Second Wisconsin regiments. One of the men in Company H of the Twenty-Second was Edmund C. Davis, Esther's cousin.

Colonel Coburn and about two hundred of the Twenty-Second, including their commanding general, Utley, were among more than a thousand Union troops captured and sent to Libby Prison in Richmond, Virginia. More of the Twenty-Second were captured at the smaller battle of Brentwood, Tennessee, ten days later when the Federals under Lieutenant General Bloodgood tried to defend the Brentwood station on the Nashville and Decatur Railroad (Quiner, *Military History of Wisconsin*, 698–701).

Thompson's Station, Tennessee, is thirty-five miles west of Murfreesboro, Tennessee, and about two hundred miles southeast of Columbus, Kentucky. Brentwood, Tennessee, is about twenty miles north of Thompson's Station.

2. In 1863, the domestic letter rate east of the Rockies was three cents per half-ounce.

∾

Columbus
March 12, 1863

Dear Esther,

I received your letter at noon today. I am now on guard at the prison guarding Rebels. My post is number 2 of the 1st relief. I came off at 12 and go on at 4. Meantime I improve the time writing to you which always gives pleasure.

My health is good. Not one in the company but what has been more or less complaining and some very sick.

I have conversed with several prisoners today; they are all loyal and do not wish to express another sentiment. I have but little faith in any of the inhabitants in this place, though they profess to be very loyal when talking with them; but every reverse in our army is spoken of and talked much about; but when it is otherwise but little is said.

There is a great stir in camp today. 3 regiments are leaving and going up the river: the 3rd Minnesota, the 25th Wisconsin, and the 111th Illinois.[1] They are expecting to be called on to fight.

You wish to know how I feel about the part I am acting in the war, and whether if I see an enemy when on picket duty, if I could shoot him. It does appear to me that the part I am acting in a military point of view is of trifling importance, but perhaps I do not see its full extent. As to the taking the life of my fellow man; the thought is a terrible one to me, and if in the course of events I shall never be called upon to shed the blood of my fellow man during my stay in the army I shall rejoice, but If I am called to meet the enemies of my country in deadly conflict I trust I shall do my duty as a soldier should.

You will doubtless [have] got my last letter before this. I was somewhat afraid that it would not go safe on account of its bulk. I said that I got my pay to the 1st of January, $19.05 in all. I also said that I should send some home by John Roberts who lives in about 5 miles from Merton; but he has not got his discharge as yet, but expects it soon. I shall send home 14 or 15 dollars when he goes, and if you should want it before it comes you had better get some from Uncle John. If he should not go soon, perhaps I shall send it by express.

I also said in that letter that Elton did not write what you were going to trade for the cow and 15 dollars, and said you might trade to suit yourselves.

There is an excitement about camp life that is peculiar. To rise in the morning not knowing what will be the orders, or whether you will go and perhaps, as was the case with me today, be ordered to go on guard with but about 5 minutes to get ready in. I say there is an excitement, which to me is pleasing and helps to break the monotony of camp life. Time passes rapidly away, and the week is gone sometimes before I am hardly aware of it.

I enjoy myself much better than I ever thought I could under like circumstances, and think that I can do some good in a moral if not in a military point of view. I trust I shall be true to my trust as a Christian and daily receive that grace which alone can support and sustain me. I hope you all will be sustained and comforted during my absence and that we all shall meet again.

From Your Husband,

Gilbert Claflin

[Upside down at top of first page]

I would like to have you send in your next a little of that powder that I make eye water of. It is in where you keep such things in a morphium bottle.[2] I have not had occasion to use any but may have. I do not want but little.

[At top of first page]

PS: The boys had better look around for seed wheat as soon as they can if they have not done so.

I perused yours first this time but the last one before, Elton's.

[Gilbert begins a letter to his son on the same page]

Dear Son,

I was glad to have you write to me, and I will tell you what I saw when standing on guard the other night. About 11 o'clock I saw a light on the point of my bayonet. It was a bright spark about the size of a number 6 shot, and the radiance of the light that issued from it was ¾ of an inch in diameter. You could distinctly hear a snapping sound. I called one of the guards to see it, and his bayonet was the same as mine. We put them together and it would go out but when separated the light was on them. It seemed to be in a spot about 5 ft from the ground and about 2 ft thick. It lasted about an hour and was caused by electricity, and was one of the most beautiful sights I ever saw. I expect that some would have thought it was spirits but I have seen the effect of electricity, and was much amused by the appearance and its effects when I put my hand towards it.[3]

Your Father,

Gilbert Claflin

NOTES

1. On March 12, 1863, Major General Hurlbut ordered an expedition to retake Forts Henry and Heiman from Rebel occupation. These forts were about seventy miles east of Columbus, Kentucky, on either side of the Tennessee River, an important supply line (Scott, *War of the Rebellion*, vol. 23, pt. 2, 137). Read more about the action at Fort Heiman in Appendix D.

2. *Morphium* was the name given to morphine by Friedrich Wilhelm Sertürner who first isolated the sleep-inducing, pain-relieving drug from opium poppies in 1805. It was commercially available by the early 1820s (Booth, *Opium: A History*, 68–70; Hodgson, *In the Arms of Morpheus*, 79).

3. The spark Gilbert saw on the windy night with low overcast skies was probably an electrostatic discharge from the sharp point of his bayonet.

∽

[March 14, 1863]

Dear Esther,

I have just returned from picket and found a letter from home as I expected. I hope that e're this reaches you, you will be well. My health is good, but a number of the boys are sick or on the sick list. Strong drink has a good-deal to do with it.

You said you felt bad when you learned that I was going into the artillery. Our camp mans the two 24 pounders in Fort Quinby which is part of the fortification here. I like the drill better than infantry drill. Our guns are splendid ones, and are just the right size to handle good. They swing in half a circle. 3 men can swing them with ease. It is not likely that we shall get to be very proficient marksman during our stay here, and I think unless something new turns up we shall be likely to spend our time here. It is possible that we may be attacked here but not probable, as it is a difficult matter to get a large force here as the woods are nearly impassable and the roads leading to this place are well guarded. If an attack should be made it will probably be guerrilla raids which would be of little service unless they could spike the guns in the fortifications.

I read some of the papers but do not get the connection of events that I did before I went into the war.

March 15:

It is one of earth's loveliest mornings. The balmy air of spring fans me as with measured tread I pace to and from my sentinel post. The sun has just cast its light across the landscape, filling my poor heart [with] joy and causing hundreds of the feathered songsters to send forth their sweetest melody. Near me on the right are the long line of breastworks extending more than a mile in a zigzag form. In the distance is the residence of a planter with his little ville to accommodate his domestics. On the left I can count by hundreds the mud fireplaces to the cabins used by the Rebels when in camp here and which previous to the evacuation were burnt. In the distance stand the frowning batteries of the Forts Quinby & Halleck that can sweep all points of the compass with their deadly missiles.

It is about 10 o'clock and the guards will soon be here to relieve us, as they generally put on the 1st relief at 10. We are having more picket duty to do since the soldiers that were called away left; but the most of them are expected back in a few days and we shall probably be relieved from picket duty and have only to guard our guns and magazine; and then we shall have time to drill which we do not under the present arrangement of things.

Soldier life is a lazy one and I hardly know what to do with myself sometimes when off from duty. I get all the papers I can to get the news, and have tramped all about the camp; but now our extra duty on picket brings relief. I have often thought of what John said about staying in one place so long that he purely hated the picket line. I have not got so bad as that yet, nor do I wish you to think that I am dissatisfied with my lot, for I believe it is as it should be with me, and I should do wrong to murmur or complain and yet you can readily see that to one that has been as active as I have been, this slow monotonous way of doing things seems tedious; and yet it is a lesson needful for me to learn, and one that I hope will be of permanent good to me and mine should my life be spared.

I want you to do as you think best about the money and use it as you think will be the best for the family, and I shall be satisfied.

You wished to know how much we owed Father. I cannot tell exactly as I do not know when all the payments were made but the account puts up $42.22.

If you wish to take a paper, (and I think it would be a good plan, and I should like one now and then) you may suit yourself in this matter. Also, I have not had to pay double postage on any letters yet.

Roberts has not got his discharge as yet and I have not sent the money.

Yours Truly,

Gilbert

Columbus, March 18th, 1863
[Upside down on page 1]

We have got our fatigue coats or blouses as they are called, and they are real nice.[1]

This hot weather the grass is green and the cattle will soon, at this rate, get a good living.

I have got me a portfolio to put my paper in, and I find it very convenient.

I should like to know what you think about my sending my overcoat and underclothes home by express. If I should have to move, I shall have more than I can carry on my back, and I do not think I shall need them, and it is a pity to lose them when clothes are so expensive.

NOTE

1. *Fatigue* can mean any manual work, such as cutting firewood or mowing around the fort, performed in the course of service. Fatigue coats are meant to be worn for this duty.

Columbus
March 18, 1863

Dear Son,

I was detailed for picket yesterday morning, and when down town we were being formed into different divisions. I saw a splendid sight. It was 5 large government transports steaming down the river. The 4 first were loaded with soldiers the 5th was loaded with commissary stores. Behind them was one of the gunboats painted black prepared should an attack be made upon the transports as they were passing down the river to hurl swift messengers of destruction upon the foe.

Last Saturday our regiment, which has charge of the guns of the forts, had a great time firing blank cartridges, and for a time the firing was almost constant. Those out in the country thought that the place had been attacked.

A few days since, they fired shot and shell across the river. It was a splendid sight to see the shells burst, and we could see the water fly where the pieces struck although nearly a mile distant. When the solid shot struck the water a column of spray would rise, I should judge, nearly 25 ft high.

I hope that you will be a good and dutiful son. I am aware that a good deal depends upon you and Price, and it gives me great satisfaction that you are doing so well.

If you can sell the colt I think it best to let him go.

Your Father,

G. Claflin

❧

Columbus
March 21, 1863

Dear Esther,

I have concluded not to send home but 10 dollars now. Perhaps I shall buy some clothing and send home by express if I can get it reasonable.

John Roberts' discharge came today and I must write now. He may not go in 2 or 3 days but when he gets ready I may be out on picket, and so it is best that I improve the present opportunity.

I am well and get along with soldier life first rate.

I got a letter from Celinette today. The folks are all well. She said that Cousin Amos was in the gold diggings west of the Rocky Mountains. His family are in St. Paul.

I wrote a letter to William today.

We are having beautiful weather here and the woods begin to look green and they are planting corn.

I am told some of the soldiers are around with shoes and stockings off.

We had artillery drill today, and the shot and shell were fired with fine effect. It costs about 32 dollars every time one of the 10 inch Columbiades are fired with shell and $10 or $12 for 32 pounders. Our practice cost the government between 2 or 3 hundred dollars this afternoon and it seems foolish to drill men at such an expense who do not expect to stay but a short time in the service, and in all probability will never be called upon to point a gun at the enemy, but perhaps I have not the right view of the subject.

Considerable is said here about the conscript and a great many surmises are going the rounds as to what will be the result. I hope that if the conscript is enforced that it will go off all right.

I want you should in your next letter after you get this inform me of its arrival. I must close as it is bedtime.

Love to you all and all the folks.

Yours Truly,

Gilbert

[At top of page 1]

March 23. Roberts leaves camp this morning.

I am well. Things are moving quietly along. I have done my washing this morning.

You must not worry if you do not hear from me every week as a letter might get miscarried, but calculate to write so that if nothing happens you will get one every week.

∽

Columbus
March 23, 1863

Dear Esther,

I received your letter this afternoon and was surprised to learn that brother James had had to go through so much and is in such a low state of health. But I rejoice that he has succeeded in getting home alive; and I trust that the kind care that he will now receive will speedily restore him to health and usefulness again; but if in the ordering of God it should be otherwise, I hope we shall all be resigned to His will.

Thus far as a regiment we have been favored as it respects hardship compared to what some of the regiments that have left the state; and the prospect is that we shall not be called into fighting service but shall have to do guard duty and drill.

We have had a wet and disagreeable time and it has been bad for picket and guards; and would, had we not got our rubber blankets, been very detrimental to our healths. I did not have to go out on picket but expect to go tomorrow.

It has cleared off fine but is colder than last week. I am so small that my rubber covers me so that I can stand out in the rain all day and not get wet. I am more fleshy than I have been in 18 years, and since I have been in Kentucky I have not missed my regular ration, and I think I am truly thankful that my life and health have been so kindly preserved.

Last night one of the lieutenants in company K died. His name was Dexter [David H. Dexter, second lieutenant]. He was from Wauwatosa [twenty-seven miles east of Summit]. He had a fever. He leaves a wife but no children. He is the first one that has died since we left Camp Randall. I think that it is a little remarkable that out of over 400 men in our regiment no more have died.

I rather think that our artillery drill is about done with. The last time we drilled at the 6 gun battery the regiment was taken down to the battery and formed in line, and men were detailed to man the guns. I happened to be one that was not taken, about ⅓ not being required. We could go to the side of the works and see where the shot and shell struck across the river. The first gun fired was a 10 inch Columbiade loaded with shell. The recoil dismounted the gun. The 2nd or 3rd round from the guns a 32 pounder was dismounted. The last gun fired with shell the shell burst prematurely. A steamboat was passing, and one of the pieces of the shell went through her. A complaint was entered at headquarters and our colonel got a dispatch from the general. Since that time we have not drilled on the cannons, but had infantry drill.

The 25th, the 31st, & 34th Wisconsin Regiments are here and some regulars—cavalry and infantry.

Considerable is said in camp about the conscription that is talked of, and will probably take place. Most of the drafted men here, if not all, think that they were fortunate in being taken in the first draft, but that remains to be proved. I hope that the war is not a going to last much longer than our time, but it is hard to tell when it will close.

I send the boys a paper [the *War Eagle*] published in Columbus.[1] The first article entitled "The Expedition" the men left here about 3 weeks since and was composed of 3 men [from the] 40th Iowa & 111th Illinois, and some regulars. The 25th, all but 4 companies, went to Cairo to do guard duty. We had, for about 12 days, all the guard duty we wanted to do. But the 25th have come back and the regulars; and we have it easy now.

In the paper is a reference to the Columbus House. It was a terrible affair and resulted in the death of the man who commenced the affray. But not before he nearly killed Mister and Mrs. Casey. Lieutenant Feirer referred to was shot through the lungs by a ball shot at the man who was doing the fearful work. He succeeded in cutting 7 or 8 before he was killed. The man was probably insane.

John Roberts got his discharge and started for home last Monday. I sent a letter by him and enclosed 10 dollars for you. He will put it in the office at Merton. I will send you some more if you do not get any from another quarter. I understand that we are to get pay before long up to March. If we do I shall be able to supply you with some funds again.

I think that it was all right in sending a line to Mr.—. They ought to pay it back.

I was in hopes you would get something from the state soon. If you do not I can spare 4 or 5 dollars that I now have. I have got 9 dollars, and if I have my health shall not want to use but little if it.

You wish to know what I want of eye water. I have no use for it now, but I may have; and as I had it, thought I would send for it, as it would be but little trouble.

I hope you will not worry about me. I am very careful of my health and wash all over twice a week.

Gilbert

[Marginal writings]

I want the boys to inform me about how they get along, and how they get along with the work. I hope they will get along well together and try to do the best they can do; not try to do too much. I should like to have you inform me about the wheat and have you succeeded in getting seed wheat.

I hope you will not worry if things do not move along about the farm as well as could be desired. You have, I am sure, much to see to, but do not injure your health by over exertion or exposure.

I take more comfort out on picket than any other place. It is so quiet; and during the silent hours of night when standing alone at my post, in imagination I have been among you as you lay quietly at rest; and the thought that the same kind Father watched over you that did me filled my heart with joy and peace.

NOTE

1. The *War Eagle* was a small paper edited and published in Columbus, Kentucky, by Sergeant H. L. Goodall of the Second Illinois Cavalry, Company D. First published in February 1863, it appeared occasionally until sometime in 1864 (Library of Congress, "Chronicling America," http://chroniclingamerica.loc.gov/lccn/sn83025557, accessed July 8, 2013).

One of the features was the "Telegraphic Summary for the Week," with headlines that were mostly bad jokes. In December's issue, the dispatch headlines included "Ye Cods and Little Fishes" about a Federal steamer captured off Cape Cod; and "How Are You Conscript?" (the title of a popular song by Frank Wilder) about a recommendation to repeal the $300 clause of the Enrollment Act (*Columbus War Eagle*, December 12, 1863).

March 26, 1863

My very Dear Gilbert,

The task before me is pleasant and yet it is unpleasant. It is pleasant to write to you, and yet it is unpleasant to realize as I now do, that our intercourse cannot be more direct. It seems as though I never so longed for you as I have today. I know that I have my Savior, my children, my house, and very many things to be thankful for; but nothing else can fill the place in my heart which you do. I hope and yet I dare not hope that we shall be spared to each other for years. It seemed from the first as if we were separated not to be united for any length of time again.

The burdens of life are more than twice as hard to bear alone. You know my life must be one of some action. It cannot be entirely passive. I must take responsibilities and then bear the blame if blame there is. Really my dear one, I am complaining to you more than I meant to or ought to.

I am quite as well as usual, but Price has been ailing for a week. I think he is threatened with lung fever. He keeps round but is not able to do much. I have given him one pack and if he is not better, I shall give him another tomorrow.

School closes tomorrow. Elton has not been since I told you. I thought he would not go any more. He don't want to go. He told me he would not care if he never went another day. Price has been quite steady. He did not seem to want to lose a day. Elton's mind seems to be mostly occupied with the work. Price has got library books and read other reading more than he ever has before. And since he has been too unwell to go to school, he has occupied himself considerably with his arithmetic and slate.

Billy has been so lame ever since Tuesday night that he cannot lie down, and Mr. Eastman has been up today to see him. And he says he has the stiffles.[1] He told Elton to go to Bill Dodge and get a receipt, which he says will cure it in a few days.[2] Elton has not got back. There was a man here Monday and offered 65, but probably he won't want him now.

Did you ever hear of such a thing as a white crow? Elton saw one and heard it make its noise. And the next morning Price saw it and heard it. I heard a blue bird nearly two weeks ago, and the boys say that larks have been here this long time.

It has been pretty cold yesterday and today. I have been cleaning house this week. I thought I would take the bugs in season. I have not whitewashed, but done the rest today. We set up the bedsteads and we shall whitewash when time comes. In market we did not find but three or four bugs.

The next day after I wrote my last was a mild day, and Elton got Mr. Eastman's sled and took James to Delafield [about five miles southeast of Summit]. He could ride in that way when he could not go on the cars. Anna has written since he went down there that he was worse.

When it comes hot weather, if you have more clothes than you need, I think it would be better to send them home than to throw them away. But John says the nights are cool all summer, and you may need more than you think for.

If I were you I would send for a paper, and if you should move you can write to the publishers to send it to me and I can send it to you. I think you ought to have reading enough to occupy your mind when you want it. If you have so much spare time, it would be a good thing for you to get some book that you could study and make yourself master of some science while you are in the army.

Don't stint yourself. Make yourself as comfortable as you can. Now you have money, buy what will conduce to your health and happiness. I was sorry you did not take that patent office report. I think it would have done you more good there than it ever will at home.

I often think when you are describing some of the sights that I should like to be there and enjoy the seeing with you. But I don't know as I should enjoy it. For I guess I should think all of the time of the dreadful necessity that has compelled our government to expend so much money in that way.

It is ten o'clock. Good night my dear.

Esther Claflin

[Upside down over top of the rest]

Friday morning. It is pleasant but cool. Elton is out splitting rails. He has fixed up the barnyard fence real nice and is preparing to fix the others.

Wool is one dollar a pound and clothing proportionately dear. I think I shall work up part of the wool into flannel; cotton is so dear.

Price is better this morning.

What do you think about getting Mr. Kendall to make the window sash for the new house?³ Are they to be just like Uncle John's?

NOTES

1. A horse's stifle joint is a very large, complex structure similar to the human knee, and found on the hind limbs only. The joint can be "locked" naturally, allowing a horse to sleep standing up; but sometimes it refuses to unlock. Damage to any of the many parts of this joint can cause swelling and inflammation. Either locking or inflammation can cause lameness ("The Problem with Stifling," Horses and Horse Information, http://www.horses-and-horse-information.com/articles/0197stifl.shtml).

2. The Dodge brothers, Miles and William, and their families lived on adjacent farms on the shore of Oconomowoc Lake in Summit, about two miles east of the Claflins. Bill Dodge was about the same age as Gilbert and had seven children aged five to eighteen years (*Atlas of Waukesha Co.*, 27; 1860 census). For more about Miles and William Dodge, see Appendix B.

3. Charles F. Kendall, the carpenter, was a close neighbor of the Claflins and Eastmans and of Esther's Uncle John Metcalf. At the time of the letters, he was forty-two years old, just a bit older than Gilbert (*Atlas of Waukesha Co.*, 27; 1860 census). For more about Charles Kendall, see Appendix B.

March 29, 1863

My Dear Gilbert,

The very day my last was put in office, yours with the money was received all right, mailed at Milwaukee. I went down that evening as Elton had been every evening during the week before, and Price was not able to go. I had been very well, but the walk was too much for me. I find I can do but little out of the ordinary line of labor and walking seems to be especially hard. It is the first walk I have taken since the 1st of March farther than the barn. I wanted to go to church today, but knew it would not do, as I coughed all that night after I came home. Margaret's cherry syrup is taken up, and as I expected, it only relieved while taking it. I have dreaded the use of water this winter almost as much as a dog with the hydrophobia.

So you see I have not done much for myself but to eat. My appetite is good as ever. I don't want you to think I am sick. I am as well to all appearance as I was 5 or 6 months ago. My skin and eyes are clear, or I might think my cough was induced by a diseased liver. But really, Gilbert, I have thought it was caused by diseased lungs or bronchial tubes. It may be whimsical, but I thought I would write this particular about myself while I can. I *may* live an invalid many years to be a tax on your goodness and patience. For myself I feel as though it would be better to depart. But the One above knows best, and I only ask to *know* and *do* my duty faithfully and submit *cheerfully* to every dispensation of Providence. I hope what I have said will not cause you much pain, & feel almost guilty to say so much about myself for I certainly am no great sufferer. And I have enough of the comforts of life, while you are enduring the hardships of war.

I have planted the corn and cotton in boxes and one spear of corn is up. The bluebirds are singing today but it has been so cold that I have kept my shawl on nearly all day.

Elton says they had an April Fool sermon today.

March 31:

Today has been a regular March day. It snowed a little last night, and it has blew like March all day. I received yours of the 25th last night, and I have often thought in the night when I have been awake that very likely you were on picket while I had the privilege of repose.

Price has just caught a rat in his trap although it is hardly dark. He catches them off as fast as they come in.

He is better, although he ought not to do anything hard. He has hard coughing spells, and this morning his coughing caused him to throw up his breakfast. Elton bought 1 lb of maple sugar last night for 15 cents and we had some pancake and molasses for breakfast. So Price lost his four cents worth.

The boys made considerable fun of your *War Eagle*. Elton told Price to read the headings of the telegraph dispatches.

We have all been shoemaking today. Elton has been tapping his boots and Price has been making a pair of slippers of his *gaiters*, and I turned and sewed the mate to that shoe which you sewed more than a year ago, and fixed up 2 pair of cloth slippers for myself. So I think I shall not have to buy any shoes for myself.

I have, this winter, repaired almost everything I can think of. I have mended 11 pairs of summer pants, so I hope they will get through the summer for everyday without buying. And I have mended all of the cotton shirts, which makes quite a pile.

Elton has thrashed a flooring of oats today for seed, and he says he shall feed the rest in the bundle. They are intending to get a load of straw tomorrow and then they think there will be feed enough.

Elton got his medicine for Billy and applies it three times a day and it is getting better.

April 1:

We have not got any seed wheat. The boys did not like to do anything about it until they got the money. Price saw Mr. Eastman yesterday. He told him if Cooledge did not want it he could get it there, and he said he could get it of the wheat buyers.

Elton is very much afraid you will buy military clothing for him to wear. I don't think he could be persuaded to wear them outside. I presume you know that there is a law prohibiting citizens wearing full military costume.

You had not better send home money to make yourself short. We have not been out yet. William's school closes next week, and it may be he can get the state pay then.

John says you will need your overcoat as late as May.

The last time I heard from James he was worse. Mother has gone over to stay a few days with him.

I am afraid my letters sound melancholy, but I am sure that I never felt more reconciled to my lot than I do now. And I pray to be delivered from selfishness and that you may have grace to sustain you always, and if it is His will we may be united again.

Esther Claflin

[Marginal notes]

Don't write anything in reply to what I have said about my health, for you know everybody sees your letters.

March 31, 1863

Dear Esther,

I was glad to find a letter this morning when I returned from picket; and to give you some idea of the interest there is felt in camp about letters, one of the boys in another company, as I was passing his tent said, "Claflin, there is a letter for you down in the tent," referring to the tent where our company get their letters. I was a little surprised as I perused the first few lines of your letter at the tone of it, but as proceeded farther it changed so suddenly that I was a little amused, no, to tell the truth, I am inclined to think that the first was the real feelings of the heart, and that when you began to make amendments you done it [to] ease my mind in the matter.

As to the prospect of my returning, I have had but little anxiety about the subject further than the passing of the time has been concerned; but it is a thought ever present with me that we are mortal and the time of our departure none but the Unseen One knows.

I can imagine something of that loneliness you speak of, and I realize that a large share of the responsibility rests upon you. But you must not allow every thing that comes along that is not exactly right to sink down into your heart, but banish them at once. And if you thus do, you will find that much that might be burdensome will pass away. I say this judging by my own experience in the matter.

I was somewhat anxious to hear from you that I might learn about the sick. Price, you said in your last, was quite unwell. I hope that he will get well soon. I thought that quite likely James would be worn for a while after he got back. The journey and excitement would be too fatiguing to have him show much signs of improvement for some little time.

I am sorry that Elton has got his mind so much upon his work that he does not want to go to school any more. If he could see as I do young men that have to get other young men to write letters for them home, I think he would be anxious to improve. I heard a young man say the other day he wished he could go to school again. He thought that he should improve his time.

I think that the colt will be all right if he is attended to in time, and if he is not, it is not best to be troubled about it. I shall not.

I never saw a white crow, but have heard of them; and white blackbirds. I saw a white pigeon once.

I think you are taking the bugs in time this spring.

You speak of reading matter and regret that I did not take that *Patent Office Report.*[1] I am not, as I had all that I ought to have carried when I left Camp Washburn; and that day's work going to the cars is impressed upon my memory a hundred fold more than any other day that I have spent in camp. I am getting more acquainted, and get more papers and the boys in our company get more; and as it is a matter of uncertainty how long we may stay here I think I will let it be respecting a paper for the present. There is a report in camp that we are going back to the state the first of May, but I do not know the truth of the matter. Before this reaches you, however, our time will be half out, and at longest will soon be past.

I trust that our lives and healths will be precious in God's sight and that we may be permitted to enjoy each other's society again.

Last Sunday I attended church in Columbus. When the Rebels occupied the place they tore out the slips and used the building as I am informed to accommodate their soldiers in. They tried to burn it but did not succeed. It is now used for a church again. Reverend Mr. Talbot is the minister of the place and was in Columbus during all the time the Rebels occupied the place, and was twice arrested and brought before the general commanding for his union sentiments but was released. Last Sunday the chaplain [Thomas C. Golden] of the 25th and the members of different churches belonging to his regiment held their communion season. Members from other regiments was invited to partake with them. His preparatory address was from Luke 22nd chapter and 12th & 20th verses.[2] It was a profitable occasion, and although a stranger to all but one (Henry Higgins of our company who went with me), I felt that they were brethren. There were present who communed, 4 ministers, 21 soldiers, and 3 ladies. I can say that God is the same covenant keeping God in camp as well as at home.

Gilbert

[Upside down at top of page and around the margin]

You wish to know about the window sash. If Elton will find out what he will make them for, and let me know in your next, I will let him know about the job. They are like Uncle John's.

I hope that Elton will not attempt to do too much. Better do less and do it well than attempt too much and get sick.

The time passes along fast and I am cheerful and happy in the thought it is all well. I can do more good here than I can in the community around

home, and but for the dear relations of home I think I should stay in the
army contented to encounter its trials and bear its burdens. But if I can
serve my country at home when my time has expired better than I ever
could have done had I not been in the army. I know something of the special wants of the soldiers and believe me it is great.

NOTES

1. The *United States Patent Office, Annual Report of the Commissioner of Patents*, also
known as the *Patent Office Report*, was put out by the Government Printing Office from
1843 to 1965. The report varied in format, but usually consisted of two parts: Agriculture
and Mechanics.

2. Luke 22:12: "And he shall show you a large upper room furnished: there make
ready." Luke 22:20: "Likewise also the cup after supper, saying, 'This cup [is] the new
testament in my blood, which is shed for you.'"

∽

April 1, [1863]

This morning is a beautiful one, and I wish that I could give you a few
comforting words that would satisfy the longing desire in your heart to see
me. But I expect that all my efforts will fail. But Esther, I hope you will
be sustained under all your accumulated burdens, and have that physical
and spiritual strength daily that you need, and that we all shall once more
be permitted to enjoy each other's society and be prepared by this separation when we meet again to discharge the relations that we sustain to each
other in a purer and Holier sense than we ever anticipated before. I am full
in the faith that God orders it and I must not repine.

Gilbert

The boys are nearly all of them following my example in washing all
over. When I went into camp, I was the only one that washed. Now the boys
begin to see that it does some good; and when I come round, one and
another say, "I have washed, and I feel a good deal better." Well this looks
some like bragging but it is in a good cause and you will not show this to
anyone.

I was a little pleased at the great faith you had in your cherry that I should
be satisfied if you only took something. I hope it will do you good.

Gilbert.

∽

April 5, 1863

My Dear happy hearted Gilbert,

I am glad if you found anything in my letter to amuse you, if it was nothing more than the style.

I feel as though I had done a very selfish thing to repine so much about myself as I have in my two last. I try to be very heroic and I almost always feel glad that I can suffer with my country. I am willing to sacrifice. I don't wish to be exempt while our country is engaged in this terrible struggle, and if it were not for these boys who need a father's advice and restraints I should say to you, "stay to the end of the war if your life and health is spared, if you feel that you can do good." It may be that you have just found the vineyard that you should labor in, and far be it from me to wish to call you from the Lord's work that you may labor for me.

We have lived just as comfortably this winter as we should if you had been here. It is only your absence that makes us feel as though we were sufferers. When I think of the sufferings of Unionists in the border and southern states and of families driven naked from their homes I am ashamed of myself.

Poor old Grandpa Eastman [father of Amasa and Cooledge] died last Friday after an illness of three days. He was perfectly senseless and motionless for a day and a half before he died. He was taken with a diarrhea. The doctor told them it was old age. The funeral services are at our church this afternoon. It is now evening and I have spent the most of the afternoon at Mr. Eastman's. There was not a neighbor that offered to stay there or do anything for them. Mr. Eastman said he had to go and get men to come and put his Father in the coffin. I sent Price down this morning to help them and Elton went down Friday to help. I did not offer to do much for I was afraid I should overdo and get sick (you know Gilbert is not here to cure me). Mrs. Eastman said if Mr. Claflin had been here he would come without being asked.

April 8:

The boys have got their seed wheat and are now getting it in. They procured it at Mr. Brakefield's.[1] He charged 10 shillings per bushel. They bought 4 bushels. We should not have had the money if you had not sent it.

William came home yesterday. He says that he can stay only about a week. This morning he sowed the ground they had ready, and then went over to see James.

I am quite as well as usual. I think March was a trying month for me, and think I may be better as it grows warmer.

Price is well and the colt is nearly well. Mr. E. thinks he can get 65 for him.

April 9:

Last night a letter came with 15 dollars from the State and now I shall pay Mr. Eastman and buy some salt, and if there is enough get Elton a coat. Of course I shall not pay out everything, and I don't want you should feel troubled about our funds. I think we shall get along comfortably if we keep well.

I let Price take a dollar this morning to get some ammunition. They have not bought any nor asked to before. They attend to the work very steady for boys, and I want they should hunt occasionally. They have been a-fishing a few times and caught some once.

I have not been to prayer meeting in some time, and think I should not go out evenings until it is warmer. We have quite cool but pleasant weather this month. The birds are singing all around us, and it seems so good to have spring come. You know how I always like it.

I am very glad you have had one opportunity of social worship, and hope it will not be the last. Do the soldiers have prayer meetings where you are?

I am very truly yours,

Esther Claflin

NOTE
1. Thomas Brakefield had the neighboring farm to Cooledge Eastman's in Summit, about two miles south of the Claflins' (*Atlas of Waukesha Co.*, 27). For more about Thomas Brakefield, see Appendix B.

∾

April 9, 1863

Dear Father,

Ma wants to have me write a little to you and tell you the news so I will. Mr. McConnell is married to Miss Nancy Mann.

We are getting along first rate with the work. We have begun to get in the grain and are plowing some.

You wrote a letter to one of us two or three weeks ago, but did not tell which one of us it was.

Mr. Wood is a-going to get 2 bushels of oats up here this afternoon. I have got it all cleaned up for him, but the bottom of the half-bushel is out. We sent Henry Kendall down to Mr. Eastman's after one.

Price

❧

Columbus
April 5, 1863

Dear Esther,

Your letter has just been perused, and as I cannot go to meeting I will answer it.

Yesterday morning when I was on picket about 3 o'clock, the long roll was heard on the picket line from the camp causing many conjectures among the pickets as to cause as there had been no alarm on the line.

When we came in we found the camp in a very excited state. A dispatch had been received that the Rebels had taken Hickman, a place 10 miles from here [to the south], and were marching towards Union City, which is some 20 miles from here [also to the south].

Order came that four companies from the 25th, 27th, & 31st; and one company of the 34th; and two companies of regulars with two days rations be ready at a moment's notice to start. When I got in five companies had gone.

Our regiment (with the exception of company B who were under marching orders), were at the guns on the fortifications drilling, and the pickets were ordered to get something to eat and then go to our company at the guns.

I waited 'til after dinner and then went up to the fort. We carried dinner to the boys. I then lay down in the sun and slept about 2 hours 'til they got ready to go home. Fort Quinby where our guns are is about ½ mile from Fort Halleck.

In the afternoon the word came that there had been no Rebels at Hickman and when the steamer came that brought the soldiers they wanted to know what they were came for.

No more soldiers have left but I believe the order is not yet counter-manded and no one is allowed to go out of the fort today, as they have not heard from those that went to Union City.

The impression is that it is all a humbug, or at most a small band of mounted Rebels that will be wearing citizen clothes in a day or two; and good union men when approached by a company of soldiers, or allowed in camp to sell butter & eggs.

I have but little faith in the Union sentiment of the majority of the people that I have seen in Kentucky, and it is no wonder to me that every move that our army makes is known by the Rebels. But I do not despair as to the final result; the rebellion must and will be put down.

Last Thursday I was partaker in a review before Adjutant General Thomas of the U.S. Army and heard words spoken by him that were cheering to my heart.[1] He said that he had been sent by the President to tell the Army of the Cumberland that it was the settled policy of the government to sustain the emancipation proclamation and that any and every slave coming to our lines must be kindly received and fed and clothed at the government expense.[2] Said slaves to be used as soldiers or teamsters or on government works as they desire, and any officer refusing this protection would be discharged from the service.

He also said he had orders to grant commissions to non-commissioned officers and privates in other regiments who could get a recommend from commanding officers and wished to serve in a colored regiment.

About 3000 soldiers were present and when the speaker closed, three rousing cheers broke the stillness for the President and for sustaining the Emancipation Proclamation. The speaker stood on the balcony of the general's quarters (General Asboth) and the soldiers were formed in the street.[3] A good many of the citizens were present, but as I was in the ranks I did not see what effect it did produce among them.

One man, a day or two before, came to our pickets and wanted them to stop one of his slaves if he came along there; but he did not get much satisfaction as to future prospects if he came.

I was glad that Price was better and hope he will be careful 'til he gets well, as it is better to be on the extreme of careful than to be at trouble of twice curing the disease.

We are having beautiful weather. The greatest trouble here during the summer I am informed is the dust when the wind blows. We have had a foretaste of it a few days ago, and it is not very pleasant, but I had rather have the dust than swamps to live in, as a plentiful application of soap and water will remove the first named but the effects of the other are more penetrating, hence more difficult to remove.

I wish that the boys would write and tell me how all the folks are getting along and what the news is about town. Anything in this line will be of interest to me, as I feel an interest in the welfare of all my old friends, and should be glad to hear of their prospects. Also how you are getting along with the work and what you are doing.

Just now I looked up and saw a sight that pained my heart. A young man has been sentenced to pass through the camp for 30 days in succession between the hours of 4 & 6 with the word thief in large letters on a card fastened to his back and breast. He left the camp without orders, and went through the picket line, and stole chickens, and was the means of inducing others to go. Two others were also sentenced; one to 30 days, the other to 30 but was, on account of being young and refusing to go a second time, his sentence was reduced to 10 days in the guardhouse. The others have 30 and every 3 days on bread and water.

I have not room to write all that I want to. You must have a hard stint to pick it out mixed up as it is.

Gilbert

[Upside down at top]

April 6:

Today I got my hat. They are like the hats that the 28th drew and are to be rigged off with a feather if we desire it.

We draw 2 months pay again this week, and I will send 5 dollars in this letter and run the risk of it going safe.

The regulars that went off to the fight are back all safe, and I heard that at Union City all was right.

I hope this will find you in the enjoyment of better health as a family than when I last heard from you.

NOTES

1. Brigadier General Lorenzo Thomas had been Adjutant General, the chief administrative officer of the army, until March 1863. At that time, he was assigned to organize colored troops in the lower Mississippi valley. He was visiting Gilbert's fort in this capacity (Budge Weidman, "Preserving the Legacy of United States Colored Troops," National Archives, 1997, http://www.archives.gov/education/lessons/blacks-civil-war/article.htm).

2. On January 1, 1863, Abraham Lincoln said that, in the Confederate states (or parts of states), slaves were freed, and would be received into the armed services of the United States. It is interesting to note that slaves in nonrebelling states or sectors would remain slaves. That included Maryland, Virginia's counties that would become West Virginia, and certain parishes of Louisiana, including New Orleans.

3. The commanding general at Columbus was Alexander Asboth. He was a Hungarian engineer who came to the United States as a political refugee after the unsuccessful 1848–49 War of Liberation led by Lajos Kossuth against the ruling Hapsburg dynasty and czarist Russia (Stephen Beszedits, "Hungarians in Civil War Missouri," Missouri Civil War Museum, http://www.mcwm.org/history_hungarians.html). More about General Asboth is in Appendix D.

[Undated letter from Gilbert]

Dear Esther,

I must say I am not a little puzzled to understand your real situation. You say, "I don't want you to think I am sick. I am as well *to all appearance* as I was 5 or 6 months ago." Well now, the question is, *are you as* well in all points of view?

I was in hopes that your cough would be better the next time I heard from you, and was glad that Margaret's cherry syrup relieved you for the time.[1] But I did not think that it would cure you enough at once. It has been of a long standing and will take time to remove it even if it can be removed by its use. I wish you would get some more, and take it again, and do what you can to improve your general health by washing and gentle exercise in the open air, especially in the morning. I would not go out in the night air more than I could help. I should like to know if you [looks like "rain"] much, and how your shoulder is, and whether your lungs trouble you about breathing, and all the particulars.

I am glad that you are resigned to the ordering of God's providence concerning yourself, and are willing to bear so cheerfully the burden of this mortal life; and that in all this you may be called to pass through you may see a Savior's hand is the earnest desire of my heart. And I trust that God in his goodness will in a short time permit us to enjoy each other's beauty again. And we [will] be better prepared to enjoy the social relations of life than we ever were before. I trust that we shall be prepared by grace divine for any and every treat that God in His goodness has in store for us to pass through if this prepared life will be beautiful.

Gilbert

[Around the edges]

I hope you will not worry about my sleeping. I get along first rate and have not felt so tired this spring as I did last. I think it will be a benefit.

I hope you will not worry about my worrying about you, and be afraid to tell me in future all about yourself and the rest of the folks when they are unwell. I am getting along well and healthy.

NOTE

    1. Wild cherry bark (*Prunus serotina*) continues to be a favorite ingredient in cough and cold remedies, primarily due to its sedative effect on the respiratory system.

Columbus
April 13, 1863

Dear Esther,

I have just perused your letter and as I have time and a willing heart, I answer.

I have just come off from guard. My post was at the magazine in Fort Halleck and it is the best post in the fort, as we can stand inside of the entrance and be protected from the cold or wet. I got permission from the lieutenant of the guard to take my blankets and sleep there, and so did one of the 31st boys on guard at the same post. We had a good time.

I was glad to hear that you had got the state pay, and if you got my last letter [I would like to hear] if you found 5 dollars in it.

The day you last wrote which was the 9th, we were paid to the first of March which was 26 dollars; and I want you to use all the money you need to make you and the rest of family comfortable. I think that I shall send some more in the course of 2 or 3 weeks. I wish you would let me know how you are off for money the next letter. I should be glad if you had 20 dollars of it now, as I have no place to put it but to carry it with me all the time in my pocket.[1] I have $29.90 and I should have nearly 10 dollars if I send 20 which will be more than I shall want if I do not get any more 'til my time is out. As Uncle Sam feeds and clothes us, and I do not use tobacco or whiskey, I shall not if I have my health be under the necessity of being too much expense out.

I am glad that the boys are doing so well and are getting along with the work as William represents to me so finely. I hope they will be obedient and good boys and work together in harmony.

The chaplain of the 31st [Alfred Brunsun of Prairie du Chien, Wisconsin] had service in camp yesterday, and I attended it although I was on guard. The text was the 16th verse of the 15th chapter of first Corinthians: "For if the dead rise not, then is not Christ raised." It was a short but interesting discourse and was listened to with a good deal of apparent interest. I have not attended a prayer since I left Oconomowoc. If I could get out of camp I could attend prayer meetings, but here in the fort every place is overheard so that it is impossible to get a place.

Our Chaplain is a perfect disgrace to the profession, and is in my opinion doing more hurt to the cause of religion by his acts daily than a hundred privates. A day or two since I was in one of the barracks. He came in and took a cup of water to drink. One of the men said, "Look here!" producing a bottle of whiskey. The water went out of the door, and the cup was presented, and a drink turned out, and he turned it down his throat. I have not heard him preach and do not intend to, as it would be time wasted in a spiritual point of view.

The time passes rapidly away and soon, if God spares our lives, we shall, I trust, meet again to enjoy each other's society and the society of dear friends in Oconomowoc.

There is but one man in our company who I believe is truly walking in the narrow way. His name is Henry Higgins of Lisbon, Waukesha County. Since he has been in the army he has lost his hearing to a great extent, and it is hard work to talk with him, but his daily walk speaks to the Christian principle of his heart. He ought to have his discharge but cannot get one. They have put him in the bake house.

Roberts that took my letter to Milwaukee was quite unwell when he left camp. He got as far as Milwaukee and could get no farther. Higgins got a letter yesterday from his father saying Roberts was very low, and his father & mother were taking care of him.

I wish you could see how clean and nice we keep things here our streets are rubbish of every kind is removed. We have to shake and fold our blankets every morning, and are required to black our boots; blacking and brushes are furnished. I think that I shall improve to some extent in an orderly point of view as every man must have some order or he would never be able to find his things when crowded together as we are in barracks and having so many trappings so near alike as soldiers must have. I have not lost anything as yet but a good many have lost clothing and gun accouterments.

I hope this will find you all in the enjoyment of better health than when you last wrote.

Gilbert Claflin

NOTE

1. Reports of costs for specific items gives an idea of what the twenty dollars could have bought. In his June 4 letter Gilbert reports buying an overcoat for ten dollars, and in her July 22 letter Esther says she bought a hundred pounds of flour for three dollars.

[Probably April 14, 1863]

Dear Son,

It is a rainy morning, and I will write you a letter. I do not know whether I wrote to you or Elton the last time, but in future I shall write to the one that favors me with a letter.

Since I wrote last we have had beautiful weather. The trees have got quite large leaves on, and I begin to think that Wisconsin is rather a cold country. But after all, there are so many disadvantages in other respects that I would not exchange my home in Wisconsin for any place I have seen since I left that state.

The 10th I was detailed to work in the magazine, and went all through it. You would be surprised to see the amount of ammunition of every description there is there.

Every form, almost, which powder, shot, and shell, and canister is used to do the work of execution is here in large quantity. We took about 5,000 pounds of powder from the magazine in Fort Halleck, and took it to the magazine at the 6 gun battery and what we took would hardly be missed from where we took it.

Yesterday morning when I was on guard, before I was relieved one of the corporals of the regulars came and wanted a 20 pound cannon shot to put in the knapsack of a private. I let him take one as he had orders to get it, and he marched that man over an hour with his knapsack full of clothes and the ball besides. Such is the way that they punish the privates when they do not obey orders.

I am glad that you have commenced getting in school. Do it well, and let me know how much you do, and how many oats you sow, and all about the work, and what the prospect is for frost. I shall expect a letter from you or Elton every week when your mother writes.

    Your Father,

G. *Claflin*

❧

April 16, 1863

My Dear Gilbert,

    Last Friday night my heart was again thrilled with motions of pleasure by the announcement of a letter similar to that which it used to experience months ago when hearing the approach of that well known footstep. Then too it was made doubly welcome by the extra contents that very necessary article *money*; not that we were out, but *you know* how much it takes to get a little, and I have no idea of making a store bill for you to pay if you ever get back, excepting at the shoe store. The boys have got them some shoes to wear to church and now I think they will get along without buying any more this summer. You see now how human plans fail. You recollect I told you that we must get our living and keep your wages for building, but it goes about as fast as it comes. You know that boys are doing the farming, and it costs something to keep them in tools, and very much must go to waste without a manager. But they try to do their best, and they are very careful of my health.

    The false alarm that you write about is evidence enough for me that you are in the enemy's country, and that you are liable to be attacked and slain or imprisoned any day. I never get a letter but I think how soon this correspondence may be interrupted. But, Gilbert, hoping as we do that we have a far more glorious and Eternal inheritance we ought not to wish for the good things of this life, and yet we have much. I know that I have more than I deserve.

    I have not had any of Emily's children since she took Anna away, though I told her I would keep one. I don't know how she lives these times, but she stays there; and Uncle John lets her have flour, and John keeps her in wood. I don't think Mother ought to keep Arabelle. I think she has raised her share of children.

    I can't tell you any news for I don't go, and no one comes here. There has not been anybody here to take tea but Mrs. Newnham since you left home, and we have very few callers except relatives. If people come when you come back I shall know who they come to see.

Price got home those potatoes today, and we have just had some for supper—the first we have had for a long time. I don't expect you get any. Don't you get dreadful tired of your diet, and have you had any change of diet since you wrote me?

Yesterday and today have been mild and beautiful days, but I think it has been a dry winter and spring. The cistern is getting quite low.

William goes back tonight. I have been very busy since he has been here fixing his things. I do but very little work since I have finished the sewing and mending. I have pieced a little and braided a little.

I have not had as much pain under my shoulder blades as I had last winter, but I have had a settled soreness in my chest and sore throat considerable. But I thought the greatest reason I had for thinking that my health was failing entirely was weakness. A pail of water seems so heavy and if I do anything a little harder than usual it uses me up so. But I am much better than I was in March. I have got more syrup.

I hear that Mr. Barton is poorly.

James is worse; his lungs have been troubling him lately. I have not seen him since he went to Delafield but I should not be surprised to hear any day that he was not alive.

That this may find you in health is the wish of

Esther Claflin

[Elton's letter is on the same page]

Dear Father,

We have sowed more wheat than we did last year, and we have got a little more seed to sow. We have commenced to build the fence that encloses the piece that we are to break.

Billy has got well. He put his stiffle out of joint. We could have another team if we had another harness.

Mr. Egerton of Summit has got married.

D. R. Tompson has got back. He says that a great many of the boys are sick.

Mr. Hoyt has died since he left the state.

Uncle John's folks have got a little boy a week old and the folks are all doing nicely.[1]

We are a-going to fix the road fence and the fence between Mr. Eastman. From Your Son,

Elton Claflin

[Here Esther continues her April 16 letter without a new salutation]

Margaret hears from J.P. pretty often. He has been troubled lately with diarrhea some. He still writes full of hope and O! I wish that our army might be successful and that there might be a speedy and righteous terminus to this dreadful war. If we live to see peace on just principles, shan't we know how to prize it.

Minona [J.P. and Margaret's three-year-old daughter] has been staying here a few days. She is a little sunshine in the house and I think a child that is easily favored.

If you should send home more money soon, I think we had better pay John. Do you think Elton can shear the sheep? He thinks he can. You may tell him what you think about it and not say that I have written. I don't think he ought to attempt it.

Esther

[Upside down over part of page 1]

Price has read a few pages of Robinson Crusoe somewhere and he is very anxious to read the book.[2] If you return safe to Milwaukee, perhaps you can find it.

Mr. Kendall says he will make the sash for the mid price including freight.

Do you ever get any papers from home? If you do, we will send more. People tell me soldiers don't get them.

NOTES
1. Holton Bradley Metcalf was born on or about April 9, 1863.
2. *Robinson Crusoe* is a classic tale of shipwreck and survival on a desert island. It was, and still is, one of the most popular adventure novels. It was written by Daniel Defoe in 1719.

[A fragment of a leaf is pressed inside this undated letter from Gilbert]

Dear Esther,

I expected a letter today, but did not get one; and as the cars do not run into Cairo on Sunday, we do not get many letters from Wisconsin on Tuesday. The result would be if I waited 'til yours is received, it would not get through this week.

I am today standing guard at the company quarters about 10 rods from our barracks. I do not like this place very well; had rather stand on picket, as there I can breathe the free air of heaven and not feel that restraint that I do when surrounded by men with shoulder straps on; but it is all right, and I do [not] let a day pass but what I learn something new, and I hope I am improving a moral and intellectual, as well as a military point of view.

Last Sunday I had the privilege of attending church, and I shall not forget for a long time the blessed privilege which I enjoyed. On the way to church I heard a voice singing "I have a Father in the Promised Land," & I looked and saw a little girl under the shade of a beautiful poplar by the side of the house that the rebel general Morgan occupied as his headquarters when he was here.[1] My mind in an instant centered on the dear children in the Sunday school in Oconomowoc; and I trust the impression then made will lead me to feel a deeper interest in their spiritual welfare than I have previously done.

But little interest is manifested in spiritual things among the inhabitants of Columbus, and there is but little among the soldiers here. There are now about 1500 cavalry and 3500 infantry here. Why so many troops are here I do not know, but think that a move of some kind will soon be made before long as there is no prospect as I can see that this place will be attacked. All sorts of rumors are going the rounds about the 34th, and considerable money is bet that we shall go back to Wisconsin the first of May. I think that we shall leave here before long myself, but where I do not pretend to predict. It matters but little with me where I go so long as I am in the service of my country and can be useful to those around me.

I am now at the guardhouse, and post is to be changed to the gate the next relief, as the man cannot read the passes. It is a better post and not as far from the guardhouse. My post was number 16 it will now be number 2.

I hardly know what to write that will be of interest. I witnessed a battalion drill of the 4th Missouri Regiment of cavalry that was a splendid sight.

"I Have a Father in the Promised Land." This is the song Gilbert heard a young girl singing under a tree in Kentucky. (Horace Waters, *Sabbath School Bells* [New York: Horace Waters, 1859], 4)

I wish that the boys could have seen it. It seemed like magic to witness the various evolutions that a thousand horsemen in a body can go through and have every change in harmony throughout the whole.[2]

I hardly know what to write about home affairs, as I have not heard since I wrote; but I want the boys to be as considerate as they can be, and not do more than they can do and do it well. They had not better do anything with the orchard or where the currants are. I saw corn several days ago that was 4 or 5 inches high.

If my life is spared I shall be home in about 4 months and then this dull formality of letter writing will be done for a time, I think, and I guess I shall appreciate its privileges.

Gilbert

[Marginal writings]

If you wish to know anything I shall answer soon.

I hope this will find you in the enjoyment of good health and the blessing of a quiet and contented spirit which I find by experience relieves the burdens of life.

Give my love to all.

NOTES

1. At the time of this letter, John Hunt Morgan, the famous Confederate raider, was conducting raids in Kentucky about three hundred miles east of Columbus.

2. The Fourth Missouri Cavalry Regiment had just come to Columbus at the time of this letter. They were a regiment of horsemen with battle experience at Pea Ridge. More about the Fourth Missouri Cavalry Regiment is in Appendix D.

April 20, 1863

My Dear Husband,

Your very welcome letter was received Friday night, and found us all in our usual health.

And that afternoon I spent at Mr. Goodall's. She told me to give their love to you. He has set up a Coffin Store over "our store." His health is very poor. He had a fit a few weeks ago in Church. They have given up their Sunday School at Oncochie.

Uncle John's people are prospering. She got along with very little sickness and she was pleased about it. I assure you they have a large, healthy, smart-looking boy. He looks as much like living as any child I ever saw.

I guess Frank is ruined beyond redemption. She left school in the winter, and has been toting about here and there, and out with Baxter almost every night; and now she is in Summit at his mother's part of the time. It seems a great pity that Uncle John has so much trouble with other people's children; but this world is a paradox. It will all come right by and by. We have only to do our duty and then wait patiently the Lord's own good time to do His work.

Last night I dreamed I was on a battlefield and when the conflict was over I was anxiously searching for a lost friend, but was unable to find him. Having friends where some of mine are, such a dream will have some impression.

James is no better. He has sent me word that he is very anxious to see me, and I shall go over tomorrow if it is dry enough. It has been a wet afternoon, although little rain has fallen.

I am 33 today, and I thought would write a little to you my best beloved. I am not as young as I once was, but I have no desire to go back to youth and live my life of errors over. It is 9 o'clock, so good night.

Friday Evening, 24th:

I have been over to see James today and found him some better. His skin looks much fresher and he is a little more fleshy, but it may not be anything lasting as he is under the doctor's care and is probably stimulated.

Anna is a good deal worn down with care and anxiety. I think James' lungs a good deal affected. But Gilbert, I am afraid you are not as well as usual. You have not said anything about your health in your two last. Do tell me if you are not well. *Is not sympathy* worth something? I have just received your last, which I think was written Tuesday (you did not date it) and I feel almost certain that you are in low spirits or poor health or both.

I have put off writing this week. For the last two or three weeks I have put a letter in the office the very day yours came so you would not get an answer in two weeks.

Before tomorrow night the boys will have got in that northeast lot to wheat and oats, and that which was ploughed last fall is got in to wheat. Elton feels very ambitious to do a great deal of farming. You write for them not to plough the orchard. I am sure I don't know where they will plant if they don't plough it. The currant bushes are not disturbed; only what people have come and took. And Elton is worrying about a place to sow buckwheat. Would the lot next Eastman's be good to raise anything on this year if it was ploughed?

Some of the trees in the orchard are completely covered with bark lice. What can we do for them? I think it is going to blow pretty full this spring. I see by your leaf that you are having summer, but never mind; we shall have summer too, by and by.

I have just measured my corn and it measures six inches. But you know I have to bring it in every night. The cotton seed rotted. The cattle and horses are in good order; better than they ever have been this time of year. The sheep have not got any lambs yet.

I heard that you had moved from Columbus and I thought it was not best to send a letter until we had one.

Mr. Hinkley [one of the directors of the Oconomowoc Bank] let me have six dollars about a week ago, and I have let John have seven and now we have five and some change. I keep account of everything so if you come back you will know how I have spent your money. And I don't believe you will say that I spent it foolishly. I have not bought a thing for myself since you went from home. Price says that Grandma worries a great deal about my having so much money and spending it, but I know you will not find fault with my managing.

Yours truly,

Esther Claflin

[Upside down at top]

I think you had better send home part of your money at a time, for if you should go further south, which I fear you will, you know the mails are more precarious; and I believe they are perfectly safe between here and Columbus.

I don't believe you will come to Wisconsin before next August.

My daily prayer is that your life and health may be spared.

We are all well. I am quite well.

∾

Columbus
April 23, 1863

Dear Esther,

As I anticipated, your letter did not reach its destination in time to answer it this week so that you would get it this week. I was glad to hear of your prosperity, and can inform you that I am doing as well as I could ask for.

I was sorry to hear that James remains so poorly. I was in hopes that he would, under home treatment, soon recover his health, and still I hope he will recover.

You said that J.P. had got the diarrhea. I have not been troubled at all as yet with it, but most of the boys have; and some of them have been quite bad off.

John Roberts, the young man that took my money to Millwaukee, is dead. He never got home alive. I can hardly realize that he is gone, that his probation state is ended, but so it is. Ever since he was drafted his friends have exerted themselves to the utmost to get his discharge on the grounds that he was a British subject, although he was born and brought up in Waukesha County, Wisconsin. When he was in Madison a discharge was sent to the Governor but on some account it was returned. Another was obtained from the British Consul at Washington, and his brother came here and brought it and spent a month here in camp before it could come round so that he could be discharged, as the discharged had to be sent to General Grant before it could be applied as a release. When it came he was quite unwell; and when he left was hardly able to sit up. He got to Milwaukee, and died last Friday the 17th. Perhaps no parents have felt a greater anxiety, or exerted themselves more than did his parents to return a son from the army and to their quiet home; but as that bright hope was about to be realized, as they thought, suddenly it was destroyed; and they are left to mourn for a son & brother departed. Such are earthly hopes and I trust I shall profit by the lesson that it teaches, and in future not be over anxious about the affairs of this mortal life which is short; but daily see a Father's hand & receive a Father's blessing.

April 24:

I am on guard today, and am now writing in the guardhouse. I expected to be out on picket, but have now been detailed for fort guard time. The two last times I have generally been 4 times on picket to 1 fort guard.

You spoke of my being in an enemy's country. It is true. But Esther, I feel as safe when out on picket now as I do here in camp; for I do not anticipate an attack on this place; for it is impossible in the nature of things for the Rebels to get here with a land force sufficient to take this place without our being aware of their coming some time before they got here; and even if it could be taken, they could not hold it as the gunboats would soon drive them out. It is true that a small force of cavalry might get on the picket line and take a few pickets; but they could do no more. And it is a hundred chances to one that not one of them would get away alive if they should come, as our cavalry are stationed or camped right on the line of pickets and a 1000 of them would be in the saddle in fifteen minutes after the alarm was given. But so far as my life is concerned I have but little anxiety about the matter.

Every day brings its duties, and with a cheerful heart I endeavor to discharge them. If in the ordering of things I must fall or be taken prisoner it will all be right. I do not want you to worry about my living. I have enough, and that is good enough; and what is better, a good appetite to eat my rations, or what is needful, as I do not eat what the government allows. We get dried apples quite often, and you will remember that I got some dried apples and peaches sometime ago. I have not cooked any but once and I have got nearly all the dried fruit you sent me. So you see that I have not been very bad off for something nice to eat. I looked at that bottle of honey a short time ago, and it had candied. I have eat some 3 times I believe.

I have got several papers from you, and William has sent several. Some of our boys had papers sent regularly from the office, but sometimes they would be several days behind time and hence produced dissatisfaction, as a man in the army when a thing is due wants it.

I am glad that you have got your sewing and the like done, and I think that you had not better try to make any cloth, but under the circumstances sell all the wool but what you need for stockings, and what Mother wants to work up, and take the money and get cloth ["the wool" is inserted very tiny above "all but," and "for stockings" very tiny above "need and"]. I should like to have you give your opinion on the subject now I have expressed mine so freely, and if you can make it appear in a satisfactory light in my view that it is for the best all things considered, I will yield the point when I get at the end of the point. I found that I had failed to make a point for you will see that at the word "need "I forgot to put in "for stockings."

We are having most beautiful weather and I enjoy the prospects from the bluff very much. The other evening as I stood there, 3 large steamers were moving in the river. The sun had just set and the steamers Ruth & Liberty were coming in, and the steamer Memphis was leaving port. It was one of the finest sights I have witnessed since I have been in Kentucky. Two other steamers lay in port. There is a landscape view as you look towards Cairo from Fort Halleck which is the finest one that I think I ever looked upon before. During the course of time the river has changed its bed and on the east side a belt of land has been formed nearly 2 miles in length. This is thickly covered with cottonwood, the trees most remote from the river on the land first formed are of large size those nearer are smaller 'til you come down to the mere bush bordering on the river. As you leave the bottomland, the land gradually rises covered with dense forest. The green foliage of the cottonwood as the sun is setting produces a pleasing emotion in the mind of the lover of nature and enables him to bear more cheerfully much which the eye rests upon that is not pleasant to behold. I wish you could for once look upon the scene, as I shall in about 5 minutes going from the guardhouse to get my supper.

I am on post 3; 3 relief and go on at 6 off at 8 on at 12 off at 2 on at 6 off at 8. I shall get about 5 hours of sleep during the night if all goes right.

April 25:

I have just come off from guard, and it is very warm for the time of year. I saw cattle eating grass in the ditch front of the earthworks which form the fort that had grown as much as 14 inches this spring. That is a little ahead of Wisconsin, I think.

In my last I spoke of our leaving this place. I hardly know what to think of it now, and guess that no one in the regiment knows when or where we shall be the next 3 months. I think most of the regiment wants to move to some other place, and would be glad to go soon. I think that it is better for men not to stay too long in a place, as a change of place produces change of scenes and relieves the dull monotony of camp life; but I do not think that while we remain south we shall find a more healthy place than it is here; and I could be contented to remain if it is for the best.

We have had a regular time cleaning house. It was on the 23rd. We whitewashed our barracks all over in the inside and they look quite neat. We also whitewashed the front of them. It will add to the appearance of the camp and be beneficial to the health of the men.

I do not know as you can make this out but perhaps you can if you take time for it.

I shall send home 10 dollars in this letter. You can use it as you think best.

Yours Truly,

Gilbert Claflin

[Gilbert's letter to his eldest son Elton is on the same page]

Dear Son,

I was glad to get a letter from you and hear of your prosperity in the farming line.

I did not think that you would sow more wheat than we did last year. I should like to know how many oats you are going to sow, and how much corn you intend to plant.

I did not expect that you and Price would break up that piece of land; and I think you will have enough to do to do the other work and do it well.

I guess that you had better repair the fences, and fix them up so that the stock will not get in the grain, before you build the fence you speak of building.

I am glad that Billy has got well. I think that you will get to be quite a horse doctor if you keep on. I did not expect that he would get well so soon.

I should like to have you inform me what the prospect for fruit is this year, and whether the orchard is going to bloom fully. Apple & pear trees have got fruit on them here.

The boys of the various regiments are having some luck in the fishing line about these days. The fish caught here are: shovel fish, sheep heads, and buffalos, & catfish.[1] Considerable fishing is done by the inhabitants around here. They sell all that they get at 10 cents a pound. I have learnt how to make a fish trap that they say will work to a charm, and supply a family in fish during the summer.[2] I think that I shall make one when I get home, if you and Price will tend it.

There are some wild turkeys here. Some of our boys saw 3 one morning in the picket line; but did not dare to shoot at them, as it would alarm the picket line and the men in the fort.

The steamer Illinois came up from Memphis the other day with a lot of rebel prisoners on board they stopped to report and started up the river before the officers at headquarters got ready. They fired a blank cartridge at them but they did not stop. Soon a ball went whistling over her smoke stacks or chimneys, which soon caused her to return, as the next ball would have gone into her had she continued on her course.

The 23rd I saw an iron ram pass down the river.[3] It had an iron turret where the guns are mounted. It was the most singular looking craft that I ever saw, and was the most formidable looking boat that I have seen on the river. I did not learn the name of her. I suppose her destination is Vicksburg, as that is the point of interest especially for this class of boats at the present time.

The same day, whilst out on drill, the order came for a detail of 7 men: 2 corporals, 1 sergeant & 1 lieutenant to report at once to the general's quarters to guard some hay boats down to Memphis. When the order came to pull out those who wished to go, there was no lack of men ready to go & privates went from our company.

I want you and Price to work together like good boys, as I hope you do, and strive to improve your leisure hours in improving your minds by reading and study. You may learn much during the summer that will be more valuable to you than gold because it will be a permanent good and be a means of fitting you to discharge more efficiently the duties of life as you ought to God and your fellow men.

I shall expect you to do with the horses as you think best.

I expect you will have to get someone to shear the sheep. You can find out by Mister Eastman who will do it, and what they charge, and can pay when the work is done.

I shall expect an answer to this letter. I want to know your plans and how you get along.

Your Father,

Gilbert Claflin

NOTES

1. Shovel fish are also called spoonbill, or paddlefish, because this fish has an odd paddle-shaped snout. Sheepshead are sometimes called convict fish because of their dark vertical stripes; this fish has strong incisors that can pick up mollusks and scrape barnacles off rocks. Buffalo fish are also called suckers because of their protruding lips; they are similar to carp.

2. Many fish traps are a frame box covered with some kind of mesh. One or more funnels allow fish into the baited box but make it very difficult for them to escape.

3. Charles Ellet Jr. first put forth the idea of a fast vessel with a sharp reinforced prow—to intentionally ram a larger but slower and less maneuverable warship—in 1855. The February 22, 1861, issue of *Scientific American* endorsed Ellet's views and argued that all "iron war steamers" should have strong iron prows that could be used offensively.

Within a few months of the standoff battle between the ironclads USS *Monitor* and CSS *Merrimac* in March 1862, the navies of both sides were using both ironclad warships and iron ram steamers.

Ellet convinced the army's quartermaster to purchase seven river steamers and have them converted to rams according to his specifications. He commanded the ram fleet, and it remained a US Army unit under independent command throughout the war (Nosworthy, *Bloody Crucible of Courage*, 359–67; Wideman, *Naval Warfare*, 47).

Columbus
April 30, 1863

Dear Esther,

I received your letter this morning and was pleased to hear that you all were well. I am in the enjoyment of good health.

You have doubtless received my last letter before this enclosing 10 dollars.

I did not think when I wrote that morning that such a change would take place in camp as has since taken place. In the afternoon of that day, the 25th, companies I & G of the 34th were ordered to get ready at once and report to headquarters. That night they went by steamer [to] Cairo.

On Sunday the 26th I went on picket about 3 o'clock. The next morning I was awakened while sleeping in the picket house by the [blank space in letter] from the 27th regiment which was camped about ¾ of a mile from the picket line. They and the 25th had got immediate marching orders for Cape Girardeau, which is about 40 miles above Cairo, as the Rebels were marching on that place. Several companies of cavalry also got marching orders and left. I should judge about 3000 soldiers left Columbus within 3 days.[1] When I got back to camp that morning from picket I found Company A [of the] 34th had got orders to leave Fort Halleck and go to Fort Quinby to man the guns and repair the fortifications. We according packed up and got tents and marched to Fort Quinby where we now are.

We are now camped on the bluff right back of Columbus. The buildings come right up to the bluff. It is a pleasant place where we now are, and will not be as dusty as in the place we left. Summer improves the looks of Columbus. The town now is dry, and the flat covered with grass instead of water.

The 28th [of April], the 25th & 27th Regiments returned as the fight had passed at the Cape and the Rebels were retreating pursued by our cavalry which were pressing them hard.

The First Wisconsin Cavalry were in the fight back of the town and were somewhat cut up. I saw a list of the killed and wounded but did not see any names that I knew.

We are now on detached service and shall not have any picket duty to do, and for the present no guard duty of any kind. We are more at liberty here than we were at the other fort and are not (for we are not inside of the fortifications) compelled to get a pass to walk out around the place.

The 25th do the guard duty on the fortifications now and probably will for some time as we have got to drill and fix the works up in shape so that they will look nice and be serviceable in case of an attack.

Yesterday our boys were all at home for the first time in nearly 3 months as we had no one out on guard. Today is fast day, and I am writing under the shade of a locust bush.[2] We have just had inspection and have been mustered for pay, and shall probably be paid next week. We do not have any drill today and the boys can go down town; all of them that want to.

I fear that many of them will not be the better, but the worse, for this day's opportunity.

I feel that it truly becomes us as a people to humble ourselves under the avenging arm of God's justice to us as a nation on account of our sins and humbly seek with penitence His favor, which is life, and His loving kindness, which is better than life, by so doing. Success would, I believe, attend our efforts and the rebellion would soon be crushed, and the instigators have their just deserts.

I do not know what to say about the work. I did not think that the boys could plow the orchard as it is a very hard job and a difficult one, but if they think they can and not injure the trees I am willing.

As to the north lot, I should think that they would need it for pasture but will leave it to the boys to decide the matter. I do not want that they should undertake to do too much. They had better do less and do it well, as it will be more of a job for them to harvest than to get it in.

I did not expect that they would sow so much wheat & oats, but guess it will come out all right. If they conclude to do anything with the orchard they had better plant part and sow part to buckwheat. They would get more by plowing the north lot if it was not wanted for pasture.

Gilbert Claflin

[At the top it says]

Direct the same as usual

NOTES

1. Starting on April 17, 1863, Confederate General Marmaduke led a raid into Missouri to attack Union forces under Brigadier General McNeil at Bloomfield in the southeastern part of the state. McNeil was able to take his forces to the fortified Union supply base at Cape Girardeau, Missouri, on the Mississippi River, about sixty miles north of Columbus, Kentucky. At Cape Girardeau, General McNeil was reinforced with troops from Columbus. General Marmaduke's Confederate forces retreated southward to Chalk Bluff where, the night of May 1–2, there was a battle as they crossed the St. Francis River into Arkansas. The part played by the soldiers from Columbus in repulsing the Confederates from Cape Girardeau is in the official correspondence of their commanding general Alexander Asboth, in Appendix D under "Battle of Chalk Bluff" (Scott, *War of the Rebellion*, vol. 22, 281–88; "The Battle of Chalk Bluff, May 2, 1863," Civil War Buff: The Civil War in Arkansas, http://www.civilwarbuff.org/Places/Clay/StFrancis.html, accessed May 26, 2013).

2. On March 30, 1863, President Lincoln proclaimed that April 30, 1863, would be a day of national humiliation, fasting, and prayer, hoping that God would pardon our national sins and restore the suffering country to its "former happy condition of unity

and peace." Lincoln wrote that the country might "justly fear that the awful calamity of civil war, which now desolates the land, may be but a punishment" because "[w]e have grown in numbers, wealth and power, as no other nation has ever grown. But we have forgotten God" (Basler, *Collected Works of Abraham Lincoln*, 6:156–57).

❧

April 30, 1863

My Dear Gilbert,

Yours of the 23rd, 24th, and 25th was received last night and read in bed as most of your letters have been this spring, as the boys don't get home until after I go to bed.

At the time, and after reading yours, my mind was reaching out to you away down in Kentucky—a *soldier* ready at a moment's call to shoulder your musket and face the enemy. And yet my thoughts of you were not particularly painful. In all my thoughts of you there was a delicious sensation; I had heard from you, and you seemed contented and well; and that was joy enough for the present. I expected a letter from you, although it was earlier by three days than we had had one for many weeks, and should have been disappointed without one. I lay awake until after 12 o'clock which is quite a common thing after getting a letter. So you see I am not quite so much of a sleepy head as you knew me to be.

We have had a very nice spring; no hot days to wilt boys and cattle, no wet weather to prevent working the land, and it has not been too dry to work. Winter wheat looks well, and so does spring wheat, what we can see of it.[1] We heard whippoorwills last Sunday night for the first time, and now they serenade us nightly, and all the old birds have come back with their morning songs. But we want one more from the south to make the whole complete.

Yesterday while thinking of you, I felt as thought I had lived the life of a parasite. It seemed as though I had expected you to hold up my head and heart and it looked selfish. But you know I am not of that independent self-sustaining character as many. Margaret seems to thrive. I think she rather enjoys being her own mistress and doing business independent, and it is well. I wish there were more women like her. *Too many* will be left with no one to lean upon, and if they can only feel competent I am sure it will be much better for them and their children.

I wish you would tell how often it comes your turn to do guard or picket duty; and also if there are rebel prisoners now to guard; and what is your opinion respecting the morals and intelligence of the Rebels, if you have had a chance to see anything of them.

Your boots and stockings must be worn out. I hope you won't wear ragged stockings if you can help it. You can take the worst pair to mend the others.

Is your fine comb good yet, and do you keep clear of *lice*? They tell me it is impossible to keep clear of them in old camps. Poor James came home covered, but you know he was sick and had but one hand and had no fine comb. His brother-in-law Patterson refused to lend him his comb.

You may not be aware that today is National Fast Day.

I did not go to meeting, for I have both of Emily's little girls this week, but Elton went and Mr. Goodall's people have just gone from here. They thought I was sick the reason I was not there. They say Mr. Montague preached a most excellent sermon and the house was full. I guess you go to meeting now oftener than I do. Last Sunday is the first time I have been since the last communion. Tomorrow is preparatory lecture and I shall try to go, but I am able to walk now, and shall go more. I cough yet, but not so badly. I am satisfied now that the seat of my cough is in my throat, for it is sore all of the time, though not sore enough to be very troublesome, and I feel very well; better than I once thought I ever should.

J.P. is now under the surgeon's care though not in hospital, and he writes that he is better but I fear for that terrible scourge.

I don't know but Emily will work for Charles Osborne and take one child this summer. If so, I told her I would take care of Florence. She wants to keep Anne and from what I have seen of the children, Florence is the least stubborn of the three.

We have sowed some beets, parsnips, onions, peas, and set out a few strawberries, and Price has planted some potatoes.

May 1:

Price went to Delafield yesterday and says James is better so that he is out in the street. They are living at Mr. Jaynes.

Yours as ever,

Esther Claflin

[Marginal notes]

The ten dollars was received.

Will you give the receipt for making grafting wax?[2] I guess I've forgotten.

It may be best not to work up any wool, but I thought I could make some colored flannel for shirts that would do to wear without cotton.

Tremain is Sabbath School Superintendent again.

Beverly W. sent home 5 dollars.[3]

Old Mr. Perkins is crazy and is very troublesome. How can anybody want to live to be old?

[This is on the back of Esther's letter of April 30/May 1]

May 1, 1863

Dear Father,

You wrote to Elton, but he is out plowing, and Ma wants to send the letter off this morning so I am a-going to answer his letter.

I went over to Delafield yesterday and Uncle James is much better. He walked all over town most, and goes to the table, and eats what other folks do.

And Elton went a-hunting with John. They got a small fox alive and would have got its mother. John snapped at her, but the gun did not go. It is the first time it has missed this spring. Elton said it was as much as 18 inches in height.

You wished to know how the orchard was getting along. The pears and plum and apple and cherry trees was never a-going to blow so full.

We cannot see any other way than to plow the orchard if we plant anything. I think we can back furrow a strip between the rows and not hurt the trees any. Elton is sowing a little piece of oats the backside of it, and the rest of it we are a-going to plant to corn and beans. We are not a-going to plant many potatoes, but more beans.

Yours as ever,

Price Claflin

NOTES

1. Winter wheat is sown in fall. It sprouts before the ground freezes, then lies dormant all winter. Spring wheat is sown in spring. Winter wheat has more gluten and therefore is better for bread than the softer spring wheat. Spring wheat is better for cakes.

2. Grafting wax is used to hold and seal the new branch to the stock. Most often grafting in fruit trees is done so branches from a tree that produces the best fruit can be grown on rootstock that is more tolerant of cold winters, or is a dwarf variety with higher yield and safer harvesting.

3. Beverly Woodruff was a Summit farmer who served in Wisconsin's First Cavalry Regiment. His father, seventy-two-year-old Allen, was a deacon of the First Congregational Church of Oconomowoc ("Roster of Wisconsin Volunteers"; 1860 census). Read more about the Woodruff family in Appendix B. Read more about the First Wisconsin Cavalry in Appendix D.

∾

[Letter from Gilbert without date or salutation, probably May 2, 1863]

I picked up the lines which I send in the tent. They are sadly soiled, but the sentiment is there.

If the last money that I sent goes through all right I will send some more.

Whilst I am writing a gray squirrel is running up and down my back having fine times. He belongs to the boy that sleeps next to me. The squirrel is a great favorite with the boys and is truly a great pet.

I got a paper from William day before yesterday.

[This next is written upside down over some of the lines]

A three cent silver coin fell out of the letter when I opened it. I did not find in the letter what was to be done with it.[1]

I hope you will not stint yourself as to things you need to make yourself comfortable. Mother ought to be satisfied to let you pay the debt. You will let her have enough to make her comfortable and disperse of the rest as you think best.

I was glad to hear that James was better.

I want you to give my love to Mr. and Mrs. Goodell and Uncle John's folks and all the friends.

I hope you will not worry about my health if I do not specify exactly how I do. I never enjoyed better sights in my life than I have in Kentucky, and I have not been excused a moment from duty.

NOTE

1. The United States issued three-cent silver coins from 1860 through 1873. They were decorated with images of a star and shield (Varhola, *Everyday Life during the Civil War*, 41).

∾

May 4, 1963

My Dear Gilbert,

Your letter was read last night.

The news of the attack on Cape Girardeau had come before, but I did not suppose that any of your regiment was called out. I sometimes feel so full of joy when I think that you have only a little over three months longer to stay that I think I can wait without a complaint, and then the awful feeling creeps over me that three months is long enough to die by the sword or disease, and then it is, Gilbert, that I feel I have not given up all.

[I] believe many flatter themselves with vain hopes, and when the hour of trial comes, they have no anchor. I believe I have received Divine Strength in days past and I will trust in Him for what is in store for me to come.

Asa has written to Mother to the effect that he can have 15 days furlough, and he may come home.

J.P. has been and I suppose still is quite sick with diarrhea. Margaret packed a box last night for him, and I suppose started it this morning. I put in some dried fruit and a bottle of asparagus. We have had very little asparagus yet. Elton manured the beds this spring, which I suppose prevented the frost coming out.

We have been having a regular snow storm today and the ground is white with snow. The fruit trees are all green and some of the blossoms show the white and red. I am a little fearful for the result, but you know I never *worry* about such things.

Last Saturday I weeded and hoed out your bed of Wilson's Albany and made a fence round it of those sticks X [Esther put an "X" in her letter at this point. It is not clear if this is meant as a picture of the fencing style or to cross out an error.] that lay across it, and I guess I turned my left hand doing it, for it pained me Sunday and Monday, and today it is considerably swollen.[1] I feel a little rheumatic in both hands and arms, but I think it will pass off with the storm.

We have been having stormy weather these three days; and we needed it. We drew the cistern dry Saturday, and the boys swept out a great deal of mud.

Last Sunday was expected to witness the union of two churches [Summit and Oconomowoc Congregational churches], but it was a stormy day and the boys said there was no one from Summit but Mr. Danforth, so it was deferred. At the Church meeting it was recommended that two new

Deacons be appointed which will probably be done at the next meeting. Grandpa Williams has come back and is a regular church attendant.

I find on looking that I have received 48 dollars since the first of March, and it seems a large sum. And I have endeavored to be economical, but almost everything costs double. We have 12 dollars now in bills. I let Mr. Montague have 2 and think we had better pay Uncle John some. I suppose it will cost several dollars to get the sheep sheared. We have not bought any clothing yet. When I went to Nashotah they had not any coats. He wears yours yet. I don't know what to do about getting one here.

That 3 cents was a freak of Price's. He put it in while taking it to the office after it was sealed.

The boys tell me the news. Last night was that Fredericksburg was taken and the South had surrendered.[2] It seems as though Vicksburg was being girdled by Union troops.

I shall send you the Tribune weekly now William has it stop here, and he told me to send it. We hear cannons today and the boys are crazy to go, so this is finished in a hurry.

Yours Affectionately,

Esther Claflin

[Elton's letter is written on the same page]

Dear Father,

We have got in the lower part of the orchard in to oats and we are going to plant the rest to corn and beans. We have been drawing rails and are going to put a fence through the back lot so that we can pasture part of it.[3]

We have got 4 lambs. They are all smart. Three of them are ewes.

Colonel Lewis [is] at home on furlough. He has sent home some contra-bands: Charley Stansbury, and one of the Levit boys, and another boy from Summit. The Levit boy shot his arm. Charley Stansbury brought a hound home for Lewis' boys. He came before Lewis.[4]

From your Son,

Elton Claflin

NOTES

1. James Wilson was a Scottish gardener and nurseryman in Albany, New York. About the middle of the nineteenth century, he sowed seed of Hovey, Black Prince, and Ross Phoenix strawberries and from the resulting seedlings two years later selected the

variety that now bears his name. This alone changed the strawberry from a fruit grown by a few for the few into a fruit grown by hundreds of thousands from Florida to Maine and west to California and Washington (George M. Darrow, "Notable Early Strawberry Breeders of America," chapter 12 in *The Strawberry: History, Breeding, and Physiology* [New York: Holt, Rinehart and Winston, 1966], 11.)

2. The Second Battle of Fredericksburg took place on May 3, 1863, near the town of Fredericksburg, Virginia. It was part of the larger Battle of Chancellorsville, April 30–May 6, 1863. The Second Battle of Fredericksburg was, indeed, a Union victory; but the overall Battle of Chancellorsville was a Confederate victory.

3. *Drawing rails* meant hauling or pulling fence rails, usually with a team of horses.

4. James M. Lewis of Oconomowoc was colonel of Wisconsin's Twenty-Eighth Infantry Regiment, stationed at Helena, Arkansas. Of the 109 boys in Lewis's Company C, 80 were from Summit and Oconomowoc. Between mid-February and mid-April 1863, 4 of those boys from Oconomowoc and 2 from Summit died of disease. Three boys from Company C were discharged April 16 on disability: Charles H. Stansbury of Oconomowoc, Theodore F. Leavitt of Summit (who was wounded March 24 on picket, or advance guard, duty), and David L. Webster of Summit ("Roster of Wisconsin Volunteers," 372–73). More on the Twenty-Eighth Wisconsin Infantry Regiment is in Appendix D. More on Colonel James Lewis and the boys is in Appendix B.

Columbus
May 5, 1863

Dear Esther,

As I have plenty of time today having nothing to do, I improve a leisure hour or two in letting you know of my present prospects, as I now have no future plans of a worldly nature here, and await orders day by day.

Since we have been here we have had a pleasant time with but little to do in the fatigue line, and no guard duty since the first night we came here.

I am well and enjoy myself better than I ever thought I could under like circumstances; and did I not see the path of duty plain before me, I fear that I should, like many around me, murmur and complain at what we are called to pass through. I mean the petty tyranny of our captain. He has had considerable trouble with other officers and has been tried by court marshal once but got clear, and he is in hot water all the time; as everybody that has anything to do with him hates him; and he can vent his spite on no one but soldiers.

The other day he ordered the sentinels that guard the fort not to sit on the guns. The sentinel was sitting on a 128-pounder, and he told our captain if he bent the gun by sitting on it, he would take it down town and get it straightened. The 25th boys guard the fort, and some of them would as lief as not try a bayonet on him if he did not walk the mark exactly. He has no right to interfere with them when on duty, and some of them are smart enough to know it.

He ordered the corporal of the guard under arrest the other day. The colonel of the 25th [Milton Montgomery] was immediately informed. The colonel sent word back to the corporal to attend to his business, and not mind what he said. All these things irritate our captain, and crush his aspiration. I once had a talk with him about the feeling that existed between him and the company. He told me that when he called them names he did not mean anything bad, and carried the idea that it was all the impulse of the moment, and was caused by the men's not doing as well as they might, which I think is to a great extent true. He had always granted every favor that I have asked of him, and I have never given him occasion to use me otherwise than respectfully; but I have been reproved by him when drilling along with the rest because we did not execute the movements to a complete success at once. He thinks that we ought at one explanation, and that in broken English, to understand and comprehend the whole. But it is about played out as the time is drawing to a close; and the 2nd lieutenant [Michael A. Leahy] has charge of the company now; and the 1st sergeant [August Beecher] drills us; and we have fine times when out, the boys doing as he wishes them, and he doing that which is for the good of the boys.

I guess you will think that my mind runs in a different channel than what it has before, and perhaps may think that I have got the blues; but I have not, and this morning I am as near the top shelf as I have been since I have been in the army to use a common expression.

Last Sunday, in company with Brother Higgins, I went to the colored meeting. It was a very interesting occasion in some respects, and in others mournful. It was a funeral occasion. About 2 weeks since some slaves, in making their escape from their master who lives on Island Number 5, which is right in sight of this place, were fired at by him.[1] The ball struck a young man in the shoulder and caused his death. Two expeditions have been on to arrest the man but did not find him. After the discourse, a Mrs. Haverland of Michigan, a sanctuary agent spoke a few words. In the evening I attended their meeting again. Mrs. Haverland addressed the meeting again. The house was crowded with Negroes and soldiers, and it was one of the most interesting ones that I have attended since I have been in Kentucky.

I have just got your letter and was very glad to hear of your prosperity.

You wish to know whether there are any rebel prisoners here; I do not know how many, but think somewhere between 1 & 2 hundred. When the prison gets full, they send them off. Today they sent off about 40 up the river.

Last week our cavalry brought in 10 guerrillas and their horses. They passed right by where we are camped. They were a rough looking set. They were captured near the Tennessee line.[2]

You wish to know about the intelligence of the prisoners. I have conversed with a number of them, but it [is] evident to the beholder that as a whole they are lacking in intelligence and many of them are very ignorant. There are some exceptions. The last time I was on guard, one of them showed me the likeness of a young lady. I should judge she was about 18. It was taken, I should judge, and presented to him as he was leaving for the strife of war. I have never looked upon a picture that showed such a calm resignation, and yet such a determined spirit to bear the separation; and filled him with her blessing. He was a Tennessee.

You wish to know about my boots and stockings. All my boots are as sound yet. My stockings are good yet and will last me all summer good. They are not worn out but little, and I have kept them darned; and first rate. My boots do not wear them bad.

[Upside down at top of letter]

You have doubtless have got the company record that I sent you. I got the papers that you sent. We get the news now quite regular, and I get considerable to read.

You wished to know about the grafting wax. It is 3 parts rosin, 1 tallow, 1 beeswax. You know how to mix it.

Gilbert

NOTES

1. The first book of navigation charts covering the Lower Mississippi was published in 1801 by a man with the improbable name of Zadok Cramer. Cramer's charts were crude, but his text was useful and he performed a unique service when he ignored the names of most of the islands in the river and gave them numbers. Until that time, some of the islands had had several names, and it was always difficult for a flatboatman to obtain and remember useful information about reaches of the river that contained no distinguishing characteristics except an island or two. The island numbers made it easier to pinpoint and identify the difficult passages on the river. Cramer's book, *The Navigator*, proved to be so useful and so popular that twelve editions were published, followed by those of many imitators who either copied him brazenly or leaned heavily on his book for information. Island Number 5 was also known as Wolf Island. Cramer

described it as a very large island with about 15,000 acres of fine land and an open prairie in the middle where cattle were pastured (Bragg, *Historic Names and Places on the Lower Mississippi River*, 10, 18).

2. The report of General Asboth on this incident, known as "The Affair at Obion Plank Road Crossing, Tennessee," is found in Appendix D.

~

Gilbert's company record. It is interesting to note that thirty-two members of Gilbert's company, those marked with an asterisk, deserted.

Columbus
May 6, 1863

Dear Son,

I was glad to hear from you and learn that you and Elton were prospering in the work line. You and he know before this what conclusion I have come to respecting the orchard, as in my last I said you could do as you thought best. I guess you had better try and save the plums if there is a good prospect of a crop.

I am getting along with soldier life and soldier fare first rate; can lay my rubber [rubber blanket issued to each soldier] on the ground and sleep as well as I could in a feather bed and I guess a good deal better now that I have been used to a hard bed so long.

It is raining this morning, and we shall have another day of rest from fatigue work. We are having an easy time of it; we work one hour and are having 3 reliefs. It will take 3 or 4 weeks to do the job unless we have more men detailed from some other company; but perhaps a change will take place, and we shall move.

It is hard telling what a day will bring—It does not take long to give orders and they must be obeyed. I think that we have a good prospect of doing the work. I hope you and Elton will strive to be good boys and obey your mother.

I shall be glad to hear from you.

Your Father,

G. Claflin

[On the other side]

May 6:

It is quite cool this morning; and I am writing, and all the rest of the boys, 10 in number, are sleeping. The morning gun at Cairo has just fired and soon ours will which will awaken them for roll call.

You wished to know about lice. I found 2 on me about a month ago, but have seen none since. I change my clothes regularly and wash them in strong soapsuds; wash myself often; and carry camphor gum in my undershirt pocket. Some of the boys have had them nearly all the time; and they are the pest of this camp, as they are too lazy to keep themselves clean. My comb is good yet, I have not broken out a tooth. I do not believe there is any need of having lice in camp if men would not live like hogs; but the truth is many men get so lazy and indolent after they have been in the service some time that all they want to do is eat and lay round.

I am glad that James is getting better.

You say that J.P. is under the surgeon's care. I suppose that is the same disease you spoke of in your last letter.

I think that the best thing that anyone can do to keep his health in this climate is to keep clean, drink but little water, and be careful what you eat. I daily see the seeds of disease from men drinking strong drink to keep them well, and they are sure to be sick every time they go down town or aleing.

I must close.

Yours Truly,

Gilbert

Columbus
May 10, 1863

Dear Esther,

It is quite an exciting time here; notwithstanding it is the day of Holy rest. The 34th (with the exception of our company) and the 25th have got marching orders for Memphis. But as orders are given and countermanded so often, it is not fully certain that they will go. But the 25th have got packed up, and some of the tents have been taken down.

We were not permitted to leave camp to go to meeting; but I went to the post hospital to carry some things to one of our boys that is sick, and went past the colored church. I stopped awhile, and listened to the discourse. On my way back it was crowded to overflowing and a good many outside.

It is very warm, and but for the wind that is blowing it would be very uncomfortable.

I am in the tent. We have the large Sibley tent and have 2 doors in it right opposite each other, and a fine draft of air passes through as I write.[1] I will give you the plan as it is fixed off for our bunks. I sleep alone and have got the best bunk in the lot. I let the others fix to suit themselves and took what was left of the room. There is 11 in the tent. I have got nearly as much room as any 2 that sleep together, and I had much rather sleep alone than have company, and can keep my things by themselves, and keep cleaner than I otherwise could. I have got a fine plan to put my things on outside of the bunk and can sit in my bunk and look all over the town and see the steamer pass up and down the river. The boys say it is the best as I have got it rigged.

I suppose I must inform you how I get along. I am well and everything moves along in a soldier like manner. The time passes rapidly along; and did I not keep a note of daily occurrence, I should hardly keep the day of the week. I like this place much better than I did the place we left, and I think it is more healthy, and as a general thing shall have a better chance to go to meeting as I do not have to get a pass here.

The fine steamer Memphis is now passing up the river. I wish the boys & you all could see it—and then I could see you all.

I was glad to hear that you could go to meeting again. I hope that you all will attend as often as you can. I intend to improve every privilege granted to me, and if permitted to return in a few months, I trust I shall be prepared to better appreciate the privileges that I may be permitted to enjoy than I ever did before.

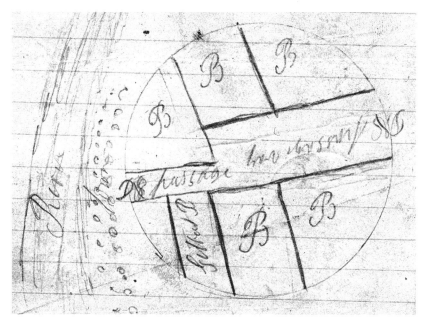

Gilbert's sketch of his tent layout. His bunk is marked "Gilbert B"; the other bunks, for two men each, are marked "B." He has labeled the palisade of Fort Halleck and the Mississippi River just outside the tent.

May 11:

We have to do guard duty now as the 25th are under marching orders. Six companies of the 34th went on board a steamer [the *Sultana* bound for Memphis, Tennessee] last night, but they have not gone yet, and may not go.

I am on guard today. It is the best place to do guard duty that I have found. When off from guard, we go and sleep in our bunks. The corporal comes and wakes us when it is time to go on. The farthest guard stands about 80 rods from the tents.

The war news is creating great excitement here in camp and if true I think the rebellion is pretty well played out. If Richmond is taken, and the number of prisoners reported taken are actually taken, and the report that Grant has cut the RR and between Jackson & Vicksburg be true; it is news that will cheer many hearts.[2]

The 21st Illinois [probably the Twenty-First *Missouri* Infantry Regiment] has just marched by and are going to Memphis along with the 34th. The 25th are going to Clinton as report says now. I expect that the letter which is due me in a day or 2 will go to Memphis unless the captain tends to it at once as the regiment postmaster goes there with the regiment.[3]

I hope this will find you all well.

Yours Truly,

Gilbert

[Gilbert wrote a letter to Price on the same page as his May 11 letter to Esther]

Dear Son,

I sent a paper home a short time since, and you doubtless found a small piece of wound wire. That was part of the wire that was laid in the ground for the purpose of blowing up the magazines here and destroying the fortifications. There is a lot of it in the magazine that has been taken, out of the ground by our men that will reach as much as 2 miles. I got that off from a piece that stuck out of the ground a half a mile from the magazine. The powder and torpedoes were to be fired by a galvanic battery and had the thing worked as the Rebels calculated, it would have destroyed the whole works and all the men in them.

You remember the thorns that John brought home? I have got one from the honey locust that is 14¾ inches long with 2 spurs on it. The united length of the whole is 3 feet and 11 inches. I wish I could bring it home.

Yesterday one of the boys belonging to our regiment Company F was drowned when out bathing. The cramp took him, and his body has not been found.[4]

I think that you and Elton are doing lots of work. You must not get so much work in hand that you will have to work too hard.

Your Father,

Gilbert Claflin

NOTES

    1. The tents commonly furnished for the rank and file were the "A" and the Sibley patterns. The "Sibley" was a simple cone, suggested by the Indian "teepee," with an opening at the apex for ventilation and the exit of the smoke of the fire, for which provision was made in the center of the tent by the use of a tall iron tripod as a foundation for the pole. It comfortably accommodated fifteen or sixteen men lying feet toward the pole, and radiating thence like the spokes of a wheel. (Johnson, *Campfire and Battlefield*, 496)

    2. Richmond was not taken until April 1865. Grant did not cut the railroad lines at Jackson until May 14, 1863. Vicksburg finally fell in July after six weeks of a siege that began May 22, 1863. Once again, rumors abounded.

    3. There is a letter from Asboth, the commanding general at Columbus, dated May 11, 1863. In that letter he describes sending the Twenty-First Missouri Regiment and six companies of Gilbert's regiment, the Thirty-Fourth Wisconsin, to Memphis. He also details where the remaining four companies of the Thirty-Fourth are stationed (Scott, *War of the Rebellion*, vol. 23, pt. 2, 323–24). The full communication is in Appendix D.

    4. Sebastian Rothwinkler from Preble, Wisconsin, drowned May 10, 1863.

May 17, 1863

Dear Son,

I was glad to get a letter from you and to learn of your prosperity.

I wish you could sit by my side and see the 5 large government transports and the telegraph boat that have just come down the river and are now anchored on the Missouri side. The telegraph boat is now crossing the river to the general headquarters. The names of the transports are 1st Autercrat, 2nd is Diana, 3rd BJ Adams, 4th Baltic, 5th John Rains. There are 2 other steamers at the wharf: the Memphis & Rob Roy. The large hospital boat, the name is Woodworth, has just come down and is now anchored with the rest. There are 3 rows of windows one above the other on the sides and around the ends and will probably accommodate 800 or 1000 sick men. They will stay overnight here and are probably bound for Vicksburg or that vicinity.

I think that you and Price are doing big things in the farming line; but be careful not to over work and get sick. I hope you will try to be a good boy in every sense of the word, and endeavor to make those around you the better by what you may say or do.

I must close.

From Your Father,

G. Claflin

[Gilbert's letter to Price was written on the same page as his May 17 letter to Elton]

Dear Son,

I think that you are having good luck with lambs this spring. I hope that you will have good luck with chickens.

I think that fox of yours and Elton's will have to be watched a little or he will be apt to help himself to chicken.

The 3 cent you put in the letter dropped on the ground when I pulled out the letter. I have got it all safe.

Gilbert

Columbus
May 17, 1863

Dear Esther,

Your letter came through all right, but not in time to have answered it so that you would have got it the same week; and as it did not necessarily need an immediate answer, I deferred all answers 'til my next letter.

It has been a beautiful day, and the sun is now gradually sinking to the west. It is at the shade of evening that my thoughts center upon home, and could I now and then look in upon and converse a while with my dear family it would be truly gratifying. But I do not feel to murmur or complain so long as duty calls and my health is precious in God's sight.

The 25th Wisconsin is camped about 30 rods from us; and the chaplain [Thomas C. Golden] preached on the drill grounds this forenoon. I attended. It was a good discourse. The subject aimed at was to prove that God rules in the earth and doeth His pleasure among the children of men and that man's paltry arm is powerless in thwarting the great designs and purposes of God. He said that he did not believe that as a nation we should fall because as a nation we recognized God as a supreme ruler and governor; and when the great purposes of God in humbling us had been accomplished we should be better prepared as a nation to occupy that true position before God and the world that we ought to occupy.

I went to the Negro meeting this afternoon or evening as they call it.[1] It commenced at 5 o'clock. I did not get there in time to hear the text. The house was crowded and a good large crowd outside. You have read of Negro camp meetings and so had I, but I have come to the conclusion that I had but a vague idea of the extent of the enthusiasm that must be manifest judging by the 100 or 150 here and the hundreds that collect on camp meeting occasions.

I just heard the orderly sergeant call, "Claflin, Claflin." I looked out and he showed me a letter which I soon had in my hand.

I was glad to hear that you were prospering, and that everything is moving along in the farming line so well.

I should think that the boys might go to school this summer and do what work there is to do; but I do not wish to urge the matter, and will leave them to decide the matter for themselves.

I was surprised that you had not got that company record that I send the 2nd of May. It cost 75 cents and I would not have taken 5 times that amount for it if it had got home all safe. Perhaps it is in the post office in Oconomowoc. It could not have been put in our box on account of its length. I wish if you do not get it before the receipt of this you would have the boys enquire at the post office.

I do not think the rain storm would hurt the fruit at all. I saw peaches today on the trees that were 1¼ inches in diameter; the trees are loaded with them.

This is a great fruit country, and were it not for the blighting curse of slavery this would be a beautiful place to live in. But its effects on the country will be felt whilst the present inhabitants are on the stage of life even if every slave should become at once free.

You write about using for diarrhea the sweet gum remedy.[2] The sweet gum grows very plenty here, and I have heard of its use in cases of diarrhea; but I have never had occasion to use any remedies. Nearly every one of the boys have been troubled, some have been very sick. I have changed my whole manner as it respects eating. Instead of taking 5 minutes to eat I now take 25 or more and think it pays in the health line.

I was pleased to hear that James was improving and that J.P. was better. I was also pleased to hear that Asa was well. I had thought of him quite often of late. I hope he will come home on furlough.

May 18:

It is a fine morning; and as I looked across the river I saw that during the night another of those large transports which I spoke about in Elton's letter has come down and 6 of them are now at anchor instead of 5.

It is a singular fact that more than double the steamers arrive here about sunset or sunrise than any other time of day.

I have got a line to hang my clothes on when I wash. It is fixed up in the angle of the stockade side of the fort, as nearly ½ of the fortifications is stockade with loopholes for sharp shooters. I have kept my clothes mended up and the pants that I took with me & wore have worn first rate, and will last I think nearly or quite my time out. But I have got a new pair.

I must close as I must fall in to drill with musket.

Yours Truly,

Gilbert

NOTES

1. Camp meetings were part of the Great Revival in Kentucky, organized by Presbyterian ministers who modeled them after the extended outdoor "communion seasons" used by the Presbyterian Church in Scotland. These meetings frequently produced emotional, demonstrative displays of religious conviction.

2. Sweet gum (*Liquidambar styraciflua*) is a tree in the witch-hazel family. Its inner bark and resin have antiseptic, anti-inflammatory, antimicrobial, and expectorant properties. The resin was traditionally chewed for sore throats, coughs, colds, diarrhea, dysentery, and ringworm. In addition, it was used externally for sores, skin ailments, wounds, and piles. The mildly astringent inner bark was used as a folk remedy, and boiled in milk or water for diarrhea.

May 20, 1863

My Dear Husband,

I seat myself to write a good deal out of tune; you know that is nothing very strange. Little things are happening every day, but some days are fuller of them than others. The responsibility comes entirely on me, and I am unable the most of the time to make things any better.

Yesterday I went to the village to do some trading, and when I presented the five-dollar bill that Mr. Hinkley let me have, Mr. Richard said it was not good. Small business for Hinkley wasn't it?

This morning when I got up, I found a hole in the ground in the place of your southern corn, which had been transplanted. The fox had got out of his box, and his chain was long enough to let him do the mischief. I felt worse to lose that than I did the five-dollar bill.

Elton hunted until 9 o'clock for the cow, and when I milked her she gave about a pint. I was just ready to cry thinking somebody milked her every day or two, but Elton told me she leaked badly while he was driving her; and Ti—g told him she always did.

I might enumerate other things, but I forbear for your sake and mine too. It is a womanly weakness I suppose; but when things are happening I think, "If Gilbert was only here I would not care." After all, Gilbert, we get along on the whole better than I ever thought we could without you.

Price has commenced going to school today, and Elton . . . has gone hunting. I expect he must want to work very steady while Price is at school. I wish he would go, but he says he can't. It is a beautiful day: the most like summer of any day we have had; and while I am writing in the back room the sweet fragrance of the fruit blossoms are wafted in through the open windows reminding me of the one that planted and cared for these trees so many years, and hope he will return to reap the *fruit* of his labor. The apple trees are many of them in full blossom, and nearly all will bloom full. The prospect now is of a much greater crop of fruit of all kinds than we have ever had; and grain looks the best it has for many years.

The farmers say some of our peas, parsnips, and beets have come up; but the pigs have been in and mutilated the beds some.

Don't you think if the fruit grows we had better let Coe have all his father's folks will take for lumber?[1]

And you did not say whether you would give Mr. Kendall the job of making the sash.

I hope we shall be able to market a few currants at home, otherwise I suppose we shan't sell any.

I forgot to acknowledge the receipt of your company record, and the wound wire, and two dollars.

I think I should go to prayer meeting tonight.

And I expect a letter. I got one last night from William and last Thursday night from you.

And you have found out long before this that the news which you thought so cheering was false, and I fear still more for the country when the next conscript takes place. But there may be no more reason to fear than at the first; but you know throughout the country men have been organizing to resist. My faith, you know, is always small; but I still hope and faintly believe that our government is strong enough to eventually crush this wicked rebellion.

Our neighbors and friends, so far as I know, are well. James was up last Friday. He is improving, but is not free from diarrhea or cough. He probably never can be a sound man.

Mother has let Arabelle go to her mother. She got so she could not do anything with her.

Emily has trouble heaped upon trouble. Father told her to go out of there, and she rented the place over Parsons old grocery. But how she will ever pay rent and support two children these times is a mystery I can't solve.

I keep Florence. I get along with her without trouble. She is no baby at all. I have not had occasion to whip but once and she has been here three weeks.

Homer Hurd died last week.

May 21:

I got a letter last night as I expected; and I called at Mr. Montague's, and he read me a first rate letter from you.

I stayed all night with Mother. She has had a letter from Asa since the battle. He was in that awful battle at Fredericksburg;[2] had his gun shot from his hands, but got off without any scratches save what the bushes scratched him.

Elton brought in a duck and partridge last night.

When I came hope this morning our oxen were in Mr. E's clover, and Nelly was on our wheat; tore clear through the fence.

Now those Negro meetings must be novel and interesting to you.

Yours in love,

Esther Claflin

[Page 2 has "we are all very well" written at the top]

NOTES

1. What we know of Mr. Coe is an advertisement in the *Oconomowoc Free Press* in June 1862, which says that E. D. Coe has opened a new lumber yard in Oconomowoc. The text of the advertisement is in Appendix B.

2. Esther's brother Asa was in the Battle of Chancellorsville, April 30–May 6, 1863, at Fredericksburg, Virginia. The battle was a Confederate victory, though the Union forces greatly outnumbered them. It was at this battle that Stonewall Jackson was mortally wounded, accidentally, by his own men.

Columbus
May 25, 1863

Dear Esther,

Your kind letter was received this morning, and I was glad to hear that you all were very well.

I am still in moving order, and have not as yet had a touch of diarrhea; but nearly all of the boys have, and some of them are very bad. But it is no wonder to me that they are so. They have been in the habit of taking a large supply of pork, and then frying their bread in grease; and when we had beef soup they would take a cup or two of that (by beef soup I mean the water and grease that is in the kettle when the beef is taken out). I use a little meat every day but I have not eaten a spoonful of grease, I do not believe, since I have been in Kentucky—only in meat.

I drink but little water to what I used to in Wisconsin. I carry the bark of the sassafras tree, or the bark of the roots, in my pocket; and chew a small piece after every meal, which serves a double purpose, quenching thirst and thinning my blood as coffee has a direct tendency to thicken it. And I use it from force of circumstances, as the water is very poor, being drawn in barrels and soon becomes warm.

We have enough to eat; or at least I get enough. But a good many complain; not about the quantity, but the quality; and are continually sighing for home fare, which does not help them much so far as satisfying the craving desire within them. But some men are never satisfied under any circumstances.

I got a paper the other day. The wrapper was from William, but some of the contents was from you. I suppose it was rather dry; but I put some vinegar in them, and they went quite good.

I hope you will return that 5-dollar bill to Mr. Hinkley at once if you have not done it. First be sure that it is not good, and then let one of the boys take it to him. If he refuses to take it back, let it pass without further notice as it will be of no use to multiply words or feel bad about the loss.

You need not feel bad about the corn, as I do not think it would do very well in Wisconsin. I think the boys' fox will be rather a troublesome fellow, and will need considerable training before he can be trusted in every place. I should think the dogs would trouble him that are passing.

I went to the Negro meeting twice yesterday. In the forenoon a Negro preached from the words found in 3rd chapter of John, 14th & 15th verses: "And as Moses lifted up the serpent in the wilderness &so."[1] I have heard many more fluent discourses; but there was a simpleness of expression, an aptness in illustration and the applying of scriptural truth that was impressive and interesting.

In the afternoon the chaplain [Anthony Wilford] of the 3rd Minnesota preached. I did not get there in time to hear the text, but when I got there he was describing Moses' passage through the Red Sea leading the children of Israel through safely; whilst the Egyptians were destroyed. It was a good discourse, and calculated to awaken strong feelings in the hearts of his colored listeners.

They are having a revival; and after the discourse, those seeking religion were invited to come forward. 8 or 10 came forward whilst they were singing. A prayer was offered, then they sung for 10 or 15 minutes, then another prayer was offered, and so on. Meantime the groans and cries of the mourners and the convulsive efforts of the body were terrible, requiring in some instances 2 or 3 to hold them. Added to this the shouts and clapping of hands of those around them and you can have a little idea of [the] scene that was before me. After a while one of them began to shout for joy; and the excess of joy was more impulsive than her sorrow had been as apparent to human view. And then such a shaking of hands, and falling upon each other's necks, and weeping for joy that another soul had felt the power of Jesus hardening love. Notwithstanding all, but few I believe can look upon such a scene and have a heart to ridicule or disturb them. I have conversed with a good many of them about their former condition and all, without a single exception, prefer freedom to slavery.

Between 4 & 5 hundred have enlisted here.

Gilbert Claflin

1. John 3:14–15: "And as Moses lifted up the serpent in the wilderness, even so must the Son of man be lifted up that whosoever believeth in him should not perish, but have eternal life."

☙

May 26, 1863

Dear Esther,

Perhaps you would like to know what I have been doing this morning.

Well in the first place I must tell you that I have charge of the hospital, and I have been waiting upon the sick (the boys, with 2 exceptions, are improving fast). There are 5 now under the doctor's treatment.

I do not do any duty, but how long I shall stay in the business will depend on circumstance. The boys want me to stay. I have not as yet had to be up any nights.

I hope that you will not worry about the affairs at home too much. I know that a greater responsibility rests upon you on account of my absence; but endeavor to rise above those petty annoyances. Endeavor to walk in the path of duty and leave the result with God. He will sustain.

Last night just before sundown quite a severe shock of an earthquake was felt here giving one something of an idea of the terrible effects when they are hard, destroying all before it.[1]

So far as the window sash is concerned, if Mr. Kendall has a mind to make them I am willing on the terms you wrote me.

If Mr. Coe wants any fruit and pay lumber for it let him have it.

I had felt quite anxious to hear from Asa. I saw a list of the killed and wounded but did not see his name. I am glad that he escaped alive.

Yours Truly,

Gilbert

Last Saturday quite an affair took place here. A slaveholder from Tennessee came here and found a family that he used to call his slaves. The woman was who. He came up to her whitewashing the new church, which they have been building. The master asked what the building was for. She told him, and added it was for a schoolhouse, which it is to be used for. He wished to know how they got the means. She told him that the Union soldiers helped build it. (I have got a small sum there invested.) He then tried to get them to go back, offering them all 10 dollars apiece in gold or silver, but it was no go. He then tried to scare them by telling them that the south would overrun the country and take them all and make slaves of them again, but that did not do. He then threatened the Negro. This had him arrested and taken to the Provost-Marshal.[2] It so happened that a white man was in Columbus that knew him in Tennessee. The testimony of the 2 convicted him; and Mr. Rebel is now in prison, and his horses and wagon will help pay his board.

There has between 4 & 5 hundred Negroes enlisted here.

NOTES

1. The New Madrid Seismic Zone lies in the central Mississippi Valley and includes much of northeastern Arkansas, southeastern Missouri, western Tennessee, western Kentucky, and southern Illinois. Historically, the area has been the site of some of the largest earthquakes in North America.

The New Madrid Seismic Zone is so named because the town of New Madrid, Missouri—which is approximately twenty-six miles from Columbus, Kentucky—was the closest settlement to the epicenters of a series of huge earthquakes in a three-month period in 1811 and 1812. During that period, there were four earthquakes, with magnitude estimates greater than 7.0. Some of these earthquakes were felt throughout much of the United States and as far away as Quebec ("The Great New Madrid Earthquake," *The Virtual Times*, http://www.hsv.com/genlintr/newmadrd/, accessed May 25, 2013).

2. The army staff position of provost marshal was created in 1861 by General McClellan, and the person assigned that job was responsible for a wide variety of duties. These duties included the suppression of marauding and depredations on private property, the preservation of good order, the prevention of straggling, the suppression of gambling houses or other establishments prejudicial to good order and discipline, and the supervision of hotels, saloons, and places of resort and amusement generally. Additional duties included taking custody of deserters from the opposing forces and of prisoners of war, issuing passes to citizens, hearing citizens' complaints, and making searches, seizures, and arrests. Thus the provost marshal had to have the temperament of both a chief of police and a magistrate (Thompson, "The Provost-Marshal and the Citizen").

∾

May 28, 1863

My Dear Gilbert,

I seat myself hardly knowing what to say, for I have not had a letter this week notwithstanding *I went to the office myself* last night. Don't you think I ought to get one after taking so much pains?

I went to prayer meeting; met Mr. James Woodruff. He was very cordial and made inquiries after you, but somehow the prayer meetings don't seem as they used to. I can't hardly keep my mind on the subject of the meeting. It is continually wandering away to you in spite of myself. Perhaps if I went every week it would not be so. Old Deacon and Mrs. Woodruff always treat me very cordially and always inquire after you.[1]

The people about here are a good deal excited and frightened just now. The smallpox has been coming this way for three weeks, and yesterday there was a man buried in Ixonia who died of the smallpox. William Skinner died with it some time ago.[2] I think there is no doubt but it will be in our place. Price has been twice to Dr. Tucker but could not get vaccinated. The Dr. told him to come today noon and he would do it. Price goes to school now.

Farin Osborne has been to war and come home with a broken constitution.[3] He is out here now on a visit. Mrs. Eastman tells me he has spinal complaint. Mrs. E. is able to be up this spring and visits some.

I hear that Alsy Rendall and Albert Harshaw are dead.

Old Mrs. Wood, JK's mother was buried Monday.[4]

Gilbert, I wish I could write more cheerful letters, but it seems as if there was nothing cheerful to write about, if I state facts; for we are being cursed with war and pestilence, and if we live long enough we shall see famine; indeed the South already feels that terrible wolf.

O that God would bring this war to a righteous termination. But it seems His time is not yet, but if His people are humble and faithful why may not this nation be saved. But no human mind can tell what is yet in store for us.

I hear very little news. The Tribune has not come this week. I hear of Vicksburg being taken and then it is not, and so on to the end of the chapter.[5] And I don't read enough to know whether the war prospects are more favorable.

The forest has now got on its best dress and everything that grows looks thriving. The oaks are full of blossoms.

The fruit is not hardly forward enough to tell whether much will hang on. I should not think there would be a very heavy crop of pears, nor many cherries excepting on the large tree by the new house.

While I am writing, as I look up occasionally and my eyes rest on the snowball, which is in full blossom and it looks larger and taller than ever, (the gnats bite so I can't hardly write).[6] We have threatening weather all the week, but not much rain. I expect you have any quantity of insects to sing you to sleep, or I might say to keep you awake. I wonder how you live if mosquitoes disturb you as they used to.

It is now seven and the cars are just coming in, and I expect I have got a letter on board.[7]

May 29:

It did come last night. I was sure it would. And it brought a light with it similar to the light which that face brings in the house.

I was glad you were in the hospital caring for the sick. Seems more in keeping with the character of a Christian than learning to fight; but perhaps it may not be as good for your health.

Uncle John says when he used to run the river, the men carried the bark of the sweet gum tree in their pockets, and if they had an attack [of diarrhea], chew it and they would be well the next day.

Tell Cousin Celia, we feel the effects of the war very sensibly.

You remember the Methodist Minister Martin? He lives in Madison and is the Martin that makes out soldiers records.[8]

The 2 dollars came safe. Don't send yourself short. It seems wicked to use up your earnings, but don't see how we can help it.

William has sent me "Vitche's Lectures on Consumption."

We had a heavy shower last night.

My dear Gilbert, I feel a trembling which is inexpressible when I think your time is so near expired and still you are exposed to the thousand accidents of war. But may our Father in heaven preserve you to us. I know I am selfish.

Yours as ever in the bonds of conjugal love,

Esther

NOTES

1. Deacon Allen Woodruff was seventy-two years old in 1863. He lived in Oconomowoc with his wife Roxy, two years younger, and the youngest of their six children, Maria. Like many in the area, the Woodruffs were a farming family who moved to Summit from New York State. They came to Summit and settled about two miles west of the Claflins in 1845, the same year that Gilbert and Esther married. Deacon Woodruff was one of the most zealous workers during the construction of the parsonage in 1853; he drove an ox team to Fond du Lac, about fifty miles north, to get lumber for the building.

James Woodruff was forty-four and lived with his wife Elmira and their two children in Lisbon, Wisconsin, about fifteen miles from Summit. They used to be closer neighbors; in 1850, they lived next door to Allen and Roxy Woodruff and their six children (*Oconomowoc Free Press*, November 4, 1858, to August 16, 1862; *Atlas of Waukesha Co.*; 1860 census). More about the Woodruff families is in Appendix B.

2. Reuben William Skinner was born in New York and settled in Oconomowoc. He was thirty-two, a year younger than Esther, when he died of smallpox, leaving a wife and two young children (1860 census). More about William Skinner is in Appendix B.

3. In 1863, Farin E. Osborne was thirty-six years old and lived in the town of Harmony, Wisconsin, about thirty-five miles from Summit. He served in Company E of the

Twenty-Second Wisconsin Infantry, and was discharged December 19, 1862, on disability. In 1850 he lived in Oconomowoc with his parents and four younger siblings ("Roster of Wisconsin Volunteers," 215; 1850, 1860 census). More about the Osborne family is in Appendix B.

4. Mary Wood was seventy-nine years old when she died in 1863. She and her husband Asa Wood, seventy-eight, had been living at the home of their son, fifty-four-year-old Jedediah (J.K.), along with Harriette Wood (fifty-eight), Charles Wood (twenty-two), and Asher Wood (forty-six) (1860 census). More about the Wood families is in Appendix B.

5. Vicksburg, Mississippi—about four hundred miles south of Columbus, Kentucky, where Gilbert was stationed, and about two hundred miles north of New Orleans, Louisiana—was a key stronghold of the Confederacy. When the war began, the Union was quickly stopped from using the southern section of the Mississippi River, a major route to the Atlantic and the rest of the world. If the North gained control of Vicksburg, it would have control of the lower Mississippi and then the rich produce from the northern interior could again reach world markets. In addition, vital southern supply lines would be cut, and the South effectively would be split in two.

It was Grant's responsibility to bypass or to take Vicksburg. Beginning in mid-October 1862, he initiated the Battle of Chickasaw Bluffs, the Yazoo Pass Expedition, Steele's Bayou Expedition, and a direct assault on the city of Vicksburg itself. All failed. Grant finally ordered his engineers to begin siege operations.

The Siege of Vicksburg began on May 23, 1863. Five days later, when Esther wrote her letter, the need continued for still more soldiers to carry out the plans to establish a line of works around the beleaguered city and cut Vicksburg off from supplies and communication with the outside world. On May 26, Union forces began constructing thirteen approaches along their front aimed at different points along the Confederate defense line. The object was to dig up to the Confederate works, then tunnel underneath them, plant charges of black powder, and destroy the fortifications. Union soldiers digging the trenches were protected by constant bombardment of artillery ("Vicksburg Campaign and Siege March–July 1863," National Park Service, http://www.nps.gov/vick/history culture/vickcamp-siege.htm, accessed May 26, 2013; Scott, *War of the Rebellion*, vol. 24, pt. 1, includes reports dealing with Yazoo Pass Expedition and siege of Vicksburg).

6. "Snowball bush" can refer to several different shrubs, most in the genus *Viburnum*. Esther's snowball bush is very likely *Viburnum opulus* 'Roseum,' a well-known heirloom cultivar. This snowball bush is a large, rounded shrub reaching ten to twelve feet, with many three-inch, round clusters of double flowers in mid-May. The flowers are first apple green, but change to pure white and last a long time. All the flowers are sterile, so there is no fruit.

7. The Milwaukee and Western Railroad ran between Milwaukee and Sun Prairie, Wisconsin. There was one round-trip each day carrying passengers and mail. The westbound train left Oconomowoc at 6:30 p.m., the eastbound train at 9:20 a.m. (*Oconomowoc Free Press*, August 9, 1862).

8. Gilbert's company record was made out by "S. W. Martin, Clerk's office of the District Court."

❧

[Gilbert later acknowledges that this brief letter written in pencil should have been dated May 30]

May 27, 1863

Dear Esther,

We have got march orders and are all packed up ready for a start. Whither we do not know.[1]

I had so much that I could not carry it and I sent a bundle home by express. I did not pay the charges, for if the bundle didn't get through I should not lose the $1.00 that was the charge for carrying.

I have 12 dollars on hand, and if nothing happens more than has happened I shall not need more than $2.00. We have not got one last pay. I shall inform you as soon as we start where we are; and if you want any more money I will send it you.

And now do not worry about me. I shall still be under the kind care of my Heavenly Father and what He sees best for me to pass through will be all right. If you do not get a letter as soon as you expect, do not be over anxious about it.

I hope this will find you all well.

Yesterday the captain called me to his tent and gave me charge concerning the sick as he was going to Memphis in a Court Martial, but the order came to march and all his plans are frustrated.

We know not what or why will bring faith in the army. The boys are not much cast down about moving but appear as jolly as ever.

I must close.

Yours Truly,

Gilbert

NOTE

1. Letter from S. A. Hurlbut to Brigadier General Asboth, May 29, 1863, 8:30 a.m. Send, with all possible dispatch, the Third Minnesota, Fortieth Iowa, Twenty-fifth and Twenty-seventh Wisconsin, by steamer to Vicksburg, reporting here for orders. Let them take five days' rations, 6 wagons to a regiment, and 100 rounds per man. No tents except shelter tents. Reduce baggage to the minim.

   Abandon Fort Heiman. Send the One hundred and eleventh Illinois to Paducah or Columbus. Bring away all Government property or stores worth moving. Send all companies of Second, Fourth, and Fifteenth Illinois Cavalry by land through Covington. Let them rendezvous at Fort Pillow. Heavy baggage and stores to follow by steamer, under light guard. You must use the Fourth Missouri and Fifteenth

Kentucky for cavalry duty. Send the remainder of Thirty-fourth Wisconsin to Memphis. Let all this be done promptly. (Scott, *War of the Rebellion*, vol. 24, pt. 3, 364)

૮ᴗ

4 o'clock May 30, 1863

Dear Esther,

You will have some idea of the uncertainty that is continually resting upon a soldier when I inform you that our marching orders has been countermanded. We had got everything ready, drew our shelter tents, got 5 days rations and ammunition. The order had been fulfilled to the letter, and we had sent to the express office our bundles, and expected soon to go on a steamer to some place.

I had written a letter to you in a hurry with a pencil stating the facts in the case as I then supposed. I guess I dated it the 27th but it was this morning that I wrote it.

I expect you will think me foolish in sending home some of the things that I did, but I thought this matter all over and came to the conclusion as you will discover when you open the bundle. I have got enough to wear and my pants will last good, I think, my time out; and if they do not, there are plenty more where they came from.

I think that we should have gone down the river. The 25th & 27th are still under marching orders, and will probably go. Should we leave this place it is not likely that we should ever have a more comfortable one unless we could have our choice. I think that we might, in that case, improve considerably upon our present situation. But I have no reason to complain. We are comfortable and pleasantly situated here, and I could pass the remainder of the time here and do all the guard duty and all the fatigue necessary and not feel it a burden if it is for the best; or if it is necessary that we should go, I can cheerfully go.

Our hospital is broken up. Those that were not able to go went to the post hospital. I shall now do, most likely, my regular duty. It was quite as hard to tend the sick as to do the other work, but it was pleasant because that I could make plans and have a variety of occupation, which you know suits me.

The boys are most of them better, but 2 or 3 that I think will not get along soon. One will probably never get well. I think he has got nearly or quite beyond the reach of human skill.

I should judge by what you and Mother write about the prospect of fruit that if nothing befalls it that there would be an abundant harvest.

You will doubtless remember Wash Phillips that used to work for Seely. He is in the 31st Wisconsin. One of Harry Lester's wife's brothers is in the 25th. I used to know him years ago (so well I got that last piece of news in rather back handed). I like to talk with them about old times and old friends.

This has been written in a hurry and you must not scrutinize it too close.

I shall expect a letter tomorrow and should not have written this had it not been just as it is to counteract the impression of the one I wrote in the morning.

My love to you all,

Gilbert

∾

Columbus
June 4, 1863

Dear Esther,

Your letter was received Tuesday night, and the corporal brought it to me, and I perused the letters standing guard, which is not exactly according to regulations.

I was glad to hear from you all, and that you are well as usual.

You say that the smallpox is coming. Since I have been in the army I have often thought of Price and that he ought to be vaccinated, but when I have written home I did not think of it. When we were in Fort Halleck they had the smallpox on both sides of us within a stone's throw of our barracks, but it did not spread much as they were soon removed. I hope that he will, if not already, be vaccinated.

Before you get this, my bundle that I sent home will be received. In the hurry of packing I forgot to take out the eye medicine you sent me. I had not had any occasion to use it, but yesterday I felt a soreness in my left eye and today it is quite red. I got some white vitriol and put it in some rainwater but the other component part of the eye medicine I have not got as yet and do not know that I can.[1] I wish that you would send me some more in your next letter. Now I don't want you to keep awake more than 23 hours out of 24 for fear that my eye will not be cared for, for if it comes to a point

I shall have nothing to do but take care of my eye and eat, but I think that it will soon be well again.

Some more of the boys have been taken sick and the doctor has issued the order that I should take charge again, which I have done. Those that were sent to the post hospital still remain until they are well. I have 4 in charge today, but none of them very sick.

You seem very discouraged about the war, but I never felt more encouraged. The government is on the right track when it places the musket with the accouterments belonging to it in the hands of the slave, and day by day I am using my tongue if not my musket in it. I intend to do all in my power to enlighten the Negroes respecting the plans of the government respecting them, and urge them to enlist with the determination to do all in their power to put down the rebellion. A regiment is now being organized here.[2] I have talked with some that have such a burning hatred towards the slave master that they would not hesitate a moment were they in their power to strike the deadly blow. They ask no quarter, and do not expect it, and say they will not give it in return. You know that I always said I believed that there was available means enough in the South to crush the rebellion. I think so still.

You say you expect we have any quantity of insects to sing us to sleep, and wonder how I sleep if mosquitoes trouble me as they used to. Well I will tell you in the first place, we do not have many. I have killed more in one night with a candle in our house than I have seen here in Kentucky, and this is true. Occasionally one comes round but they are very sedentary, but the wood ticks are very numerous in the woods. I do not go in them on this account. I have not found but one on me yet, but some of the boys that have been out have found 10 or 12 on them.

The 25th & 27th Wisconsin Regiments left last Sunday and went down the river. The 2 companies of our regiment that were in Cairo have come here and are now in Fort Halleck.

I have got me a fine bunk right now. It is in [a rectangle drawn enclosing the words "it has 4 thickness of bagging for bottom"] this form and is very comfortable.

I have got another overcoat. I gave $3.50 for it and intend to keep it, 'til I get through, with me; and if I should be obliged to leave anything, I shall leave my blanket and carry my overcoat. But I do not think that we shall leave here soon, but cannot tell. Report says we are going to Wisconsin to guard prisoners, but I do not place any confidence in any reports of the nature.

The paymaster is here, and we shall probably get our pay tomorrow, which will relieve the minds of most of the boys as they are nearly all out of money; and for a short time they will have plenty of fine things to eat, which will prove a damage to them in a health point of view.

I intended to have written an answer to Mother's letter this time, but it makes my eye ache to write and I will answer it next time.

It is rather cool here now with occasional showers.

I hope that the fruit will do well, and that I shall be permitted to return and help eat some of it.

I must close.

Yours Truly,

Gilbert Claflin

NOTES

1. *White vitriol* is another name for zinc sulfate. It is a colorless, crystalline compound that is soluble in water. Its use in eye medicine is as an astringent.

2. The US Colored Troops had 138 infantry regiments, 6 cavalry regiments, 1 light artillery regiment, and 14 heavy artillery regiments. The Second Tennessee Heavy Artillery Regiment (African Descent) was organized at Columbus, Kentucky, in June 1863. In April 1864, they were designated the Fourth United States Colored Heavy Artillery Regiment. Most of their time was spent in garrison duty at Fort Halleck in Columbus and at Union City, Tennessee (Dyer, *Compendium of the War of the Rebellion*, 1721).

Columbus
June 7, 1863

Dear Esther,

I will improve a few moments in writing to you this morning.

My eye is some better; the pain has left it but it is still considerably inflamed. The doctor said it was the inflammation of the optic nerve of the eye. I was cupped twice in the back of my neck, and had a blister applied on the cupping.[1] It stopped the pain and is now operating as a counter irritation with good results.

My general health is good. I have stopped the use of meat, tea & coffee, and use potatoes, fruit and bread; have plenty of sweetening.

I am the only one, with the exception of the captain, that has not had diarrhea; and in many of the boys it is assuming the chronic form. They take medicine that will check it a short time and then it comes on again. Most if not all have a craving appetite, but what they eat does not satisfy them. It is no uncommon thing for men to take 3 slices of fat pork at a meal here, and other things in proportion.

The boys are quite cheerful at the prospect of soon returning home. They count the days now, and say that they will soon pass by but think the last month will be a long one. I do not think it will seem any longer to me as there is one thought when the subject comes before me that settles the matter, and that is that time passes with the same rapidity and no variation from year to year.

I got a letter from brother J.P. today. It was dated Fort Donelson, May 20. It was postmarked St. Louis, June 4. I do not understand how it came to St. Louis before it was put in this post office unless he has gone there, but he said nothing in his letter about it.

June 8:

My eye is better this morning.

Things are moving along about as usual here. A little excitement now and then does the boys good. Last Saturday night about 11 o'clock the long roll sounded through the camp, and the order fall out fall out went from company to company. Our boys got out as soon as possible and formed in line and stood for some time awaiting orders; but no order came, and it proved to be only a sell. The officers done it to see how quick the men would fall out. I did not get out of bed as I thought it was nothing serious and my eye, you know, was sore.

Yesterday 4 steamers passed down the river loaded with soldiers. I was told that the 20th Wisconsin was one of the regiments passing.[2]

They are having stirring times about Vicksburg, I suppose. There seems to be no doubt but what Grant will take it, and it will be a hard blow on the Rebels and soon place the whole river in our hands.

You spoke in your letter about the prospect of famine and that the South already feels it. That idea of starving out the South has exploded long ago with me. That they are suffering for many of the luxuries I do not doubt, but they are far from a starving condition.

In my opinion take them as a whole I should like to have you or the boys rather give me the grain prospect and what is said about the draft. If you sell the wool, the boys had better get Mr. Eastman to help market it when he does his, as he can judge better as to the best time to dispose of it.

I have got 2 months' pay and shall probably send some home before long. I like to wait a short time after payday as I think it is safer, but should you want any, let me know at once and I will forward it.

It is astonishing how men spend money here. Since I have been writing one of the boys, and he is not on duty because he is not well, eat a box of small fish put up in oil that cost him 40 cents without stopping; and yesterday he eat a whole chicken for dinner. I tell you, the boys most of them live high whilst the money lasts; and that is what makes many sick.

I guess you will think that I am getting fond of writing by the way the letters come.

I guess that my eye will be well before the medicine you send will get here.

Yours Truly,

Gilbert

[Upside down at top]

Brother J.P. said he was doing duty now. If you will send his company address I should be glad, as I am not certain about it.

This letter looks hard. I did it with one eye; but it is better.

NOTES

1. *Cupping* involved heating small glass cups and applying them to the skin, often over a small incision, to cause a vacuum effect. In *blistering*, the patient was given a second-degree burn and the resulting blister drained. Both were supposed to draw inflammation out of the body. By the 1860s, these practices, along with bleeding and purging, were in serious decline.

2. The Twentieth Wisconsin served in southwestern Missouri and northwestern Arkansas starting soon after they were mustered in August 1862. On June 3, 1863, they moved to St. Louis, then down the Mississippi River to participate in the Siege of Vicksburg. Albert J. Rockwell from Oconomowoc was the first lieutenant of Company G of the Twentieth. About two dozen Oconomowoc men were in that company (Dyer, *Compendium of the War of the Rebellion*, 1682; Quiner, *Military History of Wisconsin*, 675–80; "Roster of Wisconsin Volunteers," 154–56). More on the Twentieth is in Appendix D.

June 9, 1863

Dear Gilbert,

Your letter came to hand last night and I was very sorry to learn that you had an inflamed eye, for I fear you won't get over it immediately this time of year. And I hope you won't be up nights with the sick if you can help it.

Your package arrived last Thursday night. The cost was 75 cents.

I think you are a pretty nice washer.

James took that bill to the banker, and he said it was good. And I think when we get enough together I had better get Elton a coat. There is no second hand clothing now at Nashotah, but Peters the tailor has coats for $10.[1] It seems a great deal, but I guess we can't do any better at present. Elton has left off going to church for the want of a coat, and he says he is "not going to Sabbath School any more. There is no boys of his age that go."

The boys are at work today on the road. Mr. Hinkley told me your tax was $2½. Price spoke to Uncle John about working his tax, but Elton seems to think they had not better.

They are expecting to wash sheep the last of the week. And what shall we do about selling the wool? I don't know what the price of wool is, but all goods have fallen some.

There seems to be very few currants, but very likely there is as many as we can pick. I am not going to have a lot of children here picking. I have seen Mrs. Hubbard and Mrs. Topliff and they both said they would like some.[2] Mrs. Topliff and Almaria wished to be remembered to you.

We still hear reports of cases of smallpox, but none nearer. After the first excitement was over and Price could [not] get vaccinated at the doctor's, I concluded that he might wait and we would get the vaccine of some one that we know. And I shall go soon and see if I can get it of Mr. Montague's children.[3]

As yet we have had no hot weather. Yesterday and today have been bright days. But it has seemed cold enough for a frost nearly every night for the last two weeks. But we have not had any yet. Grain and grass and the foliage on the trees look very thriving, but other things don't grow very fast.

Is there not something you want that I can send you?

Gilbert, I ain't much of a heroine. I feel all the time as though I wanted somebody else to take the responsibility. Selfish ain't it?

Margaret thinks J.P.'s well or nearly so, but he wrote to James the 30 of May, and I should judge from his letter that he was growing weaker all the time.

Esther Claflin

NOTES

  1. Peters's ad from the June 21, 1862, *Oconomowoc Free Press*:
    Summer 1862 / CLOTHS & CLOTHING / AT THE / STORE and SHOP / KEPT BY / H.M. PETERS, / Main-street / OCONOMOWOC.

His new Stock consists of Cloths, Sattinets, Men's Clothing, Hats, Caps and Tailors' Trimmings, with Gentlemen's Furnishing Goods, &c.

TAILORING / Also done at this establishment, in the best style and on short notice.

All Prices Very Cheap.

2. Mr. and Mrs. Dyer Topliff moved to Wisconsin from New York. In the 1860s they ran a boardinghouse in Oconomowoc. Mrs. Topliff was Elmira, aged forty-six. Almeriah, aged twenty-six, was the eldest of their four children (1860 census). Read more about the Topliff boardinghouse in Appendix B.

Mary Hubbard was the wife of a cooper, Charles Hubbard. At the time of the letters, they had four children and lived in Oconomowoc with another cooper and his wife and child and with a cooper journeyman (1860 census). For more on the Hubbard family see Appendix B.

3. By the mid-nineteenth century, vaccination with cowpox had eclipsed inoculation with live smallpox. One could, if necessary, inoculate the old-fashioned way, with "matter" from someone with smallpox.

ᕫ

Columbus
June 10, 1863

Dear Esther,

Your letter was received last night and I was glad that you unburdened your heart so fully to me.

I sent a letter home yesterday and have but little to write, but thinking you would like to see J.P.'s letter and wishing to answer some questions, I will enclose a few lines.

I think my eye will soon be well.

We are having a very wet time now and I think it will tell on the health of the boys, but perhaps it is better than if it was very hot.

I want you, by all means, to do as brother William wants you to. The 15 dollars is nothing, and you need not think of it a minute.

You may tell Elton if he will be a good boy and do as you say that when I get home he shall have the colt for the sheep.

I hardly know what answer to give you about my being homesick. I often feel a longing desire to see home and dear ones, but the thought is ever with me that I am treading a path that is marked out by others for the present. But I trust that soon I shall be permitted to return again to enjoy the quiet of home and feel its endearing relations.

I hardly know what to say about home matters. I want the boys to fix up the fences as well as they can, and do the best they know how to keep things as snug as possible. I know that it requires constant attention to keep everything as it should be; but I did not expect that things would go on as well as if I were there. But I must say that judging from your letters as a whole; things have gone better than I anticipated. I hope the boys will endeavor to do as you advise them, and be good to each other, and work harmoniously together. If William has a vacation in harvest, I think that he will perhaps help the boys cut the grain and I will make it right with him.

Yesterday the river was lined with steamers loaded with soldiers from General Burnsides' army on the way to join General Grant's army before and around Vicksburg.[1] At 6 o'clock last night 12000 had passed and 8000 more were coming. They must soon take it, I think, as our army must be able to worry them night and day, they getting but little rest whilst our men can be relieved. I trust the day is not far distant when it will be ours, and the Rebels inside prisoners.

You must not be discouraged if all things do not go as you would like to have them. Walk in duties path and God will bless you.

Your Husband,

Gilbert

[Upside down at top]

I want you should let me know whether you get my bundle that I sent home, and what you think about sending some more clothes, if I can get them reasonable.

I do not think it best to send currants here. It would not pay, as this is a good fruit country. I would not try to do anything with the currants but you can do as you think best.

Steamers loaded with soldiers are passing today.

You must not expect letters quite as thick all the time. I intend once a week.

NOTE

1. On May 29, Grant sent a message to H. W. Halleck (general-in-chief over all Union land forces) that "the enemy under Johnston is collecting a large force to attack me and rescue the garrison of Vicksburg." Grant reported that up to 45,000 additional Rebels were expected (Scott, *War of the Rebellion*, vol. 24, pt. 1, 40).

Halleck pulled large numbers of troops to reinforce Grant, including 8,000 troops that Ambrose Burnside had ready to invade eastern Tennessee. Halleck told Burnside on June 3, "If you cannot hire river boats, you must impress them" (Scott, *War of the Rebellion*, vol. 23, pt. 2, 383–84).

Columbus
June 15, 1863

Dear Esther,

Your letter postmarked June 10 came to hand June 13, and I am now using the powder your hands put up for me. My eye is getting better.[1] The inflammation is out of it, but it is still weak, but does not pain me any.

We are having hot weather now, and the boys look for the shady side; but we have got things fixed up in good shape; have a bough shade over our tables, and it is a fine place to sit in as the wind can blow under from all directions, and we are so situated that if a breeze blows we are sure to feel its cooling effects.

I do not have much to do in the hospital now as the boys all help themselves now. I have to go and get the medicine, and that is all. A new order of things has been instituted and we have got no doctor, he having been appointed to take charge of the Negro hospital. But by request of the general he comes and sees our boys and gives us medicine for the present. I do not think I shall stay longer than it takes for my eye to get strong enough to stand guard unless the doctor stays and urges the matter.

I shall leave this hospital, as there are several of the boys that are bound not to do any duty and are in the hospital. 2 of them are old soldiers and have got the upper hands of the captain and all the officers.[2] They have put them in the guardhouse time and again and they will go there before they will do duty.

The other day 1 of them was put in the prison down town, the other packed up and went down also, and they had to send a guard and fetch him back. The captain dare not put his threats in execution, and when he threatens they threaten back. They pretend to be sick, but drink hard and eat everything. It was one of them that eat the fish I wrote you about. It is no wonder that they do not feel well. They were sergeants in other companies, and were reduced to the ranks, and then transferred to our company; a very unfortunate transfer for us in most respects, but in some it was not as it has stopped some of the captain's private notions upon us as a company. I have not had any trouble with them, but they are about constantly growling about something, which makes it very unpleasant.

The 22nd Wisconsin is expected here every day. They have been exchanged. I think you have a cousin, or had one, in the regiment. I should like to have you inform me as to the correctness of my impression. The regiment was at St. Louis a few days since I was told.[3]

All the news we got from Vicksburg informs the first reports: that Grant is holding the place with an iron grasp, and able to continue the siege as long as they will probably want him to, and that all the efforts the Rebels may make to raise the siege will be of no avail.

There are now about 400 Negroes here in camp. They take a great deal of pride in being soldiers, and it is truly pleasing to see them stand guard and hear them challenge the person that approaches their sentry path. They know what awaits them if called to fight and are taken prisoners, and I know from what I have seen and heard them say that in the heart of many of them there is a burning hatred against slave masters that will be satisfied only by drawing the life blood of the oppressor.

I tremble when I think of the future prospects of the South. It looks to me as if the storm that is to furnish the whirling is but just gathering; and that when the tempest is past and quiet again restored the passer will look upon one vast scene of destruction. I also believe that as a nation we shall tread upon the verge of ruin. Our sins as a nation have well nigh closed every avenue to which we might reasonably look for deliverance, and were it not for that Hand whose forgiveness is great and His mercy infinite I should despair.

But I still believe that there is a bright future in store for us, and that as a nation we shall yet stand a beacon light sending forth rays of gospel light that shall be free and pure as the light of heaven. What a blessed thought it is that we may participate in this reformatory work, beginning with our poor sinful hearts, & enlarging our field of labor as opportunity offers. I hope you will be sustained under the many responsibilities that must of necessity rest upon you.

I think as you do about the coat and hope that Elton will go to Sunday School every Sunday, and that he and Price will do as well as they can. I shall expect a letter from one of them when you answer this.

Love to all.

Gilbert

[Upside down at top]

We live first rate now; have butter often, potatoes, beans, rice, cornmeal, plenty of bread and crackers, dried apples, and good corned beef, and smoked shoulders of hog; and a company fund of over 50 dollars on hand to draw upon as occasion requires. I guess we shall not suffer in this direction.

It is dinner time and the boys are washing up.

NOTES

1. The most likely explanation as to Gilbert's condition would be "iritis" or "anterior uveitis" (different terms for same condition)—notoriously chronic and/or recurrent, often involving just one eye (and recurrently the same eye), characterized by notable pain, exacerbated by light and/or focusing effort (e.g., reading, as he notes in one of his letters). As for the dissolved "powder" he found some relief from, . . . it's anybody's guess. Odds are it was some sort of ydriatic/cycloplegic agent, either prescribed or discovered accidentally (e.g., atropine, belladonna, etc.), which inactivates the inflamed structures inside the eye and helps to gradually quell the inflammation. We still use them commonly "nowadays," but in conjunction with steroids (which I doubt he would have had any access to in 1863, but who knows?). (Kevin Webb, OD, Kittery, Maine, e-mail message to author, March, 2008)

2. Adolph Knittel and August Zosel are listed as sergeants in Company E of the Thirty-Fourth Regiment who were transferred to Company A on February 15, 1863. Adolph Knittel had previously joined the Sixth Wisconsin Regiment in May 1861. He was corporal of Company F of the Sixth for three months, then transferred to Company H of the Sixth, and was finally discharged on disability in July 1862. Four months later, he signed up for the Thirty-Fourth Regiment. August Zosel (also spelled Zozel and Zoel in the records, and Zoesel on the company record) enlisted as a substitute in Company E of the Thirty-Fourth on January 10, 1863 ("Roster of Wisconsin Volunteers," 518, 527–28, and 536–37).

3. The men of the Twenty-Second Wisconsin Regiment were captured and made prisoners at the battles of Thompson's Station and Brentwood in middle Tennessee in March. Later they were released in exchange for the release of Confederate prisoners. St. Louis was where the Twenty-Second Regiment soldiers were being re-equipped before being sent back to the field of operation after their imprisonment (Quiner, *Military History of Wisconsin*, 698–701). A short history of the Twenty-Second is in Appendix D.

∾

June 18, 1863

Dear Gilbert,

Yours of the 10th was received last night. They most always come when I need them most. When the week winds up, it seems as though it must be that you will be here Sunday. I can't get used to it, but I feel more reconciled to your absence than I should be if I did not think your locality was rather a favorable one for you, considering that you are a soldier, and I thank God that your health has been so well preserved. But still I greatly fear for your eyes. But why did you let the surgeon scarify and blister you if you could help it?

For three days it has been very hot. The first summer weather we have had, and the ground is getting pretty dry.

There are still cases of smallpox occurring about us, but nobody seems frightened now. Price has been vaccinated, but it has not begun to work.

June 19:

William very unexpectedly stepped into the back door yesterday morning. He said that he came home for some strawberries, but his school was suspended because the smallpox had made its appearance in his ward, and some of his pupils had been exposed. He himself went into a house where the people were sick with it. He did not know it until sometime after, but he would not come home until the time expired that he would be taken down. He goes back tomorrow night to resume his school Monday.

Margaret and others have had letters from J.P. of later date than yours, and says that he is getting better. I guess I never wrote you that last winter, immediately after his writing to you, Fort Henry was evacuated and the forces went to Donelson where he now is. His address is Ft. Donelson, Tennessee, Company H 13th Wisconsin Infantry.

Mother has sold her place for $200 to Mr. Alvord for Lew's family. She done it for the sake of giving James a start on a new place. It seems like a wild scheme but perhaps it will succeed. James says there is a great deal of government land in Michigan, and by taking advantage of the homestead bill, and using her little means for a start, they think they can get a home.[1] If James had any health, I should think the project a good one, but with his present health it looks very uncertain. But I think his health is improving. His lung difficulty seems better. He is still troubled with diarrhea and bloats badly.

John and the boys have sheared the sheep. They done it in a little more than a day; finished yesterday. Price has commenced attending school again. The hoeing is not all done, but they seem to think they can make a short job of it. Elton has gone this afternoon to cut hay on Goodell's marsh on shares. I presume a half-day will wind up the job.

I know so little outside of the house and farm that I hardly know what to write you. The enrolling officers have taken the militia roll in some places, and in some they are afraid to do it. Mr. Luddin don't dare to do it in Ixonia [a town about nine miles northwest of Summit]; one man was shot in the town north of Ashippun [a town about ten miles north of Summit] and he was not expected to live. In Milwaukee they have been attacked by the Irish women and stoned. The fear seems generally expressed that we shall have more serious work at home than ever had. Dark days are these for our nation. You doubtless are aware of the prospect of another Northern invasion.

Esther Claflin

[Marginal notes]

I think it would be well to send home clothing. Ex[press] charges are small. We did receive your bundle. The cost was 15 cents.

It still remains hot and dry. Currants are small and very few.

It is only two months more, and then there will be an end of this letter writing.

NOTE

1. The Homestead Act was a vast giveaway of public lands that went into effect on January 1, 1863. The new law stated that any US citizen, or intended citizen, who had not borne arms against the United States and who was at least twenty-one years of age, the head of a family, or a military veteran was qualified to claim land. A small filing fee gave a homesteader the temporary right to occupy and farm 160 acres. The land did not become the homesteader's immediately; the law said that the land had to be improved, lived on, and maintained for five years by the homesteader before the person would own it.

Columbus
June 21, 1863

Dear Esther,

I have not received a letter in answer to the 3 last I have written, but expect one tonight as we did not get any last night. The steamer that carries the mail went below yesterday and did not come back 'til this forenoon. It left from Cairo about 10 o'clock and will probably come back about sun down.

It is Sunday, and I have just come back from meeting and had my supper. I attended the Methodist church. The text was in 1st Corinthians, 13 chapter, part of 13th verse: "And now abideth faith, hope, charity, these three." It was a very good discourse, but some allusions were made that plainly indicated that he was a native and was not wholly sound in his Union sentiments. In his prayer he spoke of the invader and the invaded, and cited in his discourse an incident that happened after the battle at Manassas Junction of a Federal soldier that was mortally wounded imploring a Louisiana soldier to pray with him, but he could not, but brought him some water. A Virginia soldier passed him. He asked the same favor. The soldier fell upon his knees and implored heavens blessing upon him. The dying man smiled and raised his arms to embrace him, and the spirit passed from earth to heaven.

I have left the hospital, there being none of the boys that have to take medicine. But 2 are in, and they are nearly fit for duty.

I went on guard yesterday and came off this morning.

My eye is not as strong as it was before it became inflamed, but is getting stronger every day. I use my eye water and it is as effectual as it used to be in Wisconsin.

Every day now brings some new change. Troops are coming in every day now, and there is now about as many as there was before the troops left here for Vicksburg.

Affairs move along with us as a company first rate. Our captain has not returned from Memphis yet, and we have good times under the 1st lieutenant. The boys (with the exception of the 2 referred to in my last letter that were in the hospital, one of which is now in the prison down town under arrest and will have a trial for disobedience of orders) are enjoying themselves better than I have seen them before, since we have been in Kentucky.

One thing that is cheering to us is the fact that the time is rapidly passing away that we were drafted for, and all are anxious to see home and dear friends. But a good many of the boys, if they have a chance, will go as substitutes again; but I think I shall be satisfied to stay at home, as I do not believe I am worth much as a soldier as my heart is not in the work.

The steamer did not come in last night 'til it was too late to get the letters for our company

June 22:

I received your letter, and am now writing with one of the pens that you sent.

I was glad that you were enjoying good health judging from your letter. I feel first rate.

I have to stand guard every 3 nights. We do not have to drill, and all the extra duty is to get wood for the cooks, and draw rations. It will not average ½ hour a day. The rest of the time we can sleep or read or anything we are a mind to do around camp; and if we want to go out a mile or so, we can get leave any day we are not on guard.

You wish to know why I had the surgeon scarring and blister me if I could help it. I did not wish to as I thought it would help it, and it did stop the severe pain.

I am glad that James is getting better. I hope he will recover his usual health. I was somewhat surprised to hear that Elton was going to cut hay on shares. I think he had better not do it, as I do not think it is a very good plan to wade in the water. It never paid me to do it when health was taken in to the account.

Some of the boys got letters from home. Chinch bug is destroying the wheat in some parts.[1] I should like to know if they are at work about Summit.

I do not know what calculations the boys are making about the harvest, whether they calculate to do it themselves or not; but I think that they had better get John or William to help them if they can. Perhaps you had better speak to John about it if you think of it when you see him next, and I will satisfy him.

I expect that there will be some trouble in enforcing the draft unless they make an example of some place, which will probably be done. I know it is a hard thing to take men from their families but the war that is begun may be carried on to the end; and to do this men must be supplied, and men must sacrifice. But I have no sympathy with Copperheads, and this is the class that mainly oppose the draft and are doing more to injure our cause than ten times as many armed Rebels.[2]

Yours Truly,

Gilbert Claflin

[Upside down at top]

I guess you thought that I had a poor pen to write with by your sending some pens. I had been thinking of getting some when I went down town, but had not; so they came in time.

I should like to know [how] the horse stands the weather and how many lambs and sheep we have got.

The drum is just beat for dinner and I must go.

Love to all.

NOTES

1. The cinch bug (*Blissus leucopterus*) is a North American bug that sucks the juices of grains and grasses and does much damage to crops, particularly in the Midwest. The adults are about one-eighth inch long and have black bodies with black and white wings, red legs, and red spots at the bases of the antennae.

2. *Copperhead* was the term used during the Civil War for a person in a Northern state who was a Southern sympathizer.

June 24, 1863

My Dear Gilbert,

Yours of the 15 was received Saturday eve.

It found us in tolerable health, though Price was ailing from the effects of his vaccination. Today he is better and Elton is on the grunting list. They both think they feel too bad to write.

I vaccinated Price and saved the half-dollar. That is what Tucker charges, and he must have reaped a rich harvest for almost everybody was vaccinated, and it worked in many who had been before. I shall send some of Prices to you, and I think you had better try it.

We have been having quite cool weather for a few days. We have had two light showers in the time.

All crops look very well, and William says wheat, winter wheat in particular, looks better than for many years. Ours is beginning to head out.

I weed and hoe a little, yes considerable for me, and I like it. I never done enough before to get interested in the business. I think you will eat some parsnips next spring of my raising. I have kept your strawberries wed out, and there are very nice specimens of berries. But the hens find them as fast as they turn red. According to accounts the current crop will be small about here. Ours is very light. The birds pick the Mayduke cherries faster than they ripen.[1] I guess I feel some as you used to when I hear the young birds in every direction, and can guess what they are feeding on. The plums have not been looked after, but they still hang pretty full, and the most of them are not stung.

Mother says you can have the wagon that is here for 25 dollars and pay when you get ready. But if you don't want it, let us know so that she can dispose of it otherwise.

Cousin Edmund Davis was in the 22nd Wisconsin, but he was in the hospital when they were taken prisoners, and I have heard that he is at home, discharged. I guess he might as well be in the hospital as his home.

So far as I know it has been healthy this season in this vicinity. I have not felt so well for months, perhaps I might say for years. There are some exceptions. P. A. Woodruff's wife has returned to Oconomowoc to die. Old Mr. Perkins is a complete idiot.[2] James is at Delafield. When he went away from here he seemed to be better, but he is very feeble and bloats badly, and has a diarrhea the most of the time.

I have washed five fleeces of wool for family use, and think I can get it carded with Mrs. Sheldon's.

William left some *Independents* to send to you after I read, but I have not had time to read them so I send them.[3]

This small seed (as it was thought) of slavery, which our fathers left us, has grown to fill our whole land with woes untold. Where the end will be is not in the power of man to tell. I sometimes think our nation will become extinct and the black races will supersede us and become a great and powerful nation. Our crimes toward that race are great and maybe God sees that our cup of iniquity is full. But I know that He rules and whatever He wills is right.

May He bless you abundantly and preserve you from sin.

Esther Claflin

[Marginal notes]

You know this is a hurrying time with me, and you must not expect long letters.

The Sunday Schools are to have a picnic Friday at Pine Lake.

This hymn seemed very sweet to me so I copied it for you.[4]

NOTES

1. Mayduke cherries are large, dark red cherries of excellent quality. The name may be a corruption of "Médoc," the region of France where they originated.

2. Mr. Perkins served with Deacon Gilbert Claflin and the church pastor as the committee representing the church in the summer of 1858, during a time of personal feuding and unhappiness in the church. "Father Perkins," as he is referred to in the church records, is remembered in an article from the *Oconomowoc Enterprise*, which is quoted in full in Appendix B. It states he was a graduate of Dartmouth College and, perhaps, a law partner of Daniel Webster.

3. *The Independent* was a weekly Congregationalist journal published in New York beginning in December 1848. After 1861, it was edited by Henry Ward Beecher, a famous orator known for his opposition to slavery and his support of temperance and woman suffrage.

4. There was no hymn with the letters.

Columbus
June 29, 1863

Dear Esther,

It is a warm day, and we are having very showery weather. It has rained every day or night, I think, for 2 weeks.

I have just come off from guard at 2 o'clock.

I am well and doing first rate in the general sense of the word.

There is but little sickness among the boys, and through the camps, to what there was some weeks ago.

Things around us remain about the same that they did when I last wrote you. The captain has not returned yet, and as near as we can learn he will be obliged to stay some time yet, and may not get through 'til our time is out. He has got about 50 dollars of the company fund in his hands, and I guess he will keep it, though he told me that after the 1st of July he was going to let us have it so that we could have lots of fun things to eat.

I guess I never told you the game he played on the company when he left, which was the time we got marching orders. The boys had succeeded in getting a special requisition on the commissary for 25 gallons of whiskey. They had drawn 7 gallons. A little was given to every man who wanted it every morning. When he left, he drew this whiskey and sold it, and took the money and put it in his pocket; and when the boys presented the requisition again to draw the remainder of the whiskey, they were told of the facts in the case. The boys raved some I can tell you when they found it out.

A new order of things has been instituted in this department. No more liquors go below Cairo only what goes into the commissary department. It makes the whiskey and beer sellers howl, I can assure you; but it is of no use, and it will not pay to smuggle it in as the establishment will be confiscated if found storing it. All the little groggeries were doing a big business in Columbus, but I guess business will be at a discount now in this line.

There is some talk of having a celebration on the 4th but to what extent I do not know. I do not think I shall enter into the spirit of it much under existing circumstances in our country. General Grant is still slowly at work at Vicksburg, confident that it will fall at last into his hands with the surviving garrison. I think that the only hope that they have is that Grant will be attacked in the rear, and when that hope is destroyed they will surrender and the works will not have to be taken by storm. He is confident, so report says, that he can take Vicksburg in 8 hours, but at a great sacrifice of life; and thinks it best to continue the siege until Pemberton is willing to surrender.

I have just had to leave my writing to go for the doctor. The 2nd lieutenant [Michael A. Leahy] has been out of health some time, but is worse now and has some bad symptoms. He is a noble fellow; and if life and health are granted him he will make his mark in the world. He needs but one thing; and that is the one thing needful to make him truly a blessing in the world. That God will spare his life and bestow his spirit upon him is the desire of my heart.

Tomorrow we are to be mustered for pay but probably shall not get any pay 'til we are mustered out.

I expected a letter last night and shall look for one tonight soon, but we seldom get many letters Monday night, but a good many Tuesday night.

June 30:

I did not get a letter last night, and shall send this this morning and can write another if you wish any information on anything.

I have got another bundle to send by express and shall probably put it in the express office in a day or 2. I think I shall get a little addition to it today. I think that what I have got we can use to good advantage. A large amount of clothing is changing hands, some at a low figure, but I have not went in very heavy to what some of the boys have.

I guess you had better be a little careful when you get the bundle. Perhaps there may be some livestock but I guess not. If you will take the things when they come and hang them out and let them stay a day or 2. I think it will be a good thing. I hope this will find you all well and prospering.

Love to all.

Gilbert Claflin

[Upside down at top]

We have inspection and muster at half past 8 this morning. I go on guard at 6 and shall not have to go through rigmarole of packing knapsack and the like.[1] I come off at 8 and get 3 nights in bed. The countersign last night was "Grant."[2]

We have got places built to shelter us from the rain when on guard and when the sun shines hot.

NOTES

1. *Rigmarole* is a "complex and ritualistic procedure that is characterized more by form than genuine meaning." The word comes from the obsolete *ragman roll*, meaning a long list or catalog. *Ragmane rolle* was used in a medieval game and contained verses describing various characters.

2. The countersign is the secret password that must be given to pass the sentry. Here is a verse from a poem titled "The Countersign" by an unknown author: "'Halt! Who goes there?' My challenge cry, / It rings along the watchful line; / 'Relief!' I hear a voice reply; / 'Advance and give the countersign!' / With bayonet at the charge I wait— / The corporal gives the mystic spell; / With arms aport I charge my mate, / Then onward pass, and all is well" (www.poemhunter.com/poem/the-countersign).

June 28, 1863

My Dearest Earthly Friend,

Another Sabbath day is just drawing to a close. It has been a hot day, but is now cooler with some signs of rain.

We have enjoyed church privileges this day, which always brings your case more fresh to me. We had an excellent sermon as usual on the importance of kindness, gentleness, and courteousness. I always feel exceedingly humbled after listening to such a discourse. I am very glad that you have the privilege of meetings, even if you hear sentiments promulgated that you cannot endorse. I think the schooling that you and I are now having may be of lasting benefit to us both if rightly improved. Don't you think that sometimes by our being deprived of our blessings we learn better to estimate them by their real value? I believe that if the blessing of peace and a free government is ever restored to this nation in my day, I shall appreciate it as I never have. I sometimes feel it a blessed privilege that I may, in common with many of my countrywomen, bear a little part in this great struggle. But perhaps I am like the theoretic farmer who lives in the city and never planted a potato, or the ideal poet who sings of domestic love but has not the capacity to make or enjoy it.

The rain has come, contrary to my expectations, and we are now enjoying a refreshing shower; the first of any amount for three weeks.

It is now after seven o'clock. The boys have gone down to the afternoon service. I sit by the back window writing, and the refreshing breeze comes in through the open casement. The shower is passing away and the song of the birds, the bleating of the sheep, and the sound of the distant thunder all seem to remind me distinctly that I am alone. But Gilbert, don't think that I am low-spirited. I never felt more full of joy of an earthly prospect than for a few days. In a little longer, God permitting, you will be at home; and I know if you keep well the time will seem short. When I drink of the pure cool water from your well, I think of you in the heat and dust, deprived of this refreshing draught. What do you drink? You wrote some time ago that you did not drink water. And now you say you have left off the use of tea and coffee.

[June] 29:

I can't get Elton to write, though it has been a rainy day and he has had time.

We just finished washing, etc. Washed your overcoat today. It was not very dirty, but it had the smell of the camp.

I guess the new house stands the weather. I was a little fearful in the spring that it was crumbling away, for I could hear the pebbles dropping almost every time I went out. But after it became settled weather we heard no more of it.

There are 22 sheep and 9 lambs, all doing well, only very ticky. We lost no lambs, but one ewe eat salt enough to kill her, and she would [have] had a lamb.

I have heard no complaints of the chintz bug only from Sheldon, and that was early in the spring. The boys say there is none in ours, but they complain of the wheat being thin, and since the rain a good many smut heads are visible.[1] Elton thinks they can do the harvesting without help.

John left the place over a week ago, and Mother had a letter a few days since from him saying that he had enlisted in the First Ohio Heavy Artillery.[2] He wrote from Sandusky [an Ohio town on Lake Erie about four hundred miles from Summit].

William some expects to stay after the summer term, and if he does he will not be home again until after you are.

Price took the last wheat to mill Saturday; 2½ bushels. The wheat was shrunk and it makes very little flour. I have used a great deal of corn meal for us. Do you think we had better buy a barrel of flour, or buy wheat?

Price took the wool to Mr. Eastman's Saturday and pressed and tied it. It weighed a little over 50 pounds. Uncle John told us not to hurry about selling it, and we have not said anything to Mr. Eastman about marketing it for us. Maybe it is only a fancy, but I think Mr. E. feels as though he had been troubled by us, and I had rather not ask any more favors of him than I am obliged to. You see, I am getting quite independent.

I go to Uncle John for advice occasionally, and I find that I can do business better than I ever thought I could. Uncle J. always seems glad to have me come to him. They both send their love. Their baby grows finely. I rallied him a little about beginning to raise babies after I had got through. He thought I had not better brag too soon.

I guess I forgot to acknowledge in my last the receipt of 5 dollars from you.

We sold ½ bushels of currants, but for 50 cents. Currants are very scarce this year. I have sent word to Joel W. to know if he will buy them. He buys produce and sends to Pennsylvania (we shall not have more than 10 or 13 bushels, but if we can sell them it will help).

Esther

NOTES

1. *Wheat smut* is a fungus that reduces the wheat yield and has a foul odor. Instead of producing pollen, the infected plants produce black spores that infect other wheat plants.

2. The regiment began as the 117th Ohio Volunteer Infantry on September 15, 1862; however, the designation changed to First Heavy Artillery on May 2, 1863. The men served in north-central Kentucky beginning on October 2, 1862, and constructed fortifications around Covington and Newport, Kentucky, starting in February 1863. This area was just across the Ohio River from Cincinnati, Ohio, and about 350 miles northeast of Columbus, Kentucky, where Gilbert was stationed (Dyer, *Compendium of the War of the Rebellion*, vol. 1, pt. 3, "Ohio 1st Regiment Heavy Artillery"). More on the regiment is in Appendix D.

Columbus
July 4, 1863

Dear Esther,

Your kind letter was received last night and I was glad to hear that you were all well.

I am still enjoying good health and am enjoying myself as well as could be expected, and even better than I ever supposed I could all things considered. The fact is that we have got one of the best locations so far as health and beauty of prospects is concerned. There is in this post, and I question whether there can be many better be found in the western department.

It has been very quiet here today. The national salute was fired about 12 o'clock today.[1] Most of our boys have gone down town or are going. I concluded that I would stay in camp and write a letter.

I expect that some of the boys will go in the guardhouse. It will be a wonder if they do not, as every man that gets drunk and makes any noise is sure to go in.

Last night they had quite a show of fireworks before the general's quarters, and tonight I expect there will be quite a fine display.

Our company did not take part in the grave celebration but got a nice dinner for ourselves. We bought 1½ bushel peas in the pod which cost us $3.00, ½ bushel of new potatoes $1.00, ½ bushel of onions $1.00, 7 pounds of butter $2.00, some milk 50 cents, some pickled beets 50 cents: in all $8.00 of the company fund. We had a good dinner and supper and have got nearly all the onions left, as we did not cook them; those eating them raw that wished it.

It has been a very warm day, but towards evening a fine breeze sprung up and it is a lovely night. Since I last wrote you it has not been as wet as it was previous, but warmer; but not any warmer than I have seen in Wisconsin.

The Mississippi River is rising very rapidly. It has been full 35 feet lower than at its height last spring. It does not seem possible to think of, but such is the fact.

I have lit a candle, and am reminded that it is the 4th by hearing the firecrackers. I have just been looking at some of the fireworks, and think that thus far it is not better than last night but perhaps the best is to come.

I do not have to stand guard now, nor attend roll calls, but have charge of the hospital and cook for the sick. There are 3 of the boys on the sick list, but all of them are able to get out now. I expect a new addition after today but may be disappointed. (The fireworks are very fine now. I have just been out to see them.) I do not have to sit up nights. The sergeant or corporal of the guard stays there during the night, and if any medicine is to be given, I give it to them and they give at the proper times.

I suppose you have heard of the 402 dollars bounty money which the government will give all soldiers that have been in the service 9 months and will reenlist for three years or during the war.[2] Well, it is creating quite an excitement among some of the boys, and I doubt not but that many of them will go in again; but I do not think of trying soldier's life longer than the 9 months, and if my life and health is preserved 'til the close of the term for which I was drafted, I think I shall be satisfied to return home and be contented to remain at home.

You wished to have me say what I thought about the wagon. I think that perhaps we had better take it if mother cannot do better, but you can do as you think best about it. I cannot say when as to pay if we take it.

You wish to know about what to do for flour. I guess that the boys had better take some bags to the mill and get some flour and spirits to raise bread with; or the boys may buy the wheat if you think best, if they can do it without much trouble. It takes 5 bushels to make a barrel of flour.

I think the boys will have a hard stint to do the harvesting and I think that they had better change works with Mr. Eastman, or someone else, and get them to cradle for them. I think that it will be too hard for Elton to cut it and do it all in proper time, but I may be mistaken.

I hope that you all will be careful of your healths. I am doing that which I think will preserve mine. God's blessing attending it.

I bathe every morning.

Love to all.

Gilbert Claflin

[Marginal notes]

I want you to write whether you got the bundle I sent.

You wish to know what I drink. I drink a little water, and tea, and occasionally a little coffee since my eye got better. I should like a drink of water out of the old well but do not suffer for the want of it as I have got used to the water here now.

NOTES

1. The "national salute" that Gilbert heard was most likely thirty-five guns, one for each state. West Virginia had become a state on June 20, 1863, just two weeks earlier.
  The gun salute system of the United States has changed considerably over the years. In 1810, the "national salute" was defined by the War Department as equal to the number of states in the Union—at that time 17. This salute was fired by all U.S. military installations at 1:00 p.m. (later at noon) on Independence Day. The President also received a salute equal to the number of states whenever he visited a military installation.
    In 1842, the Presidential salute was formally established at 21 guns. In 1890, regulations designated the "national salute" as 21 guns and redesignated the traditional Independence Day salute, the "Salute to the Union," equal to the number of states. ("Origin of the 21-Gun Salute," http://www.history.army.mil/html/faq/salute.html, US Army Center of Military History, accessed July 8, 2013)
2. On June 25, 1863, the War Department issued General Orders No. 191, authorizing the raising of "veteran" regiments. Any man who had already served at least nine months could re-enlist for three years, or the duration of the war. These "veteran volunteers"

would get a $25 bounty and a $2 premium along with a month's pay in advance when they mustered in. They would then get a $50 bounty on their next pay day and every six months for three years, and the final $75 of the $402 bounty at the end of the three years. Since a month's pay was $13, a bounty of $402 was considerable (Ainsworth and Kirkley, *War of the Rebellion*, vol. 3, 414–16). The details of this order are given in Appendix D.

∾

July 5, 1863

My Dear Gilbert,

Your letter came to hand Thursday night, and it seems strange that it takes mine so long to reach you. I always get yours in three days.

And no news is more welcome than to hear of your health. Has your eye got entirely well?

We are all in usual health. Mr. Eastman has been having pretty serious time with his nose and eyes being badly inflamed and swollen, but is now getting better.

Poor Mrs. Christie has been having poor health, and a few days ago she received intelligence of the death of her son.[1] His memorial sermon will be preached tonight at our church.

I attended church today. You will remember that it is Communion day. The two churches entered into covenant and Mr. Rockwell and Danforth were elected deacons for four years. There seems to be a very small representation from Summit. The words of the text today were "This do in remembrance of me." We had a live sermon and it seems as though there was not life anywhere else. How hard it must be for a minister to carry about the dead body of a church.

I saw Mrs. F. Plympton today.[2] She says her husband is well and he attributes his prosperity to praying Christian friends at home.

Mr. Tremain is again elected Sabbath School Superintendent, and I think the boys don't like to go to SS so well since.[3]

The boys attended the SS picnic at Pine Lake, and yesterday the celebration.[4] It was a basket picnic in Rockwell's Trove. Lewis [James M. Lewis of Oconomowoc, colonel of Wisconsin's Twenty-Eighth Infantry Regiment] was one of the speakers, and Price did not know the others.

I spent my fourth in the currant bushes as usual. You know me well enough to know that I could not enjoy a holiday.

But I learned today that there were telegraph dispatches yesterday of the annihilation of Lee's army, which, if true, must help turn the tide. [Lee's army was defeated at the Battle of Gettysburg, July 3, 1863.]

I picked one bushel of currants yesterday and Joel says he thinks he can afford 1 dollar per bushel.[5]

The cherries are ripening fast, and the berries have begun to ripen. So you see that I shall have plenty to do for a week or two. And I guess you won't feel hard if you don't get very long letters. You know how your time used to be occupied.

Elton has had Billy and Star pastured on Goodall's, and since the sheep were sheared, the cow has had the run of our pasture. The cattle are put in the back lot, so they have their run of stones. And lately Elton has kept Nelly shut up and cut grass for her.

The boys have broken up some new land and sowed buckwheat, but they have not finished hoeing their beans and corn.

The plums hang on the trees yet, but there is not going to be many pears.

I have paid Mr. E. 5 dollars on the 11 that we owed him for wheat, and I have bought myself a pair of 14-shilling gaiters; the first article of dress since you went away.[6]

I think you will be pretty well clothed when you get back. You have got four pairs of woolen pants. But I want you should, when you get to Milwaukee, get yourself a nice dress coat. And be sure not to forget it.

I am glad your pet captain is away. I think you can afford to lose a dollar or two apiece if you can have a decent man at the head of your company.

I am very truly yours,

Esther Claflin

NOTES

1. Melinda Christie worked as a tailor and lived next door to Esther's father, James Colby, in Oconomowoc. She was a widow, and Leander was her only child. In August 1862, Leander joined Company C of the Twenty-Eighth Wisconsin Volunteers when they were being organized by the Oconomowoc postmaster Thomas Stevens. Leander died of disease on June 22, 1863, while he was stationed at Helena, Arkansas (1860 census; "Roster of Wisconsin Volunteers"). More about Melinda and Leander Christie is in Appendix B.

2. Frank Plympton and his youngest brother Charles came to Oconomowoc from Medfield, Massachusetts, where they were born and raised. Before the war, they farmed and lived in Oconomowoc together with Frank's wife, Sarah. In 1863, Frank Plympton was twenty-eight years old, and was another of the Oconomowoc men of Company C of the Twenty-Eighth Wisconsin Volunteers (1860 census; "Roster of Wisconsin Volunteers"). See more about Frank Plympton in Appendix B. There is a short history of the Twenty-Eighth Wisconsin in Appendix D.

3. The Tremains, a farming family from New York, had been long-time residents of Oconomowoc. There were three brothers, all of them married. In 1863, Joseph was forty-five, Ira forty-one, and Charles thirty-seven. Joseph was one of the early Oconomowoc settlers. In 1846, he bought eighty acres in Section 21, three miles north of Gilbert's farm (Barquist and Barquist, *Oconomowoc: Barons to Bootleggers*, 8; 1850, 1860 census). See more about the Tremain families in Appendix B.

4. The area around Summit and Oconomowoc has many beautiful lakes. Pine Lake, also called Chenequa Lake, is about six miles northeast of the Claflin farm. It is in the town of Merton, just east of Oconomowoc.

5. Joel Woodruff was a merchant in Oconomowoc. He was the oldest son of Gilbert and Esther's friends Allen and Roxy Woodruff. Joel's younger brother Gilbert Woodruff clerked at a store in Oconomowoc (1860 census). There is more about the Woodruffs in Appendix B.

6. *Gaiters* are a covering of heavy cloth or leather for the ankle and instep, or for the whole leg from the knee to the instep.

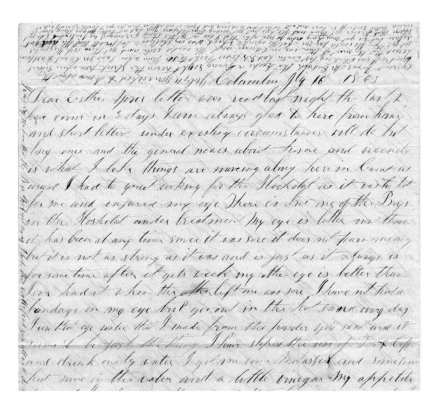

Gilbert's letter, July 10, 1863, page 1.

Columbus
July 10, 1863

Dear Esther,

Your letter was received last night. The last 2 have come in 3 days. I am always glad to hear from home; and short letters, under existing circumstances, will do; but long ones and the general news about home and vicinity is what I like.

Things are moving along here in camp as usual. I had to quit working for the hospital as it was too hot for me and injured my eye. There is but one of the boys in the hospital under treatment.

My eye is better now than it has been at any time since it was sore. It does not pain me any, but it is not as strong as it was, and just as it always is for some time after it gets weak. My other eye is better than I ever had it when the left one was sore. I have not had a bandage on my eye, but go out in the hot sun every day. I use that eye water that I made from the powder you sent, and it seems to be just the thing.

I have stopped the use of tea & coffee and drink only water. I got me some molasses and sometimes put some in the water and a little vinegar. My appetite is good. I cook occasionally some of those currants you sent me and have got some of the raspberries and gooseberries also left and dried apples & peaches; more than I shall cook before our time is out unless I cook more than I have done.

I suppose you begin to count the days, if we get our discharges, when the nine months is up. According to the time we reported, it will be the 17th of August. The general impression is that our time commenced when we were drafted, but it will depend somewhat on surrounding circumstances when we get mustered out. I do not think there is but little doubt but that we shall be back to the state in less than a month.

You have heard the glorious news of the fall of Vicksburg, and while I am now writing the cannon are being fired in rapid succession in Fort Halleck over some glorious news I suppose. Report says that Richmond is taken but I do not believe it yet.

When the official news came that Vicksburg was taken, at 12 o'clock Tuesday, 35 guns were fired, and in the evening a general illumination of the town, the ringing of bells, & bonfires, which finally ended in a general rifling of saloons and groceries of their contents by the soldiers.[1] I went down town about sundown. The orderly sergeant told me to take a blank that was signed, and make it out for as I wanted it. I put it at 10 o'clock intending to stay and see the sights, but I had not been down long before the soldiers began to flock in by hundreds, and I knew they were going to have a rough time by the motion of things and especially the 31st Wisconsin. They did not get any pay the last payday, and are all out of money; and if anyone gets anything to drink in Columbus they have to pay for it now as all spirits and beer are not permitted to go below Cairo except what comes into the commissary department and the quantity on hand here is running low. As I said the boys were short of money, and they must have something to drink; and they did have, and the crowd generally got as much as they wanted. I concluded to come home before dark and not see the result, but most of our boys went down. Quite a number of them brought home about as much as they could carry and one fellow, before he got to bed, had to have help. But none of our boys got in the guardhouse down town; but lots of the boys did belonging to other regiments. They first pitched into a saloon that was not illuminated, and soon had everything out. And when the thing commenced, it spread through the whole town. Some of the saloons handed out their liquors and saved the inside and the things were mostly returned in the glass & decanter line. Some few were knocked down, but no one was seriously hurt.

Last night I took a little walk after sundown and witnessed a scene that is not witnessed many times in one's life. I guess I never wrote about the 4th Missouri Cavalry, part of which are stationed here and part at Clinton about 12 miles out, going out on a scout about 3 weeks since in company with part of the 15th Kentucky Cavalry. They went into Tennessee and got into an ambuscade of guerrillas and had to cut their way through. 86 men went from the camp here; 57 got back. The others were killed or taken prisoners.[2]

There were several Negroes that went along as waiters. The Negro barber that lives right by our camp had a son among the number. When the men got back he did not come, and the last that the men saw of him was when they were fording a stream. His horse gave out in the water, and he jumped off and was trying to help him out. The Rebels were in hot pursuit.

The father and mother looked upon him as dead, and the old man was truly cast down and mourned for his lost son. But joy was in store for him and his family; and I was permitted, as I was passing, to witness the scene of meeting between that son and family; and no white father, mother, brother or sister could have manifested a deeper love than was manifested by that poor Negro family. He succeeded in getting into the bushes and lay 3 days without anything to eat before he ventured to start back, as the Rebels were scouring the country. After considerable hardship he got to Union City [Union City, Tennessee, is about twenty miles south of Columbus, Kentucky] and came on the train to Columbus

It is a fine day. The sun is barely visible through the hazy clouds.

Yours as ever,

Gilbert

[Upside down at top]

Currant boxes: Mr. Goodrich that keeps a grocery right across the street from where Gilbert Woodruff was clerking last winter had 24 boxes. I went to see him when I was in Camp Washburn. He said that the most of them was in Chicago and he would write and get them, or if he could not get them he could pay me what he agreed to, which was one shilling a box for all that he did not return, but we got marching orders so soon after that I did not get the thing arranged as I intended. I do not suppose that he ever got them, and he has not got many there. I believe you had not better do anything about it unless Gilbert Woodruff is there and will get the boxes and money, and I guess it will not pay then for you to trouble yourself with it.

I am sorry to hear that the boys' fox got away.

I hope this will find you all well. Do not work out and get sick, as it will not pay in a long run.

NOTES

1. On June 20, 1863, less than a month before the fall of Vicksburg, West Virginia was admitted to the Union as the thirty-fifth state. The firing of the national salute, one gun for each state, could be a celebration of a turning point toward the preservation of the Union.

2. Detailed reports of this skirmish to Major General Asboth from both William Grebe, the first lieutenant of the Fourth Missouri Cavalry, and Major Wiley Waller of the Fifteenth Kentucky Cavalry are in Appendix D. Both report that men from both cavalry regiments were ambushed and greatly outnumbered. Estimates of Rebel forces are from 1,000 to 2,000; Major Waller numbers the combined Union cavalry at 265. They made it back to Columbus, but losses were heavy and horses exhausted (Scott, *War of the Rebellion*, vol. 23, pt. 2, 628–31).

⌒

July 12, 1863

My Dear Husband,

I have just left off reading a very interesting Sabbath School book. We have a new addition of new works to the library, and Reverend Mr. Montague has a class of men and women, and today I went in it. But I do not think it so interesting or good a class as Mr. Rockwell's. But their lesson is with the school, and I think I shall remain in it when I go to church.

The text today was Zachariah, 11th chapter, 6th to 10th verses.[1]

Since I last wrote you, old Mr. Perkins has died, and yesterday Mrs. P. A. Woodruff died. So we are passing away. Life seems very short to me, and yet almost the whole of my life is spent in caring for the body. These things ought not so to be.

Tuesday [July 7, 1863, three days after the surrender of Vicksburg] evening after hearing of the surrender of Vicksburg, Old Jud started for Prices' shop where the cannon was kept, for the purpose of spiking it, and when the men arrived, he had got his foot in the window. But they took it out and fired a number of times. But I suppose through carelessness in the excitement of the moment, the powder exploded shattering the hand and destroying the eyesight of one, if not both, of W. Harrison's eyes. George Ludington also, who was assisting, had a thumb blown off, and it is feared his eyes put out. Wife expects to be confined soon. Don't you think his mother and wife have trouble?[2]

None of the friends here have had letters since the battle at Helena.[3] The 28th were in it.

I am glad you had a dinner of fresh vegetables the 4th. I had some sweetened bread for mine. Price went to the village in the evening to see the fireworks. He said they were the best he ever saw. Price would not permit Elton to go, for he went to a dancing party the night before and did not get home until five o'clock the next morning. I went to bed at dark, for I was too tired to care for the sights.

We have sold about three dollars worth of currants here, and Joel sent in 8 bushels for which he says he will give 8 dollars. We have sold one dollar and a half worth of berries, but they are bringing in the red raspberries, and I am afraid we can't sell many more. Everything is growing up to weeds. It is weeds everywhere. But Gilbert, I don't see as I can help it. I wish I could.

Didarng(?) Jones, Edmund Davis and wife were here last week. They did not know but you were at home until they got to Delafield. They wished to be remembered to you. Margaret's sister Mary has come to spend the summer with her.

I hope you have written to J.P. He is still at Ft. Donelson.

James was up a few days ago. I can see that he looks better every time. He says he weighs 41 pounds more than he did when he came home.

We have received the bundle, also the 5 dollars.

An insect has recently made its appearance in the head of the wheat.[4] No one seems to know what it is, but viewed with the microscope it has an ugly looking bill.

I was not at all afraid of money tempting you to enlist. The gladness I feel of your soon returning is inexpressible.

Ever yours,

Esther Claflin

Monday July 13, 1863:

It is 6 o'clock, and I have been at work outdoors as I have for two weeks. Have picked 8 quarts of berries and a peck of currants. There is nice feed in the currant bushes; and I watch the cow a few hours every day, and I think it pays.

We have been obliged to buy some butter this summer.

We have been having very hot weather. It is cooler now, but dry.

The boys have got the most of the timothy cut.

People tell me that you will be at home before harvest is over.

We are all well.

Esther Claflin

NOTES

1. Zachariah 11:6–10: "For I will no more pity the inhabitants of the land, saith the LORD: but, lo, I will deliver the men every one into his neighbour's hand, and into the hand of his king: and they shall smite the land, and out of their hand I will not deliver them.

"And I will feed the flock of slaughter, even you, O poor of the flock. And I took unto me two staves; the one I called Beauty, and the other I called Bands; and I fed the flock.

"Three shepherds also I cut off in one month; and my soul lothed them, and their soul also abhorred me.

"Then said I, I will not feed you: that that dieth, let it die; and that that is to be cut off, let it be cut off, and let the rest eat every one the flesh of another.

"And I took my staff, even Beauty, and cut it asunder, that I might break my covenant which I had made with all the people."

2. In 1863, William Harrison was a twenty-five-year-old Oconomowoc farmer. He had moved from Ohio to Waukesha County in the 1840s with his parents and younger

siblings. George Ludington was twenty-nine years old and worked as a carriage maker in Oconomowoc. In addition to expecting twins at the time of the accident described in Esther's letter, he and his twenty-one-year-old wife Wealthy had a two-year-old son, Edgar. George's mother and father, Mary and Henry Ludington, also lived in Oconomowoc (1850, 1860, 1870 census). See Appendix B for more on the Harrisons and Ludingtons.

3. On July 4, 1863, Union forces repulsed an attack on the fort at Helena, Arkansas, on the Mississippi River 175 miles north of Vicksburg and 250 miles south of Columbus, Kentucky. Largely eclipsed by the surrender of Vicksburg and the retreat of Lee's defeated army from Gettysburg, both of which occurred on that same day, the Battle of Helena is sometimes called "The Forgotten Battle."

Company C of the Wisconsin's Twenty-Eighth Infantry Regiment was mostly boys from Summit and Oconomowoc. Oconomowoc's postmaster, Thomas Stevens, had helped to recruit the company in 1861 and served as its captain. The Twenty-Eighth was on garrison duty at Helena when the attack was made. About 3,500 Union troops repulsed a force of 15,000. The Twenty-Eighth Wisconsin occupied rifle pits defending one of the batteries. The total casualties of the Twenty-Eighth during that engagement were eleven: two killed, four wounded, and five missing. That was far fewer than the number who died of disease while they were stationed at Helena (Quiner, *Military History of Wisconsin*, 767–71).

4. L. B. Wright wrote a letter to the *Waukesha Freeman* telling readers of the appearance in the area of a species of plant lice (*Aphis Avenae of Fabricius*). He stated, "It is easily recognized by the oval-shaped, red body, with black antennae and legs, and the two black honey tubes, which look like hairs, from the extremity of the abdomen." The letter says the insect was seen in New England in 1861, in Ohio and Michigan in 1862, and in Wisconsin in 1863. He reassures that "no mention is made of their continuance more than one season" because of their natural predators (*Waukesha Freeman*, July 14, 1863).

◌◟◞

Columbus
July 18, 1863

Dear Esther,

Your letter was received this morning and found me well. I was glad that you were well also.

Since my last to you, we have had quite a scare here, which you doubtless have heard about; but it was nothing more than a scare. So far as this place is concerned everything is in readiness for the Rebels if they want to try it on. But they built the works here and have some knowledge of the strength of them. And they could not hold it if they should get it.

The cause of the fright was the capture of 2 companies of the 4th Missouri Cavalry stationed at Union City, 25 miles from here, by some of Forrest's band.[1] They surprised them, killed 2, wounded 7, and 3 got away. The Rebel surgeon dressed the wounded men; and they then left and went back to Jackson, where they came from, taking all the government stores with them that were there. The 3 or 4 hundred men actually there were reported as 3 or 4,000 in this place, and even a greater number was named; but the thing is quiet now or at least but little is said about it.

A new post has been established this week at Clinton, 12 miles out from here towards Union City [Clinton, Kentucky, is south of Columbus, Kentucky, and about halfway to Union City, Tennessee]. The 101st Illinois and the 24th Missouri Regiments have come from New Madrid and gone there. 5 companies of the 4th Missouri Cavalry and part of the 9th Indiana Battery have also gone there.

Thus far this month the War news has been favorable as a whole. I think that the 28th Wisconsin was not at the battle of Helena. I saw a list of the Regiments engaged and if I remember right that regiment was not among the list.

I was surprised to hear of such an accident in Oconomowoc, and it must have been the grossest carelessness on the part of those handling the gun or it could not have happened. It is a severe lesson for Oconomowoc, and I hope they will profit by it, and in future demonstration the like will not occur.

I cannot realize that so many have passed away since I left Oconomowoc with whom I was acquainted; and forcibly it reminds us that we are mortal and soon must pass away. How to live and live aright should occupy our thoughts and attention day by day. The past is beyond our reach, but the future can be improved; and if improved aright will give present and eternal peace to the soul. Our motto should be now in duty's work our faith reaching the eternal throne. Did we and all God's chosen ones thus live, the world would soon be redeemed, and the fearful scenes of strife so prevalent in our land and world would cease.

I wrote a letter to Brother J.P. but have not got an answer back. I guess it is not hardly time, however.

I think you had not better send any more papers. The last one I got was postmarked the 24th of June and I got it the 16th of July.

I am glad that James is better. I think he will recover his health again.

You did not say what the last bundle cost to get it home. I had a little curiosity to know, for I some think of sending another. But If I send it will be this week.

I had heard that an insect was at work in the wheat in Wisconsin but to what extent I did not know.

I hope you will not worry about the weeds. Could you see as I have the desolating hand of war as represented in uncultivated farms, destitute of houses, and fences grown all over with weeds, the owners gone no one knows whither. Could you see this, you could realize something of the terrible effects of war in its desolating power on cultivated nature.

I went a short time since and got some blackberries. I picked them in an old orchard about a mile and a half from here. I should judge there was a 1000 or perhaps 1200 bushels of apples in it. The soldiers are carrying them off every day, and it is a great luxury to the soldiers to have blackberries and fruit.

I have not seen as much fence since I have been in Kentucky on the farms around as I have got on our place.

I suppose the people of Wisconsin are anxious about the draft. I hope that the people will not resist, as I am satisfied it will be of no use, as men must be raised and the government must be sustained, and to do this personal sacrifices must be made. I know something by experience what it is. It is true that I have passed through but little physical trials.

Love to all.

Yours Truly,

Gilbert.

[Marginal notes]

For the last week it has been quite cool here the last 2 nights. I had my blanket and overcoat on me, and the first night I put my rubber blanket over me, as I was quite cold before morning. I have not seen so warm nights here as I have in Wisconsin by a considerable. In fact we have not had a night that my rubber blanket was not comfortable.

I am doing my regular guard duty now and have 2 nights in bed. I generally take the 3rd relief. Most of the boys do not like it as well, but I like it better. I go on at 12, off at 2, on at 6, off at 8, which is bedtime, and then on at 12, off at 2, which gives me but 2 hours in the night, on at 6, off at 8 next morning.

NOTE

1. Details and official reports of the surprise and capture of the Fourth Missouri Cavalry at Union City, Tennessee, are in Appendix D. The fighting was all over in about two hours with estimates of about six hundred men in the Rebel force compared to about one hundred Union men at the outpost. All who were not killed or wounded were taken prisoner, and horses and garrison equipage, books, and papers were also taken or destroyed (Scott, *War of the Rebellion*, vol. 23, pt. 1, 822–24).

July 21, 1863

My Dear Gilbert,

It is almost dark and I meant to have written a long letter today, but we have had company this afternoon (Miss Mary Eastman) which prevented my writing.

But I must tell you that I saw you very distinctly last night in my sleep. I went out to meet you, and saw you in the distance, and knew you by the walk. There has not been a day for a long time that I have felt so much of your presence, and I guess if you will remember; your mind has been more on home today than usual. While I was ironing with my back to the door, I could not help thinking of that roguish boy that used to come in on tiptoe and touch his fingers lightly under my arms.

Today is the anniversary of the great Bull Run Battle [First Battle of Bull Run, July 21, 1861].

Elton has just returned from the village and brought me a letter. They are the most precious things I get.

But I don't want you to forget to tell us about your health. It seems you are out of the hospital now. Have you never had diarrhea, and are you as fleshy?

Elton says Kellogg told him tonight that he would give 60 cents for our wool if he would bring it down tomorrow.

The express charges on your last bundle was 85 cents, and yesterday I washed the clothes. I think the hardware you sent made the bundle heavier than the other, and consequently cost more, but I think the clothes will more than pay the cost.

We have had but very little hot weather this summer. Our nights as well as yours have been cold. It has been pretty dry. Last Sunday night is the first rain since I wrote you about it raining. It has been too dry for potatoes to do much, but crops generally look well, the grain crop in particular. The insect I wrote about has been much thicker; some of the heads looking black, but it cannot yet be discovered that they have injured the wheat.

July 22, 5 o'clock Wednesday morning:

I am glad you do get some fruit.

We have had quite a quantity [of currants] for the bushes, but I have not enjoyed them half [as] much as if you had been here. We have sold seven dollars worth. Yesterday we had some new potatoes and string beans. We have bought a hundred pounds of flour, which cost 3 dollars, and I have paid Eastman 11 dollars for that borrowed wheat. We have received 15 more from the state, but we [can't] pay all the debts yet. I find it costs us more to live than it did last year, and more than it would if you were here.

The plum trees hang full, and so do the apple trees. We have had calls for early apples already.

If we sell the wool had we better pay Uncle John?

James and Anna started for Michigan Monday. I have never told you how badly James' hand was crippled. He cannot open it wide enough to clasp a tumbler, and he is very far from well, I can assure you. I greatly fear for him going in a new country now.

Elton has been nearly laid up for two weeks. He is having boils. He has one now under his arm. And Nelly kicked his knee. Some time ago Billy threw him and he fell on a rail and lamed his back; but he says it is well now. The rest of us are well.

I guess outdoor work agrees with me, but it makes me very black. Don't worry about my getting sick. I mean to be prudent. Warm weather and hard work agree with me.

William has returned to spend vacation, and I tell you it seems good to have some one that is a companion to speak to.

Winter wheat harvest has commenced and they tell me that spring wheat will do next week.

Since Mother sold, she stays at Goody.

Margaret's sister Mary and children are living with her this summer.

Florence is here yet and she is a very good child; don't make hardly any trouble. Emily has Arabelle, and she don't get along with her any better than I could.

I am in ecstasies of hope, for I shall soon have a husband. But I hope I am not so forgetful of my country and fellow creatures as not to sympathize with them.

We have but one Friend who can always be with us, and I feel His loving presence this morning.

Adieu,

Esther

[Written in faint pencil on a small sheet of paper]

Columbus
July 21, 1863

This morning, which is a cool one after the heavy shower in the night, finds me well; and I have been packing up these things to send home.

The book I send contains some reading matter that I thought you would like to read. You will find a flower inside which grows on trees down here, and they are the most beautiful flowering tree that I ever saw. I have not been able to learn the name as yet.

The pod that I send is from the honey locust, the same tree that has those big thorns like those I sent home.

I send home the pair of drawers that I drew and have kept a lighter pair.

These bags that I send home will be good to put apples in.

The cap box I send home the 101st Illinois flung away. The boys can use it to carry wads in when they go hunting.

I went and got some blackberries yesterday, and am living first rate.

That part of a blouse I shall want to patch things which I wear when I get home.

I think that I shall not want a nice dress coat, as the dress coat that I have is nearly the same it was when I was at home.

Gilbert

[The beginning of this letter is undated but Gilbert dates his continuation July 26]

Dear Esther,

I have not received a letter this week but shall expect one tonight.

I am on guard again today. The last time I had 3 nights in bed. We have 3 more men now for duty; 2 from the hospital and 1 from the guardhouse.

We had a terrible stormy night last night. The rains keep the ground cool, and makes it more healthy.

We are doing fatigue duty every third day. I worked Thursday and Friday about an hour and a half mowing weeds around the fort. I guess that my hands would look rather sore should I swing the cradle as I used to all day. Soldier life is a lazy one in the heavy artillery service.

I think that it is a place to put the Negro in. Part of the 2nd Tennessee Negro Regiment is a going to man the guns in this fort when we leave.

By the way, I do not want you to set any limit when you think I shall be home. I do not know, and it will depend altogether on the action of the war department when we are mustered out. All sorts of assertions and predictions are going the rounds about it, but the fact is no one here knows when. It will not be before the 10th, and if we do not get marching orders before that time we shall expect marching orders every day 'til it comes. One report is that we shall be mustered out here, but I do not think it will be done. The time fixed by said report is the 15th. I do not calculate to worry about the matter, for when the time comes it will be done, and it does not help the matter to borrow trouble as some of the men do. I shall do my duty faithfully 'til we are discharged. I am satisfied that time is out at least when we reported. Our company got pay from that time. Company B, and I think 1 or 2 companies besides, got pay from the time they were drafted; and the whole regiment might [have], had the captains reported from that time. I hope what I have written will not give you any uneasiness, as what I have written are but scratches of the pen and will not delay the time a moment. I shall come at the earliest possible point.

I did not get a letter last night as I expected. I came off from guard this morning.

July 26:

It has been a very hot day, and I have stayed in camp and did not go to meeting. If your letter does not come tonight I shall think it has gone to Memphis, a thing that frequently happens. But they will come back after a while.

In my last to you I mentioned the capture of 2 companies of the 4th Missouri Cavalry at Union City and they're going to Jackson, Forrest's headquarters. Since, the whole of Forrest's gang have been defeated and drawn from the place with considerable loss.

The war in the southwest is progressing finely, and Louisiana & Mississippi will be under Federal rule before long. Then I should rejoice could the war close before the fall is ended, and union and peace be again restored.

But there are dark features which can be seen from a southern standpoint which to a careful observer are tokens of evil. The younger men that have been driven from home and have suffered the loss of all their property will return, and, if what I overheard from 3 of them that had been forced from home while conversing of the trials they had passed through and of their determinations if the Union army permitted them to return is a sample of the feeling that exists in the minds of all, ruin may be the result. It will be the finishing stroke.

The letter did not come and I will finish this and forward it, and if it comes and wish to know anything about home affairs I will write again.

I got a letter from brother J.P. I should judge by what he wrote that he was having a very pleasant time.

I want you should inform me about home affairs and I trust before long I shall be where I can see for myself and converse freely with you all again.

I trust that God's blessing will rest upon us as a family and his approving smile rest upon us.

Yours Truly,

Gilbert Claflin

Esther's letter, July 26, 1863, page 1.

[Upside down at top]

I sent home another bundle. It is getting dark and I must close. Give my love to Uncle John's people and all —ing friends.

❧

Sunday, July 26, 1863

My Dear Gilbert,

Not many more Sabbaths shall I go to church alone. Not many more weeks shall I have an oversight of things out as well as in doors. Not many more nights shall I dream of sleeping in your arms and awaken "to find it all a dream."

I know I never half realized, until the eight months past, how entirely dependent on each other are members of the same family for happiness. We may sometimes, in days of prosperity, and particularly in our youth, feel that the sunshine of friendship encircles us, and that our friends are many and warm. But who among them all will make personal sacrifice for us, or will give us that hearty sympathy in trials that members of the same family can. I speak of this as a fact, not because I expect or desire outside sympathy. You know that I always shrunk from having domestic concerns bruited abroad.

Perhaps what drew out these thoughts more particularly now was the treatment we have received from persons, members of the same church with us, small affairs of themselves, and nothing that causes me any trouble excepting the knowledge that persons professing godliness are not even honest.

Today is a cool, pleasant day as most of our days have been for the last two weeks. Winter wheat harvest is nearly or quite over, but spring wheat has not ripened very fast the weather has been so cool. It is hardly ripe enough yet, but some are cutting for fear the insect will injure it. It has not seemed to, yet it has grown larger and blacker and has wings. I put a head of wheat in a paper and sent you two weeks ago but presume you did not get it.

William has become a member of the Capitol Guards Company A. Lieutenant Colonel Wood having resigned is their captain.[1] He thought it the best course and I am glad he has. He tells me it will not make many interruptions in his business and will not be called out of the state.

July 28:

When I commenced this I expected to finish sooner, but yesterday I washed and picked two quarts of berries, and that used up the day; and today I done some weeding, picked one quart of berries, churned, picked up some apples and pared them, and then I loped down on the lounge and had a long nap when I should have been writing to you, but did not feel very guilty for I knew William sent one today.

Harvest apples will soon be ripe. One of the russet trees broke down Sunday. It was rather windy and the tree was loaded with fruit. I should think half of it is now on the ground. It is directly opposite the other that broke down. I am afraid more will break down, and some of the plum limbs bend considerable. I am afraid they will ripen before you get home. If they should, what disposal can we make of them? I have thought it might be better to send them in to Cook than try to dispose of them at home. He had our currants and I expect Joel got nearly or quite two dollars a bushel. How much ought the plums to be a bushel if you should not get home until after they get ripe?

Don't you think Horace Kellogg is an honest man?[2] You know he does business in Milwaukee, and I think it likely he would sell them for us. But I hope you will be here to attend to it.

I guess we sold our wool in the right time for I hear it is just bringing as much now and wheat is falling owing, I suppose, to our late victories.

It is raining and almost dark.

Wednesday morning [July 29]:

Last night we had quite a heavy rain, and this morning the weather is not settled.

Last night while I lay dry and secure in bed I thought of him who had labored to obtain these comforts for his family, and was himself now exposed to the elements as well as his country's enemy.

J.P. writes that he too has to go on guard every third night. I don't wonder men are sick if for no other reason than being so often disturbed of their rest.

Mrs. Lampman tells me the 16th are at Lake Providence and it is very sickly.[3]

We have not heard from John but once, nor from Asa since the battle at Gettysburg. Mother feels very anxious about him. I think she is not many degrees removed from insanity, and has she not had enough to make her so?

Our Wednesday evening meetings are thinly attended, but we have had one accession to the number this summer: Mr. Brocaw the jeweler.

Lester Rockwell lives where Peter I. used to.

Yours in the bonds of conjugal affection,

Esther Claflin

[Marginal notes]

We are all well. Now our harvest begins to [illegible] to cradle the most of it.

Our wool came to 24 dollars and 30 cents. William attended to the sale of it without waiting for an answer.

I paid the shoe bill. It was 18 dollars. I am a little afraid to keep bills long. The debts are now all paid but Father's, and we have 13 dollars on hand and two due from Mrs. Topliff for berries.

I have now got nearly through picking.

NOTES

1. The roster of the Wisconsin Eleventh Infantry Regiment lists Lieutenant Colonel Charles A. Wood of Madison, Wisconsin. He held that rank from September 2, 1861, until he resigned on June 7, 1863. It is possible this was the same Charles Wood who was born in 1841 and grew up in Oconomowoc ("Roster of Wisconsin Volunteers," 668; 1860 census). There is a section on the Wood families of Oconomowoc in Appendix B.

2. Horace Kellogg was a thirty-three-year-old produce dealer living in Oconomowoc with his twenty-four-year-old wife Lucy and their three-year-old daughter Cora (1860 census). Read more in Appendix B.

3. The Lampman family had lived next door to Uncle John in Summit. Oren Lampman, nineteen, was serving along with Esther's brother John and several other friends from Oconomowoc in Company A of the Sixteenth Wisconsin Infantry Regiment ("Roster of Wisconsin Volunteers," 5; 1860 census). There is a short history of the Sixteenth in Appendix D, and more about the Lampman family in Appendix B.

∾

Columbus
July 30, 1863

Dear Esther,

Your letter came in due time. I received the same day I sent my last. The trouble was my anticipations were a little in advance of your good works, but we will let that all pass on.

The query before I received your letter that day, which was not 'til late in the evening: I felt sure that something was the matter of Elton, and my impression was that he had been kicked by one of the colts and badly hurt. I was glad to learn that although he had been kicked, you did not feel concerned judging from what you said about it.

Last Tuesday night our captain got back, and when the news went through the camp there were some long faces among the boys I can tell you, but they soon got shortened up. The next morning commenced a new order of things. The captain had the 1st lieutenant under arrest. I was detailed as guard and came off at 10. The captain had the orderly sergeant and the 2nd sergeant also under arrest. A vile copperhead [Confederate sympathizer] traitor belonging to our company had informed against them, and if he is not soon reaping the rewards of his traitor's work then I am no judge. I would not take his place for one day for no consideration. I could not believe did I not see it that there could be such a change in a man's appearance. He is in physical form like R. Moree of Oconomowoc. He is a deist in belief and a Mason, and so is our captain. And through this channel he has done in the company about as he was a mind to. He has not done but one guard duty. He is a substitute and came thinking to get a lieutenant commander. He finally succeeded in getting the appointment of Atipier. He came into the army to make money, and says he did. The excitement that has been in camp today has somewhat changed the program and every new order of things has a tendency to relieve the dull monotony of the camp, which often breeds discontent.

This afternoon the captain ordered us to fall in with equipments and gun. Just as we got in line the rain began to fall in sight. He finally permitted us to go to our tents. We had a terrible shower, and [it] lasted so long that when it stopped he told us that we might take off our things. We ascertained that a deserter was to be drummed out of camp, which was done. Some of the boys went and saw the performance but I had no desire. He is to be confined in prison during the war.

The captain has just passed our tent in a great rage and has forbidden our teamster letting the 2nd lieutenant have a mule to ride. He is just able to get around a little having been very sick. He vents his rage on the officers Instead of the privates though. He knows that the boys all hate him, copperhead excepted.

I guess you will think this is a strange sort of a letter. Well now I will answer your questions. You wish to know if I have had diarrhea. I have not been troubled any as yet. My eye has got well. I am not as fleshy as I was before my eye was sore. I think that I have lost nearly 15 lbs since

I put myself right down to low diet and cured my eye. I shall soon come back again, as I have a coming appetite and fruit is coming in plenty and is cheap.

You wish to know about the wool. I do not know what is best about it. If Uncle John thinks it best to sell, sell it and pay the shoe bill.

You tell me not to worry about you. Well I do not intend to let anything worry me. I have had some lessons to read since I went into the army. I have seen men make themselves miserable over that that was as much beyond their reach as is the sun. I look upon surroundings with a calmer eye and a firmer trust in God's overriding hand than I used to, and I *believe* I am prepared, or shall be, to tread the path he has marked out for me to tread.

I am glad that you seem to get along so well. I hope Elton will soon be well. My love to you all.

Gilbert

[Upside down at top]

July 31:

I am first rate this morning.

The prospect is that we shall have rain today.

I am glad Brother William had come home to spend vacation. I think you will have a pleasant time.

I should think the boys might act time to write some.

I expect that the wheat will all be cut before I get an answer to this. I have been from home so long that I hardly know what to say about the work but if nothing happens I think it will not be a long time before I can see for myself.

ᕫ

August 3, 1863

Dear Esther,

I received your letter yesterday. I was glad to learn that you were all well.

I was on guard and came off this morning. I got a pass and went down town and took a general survey of things. All the saloons are closed, as it is the day of the state election.[1] I got back about 11 o'clock.

I write so often that I can hardly think of anything which I think will be interesting. I guess I will take your letter and work upon that.

In the first place you say that it will not be many more weeks that you will have the oversight of things out of doors. I say that it is possible that you may have to do it nearly 8 weeks longer, but I do not think it probable that we shall be kept over our time. I think that you will, judging from the past, be able to carry it through and come out all right. There is one thought sets my mind at rest and that is this: the day is fixed that we shall get our discharge and it cannot be passed, and until that day comes it will be all right to stay; for an Overruling Hand controls and directs.

I have not got the paper.

I have thought of William often when thinking about the draft and am glad he has become a member of the Capitol Guard.

If I do not get home before the plums are ripe I think that Kellogg will do as well as anyone. I do not know what the price ought to be. It will depend on the quantity in market. If I could know about how many bushels there would be I could tell better what to do, but I shall be satisfied any way. Get what you can for them, and if you cannot dispose of them, don't worry about it.

I guess what I came into the army for was to learn to take things cool. I do not think I ever shall be so much in a sweat about matters and things as I used to be.

You say that I am exposed to the elements and speak of the hardship of standing guard on account of sleep. I sleep nearly as much the night I am on guard as I do other nights, and the next day I can sleep all day if I want to. But when I am all sound I do not care to pay the bunk much, though since my eye got sore I got in quite a habit of doing it, but am now breaking off as it is hurtful.

Well I suppose you are a little interested in how we get along with the captain. I can give you no better idea of how matters are progressing than by passing the remark of one of the boys the other day when a lot of us were talking on this subject. His remark was this: "The captain is as sweet as a peach." He does not act like the same man. You will see why I end a short letter.

Gilbert Claflin

[Upside down at top]

I send home this sheet of 5 to let you see how they are struck off.[2] 10, 25 & 50 are struck off in sheets of nearly the same size. You will probably need it for change and can cut it up when you like.

NOTES

1. On July 31, 1863, General Burnside issued this order from his headquarters in Cincinnati:

> Whereas the state of Kentucky is invaded by a rebel force with the avowed intention of overawing the judges of elections, of intimidating the loyal voters, keeping them from the polls, and forcing the election of disloyal candidates at the election on the 3d of August; and whereas the military poser of the Government is the only force that can defeat this attempt, the State of Kentucky is hereby declared under martial law, and all military officers are commanded to aid the constituted authorities of the State in support of the laws and of the purity of suffrage as defined in the late proclamation of his Excellency Governor Robinson.
>
> As it is not the intention of the commanding general to interfere with the proper expression of public opinion, all discretion in the conduct of the election will be, as usual, in the hands of the legally appointed judges at the polls, *who will be held strictly responsible that no disloyal person be allowed to vote, and to this end the military power is ordered to give them its utmost support.*
>
> The civil authority, civil courts, and business, will not be suspended by this order. It is for the purpose only of protecting, if necessary, the rights of loyal citizens and the freedom of election. (McPherson, *Political History of the United States of America during the Great Rebellion*, 313)

2. Beginning in August 1862, the Treasury Department issued special "postage currency," reproductions of postage stamps on larger, thicker, ungummed pieces of paper in denominations of 5, 10, 25, and 50 cents ("Mail Service and the Civil War," U.S. Postal Service, about.usps.com/news/national-releases/2012/pr12_civil-war-mail-history.pdf, accessed July 8, 2013). This may be what Gilbert is referring to in his "sheet of 5."

August 4, 1863

My very Dear Gilbert,

Time wears away, and yet I cannot say that it seems to pass slowly there is so much need for mental and vital activity that I have no need to sit down and mourn because time is so slow. I have always had a sort of indefinable feeling that the work which God has given me to do was not half done as it should be, thus I dare not wish to kill time when there is so much left undone; though I do not pretend to say that the hours have not sometimes hung heavily, many times indeed have I longed for a sympathizing friend. But the time is not far distant, God willing, when we shall hear your glad voice and feel your warm embrace.

Think not, my dear Gilbert, because I say so much about ourselves that I have forgotten our suffering Christians. Though doubtless as a Christian we have cause to rejoice, yet we have still greater reason to humble ourselves on account of our great sins.

This terrible riot in New York is enough to send sorrow and dismay to every heart.[1] This great National trouble that is now upon us has, I believe, spread a shadow over my life that time will never obliterate.

I had the satisfaction of sending some dried fruit to our suffering soldiers. Our state agent at Memphis sent out a call for old clothes and dried and preserved fruits, and it was promptly answered by the Soldiers Aid Society in Oconomowoc.

Yours of the 30th and 31st came to hand last night and I was a little surprised that any of my letters should not get to you as soon as you would expect unless the mails were at fault, for I can't remember that I have been delinquent. I think I can realize pretty well the anxiety you feel when it is time to get a letter. I have had no occasion for complaint on that score today.

William has left for Chicago to attend the National Teachers Association and expects to return Friday night. He finished cutting the wheat, and cut part of the oats, and now I think the boys can cut the rest well enough.

Since our harvest commenced we have had hot weather, though it is a little cooler yesterday and today. The middle of last week was very hot and showery. The cistern, which was drawn dry last spring, is more nearly full; and Price has turned the water off. We have sold two bushels of apples, and if they don't get stole we shall have four or five more.

I see on looking at my book that there was no plums sold last year until September; so if you live to come home I need not trouble myself.

Gilbert, I want to beg a little now. I've tried to be a good faithful wife since you went away, and have managed your business to the best of my ability (though I expect it is poorly managed at that); but your earnings have paid part of the debts and there are more now on our hands; only Father and the wagon if you take it, and we have 15 dollars more coming from the state, and you must have something, and we shall have a good many apples to sell. Now don't you think you are able to buy a coat as I want you to? You have got plenty of other good clothes, and I don't feel as though I wanted you always to be confined to a military coat. Now if you can resist this appeal you must be impervious to all persuasion. I have been looking at my book and find that you have sent home 71 dollars, and I have paid out seventy-two for debts.

I was in hopes that your captain would stay away 'til the expiration of your term. But it won't be long that you will have to go at another man's bidding. Which do you like the best, to be under the control of a man or woman?

Mother has had a letter from Asa written from Warrenton, Virginia, July 28. He says they have been marching and battling ever since the 6th of June; was in the battles of Beverly's Ford, Gettysburg, Williamsport, and has marched over five hundred miles since that date; says he is very well.

Mother has received a few lines from Anna. They are stopping at Ed Jones' in Greenville, Montcalm County, Michigan.² Jones and James are to look land together I believe. She says they are well

I have just been ironing your linen so that you can have some clean clothes when you get home. It might be a good plan to draw one or two outside shirts before you come. It is only twelve days more.

Good bye,

Esther Claflin

[Written sideways in margin]

Dan Tompson is married to young Wilber.

NOTES

1. Draft riots occurred in numerous areas around the country. One of the worst was in New York City soon after the names of the first draftees were published in the papers on July 12, 1863. The city had a large and powerful Democratic party, and New York's governor Horatio Seymour openly opposed Lincoln and his policies. The people of New York had already heard of the thousands killed and wounded at Gettysburg a week earlier, and of Lincoln's call for 300,000 more soldiers. Many of the rioters in New York were poor Irish immigrants who resented inequities in the Enrollment Act that favored the rich and objected to fighting on behalf of African Americans with whom they competed for the lowest-paying jobs. The mob of rioters in New York numbered about 50,000 people and did more than a million and a half dollars' worth of damage. The Army of the Potomac was eventually sent to restore and maintain order in the city ("New York City Draft Riots (July 11–13, 1863)," Shotgun's Home of the American Civil War, http://www.civilwarhome.com/draftriots.htm).

2. The *Michigan State Gazetteer and Business Directory* for 1863/64 describes Montcalm County as follows:

> This County is situated near the geographical center of the lower peninsula, and is bounded on the north by Mecosta and Isabella, east by Gratiot, south by Ionia, and west by Mecosta and Kent. It has eleven organized townships, and embraces an area of 576 square miles. The county is well watered by branches of the Grand, Muskegon and Saginaw rivers, and occupies an elevated position from which the waters run in all directions. The surface is rolling, the soil various, and good in all

parts. Heavy forests of pine, oak, walnut, birch, and maple, extend over a large portion of the county. The various streams furnish an abundance of water power. The
following are the organized townships: Bloomer, Bushnell, Cato, Crystal, Eureka,
Evergreen, Fairplain, Ferris, Greenville, Montcalm, and Sidney; total population,
according to census of 1860, 3,984; number of occupied farms, 298, having 14,247
acres of improved land, and 20,223 unimproved. Number of bushels of wheat
raised, 36,144; corn, 20,339; oats, 16,379; potatoes, 13,390; pounds of butter, 55,515;
maple sugar, 51,136. Whole number of children attending school, 1,159. (Charles
F. Clark, *Michigan State Gazetteer and Business Directory* [Detroit: Charles F. Clark,
1863], 313)

The same *Gazetteer* describes Greenville as follows:

A post village in the township of Eureka and county of Montcalm, situated on Flat
River, 60 miles from Lansing, 33 from Grand Rapids, 150 from Detroit, and is the
terminus of the stage route from Ionia to Greenville. It contains 500 inhabitants.
It has three churches, to wit; Methodist, Congregationalist, and Baptist. The Flat
River affords good water power, which propels two saw mills and two flour mills
at the village. It contains also a steam saw mill, several stores, manufactories and
mechanic shops; one printing office, from which is issued a weekly newspaper;
one Masonic society (Greenville Lodge, No 96). It has a daily mail from Ionia, and
semi-weekly from Grand Rapids. *Postmaster*—Joseph M. Fuller. (Clark, *Michigan
State Gazetteer and Business Directory*, 334)

[Written in faint pencil on a small sheet of paper]

August 4, 1863

Dear Esther,

You are doubtless looking for me every night, but the prospect of our
being mustered out this week is rather slim, and when we shall be is all a
matter of uncertainty. Government officials do not hurry in their work, but
take things cool. I have got tired of staying here and doing nothing. A new
order has just been issued confining us to the city limits.

The 34th Regiment is to be organized and all the commissioned officers
are authorized to receive rent for the regiment, but if they keep us a week
longer, they will not get many that are not in the 34th. The boys are getting
savage in their talk and will, when called upon to enlist, remind them of the
way they were used while in the old 34th.

Report says now that we shall be mustered out next Monday, but there is
no telling when. I hope you will not worry about it, as it will do no good. I
think that I shall get enough of military life by the time I am out. I have but
little time to write as I must go to the post office and it will take 'til night.

Columbus
August 9, 1863

Dear Son,

I was glad to get a few lines from you again. I expect that you have got the grain all cut by this time. It is the first harvest I have not worked in a long time.

I guess that you and Elton will understand how to do business if you improve as you ought the lessons you are now taking.

I have done but little manual labor since I have been here, and expect it will be rather hard on me to commence hard work, but I shall come in by degrees.

The last 3 days we have had a fine cool breeze. If it was not for the wind it would be hot. For the past 2 months the wind has been most all of the time in the south, but we have not had such extreme hot weather this far as I expected to see, and I do not think we have had any warmer weather than you have had in Wisconsin.

I think Summit gets her share of the hard storms. I should have thought that if it tore down fruit trees so near that it would have affected our orchard some when loaded with apples.

I am glad that you are having such good luck with your chickens. I hope it will continue.

I should like to know what you let that fox get away for. I never learned the particulars.

I should judge that you were getting your hand in in the duck line. I would not object to taking a plate of stuffed duck. I think it would relish first rate.

I think if I get home all right I shall not grumble much at the fare I shall get at home judging by the past. We had for dinner pork, cabbage, potatoes and onions, bread & coffee.

Since my eye got well I drink coffee and tea. The water is so bad that I cannot go it, and I get sick of sweetened water. I drink 3 cups a day and can get along very well on that.

Your Father

[Upside down at top]

I hope you and Elton will be good boys 'til I get home and do as your Mother says.

෴

Columbus
August 9, 1863

Dear Esther,

I went to the Presbyterian Church this forenoon, and we had an excellent discourse from the 84th Psalm, 11th verse.[1] The number present was not large, but little interest is manifest among the white population in religious things. Reverend Mr. Talbot, the [looks like "student"] minister of the place, after Sabbath School spoke of the prevailing practice of church members here letting their children play in the streets during the day. He thought that they were not training up their children in the way they should go.

I received your letter last night and was glad to hear of your prosperity. I trust it will not be long before I shall see you all. We expect to be in Wisconsin this week if nothing happens, but everything is so uncertain in military affairs that we may be detained longer than we expect. We expect the 6 companies at Memphis here the first of the week, but I shall not be greatly disappointed if we do not get back to Wisconsin as soon as we now expect. I hope you will not feel bad if it should happen that we should stay longer than the 12 days you have set. I have not got the time figured down so close yet, and when we get on the cars going through Illinois I shall begin to think we are soon to see Wisconsin. I have heard so many stories about going back to Wisconsin, and so many times &ct that I do not believe hardly anything I hear on the subject.

The beautiful steamer Ruth was destroyed by fire on the night of 4th about 4 miles up the river from this place.[2] 30 lives were lost. 2,600,000 in greenbacks was also lost, 100 head of cattle & 150 mules were burnt and drowned. A large number of government stores were also destroyed. The money was going to pay Grant's army, and they will feel the loss, as they will not probably get any pay for 2 months now.

The 31st Wisconsin have not got any pay the last two paydays. All the rest of the troops in this post got their pay. It is owing to the rascality of the officers. It has been ascertained that at the last payment they got, and I guess the only payment that they have got from the government, the officers drew pay for men that were not in the service, and in some instances men got pay in 2 companies, being mustered in each to fill up the companies. The families of some of these men are actually suffering for the necessaries of life. The government would pay the men if they could, but the officers have got the payrolls of the companies, and refuse to make them out, if I have been rightly informed, as they cannot get theirs. The whole affair is creating a considerable excitement. I think the final results will be the removal of most of the officers and the instituting of a new order of things. They cannot be kept over another payday; if they are, the government cannot hold the men longer than 6 months if they are where they could be paid.

I think your appeal respecting the coat rather of a setta on me. I shall have to take a look at some if I get time when I go to Milwaukee, but how would you like to have me make the same application to you in the clothing line. I shall expect you will have things to match my fine coat which you want me to get. My clothing has cost me $42.60 the last 9 months, and I ought to be satisfied with that. I could have drawn some shirts yesterday, but it is now too late. I was a little sorry I did not when I saw what the boys got; they were white, half wool and half cotton, and suited me the best of any I have seen since the first ones we drew. I have not got a hole in those I drew first, and have worn them every day. I bought a shirt a few days ago to wear nights. I gave 62 cents for it.

I hardly know what to say about your writing any more to me here. If you do not hear from me again this week, or by the middle of next, you may send another letter. But I guess you will.

Gilbert

NOTES

1. Psalm 84, verse 11: "For the Lord God is a sun and shield: / The Lord will give grace and glory: / No good thing will He withhold from them that walk uprightly."

2. In a letter dated August 6, 1863, General Asboth in Cairo, Illinois, wrote to Major General Halleck the following details of the burning of the steamer Ruth: "The steamer Ruth, on her trip down the river with cargo of stores, and between two and three millions of money, in charge of eight pay-masters, for Vicksburg, burned last night between Cairo and Columbus. I have sent the steamer Crawford to render all assistance possible, and requested Fleet Captain Pennock, commanding navy station at Cairo, to make all efforts for the recovery of the money boxes. The wreck is in Lucas Bend, 4 miles below Norfolk. Between 20 and 30 lives are supposed to be lost" (Scott, *War of the Rebellion*, vol. 24, pt. 3, 580).

ᔐ

[Gilbert dates this letter July 16, but it clearly comes after his August 9 letter when he was still in Kentucky. The sequence of dates he mentions in this letter, and his mention that it is a Sunday, leads me to believe he was writing August 16.]

Camp Washburn, Milwaukee

July 16, 1863

Dear Esther,

We are once more here in camp. We came in this afternoon.

I am well but a little tired after such a trek. We turned in our guns on the morning of the 13th at Columbus. We went on the steamer about an hour before sundown, and left just as the sun was setting. We got in Cairo about ½ past eleven, landed, and spread our rubbers on the ground right in the street, and slept 'til morning.

We stayed 'til night, and during the day I took a survey of the place. It is quite a business place.

It rained quite hard just before we got ready to start. We had to go in boxcars, and we had a snug time of it nights. It was a short pattern and a narrow one. When we had got about half way from Cairo to Chicago one of the flues in the boiler burst and let the steam and water onto the fire—put the fire out in short order. It happened right by the water tank. All the water run out as low as the break. It hindered us 2 hours or more. We got into Chicago about daylight, stayed about 3 hours, then went on the cars bound for Milwaukee. Had a pleasant trip, but the march from the cars to camp was a hard one. The hardest marches we have had was when we left this camp and when we returned.

Lieutenant Calkins wished me to tell you he is well, and he says he is coming out to get some fruit when I get back.[1]

I cannot say when I shall be home. It will depend on how the company officers have kept the papers. I may be home before I am mustered out if it is going to take too long, but should prepare to stay 'til the work is done. The order from the War Department was to the effect that we should be mustered out the 15th.

I am now writing in my old bunk. Price will know where it is situated in the barracks. My old bunkey is with me. He was sick for a long time and was in the hospital at Mound City [an Illinois town on the Mississippi River about thirty-five miles north of Columbus] when we got marching orders, and was released. He is getting strong again but quite thin in flesh.

I think the company will average a loss of 15 pounds to the man. Before I had sore eyes I was fleshier than I usually am in the summer, but now I am about 10 pounds below my usual weight, which makes me look quite thin; but I am gaining, and if nothing happens I soon shall soon make it up.

It looks like home here, and I think we can spend 3 or 4 days quite comfortably.

The report is just circulated that our pay stopped yesterday, the 15th. If so, the officers have no more to do with us, and they will be obliged to make out our payrolls and give us our discharges at once. But so many stories are going in camp one hardly knows what to believe. I shall be home as soon as I can.

This day has not seemed much like Sunday, but I trust it is the last I shall have to spend in camp. I hope this will find you well.

Love to all.

Yours truly,

Gilbert Claflin

NOTE

1. Henry T. Calkins was first lieutenant of Gilbert's company. He was from Merton, Wisconsin, a town about eleven miles northwest of Summit ("Roster of Wisconsin Volunteers," 526).

August 24, 1863

My Dear Husband,

We have been looking for you every night. I go down to meet you, and think I am prepared not to be disappointed if you don't come, but find that I am. I feel so weak it is hard work to get home again, & my mind has been more harassed and unsettled for the last week than any other week since you have been away.

As the time neared for you to come home, I did not dare to indulge in very high anticipations for fear they might be crossed. My impression is that you are to be kept to assist in the draft, and I am sure I had rather you would fight Rebels at home than abroad, but I can't be reconciled to your living kept in this way.

You are needed here very much. The boys are running wild, and the cattle and colts are getting very troublesome.

I don't dare to leave home unless I can get the promise of a boy to stay by all of the time. We are all getting cross. I expect the occasion of it is disappointment in your not returning.

William is here yet but expects to return to Madison by the middle of next week. He helped the boys get in the grain and was very sick the next day, and has been quite unwell since. Elton has been complaining all of the week—has got a bad cold.

I guess I shall try to get the boys to commence ploughing

I don't mean to complain about your being kept, but I think there is a fault somewhere. You are in a place even to try your patience some. Can you come out and see us if you can't stay?

Your letter came to hand tonight. Mr. Collins handed it to Elton.[1]

Fruit is ripening. I don't know as we shall make a profitable disposal of it all.

Elton is fooling with the horses this morning. He is not willing to mind or do anything else. I hope the horses well be sold as soon as possible.

Adieu for the present,

Esther Claflin

Your letter came last night.

NOTE

1. Washington W. Collins was one of the earliest settlers in Oconomowoc. In 1844, at the age of twenty-two, he and George W. Fay opened Oconomowoc's first store. In the early days of the store, one could buy whiskey for as little as 25 cents a gallon. By 1860, Mr. Collins had been given the prestigious job of Oconomowoc's railroad station agent and was living in Oconomowoc with his wife Julia and their six children (Potter, Punko, and Leitzke, *Historic Oconomowoc*, 2–4; Johnson, *Illustrious Oconomowoc*, 14–15, 19; 1860 census). Read more about Washington Collins in Appendix B.

September 5, 1863

Dear Esther,

I thought when I last sent word to you that we should be mustered out so that I should be home this week, but I shall not be able to. We are now assured that we shall be mustered out next Monday, but I still have doubts. We have signed the payrolls and the paymaster is figuring up the amount due us. Our captain says it cannot be delayed beyond Monday. It will probably take a couple of days to do all the business when they commence.

I am very sorry that I cannot be home on Sunday, but I could not get back Monday morning in time as our company is the first to be mustered out. We have been told from day to day that we probably should be mustered out tomorrow, but the papers were not properly prepared, and some of the officers had to get there to do them before they were right, but they are all in and signed now and there can be no excuse in this direction any longer.

My health is good now, and what I eat does me good. I hope you will be reconciled to your lot and not be discouraged because I do not come home.

I hope the boys will do the best they can about home and get wood enough. I think that they had better begin to give the cattle corn stalk if they have not begun.

We shall not probably sell many plums in Milwaukee as the market is full of them the like I never saw, but perhaps in a short time there may be a change for the better as to marketing, but I shall not worry about it.

If I can get out of the 34th Regiment it will be satisfaction enough in a worldly point of view for a long time.

Gilbert.

⌒

[Probably early September]

My Dear Gilbert,

I some expected a line from you last night but it did not come.

If you get a coat for Elton you know as well as I about the color. Grey would be better for a boy than black if it don't cost too much. I think the waist and sleeves would need to be as much as an inch and a half longer for him than you.

I think you had better see about selling the Siberian crabs. If we don't get very big price it will be better than nothing. I guess the greengages will be ripe the very first of the week.[1]

William left for Madison last night.

Price has gone to Mr. Spinney's school today.[2] It is the last day.

Elton has gone this afternoon to see Alexander's boys.[3]

I feel anxious to hear from you, Gilbert, for I fear this cold wet weather will make you worse if you get down sick. Let me know, and I will come and stay with you while you stay.

Your emaciated purse haunts me.

I believe I shall be thankful when you are released and can come home to stay.

This fall weather a premonition of the coming winter always brings an indivertible gloom to my mind, but I guess I shan't have to live alone another winter and the best-loved one far away *in camp*.

But thank God your life is spared.

Esther Claflin

NOTES

1. Siberian crab apple (*Malus baccata*) has extremely fragrant blossoms in early spring and small red fruit, good for preserves, in the fall. Greengage plum (*Prunus domestica* ssp. *italica*) has sweet fruit that are green when ripe.

2. Charles E. Spinney was one of the registered teachers of Waukesha County. In 1863, he lived with his wife Elizie and their one-year-old daughter Bessie (*Waukesha Freeman*, May 27, 1862; "Proceedings of the Teachers' Institute of Waukesha County," *Waukesha Freeman*, April 14, 1863; 1860, 1870 census). Read more about him in Appendix B.

3. In 1863, John Alexander lived in Oconomowoc with his wife Eliza and three sons: Robert, John, and William. John, Eliza, and Robert were born in Ireland, and moved to Wisconsin in the early 1840s. William, the youngest, was eighteen in 1863, a year older than Elton (1860 census). See more about the Alexander family in Appendix B.

Epilogue

As soon as Gilbert was mustered out, he returned to his farm and family in Summit. He was finished being a soldier. Esther's brothers continued to serve in the Union army, though James's health never improved enough for him to do so, and William served for only the last nine months of the war. Asa Call Colby, Esther's second-youngest brother, was killed at the Battle of Resaca on May 15, 1864. J.P.'s wife Margaret wrote to John Colby on June 11, 1864:

> Mother had a letter from his Captain this week. He wrote that he was shot at Resaca. That when the regiment went into battle, his company were deployed as skirmishers. That after skirmishing for two hours (if I remember the time) the enemy made a heavy charge and drove them back, and that some of the company were left dead and wounded on the field, Asa among the latter. After fighting three hours longer they regained their position, driving the enemy before them. When the Captain came up he found Asa unable to rise. He was shot through the right lung, he was suffering very much and requested the Captain to take his knife and cut off his knapsack. He did so; then took Asa's rubber blanket, had four of the men lift him onto it and take the four corners and carry him from the field to the rear. They soon found an ambulance, and he was carried to the hospital. As he was taken from the field his last words to the captain were: "Captain, if I die, write to Mother."[1]

The Civil War ended with the fall of Richmond and Petersburg, Virginia. Another of my great-great-grandfathers, Enos James Montague, the

Asa Call Colby.
(collection of
Arlene Thurs)

Congregational minister in Oconomowoc, was there serving with the Christian Commission. On April 5, 1865, he wrote to his parents:

> While the army was quiet my work consisted in visiting the soldiers in their tents, talking with them upon the subject of religion, distributing to them religious papers, letter paper & envelopes & the like, & in preaching to them & holding meetings with them as there was opportunity. This kind of work continued about two weeks after I came.
>
> But when the army moved & the fighting began, a full account of which you have doubtless read in the papers, a very different work came upon us. Then we had to care for the wounded as they were brought in from the battle field. On Sat & Sab the two great battle days. we gave coffee & crackers to probably 2000. There were 9 of us together. We were at Humphrey's Station, the farthest point on the railroad, to which point a large part of the wounded were brought. From thence they were brought to the Hospitals here: & from here they are transferred to northern hospitals as fast as possible.
>
> It was pleasant to help the poor fellows & to do something to alleviate their terrible sufferings. And yet it was a very severe & painful work such as I should not wish often to engage in. It was the horrible side of war. But when so great & decisive a victory followed the battles, I felt quite cheered.

Our tent was within a short distance of a part of the battle so that we could hear the musketry & see some of the soldiers. The artillery firing on Sat. night from 10 o'c till 10. Sab morning was most terrific & incessant. It extended all along the lines & exceeded anything I ever conceived. We did not know at the time how the battle would turn, but when on Sab morning we heard that the rebel works had been entered, that Sheridan was victorious on the left & when pretty soon we saw as many as 6000 rebel prisoners brought in, & heard that our army was advancing on Petersburg our joy was very great.

But our rejoicing reached its height when on the next day we were not only assured that Petersburg was taken but were permitted actually to go into the city. I went in with the army train, past our own works, past those of the rebels & into the very midst of the stronghold of the rebellion, & staid there all night. The Chr. Com. took possession of a large tobacco store by the permission of the Provost Marshall. The blacks were most enthusiastic in their welcome of the union forces, but the whites were sullen & looked at us from behind shutters & half open doors. While we were on our way we met Pres Lincoln, returning from Petersburg. It was the first time I ever saw him. He was on horseback with a small escort & walked slowly along, receiving & returning the salutations of the soldiers & teamsters.

Three weeks later, home in Oconomowoc, Enos wrote again to his father on April 25:

I was at Washington on Tues. & Wed. of last week & had the sad pleasure of seeing the silent remains of our dear Pres. Lincoln. Such an affliction, as it seems to us, has never before fallen upon this nation. As I came along my route home everybody seemed to be in mourning—scarcely a house was to be seen without some emblem of sorrow upon it. It was like Sab. day in Baltimore & Philadelphia.

Life continued on for the Colbys and the Claflins. In March 1866, Gilbert and Esther had a third child, Alice Marion. Esther's brothers left Wisconsin. There was much talk among them of taking advantage of the Homestead Act, and J.P. did homestead in Kansas for a while. J.P. finally settled in Iowa, William in Arkansas, and James in Michigan.

Price Colby Claflin, Gilbert and Esther's younger son, became a jeweler and moved to Stevens Point, Wisconsin. In 1872 he married Elizabeth Hooker Montague, the daughter of the Congregational minister from Oconomowoc.

On October 16, 1878, Gilbert's mother died. Four months later, on February 13, 1879, Gilbert died at the age of fifty-six. They are both buried in Lot 132 of the Summit Cemetery. Esther stayed on in Summit with Elton and Alice Marion until 1884 when they all moved to Stevens Point to be near the rest of the family. Esther died in Stevens Point in 1900.

In 1888 Price and Elizabeth moved to Washington, DC, where Price became an optician. He and Libby, as she was called, had seven children: six in Stevens Point and one after they moved to Washington, DC. The last, Marguerite Esther Claflin, was my maternal grandmother. Marguerite was born prematurely and weighed only about two pounds at birth. She was not expected to live, but was wrapped in cotton wool and put in a shoebox beside the fire while Libby was tended. Price Colby Claflin died in Washington, DC, on December 28, 1914.

Three of Price and Elizabeth's children were Harry, Elsie, and Marguerite. After Price's death, Elizabeth lived first with their son Harry and his wife Eunice Claflin in Washington, DC; and then with their daughter Elsie and her husband Julius Payne near Philadelphia.

Marguerite Esther Claflin married Harold Ellsworth Warner on June 20, 1916. They, too, lived in Washington, DC. Their eldest child was my mother, Elizabeth Anne Warner. After Marguerite died in 1931 when my mother was ten years old, my mother lived for a time with her aunt and uncle Elsie and Julius Payne, as well as at home in Washington, DC.

My mother was close both to her aunt Elsie, who was like a mother to her after her own had died, and to her grandmother Elizabeth Claflin. Grandma Claflin paid for my mother's education at Oberlin College (two of Esther's brothers, J.P. and William, had visited Oberlin in 1853 in their quest for a teacher's education). It is very likely that the Civil War letters of Gilbert and Esther Claflin were given to my mother either by her aunt Elsie Claflin Payne or by her grandmother Elizabeth Montague Claflin. I found the letters in a box of "important papers" in 2002, after my mother's death.

NOTE
1. Margaret Sommerville Colby's June 11, 1864, letter to John Colby is in the collection of my cousin, Arlene Thurs of Waukesha, Wisconsin, and is quoted with her permission. Other family letters quoted in this Epilogue are in my collection.

Family

In 1862 when the letters begin, the forty-acre Claflin farm is in the most northern section of Summit Township, and Gilbert Claflin has been a farmer as long as he can remember. He has just passed his fortieth birthday and lives with his wife of seventeen years (thirty-two-year-old Esther), their two sons (Elton fifteen and Price thirteen), and his mother.[1] Gilbert's widowed mother is sixty-one-year-old Achsah Maria Kibbie Claflin; her husband Joshua died at the age of twenty-five when Gilbert, their only child, was just over a year old. She moved to Wisconsin with him when they left his uncle's farm in Massachusetts.

Esther's parents, James and Abigail Colby, had ten children (seven boys, three girls). Two of the boys died young. Then about a year ago, in 1861, James and Abigail sold their farm and separated. However, both still live nearby and help their grown children as much as they can. Many of Esther's siblings also continue to reside nearby. Esther's closest brother William works at the school in Summit and is a frequent visitor. Her other brothers are serving in Wisconsin infantry divisions. The eldest, Jonas Parmenter, is in Kentucky with the Thirteenth. James, three years younger than Esther, is with the Twenty-Fourth and is also in Kentucky. Asa and John, the youngest brothers, are unmarried and in their early twenties. Asa is with the Third and actively involved in the war in Maryland and Virginia. The youngest of the family, John, is with the Sixteenth in Wisconsin. The oldest sister, Emily, lives nearby, but she is struggling as a single mother. The youngest sister, Wealthy, has moved to Stevens Point and is married.

Outline of Gilbert's and Esther's Families

Gilbert's Family, Descendants of Joshua Claflin

Joshua Claflin (1798–1823)
+ Achsah Maria Kibbie (1801–1878)
   Gilbert Elton Claflin (1822–1879)
   + Esther Patience Colby (1830–1900)
   married November 27, 1845
      Elton Abijah Claflin (1847–1923)
      Price Colby Claflin (1849–1914)
      + Elizabeth Hooker Montague
      married October 8, 1872
         Gilbert Montague Claflin (1873–1880)
         Harry Edwards Claflin (1875–1927)
         Mabel Faith Claflin (1878–1934)
         Edward E. Claflin (1880–1900)
         Paul Claflin (1884–1884)
         Elsie Grace Claflin (1886–1985)
         Marguerite Esther Claflin (1891–1931)
      Alice Marion Claflin (1866–1947)
      + Niels Eugh Reton
      married October 14, 1887
         Leora Marguerite Reton (1890–1950)

Esther's Family, Descendants of James Colby

James Colby (1798–1871)
+ Abigail Metcalf (1803–1887)
   Jonas Parmenter Colby (1823–1901)
   + Margaret Sommerville (1835–1917)
   married May 22, 1858
      Cordelia Minona Colby (1859–1933)
      Elmer E. Colby (1861–1917)
      William Colby (1868–1940)
   Emily Colby (1825–?)
   + Evelou Crosby (?–?)
   married November 14, 1847
      Ellen Crosby (1850–?)
      George Crosby (1851–?)
      James Crosby (1853–?)
      Arabelle Crosby (1854–?)
      Florence Crosby (1856–?)
      Anna Crosby (1858–?)
   Price Colby (1826–1848)

William Milton Colby (1828–1916)
+ Mary Jane Gurney
married September 4, 1867
    Rose A. Colby (1870–1879)
    Mabel Colby (1878–?)
Esther Patience Colby (1830–1900)
+ Gilbert Elton Claflin (1822–1879)
married November 27, 1845
    Elton Abijah Claflin (1847–1923)
    Price Colby Claflin (1849–1915)
    + Elizabeth Hooker Montague
    married October 8, 1872
        Gilbert Montague Claflin (1873–1880)
        Harry Edwards Claflin (1875–1927)
        Mabel Faith Claflin (1878–1934)
        Edward E. Claflin (1880–1900)
        Paul Claflin (1884–1884)
        Elsie Grace Claflin (1886–1985)
        Marguerite Esther Claflin (1891–1931)
    Alice Marion Claflin (1866–1947)
    + Niels Eugh Reton
    married October 14, 1887
        Leora Marguerite Reton (1890–1950)
Wealthy Asenette Colby (1832–1908)
+ George N. Doty (1833–1889)
married October 14, 1861
    Bertha Doty (1866–?)
    Roy Doty (1878–?)
James Metcalf Colby (1834–1892)
+ Anna Maria Jacques (1841–1913)
married November 8, 1860
    Milton John Colby (1862–1923)
    William Tecumsah S. Colby (1864–1865)
    Maria Abba Colby (1866–1943)
    Io Vesta Colby (1869–1896)
    Alta Ruth Colby (1873–1958)
    James Metcalf Colby (1883–1960)
Smith Rogers Colby (1837–1840)
Asa Call Colby (1840–1864)
John Barrus Colby (1842–1876)

ESTHER'S BROTHERS AND SISTERS, TO 1863

The three oldest Colby children, J.P., Emily, and Price, were all born in Machias, Cattaraugus County, New York. William was born in Thompson, Geauga County, Ohio. Esther was born in LeRoy, Geauga County, Ohio. Some time in the early 1830s the family moved back to New York and the next four children, Wealthy, James, Smith, and Asa, were all born in Freedom in Cattaraugus County. The youngest of Esther's siblings, John, was born in Wyoming County, New York.

Jonas Parmenter (J.P.) Colby and Margaret Sommerville Colby

Jonas Parmenter Colby was the oldest of the Colby siblings, seven years older than Esther and just a year younger than Gilbert. Sometimes folks called him Parmenter, but most often he was "J.P." He had a farm and family of his own in Ixonia, Wisconsin, ten miles northwest of Summit.

Back in October of 1861, J.P. joined the Thirteenth Wisconsin Infantry, Company H. By 1862 when the letters begin, he had been out of Wisconsin for ten months. About half that time his regiment was in eastern Kansas joining a series of expeditions, each abandoned in turn. They marched to Leavenworth, toward Fort Scott, up to Lawrence, west to Fort Riley, and back to Leavenworth.

Eastern Kansas was an area embroiled in its own Civil War since the Kansas-Nebraska Act became law in 1854. Each of the two territories was to decide by popular vote whether it would be a slave or a free state. Nebraska would certainly come in as a free state, but thousands of settlers on all sides of the question had come to Kansas ready to fight. Horace Greeley of the *New York Tribune* used the phrase "Bleeding Kansas" to describe the resulting violence. Kansas finally entered the Union as a free state on January 29, 1861.

Since the beginning of June, J.P.'s regiment had been in western Kentucky guarding railroads and supply steamers, and keeping surveillance over guerrillas. The men had been at Columbus, Fort Henry, and Fort Donelson. At the beginning of November, they joined the pursuit of the notorious John Hunt Morgan.

John Hunt Morgan was a Confederate general who led daring cavalry raids far into Union territory. In the fall of 1862, word came that he was then in Kentucky. The Thirteenth Regiment joined a fruitless expedition in pursuit. Upon their return in mid-November, they moved back to Fort Henry where they remained most of the time Gilbert was in Kentucky.

Margaret Sommerville was one of the many first-generation Americans who moved with her family from New York to Wisconsin in the mid-nineteenth century. She married J.P. Colby in 1858. In November of 1862 they had a sunny three-year-old daughter, Cordelia Minona, and a year-old son, Elmer. Margaret was expecting a third child, but miscarried late in the month. The burden of not having J.P. at home was great, yet she was helped by visits from her sister Mary and J.P.'s sister-in-law Anna, both of whom had young children of their own.

Emily Colby Crosby and Evelou Crosby

Esther's older sister, Emily Colby Crosby, had a hard life. Late in 1847 she married Evelou Crosby, and they had six children in quick succession: Ellen (1850), George (1851), James (1853), Arabelle (1854), Florence (1856), and Anna (1858).

By 1860, Evelou was no longer in the picture. We don't know what happened to him, but Emily and her six children were living with her father James Colby in Oconomowoc when the census was taken. Evelou and the three older children are not mentioned in any of the letters. The family genealogies have their names, birth years, and for all except Ellen their place of death, but not the years.

Seven-year-old James Crosby was actually counted twice in the 1860 census. In June of that year, he was at his grandfather's in Oconomowoc with the others. In July, he was counted along with his uncle John Barrus Colby at the home of his uncle J.P. Colby in Ixonia.

Gilbert and Esther don't mention the three oldest Crosby children in their letters of 1862–63. It sounds as though the three little girls were moving about, living with various relatives, and Emily may have been living with an employer (farmers Elijah and Washington Perrin). In her November 30 letter, Esther wrote, "Perrins won't have Emily if she has more than one child."

In 1862, eight-year-old Arabelle was a bit of a problem. In her December 18 letter to Gilbert, Esther described her as full of scowls and snarls. During the course of the letters, she lived for a while with Esther; then with Esther's mother, Abigail; and finally with her own mother, Emily. None of them found her easy to live with. Six-year-old Florence and four-year-old Anna were easier than Arabelle, but they also moved among Esther, Abigail, and Emily.

Price Colby

Price Colby was four years older than his sister Esther. A handwritten obituary notice for his mother, tucked into the *Metcalf Genealogy*, tells about the events leading up to his death in June 1848, just over a year before his namesake nephew, Price Colby Claflin, would be born. "When 21 yrs he signed up with a company supposedly going to the west. In reality a conscripting scheme for the Mexican War (of which he disapproved). He contracted fever in the South and a family took him until he died and wrote of him in the highest terms. '*Died* of congestive fever in Monroe Co. Arkansas on the 23rd of June 1848 Price Colby, aged 21 yrs 8 mos. and 26 days.'"

William Milton Colby and Mary Jane Gurney

William Milton Colby was two years older than his sister Esther. They were close. Esther's letters are full of what William said and advised. When Esther sent her husband a letter she got from William in late January 1863, she cautioned that the letter was "glowing with brotherly love and full of high and noble sentiments. . . . I don't want you to think I endorse all he says about me."

William taught from time to time at the Summit school. Usually school terms were three or four months in summer and four in winter. In the spring and fall, so many of the children were needed to help on the farms that it was not appropriate to hold school. Sometimes, when school was not in session, William came to live with his sister Esther and help with the farmwork. There is more about William in the section on the Summit school in Appendix C.

The June 14, 1862, issue of the *Oconomowoc Free Press* lists William as one of twelve officers of Summit Lodge No. 184 of the Independent Order of Grand Templars (I. O. of G. T.), a temperance organization that was begun in 1850. The other names include ones we recognize from the school district: the Hildreths, Comstocks, and Kimballs. The I. O. of G. T. was one of the first fraternal organizations to admit both men and women—half the officers of the Summit chapter were women.

Wealthy Colby Doty and George N. Doty

Wealthy Colby was never mentioned in the letters, though she was Esther's sister, two years younger. On October 14, 1861, she married George N. Doty in Stevens Point, Wisconsin, about one hundred fifty miles northwest of Summit. The census of 1860 shows Wealthy Colby, a schoolteacher living with another schoolteacher in Stevens Point; and George N. Doty, a daguerreian artist, also living in Stevens Point.

The process for making early photographs known as daguerreotypes was discovered in France in 1837. An excerpt from *The Daguerreian Journal* in 1851 states, "The Daguerreian Artist should possess quick perceptive powers; an eye for the beautiful, which will enable him at a glance to decide on expression and position. He will promptly, yet judiciously, select the view of the face most favorable for the just disposition of light and shadows—having placed the seat and chosen the most graceful and becoming position for the body, draperies, &c."

In 1880 Wealthy and George Doty were living in Stevens Point with two children: fourteen-year-old Bertha and two-year-old Roy.

Wealthy and George are both buried in Block 9 of the Forest Cemetery in Stevens Point. Wealthy's dates are given as July 27, 1832, to November 25, 1908. George's dates are given as April 19, 1833, to October 26, 1889.

James Metcalf Colby and Anna Maria Jacques Colby

James Metcalf Colby, one of Esther's younger brothers, taught school in Delafield five miles away. In November 1860, at the age of twenty-six, he married nineteen-year-old Anna Maria Jacques from Nova Scotia, Canada. Their first child, Milton, was born in 1862.

At the end of August 1862, James joined the Twenty-Fourth Wisconsin Infantry, Company G. They trained briefly and then headed for Kentucky. Their first encounter was the Battle of Chaplin Hills, known in the South as the Battle of Perryville, on October 8. It is an interesting side note that many Civil War battles have two names; in such cases the Federals usually use names of natural landmarks and the Confederates use names of man-made features.

After the battle, James's regiment joined in pursuit of retreating Rebel forces as far as Crab Orchard, Kentucky. From there they marched south and east to Mill

Creek, near Nashville, Tennessee, where they set up camp on November 22. They marched more than three hundred miles in forty-two days. Somewhere along the way, James became ill. Most likely he had contracted dysentery from drinking polluted water. Dysentery was a major killer of soldiers during the Civil War and would account for James's chills, fever, and diarrhea. We don't know if he was too ill to take part in the Battle of Stones River at the end of December or whether that battle just worsened his condition. We do know his regiment had to "lie on their arms" through the night and suffered much from intense cold without fires. By March, James's illness warranted his discharge and left him an invalid for months to come.

Twenty-one-year-old Anna and her baby Milton spent a lot of time with the women of her husband's family. November 19, the Wednesday before the letters began, Anna and Milton came to the Claflin home hoping to visit with Gilbert one last time before he was off to the war. They arrived just hours after he left. They stayed most of a week with the Claflins. Esther had had experience with babies, which must have been comforting to Anna. Elton and Price were old enough to be enjoyable companions as well. Then Margaret, J.P.'s wife, had a miscarriage. Anna hurried to Ixonia to stay with her and help take care of Cordelia Minona and little Elmer. Several days later, Anna went to stay with her mother-in-law. Here again, Anna was staying with a woman who was suddenly without her partner. Abigail had separated from her husband, James Colby, and they were living in different houses in Oconomowoc.

Smith Rogers Colby

Smith Rogers Colby was the only one of Esther's siblings who did not survive to adulthood. Only his name is mentioned in the *Metcalf Genealogy*, but the *Sandford-May Genealogy* shows that he was born in 1837 and died in 1840 while the Colby family was living in Cattaraugus County, New York.

Asa Call Colby

Esther's mother, Abigail Metcalf Colby, named her two youngest children after her sisters' husbands: Asa Call and John Barrus. Most of what we know of Asa is from family letters and his military record.

When war broke out in April 1861, Asa joined the group of young men who tried to raise a company of cavalry. They called themselves the "Oconomowoc Cavalry Guards" and elected Asa a corporal. Like many others, Asa left the Guards to join the conflict as soon as he felt ready. Perhaps this constant turnover was the reason the Oconomowoc Cavalry Guards never went into service intact.

In June 1861, Asa joined the Union Army when he was twenty-one years old. He served in Company K of Wisconsin's Third Infantry Regiment. Organized at Fond du Lac, Wisconsin, sixty miles north of Summit, his regiment contained very few from Asa's hometown.

After spending the first fall and winter mostly based at Frederick, Maryland, the Third Regiment advanced, retreated, and skirmished up and down the Shenandoah Valley. On August 9, 1862, they took part in the Battle of Cedar Mountain. Asa was wounded, as were sixty-four others in his regiment. Twenty-seven were killed or died of their wounds. Asa was moved to hospitals in Annapolis and Frederick, Maryland, and Washington, DC. He was still in the hospital recovering from his wound on September 17 when his regiment took part in the Battle of Antietam. Out of the 345 members of the Third who commenced the action that day, fewer than 50 were not killed or wounded.

Life was quieter for the regiment until late April and early May 1863, when it was again involved in a series of battles in which another ninety-three members of the regiment were killed or wounded. It was shortly after this period that Esther, referring to the Battle of Chancellorsville, wrote, "May 21: Mother . . . has had a letter from Asa since the battle. He was in that awful battle at Fredericksburg; had his gun shot from his hands, but got off without any scratches save what the bushes scratched him."

Asa's regiment fought at the Battle of Gettysburg and pursued the retreating Confederates. His family did not hear from him until August 4, 1863, when Esther wrote, "Mother has had a letter from Asa written from Warrenton, Virginia, July 28. He says they have been marching and battling ever since the 6th of June; was in the battles of Beverly's Ford, Gettysburg, Williamsport, and has marched over five hundred miles since that date; says he is very well."

John Barrus Colby

John Barrus Colby, Esther's youngest brother, was six weeks shy of his nineteenth birthday on April 14, 1861, when President Lincoln called for seventy-five-thousand men. He immediately joined Wisconsin's First Infantry Regiment for a three-month term of service.

The First Regiment went to Harrisburg, Pennsylvania, and then Hagerstown, Maryland. While at Hagerstown in June of 1861 he wrote a letter to his older brother William back in Summit. The letter was published in the July 5, 1861, issue of the *Oconomowoc Free Press*.

Hagerstown, Md. June 18.

Dear Brother:—Here I am at one of the outposts of secession. We left Chambersburg Sunday noon for this place. At Greencastle, on the route, the people had prepared a collation for us. Although four thousand troops had preceded us, and all were served alike, we had enough.

On our arrival at this place the streets were crowded with people, but there was no particular manifestation of feeling either for or against us.

At the late election there were but one hundred secession votes polled in Washington Co., of which Hagerstown is the Co. seat. On the evening of our arrival here we were received by Gen. Patterson and Gov. Hicks. The General complimented us highly, and said we should go into the hottest of the fight. I guess he means it.

Last night, as I was on sentinel duty a messenger came galloping up the street to the Colonel's tent with despaches [sic]. He immediately ordered the *long roll* to be beat, and soon the camp was astir, and the voice of the Co. was heard above the din, giving orders to the officers to have the men load their pieces, and be ready to march in half an hour.

The report was, that the Indiana Reg't was hemmed in at Williamsport, and had sent for aid. The boys sprung to their pieces with a will, and were soon on their way; and we were left guarding a deserted camp.

Soon another messenger came with orders for the other Reg'ts to move:—In one hour four Reg'ts of infantry and one of horse were moving towards Williamsport, leaving the whole camp in charge of one hundred men.

All night we paced our beats, impatient for the morning.

To-day there are conflicting rumors as to what the troops are doing; one is, that they have crossed the Potomac and are driving the rebels before them; another is, that they are on their way back, so the boys are now preparing supper for them.

Yesterday, camp was thronged with visitors, all of whom were for *'The Union, the Constitution, and the enforcement of the Laws.'*

June 22.

I commenced this letter the 18th, but was so completely exhausted by being on guard almost forty-eight hours, that I could not finish.

The men returned from Williamsport on the evening of the 18th, without seeing the enemy.

It is rumored that our regiment will be ordered to Washington.

This is a beautiful and healthy country, and the season some weeks earlier than in Wisconsin. The winter wheat is already *yellowing*.

To a western man, this country seems very ancient. There is a mill near camp over one hundred years old, and I noticed a building in town with "1772" carved on the gable.

The citizens here manifest great interest in the welfare of the soldiers.— Every day the ladies send up some delicacy for the sick in the hospital.— both military men and civilians take great interest in our Regiment. They say it is the best in the place.

A few days since a lady of refinement and education, arrived here through much tribulation, from Richmond, Va. She escaped by means of a forged pass, and declares she will never return till she can be protected by the old banner of *Liberty and Union*.

J.B. Colby.

John's regiment, with the rest of Major General Patterson's Federal army, left Hagerstown on June 30 to invade Virginia.

On July 2, 1861, they participated in the Battle of Falling Waters. This was Confederate Thomas J. Jackson's first engagement with Federal forces. His competent command that day led his superior to recommend that "Colonel Jackson be promoted without delay to the grade of brigadier-general." It was later that month, at the First Battle of Manassas, or Bull Run, that he was given the nickname of "Stonewall" that stayed with him for the rest of his life.

From Virginia, their three months expired, the First Wisconsin returned to Milwaukee and were mustered out on August 21, 1861.

Wisconsin's First Regiment was quickly reorganized for a three-year term, but John Colby was not a part of it. Less than six months after he was mustered out of the First Regiment, John joined Company A of Wisconsin's Sixteenth Infantry Regiment.

The first fight for Wisconsin's Sixteenth Regiment was the battle of Shiloh, one of the severest of the war. The battle was made extra hard by want of food; the men had been called to action before breakfast, and were engaged for ten hours without rations. By the end of the afternoon, 225 members of John's regiment had been killed or wounded.

After Shiloh, their encounters included the siege and battle at Corinth, April 29 to June 10, 1862. Among the wounded at Corinth was Corporal John B. Colby. The regiment remained in camp near Corinth until November 2.

By November 3, less than a year after they were mustered in, the Sixteenth Regiment was so reduced by battles and sickness that the ten companies of the regiment were consolidated into five and half the company officers were discharged. It was perhaps from one of these men that Gilbert learned of John's promotion. It is little wonder that Esther, writing to Gilbert in late January 1863, said John, returning to war after a furlough, "looks as solemn as the grave, and he barely spoke unless asked a question."

OTHER FAMILY MEMBERS

Amos

In the letter of March 21, 1863, Gilbert reported that a letter from Celinette said Cousin Amos was in the gold diggings west of the Rocky Mountains, and that his family were in St. Paul.

Celia

In the letter of May 29, Esther asked Gilbert to tell Cousin Celia they felt the effects of the war.

Celinette

In the letter of March 21, Gilbert reported a letter from Celinette about Cousin Amos.

Edmund C. Davis

Edmund C. Davis was Esther's cousin from Raymond, Wisconsin. He was a wagoner, discharged from Wisconsin's Twenty-Second Infantry Regiment on April 25, 1863, because of a disability.

In the letter of March 12, Esther said he was in the Twenty-Second Wisconsin Regiment captured near Murfreesboro, Tennessee. In the letter of June 24, Esther reported that he was in the hospital when his regiment was captured and was now home, discharged. In the letter of July 12, Esther said that he and his wife came to visit.

John Metcalf

John Metcalf was Esther's uncle, Abigail Metcalf Colby's closest brother, two years younger. John was married to Mahala Meade and had a successful shoe store with his partner George Kinnee. An advertisement in the *Oconomowoc Free Press* in 1862 promised "All the late styles and descriptions of BOOTS & SHOES FOR MEN, WOMEN and CHILDREN, together with FINDINGS, LEATHER, and MOROCCO" as well as "Custom Work made to order, in the best style and on short notice."

John and Mahala lost infant twin daughters in 1862. We know about their loss only from a gravestone in the LaBelle Cemetery in Oconomowoc. In Section E, Lot 55, Grave 4 is an obelisk. On one side is, "John Metcalf, died February 22, 1884, aged 78 Ys 7 Ms 11 Ds." On another side is "Mahala Metcalf, 1830–1915," and below that, "Twin Daughters of John and Mahala Metcalf, January 1862."

When the letters began, John and Mahala were expecting a child in April of 1863, and helping to care for other people's children. They helped with John's niece Emily Colby and her young daughters, but most notable was Franciss "Frankie" Lockwood, the daughter of a former business partner. Frankie—from the letters of February 16, February 18, and April 20, 1863—was a troubled teenager, about sixteen years old, who had left school. The 1860 census shows John Metcalf living with thirteen-year-old Franciss Lockwood and sixteen-year-old Ellen Gridley.

John and Abigail were two of twelve siblings in the first decades of the nineteenth century, and were always very close. Esther's daughter wrote in her family record that she heard her great uncle John Metcalf say that when the family moved to western New York from Vermont in 1815, he and Abigail, aged 10 and 12 years old, rode horseback all the way. Twenty-nine years later, they moved much farther west. The *Waukesha County Land Records from 1839 to 1865* show John Metcalf and Abigail's husband James Colby both bought their first land in Oconomowoc in 1844.

In the letters, Uncle John was mentioned often. On March 12, Esther asked if they should give the bounty money to Uncle John for safekeeping. The same date, Gilbert suggested borrowing some money from Uncle John. On March 26, Esther asked if the window sashes for their new house would be like Uncle John's; Gilbert replied that they would. On April 16, Esther said that Uncle John was providing Emily with flour. The same day, Elton wrote that Uncle John had a new baby boy. Esther added, on April 20, that his family was prospering and that Uncle John's wife had had an easy labor. In the same letter, she mused that it was a pity Uncle John had so much trouble with other people's children, referring to Frankie Lockwood. Gilbert sent love to Uncle John's folks on May 2 and again on July 26. On May 29, Esther wrote, "Uncle John says when he used to run the river, the men carried the bark of the sweet gum tree in their pockets, and if they had an attack [of diarrhea], chew it and they would be well the next day." On June 9, Esther wrote that

Price spoke to Uncle John about working his tax. On June 29, she wrote that Uncle John advised against selling the wool too soon. In the same letter she wrote, "I go to Uncle John for advice occasionally, and I find that I can do business better than I ever thought I could. Uncle J. always seems glad to have me come to him. They both send their love. Their baby grows finely. I rallied him a little about beginning to raise babies after I had got through. He thought I had not better brag too soon." On July 21, Esther asked if they should pay Uncle John with money from selling the wool; Gilbert answered on July 30, "If Uncle John thinks it best to sell, sell it and pay the shoe bill." That would have been paying Uncle John since he owned the shoe store.

FAMILY MEMBERS AFTER 1863

Gilbert's Mother

On October 16, 1878, Achsah Maria Kibbie Claflin died at the age of 77 at Gilbert and Esther's home in Summit. She is buried in Lot 132 of the Summit Cemetery.

Esther's Parents

James Colby died in Oconomowoc on January 24, 1871. The 1880 census shows Abigail Metcalf Colby living with her son J.P. and his family in Irvington, Iowa, twelve miles from Wesley. Her obituary says she died August 10, 1887, at the home of her son.

Gilbert and Esther

After he was mustered out, Gilbert Elton Claflin returned to the farm in Summit. He and Esther had a third child, Alice Marion, in March 1866. Gilbert died February 13, 1879, and is buried in Lot 132 of the Summit Cemetery with his mother. Their tombstone says he was 56 years, 4 months, and 25 days.

Esther Colby Claflin moved to Stevens Point, Wisconsin, in 1884 and lived there until her death in December 1900. She is buried in Block 6 of the Forest Cemetery in Stevens Point. Her daughter Alice Marion Claflin Reton also has a stone in that block.

Jonas Parmenter Colby

In 1868, Esther wrote to her brother John that J.P. had secured a homestead in Kansas. The 1870 census shows him in Algona, Kossuth County, Iowa, with wife Margaret and their children: eleven-year-old Cordelia Minona (this census lists her as Momona), nine-year-old Elmer, and two-year-old William. At that time, J.P. was a clerk in a real estate office.

The 1880 census shows him in Irvington, Kossuth County, Iowa, with his mother Abigail and his son Elmer. His occupation is given as "farmer."

The 1900 census shows him living alone in Rush Lake, Palo Alto County, Iowa. "Headstones Provided for Deceased Union Civil War Veterans, 1879–1903" (online at Ancestry.com) indicates Jonas P. Colby, Private in Co. H Thirteenth Wisconsin Infantry, died February 5, 1901, and is buried at Riverview Cemetery in Algona, Iowa.

Emily Colby Crosby

In August 1868, Esther wrote to her brother John that Emily planned to go to Milwaukee where she hoped to find work as a nurse.

The 1880 census shows her in District 127 of Milwaukee, a fifty-five-year-old widow living alone.

William Milton Colby

William enlisted in Wisconsin's Forty-Ninth Infantry Regiment on February 23, 1865. Later that year he was promoted to Sergeant Major on March 6 and to Second Lieutenant on June 19. The regiment was stationed at St. Louis and Rolla, Missouri, where they did garrison and guard duty before mustering out November 8, 1865.

After the war, William married Mary Jane Gurney (some genealogies spell it Gurnee) on September 4, 1867, in Cottage Grove, Dane County, Wisconsin, and went to work as superintendent of schools in Arkansas. In this position he was to "take cognizance of all that is being done to educate refugees and freedmen, secure proper protection to schools and teachers, promote method and efficiency, correspond with the benevolent agencies which are supplying his field, and aid the Assistant Commissioner in making his required reports." He remained in this position until he retired in 1870. In August 1868, Esther wrote to her brother John that William's wife had visited, and that William had expected to visit Wisconsin and Michigan but, for reasons unknown, telegraphed his wife to come home. The 1870 census shows William M. Colby as the superintendent of education, living in Little Rock, Arkansas, with wife Mary J. Colby and one-year-old daughter Rose A. Colby.

The 1880 census shows a teacher, William Colby, living in Avoca, Iowa, with the Dancy family (parents and five children aged one to twelve) and a younger schoolteacher. It's quite possible this is our William since other information in the census shows that he was born in Ohio at the right time and both his parents were also born in Vermont.

An 1885 census from Algona, Kossuth County, Iowa, shows William M. Colby (fifty-six) living with Mary J. Colby (forty-six), Rose A. Colby (fifteen), Mabel Colby (seven), and Abigail M. Colby (eighty-two).

The 1900 census shows William in Wesley, Kossuth County, Iowa, as a retired teacher living with wife Mary and twenty-one-year-old daughter Mabel. Wealthy's obituary in 1908 lists William of Wesley, Iowa, as her only surviving sibling.

Iowa cemetery records show W. Milton Colby, born 1828, died 1916, buried in Riverview Cemetery, Kossuth County, Iowa.

Wealthy Asenette Colby Doty

The 1880 census shows Wealthy living with her husband George N. Doty and two of their children, Bertha (fourteen) and Roy George (two), in Stevens Point. In 1900, she is listed as Wealthy (census spelling is Welthy) Doty, widow, living in Stevens Point with Bertha (twenty-four, census spelling is Berthy) and Roy (eleven).

Wealthy Colby Doty is buried in Block 9 of the Forest Cemetery in Stevens Point, as is her husband George Doty.

James Metcalf Colby

James did move to Michigan. The 1870 census finds him living in Big Rapids, Mecosta County. He was thirty-six and his wife Anna was twenty-nine. (The census record was mis-transcribed as twenty-three. Also, James would have been thirty-five when the census was taken on June 7, 1870, but since his birthday was July 12 perhaps he was thought closer to thirty-six.) Their children were Milton (eight), Maria (four), and Io Vestra (one, listed as Jo W). James's mother Abigail was staying with them at that time, as was nineteen-year-old Eva Powers, a Canadian seamstress.

In 1880 the family was still in Big Rapids and consisted of James (forty-five), Anna (thirty-eight), Milton (eighteen), Maria (fourteen), Io (ten), and Alta (six), plus two servant women. Another son, James Metcalf Colby, Jr., was born April 13, 1883.

James died June 19, 1892, in Big Rapids, Michigan, and is buried in Delafield, Wisconsin, in the cemetery lot of Anna's father.

Asa Call Colby

Later in 1863, Asa re-enlisted as a veteran for the remainder of the war and was promoted to corporal. His regiment (the Third) guarded rail lines in Tennessee. In May 1864, he went to Georgia where he fought in the Battle of Resaca (May 15). Losses in the Third were light compared to the battles of 1862 and 1863, but of the ten men killed, one was Corporal Asa Colby. The letter J.P.'s wife Margaret wrote to John Colby on June 11, 1864, following Asa's death is reprinted in the Epilogue.

John Barrus Colby

John was discharged from Company A, Sixteenth Regiment, on May 1, 1863, "civil authority, minor." Soon after that, he joined Company M, First Ohio Heavy Artillery, and served until after the end of the war. On June 27, 1865, John, in Greenville, Tennessee, wrote to his brother James in Greenville, Michigan, that he was not planning to re-enlist.

In 1868 he was living in Elk Rapids, Michigan, where he received a letter from his brother J.P. detailing homestead options in Kansas and Missouri.

Elton Abijah Claflin

Elton lived with his sister Alice Marion Claflin Reton for the rest of his life. They continued to live in Summit for several years. In 1884 they moved with their mother to Stevens Point, Wisconsin, and after Esther died they moved to San Diego, California. Elton farmed and did carpentry. He died in January 1923.

Price Colby Claflin

Price became a jeweler and moved to Stevens Point. He married Elizabeth Hooker Montague at Fort Atkinson, Wisconsin, on October 8, 1872, and brought her back to Stevens Point. Elizabeth Montague was the daughter of the Congregational minister in Oconomowoc.

The 1880 census shows the family living in Stevens Point with the following members: Price C. (thirty), Lydia [Elizabeth] H. (thirty), Bert (six), Harry (four), and

Mabel (one). In the column on the census form headed "Is the person [on the day of the Enumerator's visit] sick . . . ? If so, what is the sickness?," Bert shows "Diphtheria." The stone in the family grave plot at Stevens Point says he died June 10, 1880, aged six years, nine months, and twenty days.

According to an entry in RootsWeb's World Connect project, "Price was a jeweler in Stevens Point, Wisconsin. About 1886, he moved his family to Knoxville, Tennessee, then to Cincinnati, Ohio, before finally moving to Washington, DC, a few years later. There, he obtained an M.D. degree and became an Optician, operating a store in that city for nearly a quarter of a century."

The 1930 edition of *Washington Past and Present* said that Price graduated from the Chicago Ophthalmic College and—after living a short time in Knoxville and Cincinnati—moved in 1888 to Washington, DC, where he established an optical business at Ninth and F Streets, which he ran until his death. Price and Elizabeth had seven children, six in Stevens Point and one after they moved to Washington.

Marguerite Esther Claflin was Price and Elizabeth's youngest child. She married Harold Elsworth Warner, and their first child was Elizabeth Anne Warner who married Hubert Edmund Stiles. Third of their four children was Judith Anne Stiles (now Judy Cook), this book's editor.

Price Colby Claflin died in Washington, DC, on December 28, 1914.

Alice Marion Claflin Reton

Alice Marion married Neils Reton on October 14, 1887. They had one daughter, Leora Marguerite Reton, on July 12, 1890. Leora married Stephen A. Nyland on September 21, 1915, and she died in Los Angeles in 1950. Alice died September 21, 1947, in Lorraine, California.

NOTE

1. Information on the family is from the letters of Gilbert and Esther Claflin; family genealogies including *Metcalf Genealogy*, a handwritten document compiled by Marion Claflin Reton, Gilbert and Esther's youngest child; the genealogy records of Arlene Thurs, great-granddaughter of Esther's brother James Colby; and federal censuses from 1850 to 1880. Exceptions are as follows: dates of Joshua Claflin's birth and death and the date of Achsah Maria Kibbie's (spelled Achsa Maria Kibbe in that record) birth are from *Massachusetts, Town and Vital Records, 1620–1988* (available through Ancestry.com); Achsah's death date is from her gravestone in Summit Cemetery; death dates for Price's children are from *Brose/Johnston Family Tree*, a family tree put together by descendants of Edward William Hooker and Faith Trumbull Huntington (Price's wife's maternal grandparents) and made available through Ancestry.com; and Smith Rogers Colby's birth and death dates are from *Sandford-May Genealogy*, a family tree put together by descendants of Esther's brother John Colby and made available through Ancestry.com. Military information in this section is mostly from "Roster of Wisconsin Volunteers" and Quiner, *Military History of Wisconsin*; both of these sources are easily accessible through the Wisconsin Historical Society's website at http://www.wisconsinhistory.org/civilwar/regiments.asp.

Neighbors

Surnames and the Census

The spelling of names in old records is variable.[1] Take the Newnham family as an example. Howard's and Henry's military records, as well as the censuses of 1870 and 1880, have the surname of Newnham; but the 1860 census is Newnahm, the 1850 census is Newham, and Esther Claflin spells it Noonham.

In addition, the various censuses list Mr. Goodell as P. W. Goodell in 1850, as P. Watson Goodel in 1860, and as Prescott Goodell in 1870. Esther and Gilbert sometimes write Goodall and sometimes Goodell.

Even Gilbert and Esther Claflin appear as Gilbert and Esther Claflins in the 1860 census and as Gilbert and *Hester* Claflin in the 1870 census.

Alexander Family

The 1860 census shows forty-five-year-old John Alexander living in Oconomowoc with his wife Eliza (thirty-six) and three sons: Robert (nineteen), John (seventeen), and William (fourteen). John, Eliza, and Robert were all born in Ireland. The Alexanders were a farming family.

In the 1850 census, the family was living in Sullivan, Wisconsin, with Eliza listed as Elias. This census was taken September 19, and the ages were listed as John (thirty-three), Elias (twenty-seven), Robert (nine), John (eight), and Wm. B. (five). I could not find them in the 1870 census.

In an undated fall letter, Esther reports that Elton had gone to see the Alexander boys.

William Allison

William Allison was a blacksmith in Summit. The 1860 census shows the Allison family living in Summit. William (forty-six), Margaret (forty-two), and Elizabeth (twenty) were all born in Scotland. The next two children, Cornelius (fifteen) and

James (twelve), were born in Canada. The four youngest—Fanny (eight), Andrew (five), Mary (three), and Maxwell (one)—were all born in Wisconsin.

The 1870 census shows Margaret and the four youngest children living in Elgin, Wabasha County, Minnesota, more than two hundred miles to the northwest, with John C. Allison a twenty-eight-year-old farmer. Cornelius was living nearby with his young wife Minerva. Also nearby was another farming Allison family; it included twenty-six-year-old William, eighteen-year-old Emma, and their infant son William.

In his letter of February 12, Elton wrote that Mr. Allison died of diphtheria.

ALVORD FAMILIES

It seems likely that the Lew Alvord mentioned in Esther's letters is the man listed in the 1860 census as Muric and in the 1870 census as Minich. He has a growing family with the eldest child named Louis (or Louisa). The Mr. Alvord who bought Esther's mother's house for Lew's family was probably his father, Justin. The 1860 census shows fifty-six-year-old Justin and fifty-three-year-old Sarah Alvord living in Summit next door to Esther's Uncle John. In Oconomowoc were Muric (twenty-nine), Ann (twenty-four), and their three-year-old daughter Louisa Alvord. The 1870 census shows the younger family still in Oconomowoc: Minich (thirty-nine), Ann (thirty-two), Louis (twelve, now listed as male), Jesse (eight), and Ulyses (two). Both Justin and Muric have mason listed for occupation in 1860. In 1870, Minich is listed as a bricklayer.

In her letter on December 18, Esther wrote that Lew Alvord's wife was sick with typhoid. On June 19 she wrote that her mother, Abigail, had sold her place for two hundred dollars to Mr. Alvord for Lew's family.

WILLIAM BARTON

The 1860 census shows a William Barton living in Mukwonago, Wisconsin, ten miles south of Summit.

In the letter of April 16, Esther wrote that she heard Mr. Barton was poorly.

BAXTER FAMILY

The 1860 census shows forty-nine-year-old Orpha Baxter living in Summit with her two sons: nineteen-year-old Harmon and sixteen-year-old Henry. By that, Harmon Baxter was twenty-two years old in 1863. Another source says Harmon Baxter was born September 18, 1837, and died November 20, 1881, in Granite Falls, Minnesota; thus, he would have been twenty-five in April 1863.

In his letter of February 16, Price wrote, "I expect there will be another wedding before spring. Frank Lockwood is going with Harmon Baxter to all the dances." In her letter of April 20, Esther wrote, "I guess Frank is ruined beyond redemption. She left school in the winter, and has been toting about here and there, and out with Baxter almost every night; and now she is in Summit at his mother's part of the time." Franciss (Frank) Lockwood was about Elton's age, sixteen.

CATHARINE BOYER

The 1860 census shows thirty-year-old Catharine Boyer living in Summit with John W. Boyer (thirty-one) and Eugene L. Boyer (seventeen). In the same household was another family: twenty-five-year-old Henry and twenty-year-old Harriette Bowers with their children Alma (two) and Rupert (two months), as well as a Betsey Hull (fifty-seven). This household was next to Mrs. Brainard mentioned in Esther's December 18 letter.

In her letter of February 12, Esther listed Mrs. Boyer as one of the subjects for prayer at the prayer meeting.

PHILANTHA BRAINARD

The 1860 census shows Philantha Brainard, a thirty-two-year-old woman living with her two children, Emma (ten) and Albert (seven), in Summit as part of the family of Darius and Betsey Baker. Darius was a farmer from the state of New York. He was sixty-seven, and Betsey was fifty-three. Also in the household were two of their grown children, Lucinda (thirty-five) and Dennison (twenty-two).

In her letter of December 18, Esther wrote that Mrs. Brainard was sick with typhoid.

BRAKEFIELD FAMILY

The 1860 census shows Thomas Brakefield, a farmer living in Summit with wife Mary and children Maria (nineteen), Edward (eighteen), and Louisa (eleven). The 1873 *Atlas of Waukesha County* shows their farm of one hundred fifty-five acres adjacent to that of Cooledge Eastman's and about two miles south of the Claflins'.

In Esther's letter of April 8, she said Price and Elton got seed wheat from the Brakefields.

WILLIAM CAMPBELL

The 1860 census shows a thirty-eight-year-old farmer named William Campbell (the same age as Gilbert) living in Oconomowoc with his wife Roseannah (twenty-eight) and two children, Walter (eight) and Martha (six). Next door was another New York farmer who might well be his brother: Harvey (thirty), living with Hannah (thirty-three), Charles (nine), William (seven), Celesta (five), Harvey (four), and Thimothy (one). An older woman, Betsey Campbell, who also lived with Harvey, might be the mother of William and Harvey.

In Gilbert's November 21, 1862, letter, he said he sent Esther a line out of camp with William Campbell.

MELINDA AND LEANDER CHRISTIE

The 1850 census shows thirty-five-year-old Melinda Christie (spelled Christy in the census) and twelve-year-old Leander Christie (also spelled Christy in the census) living with George and Ann Williams and their family in Oconomowoc. The 1860 census shows Melinda (forty-five, tailor) and Leander (twenty, farmer) living in Oconomowoc next door to Esther's father, James Colby.

Leander Christie (spelled Christy in the roster) mustered in August 11, 1862, with Company C of the Twenty-Eighth Wisconsin Infantry organized by the Oconomowoc postmaster Captain Stevens. After its service in the Yazoo Pass expedition, the Twenty-Eighth was engaged in fatigue duty near Helena, Arkansas. On June 22, 1863, during that duty, Leander died of disease.

In Esther's letter of July 5, she said that Mrs. Christie was in poor health and received news of her son's death.

Reverend Luther Clapp

The 1860 census shows Luther Clapp as a forty-year-old Congregational clergyman living in Wauwatosa, Wisconsin, in Milwaukee County. He was living with his wife Harriet (forty) and their children: Harriet (thirteen), Emma (twelve), Mary (nine), Wardner and Sarah (both four), and Grace (eight months). They also lived with a twenty-year-old domestic servant, Ann Pruertcom.

In her January 10, 1863, letter, Esther reported that while she listened to the church sermon, she wondered whether Gilbert might be listening to Mr. Clapp or Mr. Love. Gilbert was then stationed at Camp Washburn on the outskirts of Milwaukee.

Gilbert's letter of January 30 said he attended Reverend Mr. Clapp's church.

George Clark

The 1860 census for Summit shows a household headed by George Clark, a forty-six-year-old farmer. The household included his wife Helen (forty-seven) and their children Hattie (seventeen), Festus (twelve), Clinton (eight), and Eddy (six). Also in the household were Mary Maxwell (twenty-two, housemaid), Urania Hovey (seventy-six), and George Bino (fifty-five, gardener). Finally, there was William Clark (twenty-seven), listed as gentleman.

Elton reported in his letter of February 26 that Mr. Clark had sold his place.

E. D. Coe

There is no record of a Mr. Coe in Oconomowoc in the 1860 or 1870 censuses, but an advertisement in the *Oconomowoc Free Press* in June 1862 read:

> NEW LUMBER YARD, / IN OCONOMOWOC / — / I have opened a
> Lumber Yard at the Depot Grounds, in the village of Oconomowoc, where
> I shall keep on hand a full assortment of / PINE LUMBER, TIMBER,
> PICKETS, LATH AND SHINGLES, ETC. / which I shall sell at the Lowest
> Cash Prices. Have made such arrangements that I can fill any bill of
> Lumber that may be required. E. D. COE.

In her letter from May 20, 1863, Esther asked Gilbert if she should let Coe have all the fruit his father's folks want in return for lumber, and Gilbert answered yes.

Washington W. Collins

Washington W. Collins was one of the first settlers in Oconomowoc. In 1844, at the age of twenty-two, he and George W. Fay opened Oconomowoc's first store. In the early days of the store, one could buy the best grade of brandy for $2.50 a gallon, and whiskey for as little as twenty-five cents a gallon. In 1868, Fay and Collins's store was sold to hotelman Topliff who made it into a wayfarer's inn and then sold it to Martin Draper. Draper Hall became famous for weddings, banquets, and balls for wealthy families escaping the summer heat of St. Louis, New Orleans, and Memphis. When Oconomowoc was incorporated as a city in 1875, Washington W. Collins was elected its mayor.

By 1860, Washington Collins had been given the prestigious job of Oconomowoc's railroad station agent and was living in Oconomowoc with his thirty-six-year-old wife Julia and their six children: Sumner (eleven), Wallis (nine), William (seven), Julia (five), Solom (three), and Nellie (two). In 1870, now listed as Wallace W. Collins, he was still station agent and his household included Julia (forty-five), William (sixteen, a telegraph operator), Kate (fifteen), Earnest (thirteen), Nellie (twelve), and Charles (nine). The Collins Family Tree on Ancestry.com clears up the naming confusion: Washington is listed as Washington Wallace Collins and his fourth and fifth children are listed as Julia Kate and Solomon E.

In Esther's August 24 letter, she said Mr. Collins handed Gilbert's letter to Elton.

John Comstock

The 1860 census shows John and Sarah Comstock, both twenty-five years old, as another farming family from New York living in Summit. They had a three-month-old daughter, a farmhand, and an Irish maid living with them.

In Esther's letter of December 16, John Comstock was one of the people she listed as having died recently of diphtheria and typhoid fevers.

Thomas Cook

The 1870 census shows Thomas Cook, a forty-year-old grocer living in Pewaukee, Wisconsin, about fifteen miles east of Oconomowoc. His household included Sarah Anne (twenty-two), Thomas (thirteen), Frederick (twelve), John (nine), Wallace (seven), George (six), and Caroline (five months). It seems likely this was the Cook mentioned in the letters, though no first name is mentioned and I cannot find a corresponding record in the 1860 census.

In Esther's letter of July 26, she talked about sending both apples and currants to Cook for sale.

Danforth Family

The 1860 census shows the Danforth family in Summit: Edward aged thirty-two, born in 1827 in New York; Nancy, thirty, born in 1829 in New York; Edward, eight, born in 1851 in Wisconsin; Anna, four, born in 1855 in Wisconsin; and Mary, one, born in 1858 in Wisconsin.

The Danforths are mentioned in Esther's letters of January 10, February 12, May 4, and July 5.

MILES AND WILLIAM DODGE

The Dodge brothers, Miles and William, were farmers in New York. In about 1846, the Dodges moved their young families to Wisconsin. By 1859, the two Dodge families were living on adjacent farms on the shore of Oconomowoc Lake in Summit, about two miles east of Gilbert and Esther.

The 1860 census shows the two Dodge families with a combined real estate value of six thousand dollars compared to Gilbert's fifteen hundred. Bill Dodge was then thirty-seven, the same age as Gilbert, with a wife and seven children aged two to fifteen years. Miles, ten years older, had a wife and four children aged eleven to seventeen.

When the Claflins' colt Billy went lame in March, Mr. Eastman advised Elton to go to Bill Dodge and get a receipt, which he said would cure it in a few days.

EASTMAN FAMILY

The Eastmans were another farming family from New York State. The two Eastman brothers, Amasa and Cooledge William, were several years older than Gilbert. Each had his own farm and lived nearby. The 1850 census shows the Montagues, Claflins, and Eastmans (Amasa, Elizabeth, and Ira) in the same dwelling. The 1860 census shows the families adjacent, though Gilbert, Esther, and their family were given the surname Claflins instead of Claflin. In the 1850 census, Cooledge is shown as C. Eastman; in 1860, as C. William Eastman; and in 1870, as Cooledge Eastman.

Amasa Eastman was Gilbert's neighbor in northwest Summit. In 1860 he lived with his wife, Elisa Eastman; his younger sister, Mary Eastman; and their seventy-five-year-old father, Ira Eastman. Amasa and Elisa's three children, Henry, George, and Mary, were all under ten years old. The 1860 census also shows a German farmhand, William Cairt, living with them. Gilbert and Esther usually referred to Amasa as "Mr. Eastman" in their letters. Esther often turned to him for advice in financial and farming matters, or even for loans of money and equipment.

Amasa's brother, Cooledge William Eastman, lived in southwest Oconomowoc with his wife Mary; their two children, twenty-four-year-old Leander and twelve-year-old Albert; and an English housemaid, Eliza Austin. The Claflins occasionally went to Cooledge to ask about farm animal matters.

In mid-December 1862, Leander died during a time when there was much typhoid fever and diphtheria in Oconomowoc. In early April 1863, Cooledge and Amasa's father Ira died, apparently of old age.

The Eastmans are mentioned in Gilbert's letters November 27, January 19, April 25, June 8, and July 4. They are also mentioned in Esther's letters November 30, December 4, December 16, December 18, December 25, January 14, February 12, February 18, February 26, March 26, April 1, April 5, April 9, April 24, May 28, June 29, July 5, July 21, and July 22; in Elton's letters February 12, February 26, and April 16; and in Price's letter April 9.

EDWIN EDGERTON

The *Waukesha County Land Records from 1839 to 1865* show Edwin Edgerton bought one-sixteenth of Section 5 of Summit in 1849, but he does not appear anywhere in Wisconsin in the 1860 census.

In his April 16 letter, Elton told Gilbert that "Mr. Egerton of Summit has got married."

MR. EMERY

The 1860 census shows no Mr. Emery in Waukesha County. The 1870 shows two farmers by that name, living together in the town of Eagle.

On January 19, 1863, Esther mentioned in her letter that she heard Mr. Emery was not at the depot.

MARYANN GIFFORD

In Esther's letter of February 26, she said that Maryann Gifford, a teacher of Summit School, was turned out before the end of the term.

GOODELL FAMILY

Prescott Watson Goodell was a farmer in Oconomowoc. Like Gilbert, he was forty years old in 1862. Also like Gilbert, he had come to Wisconsin from New York State. He and his wife Lovilla attended the same church as the Claflins, and while Gilbert was away they called on Esther to make sure all was well with her. The 1860 census spells the family name Goodel and shows children aged three to sixteen years.

The Goodells are mentioned in Esther's letters of December 4, December 16, April 20, April 30, June 18, and July 5; and in Gilbert's letters of December 21 and May 2.

MR. GOODRICH

Mr. Goodrich kept the grocery across the street from where Gilbert Woodruff was clerking in the winter of 1863. Gilbert thought, in his letter of July 10, 1863, Mr. Goodrich would have currant boxes.

GOODY

In Esther's letter of July 22, she said her mother stayed at Goody's after selling her house.

MR. HARDLE

In his letter of February 26, Elton said Mr. Hardle had bought Mr. Penks's place.

WILLIAM HARRISON

Esther wrote in her July 12 letter that W. Harrison had his hand shattered and lost the sight of one, if not both, of his eyes in the cannon accident during the Vicksburg victory celebration in Oconomowoc.

Augustus Harrison, born in Connecticut about 1812, appears in the 1850 census in Ottawa, Waukesha County, Wisconsin. Also in his household were Clarissa (thirty-five), William (twelve), Helen (nine), Augustus (seven), and Albert (three), all born in Ohio.

In the 1860 census, August Harrison (forty-eight) lives with Evva Harrison (twenty-eight years old and born in Bavaria), William (twenty-two), Albert (fourteen), Clara (three), and Evva (eight months).

William Harrison was the only W. Harrison in Summit or Oconomowoc in the 1850 or 1860 censuses. There was no W. Harrison in either town in the 1870 census.

Albert Harshaw

In Esther's letter of May 28, she said Albert Harshaw was reported dead.

Mrs. Haverland

Mrs. Haverland was a sanctuary agent from Michigan who spoke at a funeral for a slave killed while escaping near Columbus, Kentucky, early May 1863. Gilbert mentioned her, the funeral, and the incident in his May 5 letter.

Reverend Helmers

Reverend Mr. Helmers preached at the church Gilbert attended on January 18, 1863, while he was at Camp Washburn.

Alinga Hendrickson

In the 1860 census, A. D. Hendrickson is listed as a forty-one-year-old schoolteacher living in the town of Eagle in Waukesha County. His household included his wife Olive (forty-one), one son (fourteen), two daughters (twelve and two), and a seventy-five-year-old cutler, Ei Densmon. In 1870, Hendrickson and his wife were superintendent and matron of a reform school in Waukesha. Their daughter Mary was a teacher and their younger daughter Annie attended school. Their household in the 1870 census included twenty-two people besides the four of them with ages ranging from a thirteen-year-old schoolboy to a sixty-four-year-old seamstress. Most of the housemates were in their late teens through thirties and included a couple of teamsters, two housekeepers, three schoolteachers, a nurse, a cook, a laundress, a gardener, a carpenter, a night watchman, and a willow worker.

It is interesting to note that in the 1880 census, A. D. Hendrickson was listed twice, five days apart in different areas of Waukesha. At the Wisconsin State Industrial School for Boys, he is listed as a widower and the assistant superintendent. The other listing shows him living with a forty-two-year-old wife, Nellon.

In Price's letter of February 16, Mr. Hendrickson is referred to as the county school superintendent.

B. R. Hinkley

The *Oconomowoc Free Press* of July 19, 1862, listed B. R. Hinkley as one of the directors of the Oconomowoc Bank. The only Hinkley family in the 1860 or 1870 censuses in Waukesha County was the A. R. or Ahira R. Hinkley family of the town of Eagle. Mr. Hinkley was listed as a farmer in both listings. The letters showed him as giving financial advice or small loans of money.

Mr. Hinkley was mentioned in Esther's letters of February 18, April 24, May 20, and June 9; and in Gilbert's letter of May 25.

WILLIAM HOYT

The 1860 census shows a physician named William M. Hoyt living in Menomonee Falls, Waukesha County, Wisconsin, about twenty miles from Oconomowoc, with a wife and four children. The 1870 census shows the same wife and three of the four children still there, but without the father.

Elton's letter of April 16 said Mr. Hoyt had died since he left the state.

HUBBARD FAMILY

Charles Hubbard was a cooper. In 1860, according to the census, he and his wife Mary were both thirty-three years old and lived in Oconomowoc with their four children: Stephen (thirteen), Charles (eleven), Mary (nine), and Ida (seven). All four of the children were born in New York. Another cooper and his family lived with the Hubbards (Ambrose and Antoinette Crew and their nine-month-old infant Charles) as well as a young cooper journeyman, George Stevens.

Mrs. Hubbard was mentioned in Esther's letter of June 9.

MRS. HUMBERT

In her letter of January 19, Esther said Anna had told her of an aged mother by this name, with one son enlisted and the other drafted.

HOMER HURD

The 1860 census shows only two adults named Homer living in the area: Homer Stevens, eighteen, and Homer Hurd, thirty-six. Both were New York farmers living in Oconomowoc. The Homer mentioned in Esther's December 28 letter could have been either, but on May 20 Esther reports that Homer Hurd died.

PETER INGEBRIETSEN

Esther's letter of July 28 said, "Lester Rockwell lives where Peter I. used to."

The 1860 census shows Peter Ingebrietsen (seventy-one) and his wife Karen (seventy), both from Norway, living in Oconomowoc with the farming family of Ole Petersen (forty-six) and his wife Maria (thirty-six). Their children were Anna (fifteen), Ingebrit (thirteen), Peter (eleven), Christian (nine), and Jacob (six). The three youngest children were born in Wisconsin; Ole, Maria, and the two older children, in Norway.

The 1870 census shows much of the same household still living together in Oconomowoc, but now the names and ages are given as Ole Peterson (fifty-seven), Mary (forty-six), Christian (twenty-eight), Jacob (sixteen), Lewis (nine), Henry (three), Peter Ingerberson (eighty-one), and Carrin Ingerberson (seventy-nine). Ann Peterson (twenty-three) is listed as a domestic servant at the house.

MISS L. JAMES

In his February 16 letter, Price said Miss L. James married Tom McPherson.

DIDARNG JONES

I have not found who this might be. He is mentioned in Esther's letter of July 12.

OLD JUD

I have not found who this might be. In Esther's letter of July 12, Old Jud went to spike the cannon after hearing of the surrender of Vicksburg.

HORACE KELLOGG

In her letter of July 21 Esther said Horace Kellogg would give sixty cents for wool. On July 28, she told Gilbert that Horace Kellogg did business in Milwaukee and would be likely to sell their plums. August 3, Gilbert replied that Kellogg would do as well as anyone.

The 1860 census showed a produce dealer named Horace Kellogg (thirty) living in Oconomowoc along with his wife Lucy (twenty-one), and daughter Kora (three months), as well as a housemaid, Mary Kellogg (fifteen). Next door to them was another produce dealer, Lyman Kellogg (forty-five), living with Emiline (forty), Harriette (eleven), Sarah (nine), Charles (seven), and Frank (three). Also in that household was Mary Lenort (thirty).

In 1870, Horace and Lucy were living in Summit with their children: Cora (ten), Lizzie (seven), Benjamin (three), and Wallace (one). In 1880, Horace is listed as a produce buyer in Oconomowoc with Lucy (forty), Cora (twenty), Lizzie (sixteen), Benjamin (thirteen), Wallace (eleven), and Grace (nine). Also living with them in 1880 was a boarder, George Cook (forty-five).

CHARLES F. KENDALL

Esther and Gilbert wrote several times between late March and late May 1863 about the possibility of Mr. Kendall making a window sash. These letters are Esther's of March 26, April 16, and May 20, and Gilbert's of May 26. Price mentions Henry Kendall on April 9.

The 1860 census shows Charles F. Kendall, carpenter, as a close neighbor of the Claflins and Eastmans, and of Esther's uncle John Metcalf. At the time, Kendall was thirty-nine, a year older than Gilbert. His wife, Emma, was closer to Esther's age. They had four children, aged two, four, six, and eight years.

MRS. LAMPMAN

In Esther's letter of July 29, she said Mrs. Lampman told her the Sixteenth were at Lake Providence and very sickly.

The "Roster of Wisconsin Volunteers" shows Orin Lampman in Company A of Wisconsin's Sixteenth Infantry Regiment. He mustered in October 14, 1861, and died of disease August 16, 1863, at Vicksburg, Mississippi.

The 1860 census shows the Lampman family living next door to Uncle John in Summit. The father, James, was a forty-two-year-old farmer. The rest of the family was Elisa (thirty-five), Oren (sixteen), Charles (fifteen), Frank (ten), and Alice (four). Also part of the household was Rachel Wightman (fourteen).

In 1870, Oren and Charles were missing from the census. James (now a grain miller), Eliza, Frank, and Alice were living in Lima, Sheboygan County, Wisconsin. Also in the household was a new brother, Harry Lampman (nine); a domestic servant, Sina Bruhmelstrohde (eighteen); and two mill workers, Edwin Littlefield (twenty) and John Rushlink (twenty).

COLONEL JAMES LEWIS AND THE BOYS

James M. Lewis of Oconomowoc was colonel of Wisconsin's Twenty-Eighth Infantry Regiment, stationed at Helena, Arkansas. The 1860 census showed two boys in James M. Lewis's household: James Lewis aged seven and Duncan McCarter aged two.

Of the 109 boys in Lewis's Company C of the Twenty-Eighth, 80 were from Summit and Oconomowoc. Between mid-February and mid-April 1863, 4 of those boys from Oconomowoc and 2 from Summit died of disease. Three boys from Company C were discharged April 16 on disability: Charles H. Stansbury of Oconomowoc, Theodore F. Leavitt of Summit (who was wounded March 24 on picket duty), and David L. Webster of Summit.

Elton's letter of May 4 said that Colonel Lewis and three of the boys were home. Esther's letter of July 5 said Colonel Lewis was a speaker at the July 4 picnic.

EMILY LITTLE

Esther's letter of December 16 said that Emily Little paid a call and had the appearance of an opium eater.

FRANKIE LOCKWOOD

Franciss Lockwood was the teenage daughter of Uncle John's former business partner Charles Lockwood. She was referred to as Frank or Frankie. Part of the time she was living with Uncle John Metcalf, but she left school and kept company with Harmon Baxter, a young man in his mid-twenties at the time of the letters.

She is in Esther's letters of February 18 and April 20 (when Esther said she was ruined beyond redemption) and in Price's of February 16.

REVEREND WILLIAM LOVE

In her letter of January 10, 1863, while Gilbert was stationed at Camp Washburn on the outskirts of Milwaukee, Esther reports that while she listened to the church sermon, she wondered whether he might be listening to Mr. Clapp or Mr. Love.

The 1860 census shows William DeLos Love was a Congregational clergyman living in Milwaukee along with his family and servants. His wife was Matilda Love. Both William and Matilda were forty years old. Their children were Katie (fourteen), Fannie (twelve), Edward (ten), William (eight), Archibald (six), Laura (four), and Henry (eight months). The servants were Jennette Powell, the twenty-four-year-old governess, and Sarah Orford, the eighteen-year-old domestic servant.

Chaney Luddin

The 1860 census shows the family of Mr. C. Luddin, a forty-two-year-old carpenter, living in Ixonia, Wisconsin, as a near neighbor to Esther's oldest brother J.P. Colby. The Luddin household also included Lousia (forty-one), Adell (thirteen), Wilbert (eleven), Willett (nine), Keene (eight), Clarrance (five), Charles (four), and Anna (two). The 1850 census shows him as Chancy Luddin with wife Louisa and children Adell (four) and Wilson (two) in Ixonia. The 1870 census shows him as Chaney Ludden (fifty), with Louisa (fifty), Willard (twenty), Keene (eighteen), Charles (thirteen), Anna (eleven), and Lewis (eight) living in Dayton, Cedar County, Iowa.

Esther's letter of June 18 said Mr. Luddin dared not take militia roll in Ixonia.

George Ludington Family

We first find George Ludington (seventeen) in the 1850 census living in Rochester, Racine County, Wisconsin, along with his father Henry (forty), mother Mary (thirty-nine), and siblings Esther (fifteen), Charlott (thirteen), Franklin (nine), and Octavia (five). Both George and Henry were listed as blacksmiths.

By 1860 they had moved to the village of Oconomowoc and the household was Henry (fifty), Mary (forty-eight), Franklin (eighteen), Octava (fourteen), George (twenty-six), Wealthy (eighteen), William (three months), and an apprentice, Courtland Vroman. Henry, Franklin, and George were all carriage makers.

By 1870 George (thirty-seven) was back to being a blacksmith in the village of Oconomowoc, living with Wealthy (twenty-six), Edgar (nine), Elmer (seven), Elsworth (seven), Frank (five), William (three), and Gertrude (seven months). (These last two children are listed on a page that is erroneously titled "Village of Delafield." I suspect it was really Oconomowoc since the page numbers are sequential and the date and census taker match.)

In 1880, there were two families of Ludingtons living in Oconomowoc. George's brother Frank (thirty-eight) lived with his wife Rosella (thirty-two) and their two daughters, Lulu Belle (two) and Hattie (five months). Next door were George (forty-six), his wife Wealthy (thirty-eight), and their children Edgar (twenty), Elmer (eighteen), Ellsworth (eighteen), Frank (sixteen), Willie (thirteen), and Gertrude (ten). Both Frank and George are listed as wagon makers.

In her letter of July 12, Esther said Mr. Ludington was injured in a gunpowder explosion while celebrating the fall of Vicksburg and that his wife expected to be confined soon—that would have been the year the twins Elmer and Elsworth were born.

Curtis Mann

In the 1860 census the Mann family of Summit consisted of Curtis (forty-five), Nancy (thirty-three), Fanny (ten), Frank (eight), Eddy (five), and Orvill (two), as well as two farmhands and a housekeeper. In the 1870 census the same family members are living together except for Frank. Curtis was now listed as a commercial merchant instead of a farmer.

The Mann farm was 335 acres immediately east of the Claflin, Amasa Eastman, and Newnham farms. Mr. Mann gave the Claflin boys straw in January 1863; Gilbert suggested asking him for more straw in February.

Gilbert's letters of January 11 and February 12 and Esther's letter of January 19 discuss these transactions.

Miss Nancy Mann

In Oconomowoc's 1860 census, the Mann farming family consisted of Joseph J. (fifty-one), Lucettie (also fifty-one), Sarah (twenty-six), Joseph (twenty-four), Nancy (eighteen), and John (twelve).

Price's letter of April 9 said Miss Nancy Mann married Mr. McConnell.

Reverend S. W. Martin

In Esther's letter of May 29, she said that Martin was a Methodist minister who lived in Madison and made out soldiers' records. Gilbert's company record was made out by "S. W. Martin, Clerk's office of the District Court."

Mr. McConnell

Price's letter of April 9 said Miss Nancy Mann married Mr. McConnell.

Ed McCuell

Esther's letter of December 18 lists Ed McCuell's wife as one of several people who had died recently.

Tom McPherson

Price's letter of February 16 said that Mr. Tom McPherson married Miss L. James.

Reverend Enos James Montague

Reverend Enos James Montague, the Congregational minister, served Oconomowoc and Summit. He had been pastor at Summit Presbyterian for several years when he came to serve the Oconomowoc Congregational Church in January 1862. A year and a half later, in May 1863, in accordance with the wishes of both churches, they were consolidated into one church as they had been for the first four years of 1841–45. The pastorate of Mr. Montague was, on the whole, twelve years of peace following a series of short pastorates and occasional feuding. Reverend Enos James Montague and his wife Faith Hooker Montague had two daughters, Elizabeth and Mary. Their son Edward died in January 1861 at age thirteen.

Reverend E. J. Montague was more important to the family history than is evident from the letters. His daughter Elizabeth married Gilbert and Esther's son Price.

Reverend Montague is mentioned in Esther's letters of December 4, December 28, January 14, February 12, March 1, April 30, May 4, May 21, June 9, and July 12; also in Gilbert's letters of December 8, December 15, and March 2.

R. MOREE

In Gilbert's July 30 letter, he said a copperhead (Confederate sympathizer) in camp has physical appearance similar to R. Moree of Oconomowoc.

JAMES NEWNHAM FAMILY

Unlike the Goodells and the Eastmans, James Newnham and his wife Eliza came from England. James was a farmer, and he and Eliza were twenty years older than Gilbert and Esther. The 1870 census shows James Newnham to be sixty-six, and Eliza Newnham sixty. All four of their children were born in Wisconsin. Sometime between 1850 and 1860, they moved from Milwaukee to become near neighbors of the Claflins in Summit, twenty-five miles to the west of Milwaukee.

On December 16, 1862, Esther wrote to Gilbert that Mr. Newnham's boys were selling straw and wondered if they should buy a load. The boys, Howard and Henry, were twenty-two and eighteen. On February 26, Elton said Mrs. Newnham visited Esther and brought word from Mr. Newnham who said they could have all the straw they wanted. In the same letter Elton wrote that Howard had gone to work in the pinery. Two years later, in 1864, both Howard and Henry joined the Forty-Third Wisconsin Infantry Regiment and spent nine months guarding railroad lines and supplies in Tennessee.

On April 16, Esther said Mrs. Newnham had been the only one over to take tea since Gilbert left.

OSBORNE FAMILY

The *Waukesha County Land Records from 1839 to 1865* shows that Chauncey Osborne bought one-eighth of Section 32 in Oconomowoc in 1849. The 1850 census shows three Osborne families, all farmers from New York, living in Oconomowoc. One of them was fifty-two-year-old Chauncey Osborne, living with Polly (fifty-two), F.E. (twenty-three), Julia (sixteen), Chauncey (thirteen), Henry (ten), and Harriett (six). There is no sign of Chauncey, Polly, or any of their family in the 1860 census, but Chauncey and Polly Osborne, now both seventy-two, appear to be living in Johnstown, Rock County, Wisconsin, in the 1870 census.

In her April 30 letter, Esther said that Emily may work for Charles Osborne and take one child (Anne) that summer. On May 28, Esther wrote to say that Farin Osborne had been to war and had come home with a broken constitution and a spinal complaint. Farin E. Osborne, from Harmony, Rock County, Wisconsin, about thirty-five miles from Oconomowoc, is listed in Wisconsin military records in Company E of the Twenty-Second Wisconsin Infantry, discharged December 19, 1862, on disability. In 1860, two other Osborne families are living in Oconomowoc. Perhaps that is why Farin comes to visit.

MR. PENKS

In Elton's letter of February 26, he said Mr. Penks had sold out to Mr. Hardle and moved to Illinois.

Mr. Perkins

Mr. Perkins served with Deacon Gilbert Claflin and the church pastor as the committee representing the church in the summer of 1858, during a time of personal feuding and unhappiness in the church. "Father Perkins," as he is referred to in the church records, is remembered in a June 29, 1929, article from the *Oconomowoc Enterprise*:

> He was a graduate of Dartmouth College and I think, but will not be sure, that he was in the class of Daniel Webster. After graduation he studied law and formed a co-partnership with Mr. Webster which lasted about four years. The young firm had a great rush of business—in fact, too much of a rush for Mr. Perkins, for his health failed and he removed to Florida and entered the mercantile business which he continued until about the beginning of the fifties, when he came North and made his home in Oconomowoc. He was about 70 when I formed his acquaintance. He had a fine forehead, a handsome nose, and bright clear eyes. It has ever been a pleasure to know him, not only for his intimate acquaintance with America's greatest statesman of whom he narrated a great number of most interesting incidents, but for his ready wit, which had no tinge of unkindness, and a boundless fund of incidents connected with our early history.

Esther said in her May 1 letter and again June 24, that Old Mr. Perkins was crazy and very troublesome. On July 12, Esther said that Mr. Perkins died since her last letter.

Perrin Family

In her letter of November 30, Esther said Perrins won't have Emily if she has more than one child. Elijah and Washington Perrin were sheep and cattle farmers in Oconomowoc. The 1860 census shows them living together with Elijah's wife Maria and three children. Articles in the Oconomowoc newspaper spoke of their wool and cattle.

Mr. Peters

In her letter of June 9, Esther said Peters the tailor has coats for ten dollars.

Wash Phillips

In his May 30 letter, Gilbert tells Esther that Wash Phillips, who used to work for Seely, was in the Thirty-First Wisconsin. The Thirty-First Wisconsin Regiment was stationed at Columbus from March to October 1863. The roster shows George W. Phillips in Company D of that regiment.

Frank Plympton

Francis W. Plympton of Oconomowoc is listed as a sergeant in Company C of Wisconsin's Twenty-Eighth Volunteer Infantry. He died of disease on the steamer *Westmoreland* in Arkansas on August 24, 1863.

The 1850 census shows the Plimpton family in Medfield, Massachusetts. Wales Plimpton (sixty-seven) was a farmer. His children were Lucy C. (eighteen), Francis W. (seventeen), George L. (fourteen), and Charles F. (nine). All were born in Massachusetts. In fact, Wales Plimpton is shown as head of household in Medfield, Massachusetts, in the 1820, 1830, and 1840 censuses as well. The 1860 census of Oconomowoc, which lists the family name as Plymton, shows Frank W. Plymton (twenty-five, born in Massachusetts) living with Sara Plymton (twenty-four, born in Connecticut) and Charles Plymton (nineteen, born in Massachusetts).

In her letter of July 5, Esther said, "I saw Mrs. F. Plympton today. She says her husband is well and he attributes his prosperity to praying Christian friends at home."

MR. POTTER

On November 21, Gilbert wrote from Camp Randall, "There is but one case of favoritism among the Waukesha boys and that is Mr. Potter who has friends in Madison. He is fisting for the office of captain, but it will be a hard berth for him if he gets it, judging by what the boys say." In her January 19 letter, Esther tells Gilbert that Mr. Potter has sent him the Patent Office report. It is possible these are not the same Potters.

MR. REED

In her March 18 letter, Esther said, "Mr. Sawyer has just called here and asked if that money had not been refunded. He said he would see Mr. Reed and give him a jug."

ALSY RENDALL

Alsy Rendall was reported dead in Esther's May 28 letter. Only one family of Rendalls was living in Waukesha County according to the 1860 census. Charles Rendall, a thirty-nine-year-old tailor, is listed in that census as living next door to Enos James Montague in Summit, along with his wife Ann (thirty-nine) and nine children. Charles, Ann, and nineteen-year-old Job A. were all born in England; the next three children were born in New York; and the remaining five children, aged ten months to nine years, were all born in Wisconsin. None is named Alsy. The entire family except for George, who was three in 1860, was living in Lura, Fairbault County, Minnesota Territory in 1865 according to the territorial census.

MR. RICHARD

In her May 20 letter, Esther said, "Yesterday I went to the village to do some trading, and when I presented the five-dollar bill that Mr. Hinkley let me have, Mr. Richard said it was not good."

ROCKWELL FAMILY

John S. Rockwell is known as the founder of Oconomowoc. In 1837, just twenty-five years before Gilbert was drafted, Rockwell and a partner bought the west half of Section 33. The land was then mostly a tamarack and ash swamp with no roads; only Native American trails existed and formed a junction at what would become the center of Oconomowoc at Main Street and Wisconsin Avenue. Rockwell drained the swampy land, built mills for lumber and grain, and saw to it that Main Street was laid out wide and straight and that the Watertown Plank Road and Milwaukee & Watertown Railroad came through Oconomowoc instead of neighboring Summit and Delafield. Through Oconomowoc's early years, Rockwell was active in the government, education, and religious matters of the town and surrounding area.

The 1850 census shows J. S. Rockwell (forty) living in Oconomowoc with his wife Lavinia (thirty-three), their three children (aged eight, five, and eight months), and his brothers Lester R. (thirty-three) and D. Henry (twenty-five). The 1860 census shows three Mr. Rockwells in Oconomowoc (and none in Summit): Anson Rockwell, D. Henry Rockwell, and John S. Rockwell. John S. Rockwell died in February 1863, as mentioned in Elton's letter of February 12. D. Henry was the only Mr. Rockwell in the area in the 1870 census.

The Mr. Rockwell most often mentioned in the letters may have been John S. Rockwell's brother David, the D. Henry found in the censuses. Or it might have been his son Albert John. Born in March 1842, Albert John would have been twenty years old when the letters were started. Both David and Albert John Rockwell lived and were active in Oconomowoc. David was village president in 1867; Albert John was mayor in 1879.

The Rockwells are mentioned in Esther's January 14, February 12, July 5, July 12, and July 28 letters and Elton's February 12 letter.

Parker Sawyer

Parker Sawyer was a Vermonter and an abolitionist with enough money to help him work for his beliefs. In 1854, at the age of thirty-six, he moved to Summit with his wife and young daughter. He purchased 262 acres adjoining the Nashotah and Nemahbin Lakes, a chain of lakes more than three miles long. In the middle of his land, he built a three-story home with six fireplaces, a billiard room, and a grand-piano music room. Then a ten-foot-diameter "root cellar" was dug, lined with bricks, and closed with a trapdoor. Sawyer never let on as to its true purpose. In his music room, the bookcase wall pivoted like a door, revealing a secret room with bed and bath for escaping slaves headed for Canada. Sawyer's outside hideaway had a door that led into a tunnel to the chain of lakes. Two huge pipes circulated air so efficiently that there was never a hint of mustiness in this well-room.

The 1860 census shows Parker (forty-two) and his wife Angeline (thirty-three) living in Summit with four young children: Clara (ten), Frank (six), Alvin (four), and Libby (two). Also in the household are two farmhands and a housemaid.

In her December 16 letter, Esther reported that Mr. Sawyer talked to the committee about refunding ten dollars. On March 12 she said, "Mr. Sawyer has just called here and asked if that money had not been refunded. He said he would see Mr. Reed and give him a jug."

MR. SEELY

Gilbert's May 30 letter said that Wash Phillips used to work for Seely.

MRS. SHELDON

On June 24, Esther said she will get her fleeces carded with Mrs. Sheldon and on June 29, "I have heard no complaints of the chintz bug only from Sheldon, and that was early in the spring."

REUBEN WILLIAM SKINNER

The 1860 census shows Reuben W. Skinner born 1831 in New York and living in Oconomowoc along with wife Jane (twenty-one) and children George (three) and Janet (eight months). He worked as a blacksmith.

Esther's letter of May 28 said that William Skinner died some time ago with smallpox. He would then have been thirty-two, a year younger than Esther.

MR. SMITH

Price's letter of February 16 said Miss C. Whipple was married to Mr. Smith, the man who went to Pikes Peak to get gold.

CHARLES SPINNEY

C. E. Spinney, along with William M. Colby, appears in the May 27, 1862, *Waukesha Freeman* in a list of registered teachers in Waukesha County. The next spring, the "Proceedings of the Teachers' Institute of Waukesha County," as reported in the April 14, 1863, *Waukesha Freeman*, included, "Afternoon Session: The chief features of the session this afternoon consisted of an exercise in Map-Drawing by Mr. Spinney; Orthography by Mr. Hendrickson; and a sub-lecture by the Rev. Mr. Smith on the use of the spelling book." This Teachers' Institute was an eight-day seminar held each April for instructing teachers in Waukesha County. Charles E. Spinney appears in the 1870 census as a teacher living in Milwaukee along with his wife Elizie and their three children: Bessie (eight), Alice (six), and James (two).

The only mention in the letters was an undated one from Esther—probably from September—in which she said Price had gone to Mr. Spinney's school.

STANSBURY FAMILY

Erskine Stansbury was another of the New York farmers. He and his wife Abby brought their young family to the town of Summit sometime between 1846 and 1848 and settled less than a mile south of the Claflins, according to an 1859 plat map of Summit reprinted in Barquist, *The Summit of Oconomowoc: 150 Years of Summit Town.*

The 1850 census forms for the town of Delafield, five miles east, were filled out by hand with each page signed by Erskine Stansbury (or E. Stansbury), Ass't Marshall.

Erskine was active in the Congregational Church, and served as deacon during Gilbert's time in the army. He was a help to Esther and was able to fill out the appropriate government forms to allow her to collect the state bounty for enlisted men's families.

The Stansburys' son, Charles Howard Stansbury—known as Charley—was the same age as Elton. At the age of sixteen, Charley, along with seventy other boys and men of Summit and Oconomowoc, joined Company C of Wisconsin's Twenty-Eighth Infantry Regiment, but eight months later on April 16, 1863, he was discharged because of a disability and brought home by his neighbor and the colonel, James Lewis. His joining and discharge are recorded in the "Roster of Wisconsin Volunteers."

In her March 1 letter, Esther said Mr. Stansbury officiated as deacon. On March 4 she said he would call and fill out some papers so she would not have to go to Summit. On March 12 she reported he filled out rate papers, which she sent to William. Elton's May 4 letter mentioned Charley Stansbury.

In the census of 1850, the family name was transcribed as "Gransbury" but written as Stansbury, and in 1860 it was both written and transcribed as "Stanbury." Both of these are clearly the same family members living in Summit.

ELIPHALET STONE

On November 23, 1862, Esther reported that Mr. Stone called and said that Gilbert had been issued a blanket. On November 27 Gilbert indicated that Captain Stone said that he would let Gilbert have as much money as he needed to get a substitute if he wanted one.

The 1860 census shows Eliphalet Stone (thirty-five) a New York farmer living in Summit with wife Nancy (twenty-seven) and three children: Percy (five), Ella (four), and Jenny (one). Also in the household are Mary Stone (sixty-eight), a farmhand, and a housemaid. The 1870 census shows the family still in Summit, though Mary was gone and there were two more children.

J. STRATTEN

J. Stratten was one of several folks mentioned in the prayer meeting in Oconomowoc according to Esther's February 12 letter.

REVEREND MR. WILLIAM K. TALBOT

William Kendall Talbot was born June 17, 1799, in Athol, Massachusetts. In 1850, he and his wife were living in Oquawka, Henderson County, Illinois, where he was an O. S. P. (Old School Presbyterian) assistant preacher and his wife was listed as Francine. The 1850 census shows three children: Mary (twenty), Mariah (seventeen), and Chalmers (seven). The 1860 census shows W. K. Talbot, a fifty-nine-year-old O. S. P. Minister living in Columbus, Kentucky, with his wife, F. Ann Talbot (thirty-eight). By 1870 they had moved back to Illinois where they lived in the town of Andover, in Henry County. His wife is listed as Fannie A. Talbot. In 1880, William was eighty-one; Francine was sixty. They lived in Henry, Woodhull County, Illinois, with a nineteen-year-old servant, Mary Russell.

Reverend Mr. Talbot was mentioned twice in Gilbert's letters, once on March 31 as a minister and then on August 9 as the minister of the Presbyterian Church.

Dennis R. Thompson

The 1860 census shows a Dennis R. Thompson, about three years older than Gilbert, living in Oconomowoc. There was no Thompson or Tompson in Gilbert's regiment.

Esther's letter of December 18 said D. R. Thompson's sister died recently. Her letter of February 12 said William Thompson was a subject for prayer at the February 11 meeting. Her August 4 letter said that Dan Thompson was married to young Wilber. Elton's letter of April 16 said D. R. Thompson got back and said many boys were sick.

Topliff Boardinghouses

Dyer Topliff and his wife Elmira ran boardinghouses. The 1860 census shows them running a boardinghouse in the city of Berlin in Green Lake County, Wisconsin. The household then consisted of Dyer (fifty-nine), Elmira (forty-three), Almeriah (twenty-three), Edgar (twenty), Ella (seven), and Frank (five). The two older children were born in New York; the two younger in Wisconsin.

In 1870, the census shows them running a much bigger boardinghouse in Oconomowoc. Of the Topliffs, only Dyer, Elmira, Ella, and Frank were still there; but sixteen additional people were part of the household. Most of them were young people in their late teens and twenties. The group included a brick mason, two hostlers, three domestic servants, two horse trainers, a music teacher, a boot maker, two store clerks, a laborer, and a painter. They came from Georgia, Massachusetts, New Hampshire, New York, Wisconsin, Vermont, Canada, Denmark, England, Ireland, and Prussia. The two older boarders were a fifty-four-year-old patent rights dealer from Vermont and a forty-five-year-old sewing machine agent from Massachusetts.

Mrs. Topliff and Almeriah are mentioned in Esther's June 9 letter, and Mrs. Topliff is mentioned again on July 28. They bought currants from the Claflins.

Tremain Families

Land records show a Joseph Tremain bought land in Section 21 of Oconomowoc in October 1846. The 1850 census shows Joseph Tremaine (thirty-two) was living with Susan (twenty-four), Charles (three), and Elizabeth (thirty-one). Twenty-eight-year-old Ira and twenty-three-year-old Rosalia Tremain were living with William Radcliffe, the blacksmith, and his wife and young son. Charles Tremain (twenty-four) was living next door with his mother, Ruth Tremain (sixty-two). All of the Tremain men were farmers living in Oconomowoc.

The 1860 census shows three households of farming Tremains living close to each other in Oconomowoc: Joseph (forty-two), Susan (thirty-three), Charles (thirteen), and Franklin (ten); Ira (thirty-eight), Rosalia (thirty-four), Harmon (seven), Orlando (five), and John (three); and Charles (thirty-three), Ruth (seventy-three), and Mary (thirty-six).

On May 1 and again on July 5, Esther said Tremain was re-elected Sabbath School superintendent.

DR. SAMUEL TUCKER

Dr. Samuel Tucker, a forty-four-year-old physician, appears in the 1860 census as living in Oconomowoc with his wife Lucy and their children Theodore, Jenny, and George. They live quite near the Allen Woodruffs, who are about two miles west of Gilbert's farm. By 1870, the Tuckers had moved to Webster, Iowa, where Samuel is still listed as a physician living with Lucy, Jennie, and George.

In her letter of May 28, Esther said Price went to Dr. Tucker twice in May but could not get a smallpox vaccination. In her letter of June 24, Esther stated that Dr. Tucker charged half a dollar for each vaccination, and she mused that he must have reaped a rich harvest.

MR. VROMAN

On November 23, Esther wrote, "We heard from you through Mr. Vroman the same day you left Waukesha." The 1860 census shows four households of Vromans, totaling eighteen people, living in Oconomowoc. In 1850 there were twenty-eight Vromans in five households; all were farmers, born either in New York State or Pennsylvania. The Mr. Vromans in each of the four 1860 households were Stephen (fifty-eight), Barnabas (forty-three), Charles (thirty-five), and Ezra (twenty-four). Ezra was Stephen's son. Any one of these men could have had business in Waukesha and brought back news of Gilbert.

MISS C. WHIPPLE

On February 16, 1863, Price wrote to Gilbert that, "Miss C. Whipple was married to Mr. Smith, the man that went to Pikes Peak to get gold."

FREDERIC WILLIAMS

The 1860 census shows Frederic Williams, sixty-seven years old, living in Oconomowoc with Charles and Henrietta Hartwell and their four children. On May 4, 1863, Esther reported that Grandpa Williams had come back and was a regular church attendant.

WOOD FAMILIES

On January 14, 1863, Esther mentions that "old Mr. Wood" was at church; then on May 28 that "old Mrs. Wood, JK's mother was buried Monday." Judging from census records, I would say these were Asa and Mary Wood.

The 1850 census shows two households of Wood families next door to each other in Oconomowoc. One was headed by J. K. Wood, a forty-one-year-old painter and glazier born in Massachusetts. He was living with forty-six-year-old Harriet Wood, sixteen-year-old Ira Wood, and nine-year-old Charles Wood, as well as eighteen-year-old Rosilla Morton (all four were born in New York). The second household was

headed by Asa Wood, a sixty-five-year-old farmer living with sixty-seven-year-old Mary
Wood and sixty-five-year-old Carey Kingsley (all three were born in Massachusetts).

The 1860 census again shows two Wood households next door to each other in
Oconomowoc. The first was Jedediah (fifty-one, now a farmer), Harriette (fifty-five),
Charles (nineteen), Asa (seventy-five), Mary (seventy-six), and Asher Wood (forty-
three, a blacksmith). The second household was the farmer Ira P. Wood (twenty-
six), Laura (twenty), Frank (two), and Fransiss (nine months).

By 1870 the census showed just one household of Woods in Oconomowoc:
Jeddekiah K. Wood (a sixty-one-year-old painter), Harriet M. Wood (sixty-four),
Minerva R. Wood (thirty-seven), Charles R. Wood (thirty-seven), Asa Wood (eighty-
six), and Minnie Wood (seven). Ira, Laura, Frank, Francis, and Willie (then nine
years old) had moved to Ellsworth, Wisconsin.

WOODRUFF FAMILIES

There were several households of Woodruffs living in Summit and Oconomowoc,
and a number of them were mentioned in Gilbert's and Esther's letters. Those
mentioned were Deacon Allen Woodruff; Allen's sons Joel, Beverly, and Gilbert;
Jack Woodruff; James Woodruff; and P. A. Woodruff's wife.

Probably the most important to the Claflins was the farming family of Allen
Woodruff. Allen, born in 1791, was not much younger than the country. Like many
in the area, he moved to Summit from New York. In 1843 he bought land in the
southeast quarter of Section 6—the northwest corner of the six-mile-square town
of Summit. Gilbert's forty acres were the southeast quarter of the northeast quarter
of Section 4. Thus Allen Woodruff's farm was about two miles west of Gilbert's
farm. In 1850 Allen's household in Summit included his wife Roxy (fifty-seven) and
six of their children: Joel (twenty-three), Beverly (twenty), Aphia (eighteen), Gilbert
(fifteen), Frank (twelve), and Maria (also twelve).

Allen Woodruff, like Gilbert Claflin, was a deacon of the First Congregational
Church of Oconomowoc. Esther wrote on May 28 that old Deacon and Mrs. Woodruff always treated her very cordially and always inquired after Gilbert.

The 1860 census showed Allen and Roxy back in Oconomowoc with Maria
(listed as Mary in this census), the youngest of their six children. Meanwhile, their
son Beverly was farming back in Summit. In 1861 their son Beverly joined the First
Wisconsin Cavalry. At the end of April, Beverly sent five dollars home to his parents
according to Esther's May 1 letter.

At the time of the letters, most of Allen and Roxy's other children were living in
Oconomowoc, though only Maria lived with her parents. According to the 1860
census Gilbert Woodruff was a clerk living with merchant Phillenio H. Woodruff—
perhaps a relative. In his July 10 letter, Gilbert Claflin suggested that Gilbert
Woodruff may be able to help Esther deal with a nearby merchant, Mr. Goodrich.

Joel Woodruff appeared in the 1860 census as a farmer living in Oconomowoc
with his wife Amanda and their month-old unnamed daughter. Also in that household are Joel's sister Maria and schoolteacher Daniel Morgan and his six-year-old
daughter. In 1870, Joel was listed as a lumber merchant living in Oconomowoc with

his wife Amanda and their daughter Hattie. In 1880, the three of them were still in Oconomowoc, and he was listed as a retail grocer. He must have been doing some grocery buying and selling in 1863, since Esther's letters talked about his buying eight bushels of currants at one dollar a bushel. Joel's birth year is listed in 1850 as 1827, in 1860 as 1828, in 1870 as 1829, and in 1880 as 1828.

The only mention of Jack Woodruff was in Esther's December 25 letter in which she said that Jack Woodruff wanted to buy the Claflins' horse, Billy. There is also a Jack mentioned in Esther's November 30 letter, but there is no indication this might have been Jack Woodruff. The name Jack Woodruff does not appear in the censuses, though there was a tinner named J. T. Woodruff in Oconomowoc in 1850.

James Woodruff was another matter. Esther mentioned him on May 28, saying she met him at prayer meeting and that he was cordial and asked about Gilbert. This could have been an older son of Allen and Roxy; in 1850 he was listed as J. W. Woodruff (thirty-one) with wife Elmira and young children Herbert and Adelle, living next door to Allen, Roxy, and the six children. In 1860, J. W., Elmira, and the children were living in Lisbon, Wisconsin, where he was listed as James W. Woodruff.

The final Woodruff family member mentioned in the letters was Mrs. P. A. Woodruff. In Esther's June 24 letter, Esther said that Mrs. P. A. Woodruff had returned to Oconomowoc and in her July 12 letter she said that Mrs. P. A. Woodruff had passed away. There was a storekeeper P. A. Woodruff in Summit in 1850, aged twenty-three and apparently single, but he does not appear in the 1860 census.

NOTE

1. Information on neighbors is from the letters of Gilbert and Esther Claflin, federal censuses from 1850 to 1880, and the 1873 *Atlas of Waukesha County*. Military information in this section is mostly from "Roster of Wisconsin Volunteers" and Quiner, *Military History of Wisconsin*; both of these sources are easily accessible through the Wisconsin Historical Society's website at http://www.wisconsinhistory.org/civilwar/regiments.asp.

Summit and Oconomowoc

When the first pioneers settled in this region, about thirty miles west of Milwaukee in southeast Wisconsin and twenty-five years before the opening of this story, the Wisconsin Territory was already divided into townships, six miles square. Two of these townships were Summit and Oconomowoc.[1]

Summit was a center of commerce for both Summit and Oconomowoc until a freak tornado in the 1850s destroyed most of Summit Center and Summit Corners. The railway that planned to go through Summit instead built its station in Oconomowoc. In 1862 Oconomowoc was a village of a thousand people and had become the metropolis of the region.

A Glance at the *Oconomowoc Free Press*

The *Free Press* was Oconomowoc's first newspaper, first published on October 14, 1858. Its final issue was August 1862 because its publisher, D. S. Curtis, enlisted in the Union army.

On May 12, 1859, the *Oconomowoc Free Press* published an article headed "Oconomowoc" that described the town from a tourism view.

> Heretofore, very little has been said concerning the many natural advantages of our thriving little town. Situated in the heart of one of the finest grain growing countries of the West; surrounded by numerous lakes, forming an immense water power whose waters abound with fish of the finest quality, and on whose placid bosom numberless flocks of wild ducks, geese, white swan, &c. abound, affording unbounded facilities for the sportsman to display his skill; on the line of the Mil., Wht. & Bar. Val. R. R. [Milwaukee, Watertown, and Baraboo Valley Railroad], and only 33 miles from Milwaukee, the metropolis of Wisconsin, and immediate connection with which, was not only very desirable, but of which very few towns of our size can boast.

We know of no place in the West which, during the summer season, affords such natural advantages for enjoyment to our city friends, as Oconomowoc. Here you can obtain *all* if not more, than is found at our fashionable watering places. A fine Hotel capable of accommodating a goodly number, and under the management of G. W. Fay, Esq., who is acknowledged by those who have once *broke bread* at his bounteous table, to keep the finest house outside of Milwaukee.

On our lakes, plenty of fine sailing boats as ever spread canvass to the breeze, can be found to take parties on excursions to the island or different points on the lakes. Take it all in all, we must say again, that there is not a more beautiful town in the West, where people may come to rid themselves of the dust and bustle of city life, than Oconomowoc; and we cordially invite those who wish to enjoy rural felicity as it is to come and try it.

The following were printed in a section headed "News Items" in the *Oconomowoc Free Press*, May 12, 1859:

—James Buchanan, President of the U.S., was 68 years old on Saturday, the 23d ult.
—There have been four hundred cases of measles at Niles, Mich., within the past four months.
—Mathew Gilroy, died at Deerfield, Oneida Co., N.Y., on Monday week, at the age of 105 years.
—A bill to prohibit the marriage of white and black persons has passed the Wisconsin legislature.
—Eighteen thousand herrings were caught on Monday week, at Squawbetty, near Taunton, Mass.
—Steamboat navigation has been resumed on the St. Lawrence River between Montreal and Quebec.

Here is a sampling of news articles from the *Oconomowoc Free Press* between 1859 and 1862. These are wonderful for giving the reader a flavor of the town of Oconomowoc about the time the letters were written.

REFORMERS:—There is a certain class in every community who make loud professions of devotion to Temperance and other reforms, but scarcely ever spend a dime or an hour's time to help the work on or relieve those who are doing *all* they can. To such we recommend the 2nd chapter of James, 16–18 verses. (July 26, 1862)

EXPLAINED.—The man who came through the upper end of the village so furiously the other day, stopped suddenly at Place's grocery and provision store, and purchased sugar, coffee, tea, and other articles enough to last his family a year. That's the place to buy cheap. (April 21, 1859)

FINE BERRIES: A good lady friend has our thanks for a little pail of handsome, delicious Rhasberries, sent to our office the other day. May blessings attend the donor. (July 19, 1862)

MUD: the mud has been all dried up, having become slightly *chilled* by the *cool* air last night. (February 24, 1859)

SPIRITUAL: The Rev. Mr. Todd, is delivering a course of lectures on the Philosophy of Spiritualism, at Fay's Hall. (February 24, 1859)

ESTRAY NOTICE. Came into the enclosure of Thomas Maloney, in the town of Ixonia, on the 29 day of March 1859, two sheep, a buck and a ewe. The owner is requested to come forward and prove property, pay charges, and take them away. (April 14, 1859)

HAYING AND CROPS: Many farmers are already briskly at work in their Hay-fields. On Saturday we took a little tour through portions of summit at it was truly delightful and refreshing to pass the bountiful clover-fields, partly cut, and inhale the rich perfume which rises from them. While the wheat, Corn and Oats look fair, they do not promise as large yield, as in some previous years. Rust has struck the spring wheat, in some places. (July 19, 1862)

PERRIN'S WOOL: On Monday morning last, as Mr. Perrin stoped in front of our office, with his load of wool, we took a look at it, and truly it was a beautiful clip, equal to any we have seen in this State; it was sold to Col. Hinkley, for 46 cts, who pronounces it a very superior staple, and in good order. Mr. Perrin is one of those farmers who believes in raising the best; he has some of the best Devon Cattle in our State. (July 19, 1862)

OUR VILLAGE: We have a population of 1,000 and one would suppose that there would be a few *rooms to let* during these hard times. But everything inhabitable is filled. There is not, we believe a vacant house or shop in town. Several strangers have been here recently looking for stores and shops, but none can be had without building them. We wonder what other town in the State is in such a condition. (July 19, 1862)

A GOOD PROSPECT: A large town or village with no side-walks, and with streets at certain seasons of the year almost impassable, is a disgrace to the inhabitants thereof, and should be avoided by strangers, as any sensible young man would avoid a young lady who eats her breakfast in the morning before combing her hair. Oconomowoc is going to have sidewalks and have her *ways* mended.—The supervisors have *incorporated* the village into a separate road district and have appointed Orville Hathaway path-master.

Now, Orville, go to work in earnest and we will all help you, for in this thing are we all united as one man. Let us have our sidewalks in such a condition, that when our country friends (including friend Cottrell) come to the village, they can get along pleasantly, without getting into the mud, or falling into some hole. Let us have the village fixed up so that our country friends will be proud to tell strangers that they live *near* the beautiful village of Oconomowoc. (April 21, 1859)

FARMWORK AT THE CLAFLINS'

With Gilbert away, the work on the farm was left to Esther and their two sons. Elton turned sixteen on January 3, 1863, and Price was thirteen. There was plenty to keep them busy. Cows, horses, sheep, pigs, and chickens all needed to be cared for. The family grew both spring and winter wheat and oats, corn, beans, and potatoes. Fruit was an important cash crop, and the Claflins grew strawberries and currants and had an orchard of pears, plums, apples, and cherries. In the fall and winter, the family wrote much of the health and feeding of animals, of threshing and storing grain, and of drying and selling apples.

OCONOMOWOC CONGREGATIONAL CHURCH

Church was an important part of the Claflins' life. Gilbert was a deacon of the Congregational Church and a member of the first Sabbath School in the town. In addition to Sunday services, there were preparatory lectures on Saturdays before each Communion Sunday, prayer meetings on Wednesdays, monthly Sabbath School concerts, and church social events, picnics, parties, and donations. Donations were special parties at which provisions of all kinds were bestowed upon the pastor.

THE SUMMIT SCHOOL

A tattered, handwritten book in the Oconomowoc Historical Society Archive titled *Records of School District No. 4. in the Towns of Summit and Concord* yields information about the Summit School. One page is an official contract for William Colby to teach the school for the four month winter season of 1857:

> It is hereby agreed between School Dist. No. Four of the Town of Summit and Wm M. Colby, a qualified teacher of said town, that the said Wm M Colby is to teach the common school in said Dist. for the term of four months for the sum of Twenty-Five Dollars per month, Commencing on the 16th day of Nov. 1857.
> And for such services properly rendered the said District is to pay the said Wm M Colby the amt. that may be due according to the terms of this contract on or before the first day of April A.D. 1857.—
> Nov. 15th 1857
> J. M. Putney, Clerk
> Wm. M. Colby, Teacher

We consent to the above contract.
Geo Comstock, Treasurer
B. C. Hildrith, Director

William Colby's pay of twenty-five dollars per month was higher than the average wages for Wisconsin teachers (male or female) as reported in the *Oconomowoc Free Press*, June 28, 1862:

TEACHERS' WAGES: The following table from the State Superintendent's report shows the average wages of male and female teachers in several States, per month:

State	Paid Males	Paid Females
Wisconsin	$24.20	$15.30
Illinois	$28.82	$18.80
Iowa	$27.68	$17.16
New Jersey	$33.60	$19.17
Ohio	$27.81	$16.25
Pennsylvania	$24.20	$18.11
Upper Canada	$38.10	$20.18

The table shows that Wisconsin pays the lowest wages to teachers of any State on the list, except Pennsylvania, which pays the same; Wisconsin pays less to female teachers than any other state. The lesson teaches that there are very strong inducements for teachers, males and females, to leave Wisconsin. The whole amount of money raised by tax for teachers' wages the past year $723,120 of which $551,422 was voted at the District meetings; the remainder was levied by county Boards as County School Tax.

Other pages of *Records of School District No. 4.* show money received from town superintendents and paid out for everything from a broom for twenty cents to the teachers' wages:

District Treasurers Report for Sept 26th 1859
    I Geo Comstock Treasurer of Joint School Dist No. four of the Towns of Summit and concord do report to the annual Meeting of said district that I have received during the preceeding year.

From Treasurer of Town of Summit	$70.09
From Town Superintrendant of Summit	49.06
From Town Superintendant of Concord	10.97
In my hands as Former Treasurer	*10.12*
Amounting to	$140.84

And that I have paid on Order of district Clerk
dated April 20th, 1858, to Lall B. Smith $1.51
Paid for Broom   .20
Paid for Chair $1.00
Paid order of Richard Twill dated Jan. 17th, 1859   8.16
do Do of W. Colby "Feb 7th"   25.00
do Do of W. Colby "Apr 10"   75.00
do Do of M.P. Landers "August 23"   *30.00*
Leaving a deficit of 3 cts.

This same record book shows the kinds of topics that were discussed at the school district meetings: school terms, firewood, teacher, bills. It is interesting that more attention was given to what kind of firewood was bought and from whom than to who should be the teacher:

Minutes of the School District Meeting
    September 27th 1858
    At the annual Meeting of joint School District No. four composed of the Towns of Summit and Concord held pursuant to Notice on the 27th day of Sept. 1858 at (6) o'clock P.M. at the School House in said Dist. George Comstock was appointed Chairman and J. M. Putney was present as District Clerk.
    John Champion was elected Director, Geo Comstock was elected Treasurer, Geo Byan was Elected Clerk.
    Treasurers report presented and accepted finding a Balance in his hands of ten Dollars and twelve cents.
    It was voted that there be 7 months of school in the year: four months in Winter and Three in the Summer by a Male Teacher Winter .
    Voted that 75 Dollars be raised by tax for Teachers wages the ensuing Year.
    Voted that Richard Twill gets 12 cords of wood for 68 cents per cord.
    An account of George Byamis of Two Dollars and Thirty-one cts as charged was allowed
    George N. Coult was elected librarian
    Ajournd Sine Dye [*Adjournment sine die* was the final adjournment of a session without definitely fixing a day for reconvening]

Minutes of the School District Meeting
    September 1860
    At the Annual School Meeting 1860 Organised by calling John Kimball to the chare the meeting proceded to business
    the treasure then made his report which was excepted the accounts was then called for and presented. P. B. Robinson 24 Dollars for Teachers board also, B. Hilbuth 24.54 Dollars which was allowed.

The next in order was the election of George Comstock treasure. the meeting then voted for to have 4 months winter School taught by a man and 4 months summer School taught by a woman. It was then motiond and Caired [carried] that we raise 100 Dollars for teacher wages.

the job was then let to R. Twill to get 12 cord of good grean oak boddy wood for the sum of 6.64 to be delivered one half by the middle of Nov the other half by the first of January 1st 61.

motion mad and cried [carried] that we rase 50 Dollars for to pay old indibtenes [indebtedness] also voted to rase 5 Dollars for to pay incidintte [incidental] expenses.

The meeting closed siandi [Sine Die]

The *Oconomowoc Free Press*, June 21, 1862, lists names of teachers "licensed by Mr. Enos." There were 108 ladies and 23 gentlemen, one of whom was Wm M. Colby. On July 19, 1862, the paper ran William's abstract of his school's register: "SUMMIT SCHOOL. Abstract of Register, for the month ending July 14, 1862. No. pupils enrolled, 58. Average Daily attendance, 48. Per Cent. of Attendance, 83. Per cent. of Absence, 17. No. of visits, 9. No. of visits from parents, four. Wm. M. Colby, teacher."

William's school was again in the news on July 26, 1862. On that date, the *Oconomowoc Free Press* ran the following article: "IN THE COUNTRY. On Thursday afternoon, we took a short trip to the town of Summit to see the fine crops which look promising and the harvesting has already commenced. We have seen several specimens of very fine winter wheat. We also visited Mr. Colby's School, and as usual, found it one of the most orderly, prosperous and creditable we have ever seen in the State. His summer term closes this week." Also in that day's paper was a report by William Colby in which he stated there was an enrollment of fifty-six pupils, and although "truancy is unknown . . . tardiness is a grievous fault." He also reported that it was not uncommon to open school with less than one-half of the pupils in their seats by nine in the morning.

OCONOMOWOC TODAY

The Claflins' house at 525 East Summit Avenue has been known as the Leaf Residence. Possibly ownership went from Claflin to Anne Horrigan to Leaf. The corner of South and Church Streets (the site of the Congregational Church that Gilbert and Esther attended) is occupied by the Oconomowoc Library.

NOTE

1. Information about the history of Summit and Oconomowoc is from three books with overlapping information: Potter, Punko, and Leitzke, *Historic Oconomowoc*; Johnson, *Illustrious Oconomowoc*; and Barquist and Barquist, *Oconomowoc: Barons to Bootleggers*. I also relied heavily on the letters of Gilbert and Esther Claflin, federal censuses from 1850 to 1880, and articles from the *Oconomowoc Free Press*.

Military

The Draft and Unrest

The Federal government did not enact the first official draft, calling for all men between the ages of eighteen and forty-five to be available to be called into national service, until March 3, 1863; but more than six months earlier, in mid-July 1862, the government had passed a law that effectively did the same thing. The law outlined draft procedures for states that did not already have them, but the actual process was left up to each state's governor.[1]

The Wisconsin draft in the fall of 1862 took place only in the counties where the volunteer quotas designed by Governor Salomon had not been met. The counties of Manitowoc, Milwaukee, Ozaukee, Sheboygan, and Washington had the most difficulty. These counties had many German and Irish immigrants. The Germans were particularly opposed to the draft since many had left Germany to avoid mandatory war service. In addition, it was especially hard for recent immigrants to have the head of household leave for months of service.

Objections were also raised on the basis of fairness. Many men who were drafted, more than a third in fact, simply did not report. Of those who did, most were discharged or released. Then there was the matter of substitutes. During the Civil War, it was legal for a drafted man to pay someone to serve in his place, but this option was out of reach for men without much ready cash.

There was resistance to the draft, including a riot in Port Washington, about fifty miles from Summit on the shores of Lake Michigan.

Later, when the Federal draft took place in March 1863, there was trouble again. On June 19, Esther wrote that enrolling officers were afraid to take the militia rolls in some of the nearby towns. She said that one of their acquaintances in Ixonia, nine miles northwest of Summit, didn't dare since a man in Ashippun, ten miles north of Summit, had been shot and was not expected to live. In Milwaukee, thirty miles to the east, the enrolling officers were attacked by Irish women and stoned.

Bounties

Bounties were sums of money offered to any eligible man for volunteering. During the Civil War, bounties existed on federal, state, and local levels. Wisconsin offered a state bounty for enlisted soldiers, and the bounty could be collected by draftees as well as volunteers. The amount was five dollars a month and appeared to be paid quarterly. There were more than a dozen mentions of the bounty in Gilbert's and Esther's letters, with the Claflins mostly wondering when the bounty would be paid and how they might use the money.

Near the end of his service, on July 4, 1863, we heard from Gilbert about a Federal bounty that was being offered: $402 for soldiers who had been in the service for nine months and who would re-enlist for three years or for the remainder of the war. Nine months was the span of time Gilbert's regiment had been drafted for, and Gilbert had little doubt that many in his regiment would accept the offer. For Gilbert, however, nine months as a soldier was enough. He was satisfied and content to return home and remain there with his wife and family.

Conscription Law of 1863

Abraham Lincoln signed the Enrollment Act, also known as the Conscription Law, on March 3, 1863. This was the nation's first Federal draft and required all men between the ages of twenty and forty-five to register. Federal agents determined quotas for new troops required from each congressional district. By mid-July, the government began calling men into military service from places where these quotas had not been met by voluntary enrollment.

The *Waukesha Freeman*, on Tuesday, July 21, 1863, devoted the first four columns of its front page to the following article clarifying who would be drafted and who would be exempt from military service:

> *The Draft.* It having become a matter of absolute certainty that the
> Government has determined to enforce the Conscription Law, in
> the prosecution of the war for the suppression of the rebellion and the
> preservation of the Republic, it becomes a matter of the greatest interest to
> every citizen to know first
>   WHO CAN BE DRAFTED.
>   In answer to this question, the act expressly declares that "All able-bodied
> male citizens of the United States and persons of foreign birth who shall
> have declared on oath their intention to become citizens, under and in
> pursuance of the laws thereof, between the ages of 20 and 45, with certain
> exceptions, to be subject to draft."
>   These persons being enrolled are divided into two classes, the first of
> which comprises all persons subject to do military duty, between the ages of
> twenty and thirty-five years, and all unmarried persons subject to do military
> duty, above the age of thirty-five and under the age of forty-five; the second
> class comprises all other persons subject to do military duty.—The latter are
> not to be called into the service of the United States until those of the first

class have been called. The enrollment of each class has been made separately, and they should embrace those whose ages were on the 1st of July, between 20 and forty-five. All persons enrolled are subject for two years after the first instant, to be called into the military service of the United States, and to continue in the service for three years, or during the war, and when called into service are to be placed on the same footing, in all respects, as volunteers during the present rebellion; not, however, exceeding the term of three years, including advance pay and bounty, as now provided by law.

And in regard to those who are thus drafted, the following
REGULATIONS
have been prepared:

Any person drafted and notified to appear may, on or before the day fixed for his appearance, furnish an acceptable substitute to take his place in the draft, or he may pay to the Commissioner of Internal Revenue in the Congressional District in which he may reside, the sum of $300. On the receipt of this sum the Collector of Internal Revenue will give drafted persons paying it duplicate receipts. One copy of these receipts will be delivered to the Board of Enrollment on or before the day in which the drafted person is required to report for duty, and when so delivered to the Board, the drafted person will be furnished by the Board with a certificate of exemption, stating that such person is discharged from further liability under that draft, by reason of having paid the sum of $300. Any person failing to report after due service of notice as herein-prescribed, without furnishing a substitute, or paying the required sum therefore, shall be arrested by the Provost Marshal and sent to the nearest military post for trial by court martial, unless, upon proper showing that he is not liable to military duty, the Board of Enrollment shall relieve him from the draft. All drafted persons will, on arriving at the rendezvous, be inspected by the surgeon of the Board, who will report to the Board the physical condition of each one; and all persons drafted and claiming exemption from military duty on account of disability, or any other cause, shall present their claims to be exempted to the Board, whose decision will be final. As soon as the required number of able-bodied men liable to do military duty shall be obtained from the list of those drafted, the remainder are required to be discharged. The persons drafted are to be assigned by the President to military duty in such corps, regiments or other branches of the service as the exigencies of the service may require.

It having thus satisfactorily been established as to who are liable to be drafted, a second question of hardly less interest presents itself, viz:
WHO ARE EXEMPT?
The act very clearly defines that exceedingly limited class to be:
Such as are rejected as physically or mentally unfit for service; also, first, the Vice-President of the United States, the Judges of the various courts of the United States, the heads of the various Executive Departments of the

Government, and the Governors of the several States. Second, the only son of a widow dependent upon his labor for support. Third, the only son of aged or infirm parent or parents dependent upon his labor for support. Fourth, where there are two or more sons of aged and infirm parents subject to draft, the father, or, if he be dead, the mother, may elect which son shall be exempt. Fifth, the only brother of children not twelve years old, having neither father nor mother, dependent upon his labor for support. Sixth, the father of motherless children under twelve years of age dependent upon his labor for their support. Seventh, where there are a father and sons in the same family and household, and two of them are in the service of the United States as non-commissioned officers, musicians or privates, the residue of such family, and household, not excepting two, shall be exempt. Provided, however, that no person who has been convicted of any felony shall be enrolled or permitted to serve in said forces.

IMPORTANT CIRCULAR

The following circular from the War Department, in relation to the commutation and substitutes was telegraphed from Washington last week:

WAR DEPARTMENT,

PROVOST MARSHAL GENERAL'S OFFICE,

WASHINGTON, July 13, 1863

To answer the inquiries made at this office, it is announced—

First—That any drafted person paying $300, under section 13 of the Enrollment Act, is thereby exempt from further liabilities under that draft, but not from any subsequent draft.

Second—That any drafted person furnishing an acceptable substitute is exempt from any service for the period for which said substitute is mustered into the service.

Third—That a substitute once mustered into the service cannot be drafted while in the service.

Fourth—That a drafted man cannot pay the commutation or present a substitute after he has reported himself to the Board of Enrollment for examination.

Fifth—That men who on the 3rd of March 1863, were in the military service of the United States as substitutes under the draft of 1862, and whose terms of service have since expired, are not liable to the present draft; but the persons for which they were substituted are liable for draft, the same as if they had not been drafted and furnished substitutes.

Sixth—That in serving the notice as required by Circular NO. 42 from this office, a reasonable time to report shall in each case be granted by the Board of Enrollment to the men in the State service who have been or may be drafted.

JAS. B. FRY

Provost Marshal General.

The question of
PHYSICAL DISABILITY
being one of such exceeding wide limits, the United States Medical
Department at Washington have deemed it well to specify such diseases and
infirmities as may be considered of sufficient gravity to exempt a drafted
person, and they are as follows:

1. Manifest imbecility or insanity.

2. Epilepsy. For this disability the statement of the drafted men is
insufficient and the fact must be established by the duly attested affidavit of
a physician of good standing who had attended him in a convulsion.

3. Paralysis, general, or of one limb, or chorea; their existence to be
adequately determined.

4. Acute or organic disease of the brain or spinal cord; of the heart
or lungs; of the stomach or intestines; of the liver or spleen; of the
kidneys or bladder—sufficient to have impaired the health, or so well
marked as to leave no reasonable doubt of the man's incapacity for military
service.

5. Confirmed consumption; cancer; aneurism of the larger arteries.

6. Inveterate and extensive diseases of the skin, which will necessary
impair the efficiency of a soldier.

7. Decided feebleness of constitution, whether natural or acquired.

8. Scrofula or constitutional syphilis, which has resisted treatment or
seriously impaired the general health.

9. Habitual or confirmed intemperance or solitary vice in a degree
sufficient to have materially enfeebled the constitution.

10. Chronic rheumatism, unless manifested by positive change of
structure, wasting of the affected limb, of puffiness or distortion of the joint,
does not exempt.—Impaired motion of joints and contraction of the limbs
alleged to arise from rheumatism, and in which the nutrition of the limb is
not manifestly impaired, are to be proved by examination while in a state of
anesthesia induced by ether only.

11. Pain, whether simulating headache, neuralgia in any of its forms,
rheumatism, lumbago, or affections of the muscles, bones, or joints, is a
symptom of disease so easily pretended, it is not to be admitted as a cause
for exemption unless accompanied with manifest derangement of the
general health, wasting of a limb, or other positive signs of disqualifying
local disease.

12. Great injuries or diseases of the skull, occasioning impairment of the
intellectual faculties, epilepsy or other manifest nervous or spasmodic
symptoms.

13. Total loss of sight; loss of sight of right eye; cataract; loss of
chrystaline lens of right eye.

14. Other serious diseases of the eye affecting its integrity and use, e.g.,
chronicopthalmia, fistula lachrymalis, ptosis, (if real) extropion, entropion,

etc. Myopia, unless very decided, or depending upon some structural change in the eye is not a cause for exemption.

15. Loss of nose; deformity of nose so great as seriously to obstruct respiration; ozena dependent upon caries in progress.

16. Complete deafness. This disability must not be admitted on the mere statement of the drafted, but must be proved by the existence of positive disease, or by other satisfactory evidence. Purulent ottorrhoea.

17. Caries of the superior or inferior maxilla of the nasal or palate bones, if in progress; left-palate (bony) extensive loss of substance of the cheeks, or salivary fistula.

18. Dumbness; permanent loss of voice; not to be admitted without clear and satisfactory proof.

19. Total loss of tongue. Mutilation or partial loss of tongue, provided the mutilation be extensive enough to interfere with the necessary use of the organ.

20. Hypertrophy or atrophy of the tongue sufficient in a degree to impair speech or deglutition; obstinate chronic ulceration of the tongue.

21. Stammering, if excessive and confirmed; to be established by satisfactory evidence under oath.

22. Loss of a sufficient number of teeth to prevent proper mastication of food and tearing the cartridge.

23. Incurable deformities or loss of part of either jaw, hindering biting of the cartridge or proper mastication, or greatly injuring speech; anchylosis of lower jaw.

24. Tumors of the neck, impending respiration or deglutition; fistula of larynx or trachea; torticollia, if of long standing and well marked.

25. Deformity of the chest, sufficient to impede respiration, or to prevent the carrying of arms and military equipments; caries of the ribs.

26. Deficient amplitude and power of expansion of the chest. A man five feet three inches (minimum standard for the regular army) should not measure less than thirty inches in circumference immediately above the nipples, and have an expansive mobility of not less than two inches.

27. Abdomen grossly protuberant; excessive obesity, hernia, either inguinal or femoral.

28. Artificial anus; stricture of the rectum; prolapsus ani. Fistula in ano is not a positive disqualification, but may be so if extensive or complicated with visceral disease.

29. Old and ulcerated internal hemorrhoids, if in a degree sufficient to impair the man's efficiency. External hemorrhoids are no cause for exemption.

30. Total loss or nearly total loss of penis; epispadia or hypospapia at the middle or near the root of the penis.

31. Incurable permanent organic stricture of the urethra, in which the urine is passed drop by drop, or which is complicated by disease of the

bladder; urinary fistula. Recent or spasmodic strictures of the urethra does not exempt.

32. Incontinence of urine, being a disease frequently feigned and of rare occurrence, is not of itself a cause for exemption. Stone in the bladder, ascertained by the introduction of the metallic catheter, is a positive disqualification.

33. Loss or complete atrophy of both testicles from any cause, permanent retention of one or both testicles within the inguinal canal, but voluntary retraction does not exempt.

34. Confirmed or malignant sarcocele hydrocele, if complicated with organic disease of the testicle. Varicocele are not in themselves disqualifying.

35. Excessive anterior or posterior curvature of the spine, caries of the spine.

[There is no 36 given within this article.]

37. Wounds, fractures, tumors, atrophy of a limb, or chronic diseases of the joints or bones, that would impede marching, or prevent continuous muscular exertion.

38. Anchylosis, or irreducible dislocation of the shoulder, elbow, wrist, hip, knee, or ankle joint.

39. Muscular or cutaneous contractions from wounds or burns in a degree sufficient to prevent useful motion of the limb.

40. Total loss of a thumb; loss of ungula phalanx of the right thumb.

41. Total loss of two fingers of the same hand.

42. Total loss of index finger of right hand.

43. Loss of the first and second phalangers [sic] of the fingers of the right hand.

44. Permanent extension or permanent contraction of any finger except the little finger; all the fingers adherent or united.

45. Total loss of either great toe; loss of any three toes on the same foot; all the toes joined together.

46. The great toe crossing the other toes with great prominence of the articulation of the metatarsal bone and the first phalanx of the great toe.

47. Overriding, or superposition of all the toes.

48. Permanent retraction of the last phalanx of one of the toes, so that the free border of the nail bears upon the ground; or flexion at a right angle of the first phalanx of a toe upon the second, with antichlosis of this particulation.

49. Club feet; splay feet, where the arch is so far effaced that the tuberosity of the scaphoid bone touches the ground and the lines of station run along the whole internal border of the foot, with great prominence of the inner ankle; but ordinary large, ill-shaped, or flat feet do not exempt.

50. Varicose veins of inferior extremities, if large and numerous, having clusters of knots, and accompanied with chronic swelling or ulcerations.

51. Chronic ulcers; extensive, deep, and adherent cicatrices of lower extremities.

[Numbers 52 through 85 are missing within this article.]

86. No certificate of a physician or surgeon is to be received in support of any point in the claim of drafted men for ex-exemption [*sic*] for military service, unless the facts and statements therein set forth are affirmed or sworn to before a civil magistrate competent to administer oaths.

87. The exempts under the first provision of section 2d of the act for enrolling and calling out the national forces, &c, will generally be sufficiently well known to the Board to obviate the necessity of evidence with regard to them. Should, however, the Board consider it necessary in any case, the commission or certificate of office of any person claiming exemption under the provision mentioned, may be required to be shown.

88. To establish exemption under the 2d, 3d, 4th, 5th, and 6th provisions of section 2 of the act for enrolling and calling out the national forces, &c., the Board shall require the affidavit of the persons seeking to be exempt, and of two respectable men, (heads of families,) residing in the district, that the man in question is the only son of aged or infirm parents, or parents dependent on his labor for support, or otherwise, according to the particular provision of the section under which the exemption is claimed. These affidavits will be made according to the forms hereinafter prescribed, and must in all cases be taken before a civil magistrate duly authorized to administer oaths. These forms of affidavit shall be published by the Board of Enrollment, in the newspapers of the district, for the information of the public when a draft is ordered.

Soldiers in active service on the 3d of March last are understood to be exempt from the first and second drafts—that is, provided they have been honorably discharged.

THE MODUS OPERANDI OF THE DRAWING

In New York the following is the method adopted by the Draft Commissioners for the drawing of names and we presume the same will be adopted elsewhere:

"The slips upon which the names of all persons liable to be drafted are written, are of white paper, about six inches in length, and one inch in width. Each slip is neatly rolled up and secured with an India-rubber band. These rolls will be placed in a revolving box, and drawn out by a man blindfolded. The name will then be announced and placed on record in a book prepared for that purpose.—Those drafted will be notified, and required to appear before the Examining Board within the following ten days, to report for duty, or pay $300 to the Collector of Internal Revenue, who will be present for that purpose. If physically disabled they will be released from further obligations."

The Conscription now about to take place for 300,000 men to serve for three years or during the war, naturally absorbs all other intests [*sic*] for the time being. It is a measure that in a peculiar manner, comes home to "the business and bosoms" of every family wherein there is an arms-bearing member. The volunteer system long since exhausted the spontaneously patriotic warlike spirit of the community. When volunteering for the love of the cause came to an end, the bounty system was brought into requisition, and money considerations induced tens of thousands to enlist who otherwise would not have done so. But the charge on national and municipal credit, of keeping up a vast army by bounties, was too great to be long borne. The Government has at last resorted to the means that all great military nations employ to raise and sustain armies; and it is the only means that in the long run can be relied on. The plan is that of general, impartial Conscription.

It is equally the duty of all who are capable of military duty to serve their country at a time like this.—But as the services of all are not required, nothing is fairer than to determine, by lot, who among those that are able to take the field shall be called out. It is this that the Conscription proposes to do. Instead of the Conscription being a hardship, ungenerously imposed by the Government upon the people, it is really an arrangement of reverse character, by which the Government remits to a majority of its citizens a duty which it might rightfully call on all to discharge—and remits, according to a plan that the majority who have to serve cannot complain of as unfair, for all run an equal risk in the Conscription.

The lot in the impending draft will be manfully met and responded to, with the exception of here and there a locality. And in this gratifying circumstance we do not fail to see the happy effect of the late important victories of the Union cause. These triumphs have acted as a decided tonic to the national courage, and at the same time imparted a much needed confidence in the trustworthiness of the Government and the capacity of our military leaders.

Veteran Volunteers

On June 25, 1863, the War Department issued General Orders No. 191, authorizing the raising of "veteran" regiments.

WAR DEPARTMENT, Adjutant General's Office
   WASHINGTON, June 25, 1863
   GENERAL ORDERS, No. 191.
   In order to increase the armies now in the field, volunteer infantry, cavalry and artillery may be enlisted at any time within ninety days from this date in the respective States, under regulations hereinafter mentioned. The volunteers so enlisted, and such of the three years' troops now in the field as may re-enlist in accordance with the provisions of this order will constitute a

force to be designated "Veteran Volunteers." The regulations for enlisting this force are as follows:

I. The period of service for enlistments or re-enlistments above mentioned, shall be for three years or during the war.

II. All able bodied men between the ages of 18 and 45 years, who have heretofore been enlisted and have served for not less than nine months and can pass the examination required by the mustering regulations of the US, may be enlisted under this order as veteran volunteers in accordance with the provisions hereinafter set forth.

III. Every volunteer enlisted and mustered into service as a veteran, under this order, shall be entitled to receive from the US one month's pay in advance, and a bounty of $402, to be paid as follows:

1st, upon being mustered into service he shall be paid one month's pay in advance, $13; first installment of bounty, $25; premium of $2; total payment on muster $40. 2nd, at the first regular pay day, or two months after muster-in, an additional installment of bounty will be paid of $50. 3rd, at the first regular pay day after six months' service, he shall be paid an additional installment of bounty $50. 4th, at the first regular pay day after the end of the first year's service, an additional installment of bounty will be paid $50. 5th, at the first regular pay day after eighteen months' service, an additional installment of bounty will be paid, $50. 6th, at the first regular pay day after two years' service, an additional installment of bounty will be paid $50. 7th, at the first regular pay day after 2½ years' service, and additional installment of bounty will be paid, $50. 8th, at the expiration of three years' service, the remainder of the bounty will be paid $75.

IV. If the government shall not require these troops for the full period of three years, and they shall be mustered honorably out of service before the expiration of their term of enlistment, they shall receive upon being mustered out the whole amount of bounty remaining unpaid, the same as if the full term had been served. The legal heirs of volunteers who die in service shall be entitled to receive the whole bounty remaining unpaid at the time of the soldier's death.

V. Veteran Volunteers enlisted under this order will be permitted at their option to enter old regiments now in the field; but their service will continue for the full term of their own enlistment, notwithstanding the expiration of the term for which the regiment was originally enlisted. New organizations will be offered only by persons who have been in service and have shown themselves properly qualified for command. As a badge of honorable distinction, "service chevrons" will be furnished by the war department, to be worn by the veteran volunteers.

VI. Officers of regiments whose terms have expired will be authorized, on proper application and approval of their respective Governors, to raise companies and regiments within the period of sixty days, and if the company or regiment authorized to be raised shall be filled up and mustered into service within the said period of sixty days, the officers may be re-commissioned of the date of their original commissions, and for the time engaged in recruiting they will be entitled to receive the pay belonging to their rank.

VII. Volunteers or militia now in the service, whose term of service will expire within ninety days, and who shall then have been in service at least nine months, shall be entitled to the aforesaid bounty and premium of $402, to be paid in the manner herein provided for other troops re-entering the service. The new term will commence from date of re-enlistment.

VIII. After the expiration of ninety days from this date, volunteers serving in three years' organizations, who may re-enlist for three years or the war, shall be entitled to the aforesaid bounty and premium of $402, to be paid in the manner herein provided for other troops re-entering the service. The new term will commence from date of re-enlistment.

IX. Officers in service whose regiments or companies may re-enlist in accordance with the provisions of this order before the expiration of their present term, shall have their commissions continued so as to preserve their date of rank, as fixed by their original muster into US service.

X. As soon after the expiration of their original term of enlistment as the exigencies of the service will permit, a furlough of thirty days will be granted to men who may re-enlist in accordance with the provisions of this order.

XI. Volunteers enlisted under this order will be credited as three years men in the quotas of their respective States. Instructions for the appointment of recruiting officers and for enlisting veteran volunteers will be immediately issued to the Governors of States.

By order of the Secretary of War.

E. D. TOWNSEND, Ass't Adj't Gen.

Military Men

Colonel Fritz Anneke

Friedrich "Fritz" Anneke was the colonel of Gilbert's regiment, Wisconsin's Thirty-Fourth.[2] He was born in Germany in 1818 and had been an artillery officer in Prussia. After he was discharged he emigrated to the United States as a refugee in 1849.

On March 10, Gilbert wrote from Columbus, Kentucky, "Our colonel's name is Fritz Anneke. He is an old artillery man and has, by a good deal of exertion, got the command of the guns and magazines here. I think that we shall be more likely to stay here if we work in the artillery service than if we were infantry." Then on March 15 he writes again detailing some misadventures during artillery drill: "A complaint was entered at headquarters and our colonel got a dispatch from the general. Since that time we have not drilled on the cannons, but had infantry drill."

General Alexander Asboth

The commanding general in Columbus, Kentucky, was Alexander Asboth. He was a lieutenant-colonel during Hungary's 1848–49 War of Liberation and one of the most loyal followers of Lajos Kossuth, Hungary's president during that time. After that revolution failed, Asboth came to the United States as a political refugee. Until the Civil War he worked as an engineer and helped to survey both Central Park and the upper west side of Manhattan in New York.

During the Civil War Asboth served as chief-of-staff for John C. Fremont, head of the Western Department headquartered in St. Louis. According to the eminent historian Allan Nevins: "Asboth was highly efficient in seeing that the new regiments drilled hard, steadily and with growing precision." Following Fremont's dismissal, Asboth remained in Missouri and participated in the Pea Ridge campaign, sustaining wounds in the battle. Later, he served as commander at Columbus, Kentucky, and fought against Nathan Bedford Forrest, one of the most famous Confederate cavalry leaders.

In recalling Asboth in his memoirs, Col. Philip Sheridan wrote: "General Asboth was a tall, spare, handsome man, with gray mustache and a fierce look. He was an educated soldier, of unquestioned courage."

The general is mentioned in Gilbert's letters of March 23, April 5, and June 15.

Lieutenant Henry T. Calkins

Henry T. Calkins was first lieutenant of Gilbert's company. He was from Merton, Wisconsin, a town about eleven miles northwest of Summit.

In Gilbert's August 16 letter, he told Esther that Lieutenant Calkins would come to get fruit when Gilbert returned.

Lieutenant Henry J. Curtice

On November 27, 1862, Gilbert wrote, "I do not spend my evenings in barracks, but in the tent of the chaplain or at the quartermaster department, Lieutenant Curtice of the 30th having charge." In his letter, Gilbert spells the name "Lieut. Certs," but the "Roster of Wisconsin Volunteers" shows no one named *Certs*, or anything more similar than *Curtice*, so I have changed the spelling to *Curtice* in the letter.

The "Roster of Wisconsin Volunteers" shows Henry J. Curtice from Wautoma, Wisconsin, in Company G of Wisconsin's Thirtieth Infantry Regiment. He enlisted August 21, 1862; was made second lieutenant September 11, 1862, and then captain February 21, 1865; and mustered out September 20, 1865.

The Civil War Pension Index shows that Maria L. Curtice, widow of Henry J. Curtice who served as captain in Wisconsin's Thirtieth Infantry Regiment, filed for a pension in Missouri. The dates of filing were July 31, 1890, for invalid class; and September 24, 1900, for widow class.

The 1870 census shows Henry and Maria Curtice living in Campbell, Greene County, Missouri, with three children: William (twelve), Charles (nine), and George (six). Henry is listed as a newspaper editor. In 1880 the census shows Henry J. Curtice in Neosho, Missouri, still an editor, still with his three boys: William (twenty-two), Charles (nineteen), and George (sixteen). However, his wife was now shown to be Louise C. Curtice. In 1900, the census shows Henry J. Curtice and Louise C. Curtice still in Neosho. Both Maria L. and Louise C. Curtice show as one year younger than Henry, but the changing wives of Henry Curtice remains one of the many mysteries in this book.

Edmund C. Davis

Edmund C. Davis, a wagoner from Raymond, Wisconsin, was Esther's cousin. He served in Wisconsin's Twenty-Second Infantry Regiment and was discharged April 25, 1863, on disability.

In her letter of March 12, Esther said Edmund Davis was in the Twenty-Second Wisconsin Regiment captured near Murfreesboro, Tennessee. In her letter of June 24, Esther reports that he was in the hospital when his regiment was captured, but heard that now he was at home, discharged. In her letter of July 12, Esther said that Edmund Davis and his wife came to visit.

Lieutenant David H. Dexter

David H. Dexter from Butler, Wisconsin, was second lieutenant in Company K of the Thirty-Fourth Regiment. He enrolled November 19, 1862, and died March 25, 1863, in Columbus, Kentucky, of disease.

The 1860 census shows David H. Dexter, a thirty-eight-year-old farmer from New York, living in Wauwatosa, Wisconsin, with thirty-three-year-old wife Mary T. Dexter and two children: Francis (nine) and Ada (three). The 1870 census shows Mary T. Dexter still living in Wauwatosa with the two children as well as two farm laborers.

In Gilbert's letter of March 23, 1863, he said, "Last night one of the lieutenants in company K died. His name was Dexter. He was from Wauwatosa. He had a fever. He leaves a wife but no children. He is the first one that has died since we left Camp Randall. I think that it is a little remarkable that out of over 400 men in our regiment no more have died."

Butler and Wauwatosa are both very near Milwaukee, about six and a half miles apart, and about thirty miles east of Summit.

Captain W. Eugene Ferslew

W. Eugene Ferslew from Spring Green, Wisconsin, was Gilbert's captain according to the "Roster of Wisconsin Volunteers." With one exception, Gilbert referred to him as "our captain" or "the captain" rather than by name.

For example, on January 18 Gilbert said, "Our captain has had a considerable trouble about his men leaving; some 12 have deserted and failed to return on furlough. The result is that he is more strict with the rest of us. I think the result will be that more will follow their example as he now refuses to grant any more furloughs 'til they return." On February 26, Esther reported, "Mr. Meigs called here yesterday to inquire after you. He wants you to remember him to the captain. He said if he and a few others had stayed that [they] would have shot the captain before now." On March 10, Gilbert replied, "Our captain is liked much better than he was at first. He is the best drilled man in the regiment. His name is E. W. Ferslew."

But on May 5 he talked at some length about "the petty tyranny of our captain. He has had considerable trouble with other officers and has been tried by court marshal once but got clear, and he is in hot water all the time; as everybody that has anything to do with him hates him; and he can vent his spite on no one but soldiers."

On May 30 the captain went to Memphis for a court-martial and was there until July 28. On June 29 Gilbert wrote, "The captain has not returned yet, and as near as we can learn he will be obliged to stay some time yet, and may not get through 'til our time is out. He has got about 50 dollars of the company fund in his hands, and I guess he will keep it, though he told me that after the 1st of July he was going to let us have it so that we could have lots of fun things to eat." On July 5 Esther responded, "I am glad your pet captain is away. I think you can afford to lose a dollar or two apiece if you can have a decent man at the head of your company."

On July 30, when the captain returned, Gilbert still talked about how everyone hated him, but finally on August 3 he wrote, "Well I suppose you are a little interested in how we get along with the captain. I can give you no better idea of how matters are progressing than by passing the remark of one of the boys the other day when a lot of us were talking on this subject. His remark was this: 'The captain is as sweet as a peach.' He does not act like the same man."

The captain was also mentioned in Gilbert's letters of February 11, February 18, May 11, June 7, June 15, June 21, and September 5, and Esther's of August 4.

Henry Higgins

Henry Higgins of Lisbon, Wisconsin, about fifteen miles northeast of Summit, was a friend of Gilbert in his company.

The 1860 census showed Henry as twenty-one years old, born in England, and living with his parents or grandparents, George (fifty-eight) and Emma (sixty). In 1850 there were three children in the household: George (fifteen), Henry (twelve), and Elizabeth (seven). In 1870, Emma was no longer listed, but Elizabeth had come back with two children of her own. The household then was George Higgins (sixty-eight), Elizabeth Salter (twenty-seven), Eli H. Salter (six), Elizabeth H. Salter (four), and Henry Higgins (thirty-two).

Henry was mentioned in Gilbert's letters of March 31, April 13, and May 5.

Second Lieutenant Michael A. Leahy

Gilbert reports at the end of June that Second Lieutenant Michael A. Leahy was very ill, but the "Roster of Wisconsin Volunteers" shows that he survived to be mustered out when his term expired September 8, 1863.

In the 1860 census he was listed as living in Portland, Wisconsin, and shown as a thirty-six-year-old farm laborer in the family of Stephen and Hanora Hanifon and their four children aged six to sixteen. Michael Leahy and all of the Hanifons except for the little girls (aged ten and six) were born in Ireland.

Michael is mentioned in Gilbert's letters of May 5 and June 29.

Richard Meigs

According to the November 18, 1862, *Waukesha Freeman*, Richard Meigs from Ottawa, Wisconsin, was one of the men drafted at the same time as Gilbert. He was discharged in early December while the regiment was still in Wisconsin.

He shows up in the Ottawa draft records of June 1863 as an unmarried, thirty-nine-year-old farmer, but he does not appear in the censuses of 1850 or 1860. In the 1870 census, a Richard Meigs of the correct age is shown living in a hotel in Sioux City, Iowa, working as a general laborer.

Richard Meigs is mentioned in Gilbert's letter of December 2, and in Esther's letters of December 4 and February 26.

Peter Olson

Gilbert's bunkmate was most likely Peter Olson from Coon, Wisconsin. The "Roster of Wisconsin Volunteers" for Gilbert's company shows three different Peters: Peter Goeden, who deserted January 31, 1863; Peter Peterson, who furnished a substitute December 9, 1862; and Peter Olson, who served his term and was mustered out along with Gilbert on September 8, 1863. Gilbert said in his letter of August 16, 1863, that his old bunkey was back with him after a long illness.

The 1860 census shows no Peter Olson, and only one Peter Olsen living in Coon, Wisconsin. He was a thirty-three-year-old carpenter/joiner at that time living with wife Ann (thirty) and daughter Matilda (fifteen). All three were born in Norway.

It is interesting that the *Waukesha Freeman* of November 18, 1862, listed three different Peters, all drafted from Waukesha County along with Gilbert on November 3: Peter Gill from Genesee, Peter Foley from Menomonee, and Peter Gaton from Menomonee. None of these three is listed in any regiment of the "Roster of Wisconsin Volunteers."

Peter is mentioned in Gilbert's letters of November 27, February 18, and August 16.

General Gideon Pillow

Gideon Johnson Pillow was appointed brigadier general by President James K. Polk at the beginning of the Mexican-American War, then became a Confederate brigadier on July 9, 1861. Throughout his career he demonstrated an amazing incompetence that left him, by the end of the war, serving as commissary general of prisoners. William T. Sherman assessed him brutally as "a mass of vanity, conceit, ignorance, ambition, and want of truth."

Pillow is mentioned in Gilbert's letter of February 3, 1863. The note following that letter quotes a letter from General Grant describing Pillow's inept idea for blocking the Mississippi River traffic with a giant chain.

Ludwig Potter

On November 21, Gilbert wrote, "There is but one case of favoritism among the Waukesha boys and that is Mr. Potter who has friends in Madison. He is fisting for the office of captain, but it will be a hard berth for him if he gets it, judging by what the boys say."

The roster of the Thirty-Fourth Regiment indicates the only Mr. Potter in that regiment was Ludwig Potter from Crystal Lake, Wisconsin. He was in Company A and deserted January 31, 1863.

The 1860 census shows Ludwig Potter, a thirty-six-year-old farmer, living in Crystal Lake with his wife Wilhelmina (thirty-three) and four children, aged one to eleven. Ludwig, Wilhelmina, and the eleven-year-old August were all born in Prussia.

John Roberts

The November 18, 1862, issue of the *Waukesha Freeman* lists John Roberts as one of twenty-nine men drafted from the town of Lisbon, Wisconsin. The "Roster of Wisconsin Volunteers" shows that he reached the rank of corporal and was discharged March 23, 1863.

The 1850 census shows two households of Roberts, totaling ten people, living next door to each other in Lisbon. All were born in England except for John, then seven, and his two younger siblings. The 1860 census shows only one household of six people. The 1870 census shows the family still in Lisbon. John, of course, was not there.

Gilbert told the sad story in his letters. March 10 he said John Roberts had got a discharge and Gilbert would send money to Esther by him. March 12 and again on March 15, Roberts had not got his discharge but expected it soon. March 21, Roberts got his discharge. March 23, Roberts left camp. April 13, "Roberts that took my letter to Milwaukee was quite unwell when he left camp. He got as far as Milwaukee and could get no farther. Higgins got a letter yesterday from his father saying Roberts was very low, and his father & mother were taking care of him." Finally, on April 23, Gilbert wrote, "John Roberts, the young man that took my money to Millwaukee, is dead. He never got home alive. I can hardly realize that he is gone, that his probation state is ended, but so it is."

Captain Thomas Stevens

Thomas N. Stevens was born in New York in 1835 but moved to Wisconsin at the age of seventeen. He was appointed post-master at Oconomowoc in May 1861 and helped recruit Company C of the Twenty-Eighth Regiment Wisconsin Infantry. The company was largely made up of boys from Oconomowoc and Summit. After the war, Stevens moved to Michigan where he held several public offices, including mayor of Greenville. He was married in 1857 and had five children.

Stevens is not mentioned by name in the letters, but the Twenty-Eighth is mentioned in Gilbert's letters of April 6 and July 18 and Esther's letters of July 12.

Adjutant General Lorenzo Thomas

In an effort to speed up the pace of organizing regiments of African American soldiers, Secretary of War Edwin M. Stanton sent Gen. Lorenzo Thomas to the lower Mississippi valley in March 1863. Thomas was to explain the administration's policy regarding these new recruits and to find volunteers to raise and command African American regiments. He was serving in this capacity when he visited the fort at Columbus, Kentucky, where Gilbert Claflin was stationed.

Colonel William L. Utley

Colonel William L. Utley was forty-eight years old in the spring of 1863. He had twice been Wisconsin's adjutant general and 1861 had placed thirty thousand Wisconsin soldiers in the field. He was colonel of Wisconsin's Twenty-Second Regiment, in which Esther's cousin Edmund Davis served. After the war he ran the *Racine Journal* for nine years, served as postmaster, and raised blooded horses. He was married twice and had four children (*The History of Racine and Kenosha Counties, Wisconsin* [Chicago: Western Historical, 1879], 613).

Utley was mentioned in Esther's letter of March 12.

Major George H. Walther

In her February 15, 1863, letter, Esther wrote about a letter from Gilbert's Major Walther.

George H. Walther enlisted July 19, 1861. He served first as a captain in the Seventh Wisconsin Infantry, and was wounded at Gainesville. On January 31, 1863, he was promoted to major of Gilbert's regiment. He was mustered out with the rest of the regiment on September 8, 1863. On December 23 of that year he joined the Thirty-fifth Wisconsin Infantry as major; was promoted to colonel October 24, 1865; and mustered out March 15, 1865.

Lieutenant Charles Whitaker

In her letter of December 18, 1862, Esther mentioned that "Mrs. Lieutenant Whitaker" was one of several people around Oconomowoc who had died recently, possibly of typhoid or diphtheria.

Charles Whitaker of Waterville, Wisconsin, was lieutenant colonel of Wisconsin's Twenty-Eighth Infantry Regiment with many soldiers from Oconomowoc and Summit. Waterville is about three miles southeast of Summit.

Lieutenant Colonel Charles A. Wood

In her letter of July 26, Esther said, "William has become a member of the Capitol Guards Company A. Lieutenant Colonel Wood having resigned is their captain."

The roster of the Wisconsin Eleventh Infantry Regiment shows Lieutenant Colonel Charles A. Wood of Madison. He held that rank from September 2, 1861, and resigned on June 7, 1863. It is possible this was the same Charles Wood, born 1841, who grew up in Oconomowoc and is discussed in Appendix B.

MILITARY ACTIONS

Gideon Pillow's Chain across the Mississippi

The following is a letter from Confederate Lieutenant Brown about the chain.[3]

MEMPHIS, November 1, 1861
    Capt. E. D. BLAKE, C.S. Army,
    Acting assistant Adjutant-General, Columbus, Ky.;
    Sir: I beg leave to state for the information of Major-General Polk that I
am now at Memphis collecting barges to be used in the construction of the
floating defenses at Fort Pillow. Owing to the weight of the chain to be used
across the river, barges will have to be relied on for buoys in place of rafts of
logs. The heavy anchors have not yet arrived, but are daily expected. The
chain is here . . .
    I Am, very respectfully,
    ISAAC N. BROWN,
    Lieutenant, C.S. Navy.

Following is a letter from Union General Grant about the chain.

Headquarters District of Cairo,
    Cairo, January 6, 1862
    Capt. J. C. Kelton,
    Asst. Adjt. Gen., Dept. of the Missouri, Saint Louis, Mo.:
    CAPTAIN: From information just received from Columbus the garrison
there is now reduced from what it was a few weeks ago by the withdrawal of
the sixty-days' men, who are supposed many of them to have gone to Camp
Beauregard. This leaves a force of probably thirty regiments in Columbus.
General Pillow has resigned and gone to his home, in consequence of being
ordered to Bowling Green.
    The rebels have a chain across the river about 1 mile above Columbus. It
is sustained by flats at intervals, the chain passing through staples placed
about the water's edge, the chain passing under the boats. Between each
pair of the boats a torpedo is attached to the chain, which is expected to
explode by concussion.
    An experiment was made with one of these machines about ten days ago
by directing a coal-boat against it. The experiment resulted satisfactorily to
the enemy. The position of them being so distinctly marked cannot be
regarded as much of an obstacle. Others are supposed to be planted in the
river above these, not so distinctly located. From information received
through a gentleman up from Memphis there are about 600 torpedoes in
the river from Columbus to that city.
    U. S. GRANT,
    Brigadier-General

Columbus, Kentucky, before Gilbert's Arrival

Kentucky as a whole was a carefully neutral state between the conflicts in the eastern states and those in Kansas and western Missouri for the first four and a half
months of the war. Many of the people of Hickman County, Kentucky, located in

the far west part of the state, were sympathetic with the South with more than seven hundred of Hickman's citizens fighting for the Confederacy. On September 3, 1861, Gideon Pillow, on orders of General Polk, entered Kentucky from Confederate strongholds in Northern Tennessee and moved to Columbus where his men began setting up and strengthening their position. The next day General Grant arrived at Cairo, Illinois, where he established Union headquarters. These actions were the final links to an unbroken front between North and South from the Atlantic west to Kansas.

The Battle of Belmont, November 7, 1861, took place in the hamlet of Belmont, Missouri, just across the river from Columbus, Kentucky. The greatest significance of the battle was that it provided battle experience to General Grant and his troops. When Grant received the erroneous intelligence that Confederates were moving from Columbus into Missouri, he personally led about three thousand troops and captured the Confederate camp near Belmont. Confederate reinforcements of about ten thousand troops from Columbus then caused Grant to remove his troops back to Cairo.

In early February 1862, Grant's forces captured the Confederate Fort Henry and Fort Donelson, just over the Kentucky border in Tennessee. This left Columbus a fairly isolated Confederate outpost. On March 2, 1862, the final units of Confederate troops left Columbus. Of the 140 Confederate guns, only two were left behind. The next day, March 3, Federal troops occupied the town and the forts on the bluff.

Below is an article from *Harper's Weekly*, March 29, 1862, that describes in some detail what Columbus was like soon after the Confederates left, about ten months before Gilbert arrived. The article includes descriptions of the bursting of the 128-pound gun "Lady Polk" and the discovery of explosives known as "infernal machines."

WE publish on page 197 illustrations of COLUMBUS, Kentucky, from sketches by Mr. Alexander Simplot. The Herald correspondent thus described the place after the evacuation:

The river batteries have been almost entirely demolished—three tiers of them—their guns dismounted and thrown into the river, the gun-carriages mutilated and magazines demolished, leaving nothing to mark their former presence save ruined breast-works and huge piles of cannon-balls and shells. Just below the upper river battery, a huge chain, which has been christened "Pillow's Folly," emerges from the water, extends up the almost perpendicular bank a hundred feet or more, and disappears under the soil, where it extends to—the Lord only knows where. This is the Kentucky end of the chain which the valiant inside-ditchdigger had stretched across the river to obstruct the passage of our gun-boats. A few feet above the chain and below the battery I counted five sixty-four pound guns which had been thrown over the breast-works, with the intention of sinking them in the river; but they had lodged in the yielding earth and become immovable. Two others lay a few rods below, which had been taken from the batteries on the bluff.

Within the breast-works on the hill there was nothing to be seen but the wildest desolation. Burning piles of rubbish, smouldering heaps of grain— the remnants of burned warehouses—charred timbers of what were once quarters for the troops, broken gun-carriages and disabled ordnance, completed the picture.

Leaving the lower town and ascending the hill in the rear, we get the most comprehensive view of the rebel works. From one point near the top of the hill my guide pointed out to me the locality of no less than eight different batteries, besides the positions of forty-five or fifty isolated pieces of heavy artillery. In all, I computed that a month ago there could not have been less than one hundred and thirty pieces of artillery, of the caliber of twenty-four pounders and upward, added to which there were over seventy pieces of light field artillery. Most of these heavy guns are now in the river, or disabled upon the works, easily fished up when the floods go down, or repaired by skillful workmen. I saw in the north fort, upon the brow of the bluff. The ruins of the celebrated one-hundred-twenty[-eight] pounder, Lady Polk, which burst in November last, coming to near causing the Very Reverend Bishop General to "puss in his cheeks." My guide was one of the gunners upon that occasion, and it was really amusing to hear his rendition of the affair:

"You see," said he, pointing to the breech of the piece, which lay precisely where it fell when the accident occurred, "dat is de butt of Lady Boke what busted. You see I vas standin' shoost here mit der sponge. Shendrel Boke shtood right dere on horsepach, und dem fellers mit der gold lace on der arms, und all over, was shtandin' all 'round; den der Shendrel say, 'Poys, look out; yen Lady Boke speaks I always sthop mine ears up.' Den he rides oop and dakes der lanyard and sherk him, and, mein Cott, you oughter see how Lady Boke she flies in leetle bieces. Her preech flies pack and shlaps ter Shendrel mit der pread pasket und makes hint double up like mine shack knife. Der Shendrel vas hurted purty pad, and his horse vas killed; but he shumps up and say, 'Never mind um, poys; dake care of dem odder fellers.' Den I look 'round, und dere was eight mens killed and more as a dozen wounded."

TORPEDOES AT COLUMBUS.

WE illustrate on page 198, from sketches by our correspondent, Mr. Alexander Simplot, the TORPEDOES AND INFERNAL MACHINES which have been discovered by our troops at Columbus. The correspondent of the Chicago Times thus describes them:

After two days' exploration for infernal machines, and to discover where the bluff had been mined, as was reported to have been done, Captain W. A. Schmitt and company, of the Twenty-seventh Regiment, discovered ridges of new earth, similar to ridges which are formed by covering up gas or water pipes in a city, and traced them to a cavern. Effecting an entrance he found a strong, rude, wooden frame, covered by earth to attract no attention.

Inside this, with the assistance of a light, he found implements similar to those used in a telegraph office, with wires running in a dozen different directions. Following the raised rows of earth he soon came to a spot where something had evidently been buried. Digging down some five feet, he came to a large iron cask, about three feet high, and a foot and a half through, in shape as near as can be described to a well-formed pear, with an iron cap fastened by eight screws. Taking off the cap we found grape, canister, and four eight-pound shell, surrounded by about two bushels of coarse powder. On the bottom of the cask there was a wooden box containing several batteries, with hollow wires attached to two larger wires, covered with a substance impervious to water, connecting with the cavern before spoken of. A dozen of these iron pots or casks were thus united with this cavern. Half a dozen of these caverns have been found, and probably 75 or 100 of these infernal machines are thus buried in the earth, some distance from the enemy's works; and the time to be exploded would be when our infantry had driven them inside their works—a sentinel would give the operator inside the cavern a signal, and he would send the electric spark through all the wires, and decamp. The result may be imagined. Whole regiments could thus be blown up and sent to eternity, without even a chance of escape. The discoveries, as far as made, are all on the north and northeast portions of their works. Probably other parts of the works are similarly mined. Fortunately their fiendish designs were discovered in time, and no damage has been done by soldiers, who are constantly on the look-out for discoveries, and might by accident have set off the train.

Another class of infernal machines, called torpedoes, have been discovered anchored in the river. They are round, about three feet long and a foot and a half in diameter, with one end tapering off to a point. The river is very high, and the number can not be made out. It took three steamers five days to sink what are in the bottom of the river. The very high stage of water has prevented any damage to either gun-boat or transport.

By the time Gilbert arrived in early 1863, the Federals held Columbus. Here they collected and guarded prisoners, sheltered and enlisted runaway slaves, and sent out occasional minor expeditions. It was a quiet corner of the war.

The Action at Fort Heiman

Fort Heiman, about seventy miles east of Columbus, Kentucky, was on a bluff across the Tennessee River from Fort Henry. Both forts were in Federal control beginning February 1862. They defended the important supply line that was the Tennessee River, and provided haven for many escaping slaves.

On March 12, 1863, the following report was made from US Major General Hurlbut to US Major General Rosecrans: "General: It being officially reported to me that Forts Henry and Heiman were occupied by the rebels, I have ordered an expedition to retake them."

The same day, March 12, Gilbert wrote to Esther, "3 regiments are leaving and going up the river: the 3rd Minnesota, the 25th Wisconsin, and the 111th Illinois. They are expecting to be called on to fight."

On March 18, General Asboth wrote to Major General Hurlbut: "In obedience to your orders, reoccupied Fort Heiman, on the 14th, in the morning. . . . I left the Third Minnesota and One hundred and eleventh Illinois Volunteers, with two pieces of artillery and two companies of cavalry, as garrison."

Battle of Chalk Bluff

Gilbert's letter of April 30, 1863, tells of great excitement in the camp between April 25 and 29. This excitement was in response to activity that led up to the Battle of Chalk Bluff in early May.

Starting on April 17, Confederate General John Sappington Marmaduke led a raid into Missouri to attack Union forces under Brigadier General John McNeil at Bloomfield in the southeastern part of the state. McNeil was able to take his forces to the fortified Union supply base at Cape Girardeau, Missouri, on the Mississippi River about sixty miles north of Columbus, Kentucky.

At Cape Girardeau, General McNeil was reinforced with troops from Columbus, and more Union troops under Brigadier General William Vandever were moving in from the west. General Marmaduke's Confederate forces retreated southward to Chalk Bluff where, the night of May 1–2, they crossed the St. Francis River into Arkansas.

The crossing at Chalk Bluff was difficult, as they had to quickly build a floating bridge for the men and swim exhausted horses across. Some of Marmaduke's forces had built a series of trenches along the last four miles of the way and success-fully delayed the Federal forces long enough for most of the Confederates to get across the river. McNeil did not follow the raiders back into Arkansas, but the Con-federates continued to withdraw toward Jacksonport.

The part played by the soldiers from Columbus in repulsing the Confederates from Cape Girardeau can be seen in the official correspondence of their command-ing general, Alexander Asboth, below.

> HDQRS. SIXTH DIVISION, SIXTEENTH ARMY CORPS,
>   Columbus, Ky., April 26, 1863.
>   GENERAL: Lieutenant Livingston, aide-de-camp to Brigadier-General Montgomery, has just arrived from Cairo, and reports that heavy artillery firing commenced early this morning at Cape Girardeau, and has continued all day.
>   I would be glad to take the enemy in the rear, but my troops here are all provided with condemned arms, worthless in the field. The Bostona Number 2 is now at landing, with over 10,000 stand of good arms and ammunition, consigned to Captain J. P. Harper, Memphis. Can I take 3,000 stand and ammunition for my troops, and will you give your consent to the movement proposed?

I will, in anticipation, take steps immediately to secure transportation.
ASBOTH
Brigadier-General
[addressed to] Major-General HURLBUT,
Memphis, Tenn.

Response from Assistant Adjutant General Henry Binmore, April 26, 1863:

Memphis,
   April 26, 1863–11 p. m.
   Brigadier General A. ASBOTH:
   The commanding general directs that if you are sure there is a real
attack, you will take 3,000 stand of arms and move up.
   Respectfully,
   HENRY BINMORE,
   Assistant Adjutant-General

Below is a report from Brigadier General Alexander Asboth the next day:

HDQRS. SIXTH DIVISION, SIXTEENTH ARMY CORPS,
   Columbus, Ky., April 27, 1863
   COLONEL: At the urgent solicitation of Brigadier General John McNeil,
commanding at Cape Girardeau, I have this morning sent him two
regiments of infantry, a section of artillery, and 100,000 rounds of
ammunition for his command, with directions to send back the troops as
soon as re-enforced by Brigadier-General Vandever, which he expected
to-day. General McNeil wrote me that he had been attacked by Marmaduke,
with four brigades, 8,000 men, and repulsed him, but would be attacked
again.
   As my troops here were all provided with condemned arms, I considered
it necessary to take from a large lot of good arms on steamer Bostona
Number 2, consigned to Captain Harper, Memphis, 3,000 Enfield rifled
muskets, as alluded to in yesterday's telegram, and had my explanatory
report ready to send by Bostona, but she left from the lower depot without
orders or permission. The report will be sent by first boat.
   ASBOTH,
   Brigadier-General
   [addressed to] Lieutenant-Colonel BINMORE,
   Assistant Adjutant-General, Memphis, Tenn.

Below are addenda to the report from Brigadier General Alexander Asboth:

SAINT LOUIS, April 27, 1863.
   General ASBOTH:

My troops have routed the rebels near Cape Girardeau, and they retreated toward Chalk Bluff. Even a small additional force at New Madrid would admit of a successful move from that point. There is some trouble crossing Little River, but this makes it safe if the enemy goes down on the west side of Little River.

SAML. R. CURTIS,
Major-General

SAINT LOUIS, April 27, 1863.

General ASBOTH:

If you can send force to Chalk Bluff, via New Madrid, you may take Marmaduke in flank, or cut off his retreat. Some artillery and cavalry would be necessary. The river swamp would be the proper base to hold, while light troops act toward Chalk Bluff and New Madrid. Infantry will co-operate.

SAML. R. CURTIS,
Major-General

HDQRS. SIXTH DIVISION, SIXTEENTH ARMY CORPS,

Columbus, April 27, 1863.

GENERAL: I this morning sent two regiments of infantry, two companies of cavalry, a section of artillery, and 100,000 rounds of small-arm ammunition to Brigadier-General McNeil, at Cape Girardeau, being all in my power to accomplish, having no more infantry or artillery that can be sent, which I regret exceedingly. I will immediately secure transportation, and send six companies of cavalry to New Madrid, to operate as desired by you, as far as possible.

ASBOTH,
Brigadier-General
[addressed to]
Major General SAMUEL R. CURTIS, Saint Louis, Mo.

Below is a report from Brigadier General Alexander Asboth and a response from Brigadier General Samuel Curtis, both on April 28, 1863:

HDQRS. SIXTH DIVISION, SIXTEENTH ARMY CORPS,

Columbus, April 28, 1863. 2:15 p.m.

GENERAL: Six companies of the Fourth Missouri Cavalry, Major Langen commanding, left last evening for New Madrid, with orders to co-operate with the commander of that post. The rebels being repulsed from Cape Girardeau, I request that my troops sent yesterday morning may be immediately ordered back. An action is now going on in the direction of Charleston, the cannonading being very distinct. I hope my cavalry is at work, and I have ordered General Buford to inform General McNeil of their co-operation.

ASBOTH,
Brigadier-General
[addressed to] Major-General CURTIS, Saint Louis.

SAINT LOUIS,
    April 28, 1863.
    General ASBOTH:
    GENERAL: Your troops sent to Cape Girardeau have started back. Accept
my thanks for this and other favors. Press the New Madrid movement. The
rebels made a stand for several hours yesterday, but finally retired and
retreated toward Bloomfield. There must be a pretty strong force.
    SAML. R. CURTIS,
    Brigadier-General

Meanwhile, on April 30, Gilbert's company, Company A of the Wisconsin
Thirty-Fourth Infantry, was sent to Fort Quinby, just north of Columbus, to man
the artillery and reinforce the fortifications. Gilbert was still there when the troops
returned from the action at Cape Girardeau.

The Affair at Obion Plank Road Crossing, Tennessee

In his May 5, 1863, letter, Gilbert wrote, "Last week our cavalry brought in 10 guerrillas and their horses. They passed right by where we are camped. They were a
rough looking set. They were captured near the Tennessee line." The Rebel band
was led by the infamous guerrilla Captain Parks. This incident was known as the
"Affair at Obion Plank Road Crossing." Below is General Asboth's report of the
incident:

Columbus, KY., May 8, 1863
    Sir: I beg to report that Company E, Fifteenth Illinois Cavalry Volunteers,
First Lieut. William B. Ford commanding, succeeded in surprising the
notorious guerrilla, Captain Parks, with his band, encamped on the Obion
Plank Road Crossing, 70 miles distant from Hickman. The rebels fired
upon our men, but were gallantly charged. One lieutenant and 3 of their
men killed and 18 taken prisoners, including Capt. J. H. Parks and First
Lieut. A. W. Henry. Thus another guerrilla company is destroyed, and I
have now 4 noted guerrilla leaders here. Scales, Cotter, Cushman, and
Parks, all to be tried as highway robbers. Tomorrow our artist will combine
the four in a picture. The officers and men of Company E, Fifteenth Cavalry
Volunteers, are deserving of all praise. Telegraphic communication is open
between here and Hickman.
    ASBOTH
    Brigadier-General
    [addressed to] Lieut. Col. Henry Binmore,
    Assistant Adjutant General.

Troop Movements from Columbus

On May 10, 1863, Gilbert wrote to Esther, "It is quite an exciting time here; notwithstanding it is the day of Holy rest. The 34th (with the exception of our company) and the 25th have got marching orders for Memphis. But as orders are given and countermanded so often, it is not fully certain that they will go. But the 25th have got packed up, and some of the tents have been taken down." The next day he wrote, "The 25th are under marching orders. Six companies of the 34th went on board a steamer . . . last night. . . . The 21st Illinois [probably the Twenty-First *Missouri* Infantry Regiment] has just marched by and are going to Memphis along with the 34th. The 25th are going to Clinton as report says now." Below is a letter from Brigadier General Asboth to Major General Hurlbut concerning these troop movements:

Columbus, Ky., May 11, 1863
    Maj. Gen. Stephen A. Hurlbut,
    Commanding Sixteenth Army Corps, Memphis, Tenn.:
    GENERAL: I have the honor to report, that in obedience to Special
Orders, No. 93, Headquarters Sixteenth Army Corps, 1863, the Twenty-first
Regiment Missouri Volunteer Infantry, Col. David Moore commanding, and
six companies of the Thirty-fourth Regiment Wisconsin Infantry, drafted
militia, Maj. George H. Walther commanding, are embarked on steamer
Sultana for Memphis, with orders to report to your headquarters. The
Twenty-first Regiment Missouri Infantry is an old regiment, and its colonel
a gallant, earnest officer, who lost a leg on the battle-field of Shiloh. The
Thirty-fourth Regiment Wisconsin Infantry has done heavy artillery duty,
and is well drilled in that service. Four companies of the Thirty-fourth
Regiment Wisconsin Infantry are detailed to serve the heavy guns in
different forts in my district—one company at Columbus, in fort Quinby,
two at Cairo, and one at Paducah, and as I have no artillerists to serve the
guns in the forts, I would respectfully request your permission that they
may continue on their present duty. The colonel, Fritz Anneke, is under
arrest, and awaiting trial before general court-martial.
    Knowing the proclivities of the people of Kentucky between the
Tennessee and Mississippi rivers, and being aware that their sympathies
are, with few exceptions, with the south and the rebellion, I consider it
unsafe for my district, and particularly Paducah, to again evacuate Fort
Heiman, which is certainly the key to the above portion of Kentucky and a
point also controlling the Kentucky and Tennessee State line. Under these
conditions, I concluded to withdraw for the present my infantry force from
Clinton, and make it a cavalry outpost.
    Inclosed [sic] I submit section 9, Special Orders, No. 109, current series,
form these headquarters, giving instructions to Maj. Gustav Heinrichs,
Fourth Regiment Missouri Volunteer Cavalry, who takes command at
Clinton.

Requesting your sanction to these my arrangements, I have the honor to remain, general, very respectfully, your obedient servant,

ASBOTH,

Brigadier-General, Commanding.

Skirmish near Lexington, Tennessee, Late June 1863

In his July 10, 1863, letter, Gilbert told of witnessing a reunion between a young African American and his parents. The young man had been last seen during a skirmish near Lexington, Tennessee, in which members of the Fourth Missouri Cavalry and Fifteenth Kentucky Cavalry were ambushed by a large force of Confederates. The young man's horse had got stuck in a river when the Rebels were in hot pursuit, and he was presumed dead. The skirmish is reported below by officers of both the Fourth Missouri and the Fifteenth Kentucky cavalries.

Report of Lieutenant M. M. R. William Grebe, Fourth Missouri Cavalry:

Fort Heiman, July 7, 1863

I arrived here last night with 2 officers and about 40 men of the Fourth Missouri Cavalry Regiment and 10 men of the Fifteenth Kentucky Cavalry Regiment. Lieutenant-Colonel von Helmrich and Lieutenant Garrett are missing, and probably taken prisoners. All the officers of the Fifteenth Kentucky Cavalry Regiment are missing.

On the morning of June 29, we left Spring Creek to go to Lexington. When within 2 miles of the latter place, we were informed that a large force of rebel troops was there, probably 15,000 men, and that another force from Jackson, about 500 strong, was to attack us in our rear. Lieutenant-Colonel von Helmrich concluded to fall back to Spring Creek to avoid the cut off. When on the march back there, we were attacked by a force of about 2,000 rebels at 2 p.m., who were lying in ambush, whom we did not see till they fired upon our advance guard. Lieutenant-Colonel von Helmrich has done the best he could do, but we met with a bad fate. As we were very hardly pursued, and not able to reach Columbus, we concluded to fall back to Fort Heiman. As all our men and horses are entirely broken down, and many men without arms, and cannot be of any assistance to the fort here, we intend to leave here by the first boat, to go to Columbus.

The whole force of the enemy under command of General [R. V.] Richardson is reported to be from 20,000 to 25,000 men, well armed, and all mounted; and the nearest pickets are reported at Paris, Tenn.

I have the honor to remain, your most obedient servant,

M. M. R. WILLIAM GREBE

First Lieut., Comdg. Detachment Fourth Missouri Cavalry

Brig. Gen. A. ASBOTH, Commanding District.

Report of Major Wiley Waller, Fifteenth Kentucky Cavalry:

Headquarters United States Forces,
   Fort Heiman, July 4, 1863
   GENERAL: I have the honor to report that in the absence of Lieut. Col.
A. P. Henry, I have assumed command of this post.
   On the 26th instant, Lieutenant-Colonel Henry, with the entire effective
force of the cavalry at this post, numbering 185, rank and file, started on an
expedition against [J. B.] Biffle. He was joined by the forces under
Lieutenant-Colonel von Helmrich, of the Fourth Missouri Cavalry,
numbering 80, rank and file, at Paris, Tenn. The forces then moved to
Lexington, and from there toward Jackson, and encountered a rebel force,
estimated at from 1,000 to 1,500 strong. A skirmish ensued under the
direction of Lieutenant-Colonel von Helmrich, which lasted some hour and
a half, when our forces retreated, and were rapidly pursued by the enemy.
The rear guard made several stands, each time inflicting severe loss on the
enemy.
   The loss from the Fifteenth Kentucky, as near as can be ascertained, is as
follows: One lieutenant-colonel, 1 captain, 3 lieutenants, 35 enlisted men,
and a considerable number of horses, arms, &c.
   Several of our men have returned paroled, and I would respectfully ask
for instructions as to what disposition to make of them.
   The situation of the cavalry at this time is bad; almost all the horses they
had were engaged in the skirmish, and, after a hasty retreat of 100 miles,
those that have reached camp are utterly exhausted, and will be unfit for
service for some time. The force also is quite small, and unable to withstand
an attack of 500 men. The enemy has a force of from 10,000 to 15,000 men
within 100 miles of this post, and some small bodies as close as 30 miles,
and but for the gunboats we might be attacked any hour. Yet we are willing
to do everything in our power, and expect to hold the place as long as
possible.
   Please let me hear from you at your earliest convenience.
   I am, general, very respectfully yours,
   W. WALLER
   Major, Commanding Post.
   Brig. Gen. A. ASBOTH, Commanding District of Columbus

Capture of the Outpost at Union City,
Tennessee, July 10, 1863

In his letter of July 18, 1863, Gilbert wrote about the capture of two companies of
the Fourth Missouri Cavalry stationed at Union City, Tennessee, twenty-five miles
from Columbus, Kentucky, by some of Forrest's band. This incident is detailed in
the reports by Brigadier General Alexander Asboth, Colonel John Scott, and Major
Edward Langen.

Report of Brigadier General Alexander Asboth, US Army, commanding District of Columbus, Kentucky:

Headquarters, District of Columbus, 6th Division, 16th A.C.
  Columbus, Ky., July 12, 1863
  COLONEL: I beg leave to report that, on the 10th instant, about 7 a.m., the advanced cavalry post of Union City was surprised by a rebel force of 600 cavalry, under Colonel [J. B.] Biffle. Our loss is from 90 to 100 men killed, wounded, and prisoners.
  I immediately ordered Colonel Scott, Thirty-second Iowa Infantry, with six companies of his regiment, by railroad, to Union City, but the rebels had left the place an hour before his arrival. Inclosed please find Colonel Scott's report, showing that the disaster was caused by the total neglect of the officers to follow even the ordinary military precautions, not to speak of my peremptory and repeated orders directing the utmost vigilance.
  As the rebel force is rapidly increasing in the District of Jackson, by recruiting and conscription, I requested Major-General Schofield to reinforce me, and last night 600 men arrived from New Madrid as a temporary loan.
  Feeling the great importance of holding our communications and river navigation open and uninterrupted, I again respectfully request that some additional cavalry and a battery of light artillery may be sent me, and now that Vicksburg has fallen, and troops can be spared from there, I ask that, if possible, Montgomery's brigade, comprising four of my old infantry regiments, may be ordered back to this district.
  Should the general commanding direct General Dodge to move a force to Jackson and above, I would request to be informed in time, so as to be enabled to co-operate as far as my limited force will admit.
  Respectfully, colonel, your obedient servant,
  ASBOTH
  Brigadier-General.
  Lieut. Col. Henry Binmore
  Assistant Adjutant-General

Report of Colonel John Scott, Thirty-Second Iowa Infantry:

Headquarters, Thirty-second Iowa Infantry
  Camp near Columbus, KY, July 11, 1863.
  CAPTAIN: In obedience to the verbal orders of the general commanding, I have the honor to report that, on the 10th instant, with the effective men of my command (164 enlisted men, 9 line officers, and 5 officers of the field and staff), I proceeded by rail to Union city, Tenn.
  I found on my arrival at that point, at about 3 p.m., that the place and Federal forces had been captured by rebel forces, said to be under colonel

Biffle, of Forrest's command, at about 7 a.m. It was a complete surprise, and no organized resistance was made. From information received, I may state the loss at 2 killed 8 wounded, about 90 prisoners, 116 horses, and transportation and camp equipage at the post destroyed.

I estimate the rebel forces at about 650. They retired in the direction of Troy. At about 2 p.m. I found the citizens engaged in burying our dead and caring for the wounded. The latter, except one man, not able to be moved, I brought to post hospital at this place. The former I left to be decently buried by the citizens.

The names of the killed are Henry Rosengoetter, private company C, Fourth Missouri Cavalry, and Henry Stribbers (or Strubberg), private Company E, Fourth Missouri Cavalry.

The only loss ascertained to have been sustained by the rebels was 1 man wounded severely.

I should mention that both officers and men of my command behaved well, and confidently advanced upon the town, believing it to be then occupied by a superior force.

Your most obedient servant,
JOHN SCOTT,
Colonel Thirty-second Iowa Infantry.
Capt. T. H. Harris,
Assistant Adjutant-General, Columbus, KY

Report of Major Edward Langen, Fourth Missouri Cavalry:

Columbus, KY, August 8, 1863
CAPTAIN: In obedience to orders from headquarters District of Columbus, KY, Maj. G. Heinrichs, commanding post Clinton, KY, ordered on the 26th day of June 1863 company C, Capt. C. Rosa, and Company E, Captain Illig, of the Fourth Regiment Missouri Volunteer Cavalry, both companies under the command of Capt. C. Rosa, to Union City, Tenn., as advanced post, and continued there until the 10th day of July 1863 where we were, in the morning between 9 and 10 o'clock, surprised by a rebel force superior in numbers.

The rebels surrounded the place, and, after a short fight, in which 2 were killed and 8 men wounded, the whole command was captured, except 2 men, who escaped to Clinton, KY.

All the camp and garrison equipage, books, and papers belonging to said companies were also taken and partly destroyed by the enemy, who left the place two hours after their first appearance, taking along with them all the officers and men as prisoners, except the dead and wounded, the former unburied, the latter to the mercy of the inhabitants of the place. Brigadier-General Asboth sent, as soon as he heard of the disaster, re-enforcements by railroad, which found the place evacuated by the enemy, buried the dead, and brought the wounded to Columbus, KY, in hospital.

Inclosed you will find a list of killed, wounded, and prisoners of both companies.

Your most obedient servant,

EDWARD LANGEN,

Major, Comdg. Detachment Fourth Missouri Volunteer Cavalry.

Capt. T. H. HARRIS, Assistant Adjutant-General

Yazoo Pass Expedition

On February 28 Gilbert wrote, "About 11 one of the iron-clad gunboats passed down the river. It was truly a formidable looking craft. In company was a government dispatch boat or telegraph boat—small but very fast—also a steam dredge and a government transport which had attached to her 4 mortar boats with mortars on them. They were going to Vicksburg, I believe, and may be used to take the place."

During February and March 1863, part of General Grant's plan to capture Vicksburg was to go through the Yazoo Pass, about three hundred miles north of Vicksburg, and proceed via the Coldwater, Tallahatchie, and Yazoo rivers to reach high ground east of Vicksburg. A short canal was cut through the east levee of the Mississippi to reach and clear the Yazoo Pass, a rapid, crooked, narrow stream leading to the series of rivers. The streams were too narrow and the lands too wet for Federal forces to mount an effective attack on Fort Pemberton—about a hundred miles north of Vicksburg. The expedition forces withdrew in April without success.

REGIMENTAL HISTORIES—WISCONSIN

First Wisconsin Cavalry

In Gilbert's letter of April 30, he said, "The First Wisconsin Cavalry were in the fight back of the town and were somewhat cut up. I saw a list of the killed and wounded but did not see any names that I knew." Volume 22 of *The War of the Rebellion: A Compilation of the Official Records of the Union and Confederate Armies* shows five killed, nine wounded, and eight captured or missing from the First Wisconsin Cavalry during the action against Marmaduke's raid April 17 through May 2, 1863.[4]

The "Roster of Wisconsin Volunteers" gives this short history of the regiment:

> The 1st Wisconsin Cavalry was organized at Camp Harvey in Kenosha between September 1, 1861, and February 2, 1862. It mustered in on March 10, 1862, and left for St. Louis, Missouri, on March 17, 1862, where it was stationed at Benton Barracks until April 28. It traveled to Camp Girardeau, Missouri, on April 28, 1862, where it was attached to a series of Union cavalry brigades that fought in Kentucky, Georgia, Tennessee, and Alabama over the next four years. The regiment fought at the Battle of Chickamauga on September 19–20, 1863, in the Atlanta Campaign the following year, and helped capture Confederate president Jefferson Davis on May 10, 1865. The

1st Cavalry lost a total of 401 men during service. Six officers and 67 enlisted men were killed. Seven officers and 321 enlisted men died from disease.

Third Wisconsin Infantry

The Third Wisconsin Infantry (Company K) was the regiment to which Esther's brother Asa belonged. He served from June 6, 1861, until his death at the Battle of Resaca, May 15, 1864. He was mentioned in letters May 4, May 17, May 21, May 26, July 28, and August 4.

The "Roster of Wisconsin Volunteers" gives this short history of the regiment:

> The Third Wisconsin Infantry was organized at Camp Hamilton, in Fond Du Lac and mustered into service on June 19, 1861. From Wisconsin it moved to Hagerstown, Maryland, on July 12 and then went on to Harper's Ferry, West Virginia, July 18, 1861. During its service it moved through Maryland, Virginia, the Washington D.C. area, and Pennsylvania. After brief duties in New York and Alabama, it moved through Georgia, the Carolinas, and ended up in Kentucky. It fought at the Second Battle of Bull Run, Antietam, Chancellorsville, Gettysburg, Resaca, and in the siege of Atlanta, and participated in Sherman's March to the Sea. It was mustered out at Louisville, Kentucky, on July 18, 1865. The regiment lost 282 men during service. Nine officers and 158 enlisted men were killed. Two officers and 113 enlisted men died from disease.

Thirteenth Wisconsin Infantry

The Thirteenth Wisconsin Infantry (Company H) was Esther's oldest brother Jonas Parmenter's regiment from August 30, 1862, until he mustered out July 5, 1865. Much of the time that Gilbert was stationed in Columbus, Kentucky, Jonas Parmenter Colby was stationed at nearby Forts Henry and Donelson. J.P., as he was usually called, was mentioned in letters January 22, January 29, February 12, February 26, March 2, April 16, April 23, April 30, May 4, May 6, May 17, June 7, June 8, June 9, June 10, June 19, July 12, July 18, July 26, and July 29.

The "Roster of Wisconsin Volunteers" gives this short history of the regiment:

> The 13th Wisconsin Infantry was organized at Camp Tredway in Janesville and mustered into service on October 17, 1861. The regiment left Wisconsin for Leavenworth, Kansas, on January 13, 1862. During its service it moved through Missouri, Kentucky, Alabama, and Tennessee, where it served on duty at Forts Henry and Donelson. The regiment mustered out on November 24, 1865, having lost 193 men. Five enlisted men were killed and 188 enlisted men died from disease.

Sixteenth Wisconsin Infantry

The Sixteenth Wisconsin Infantry (Companies A and B) was the regiment that Esther's youngest brother, John, served in from October 7, 1861, until his discharge on May 1, 1863. John was mentioned in letters November 21, November 23, January 11, January 14, January 19, January 22, January 29, February 3, February 16, February 26, March 15, March 26, April 1, April 16, April 24, May 1, May 11, June 19, June 22, June 29, and July 28.

The "Roster of Wisconsin Volunteers" gives this short history of the regiment:

> The Sixteenth Wisconsin Infantry was organized at Camp Randall in Madison and mustered into service on January 31, 1862. The regiment left Wisconsin for St. Louis, Missouri, on March 13, 1862, and then traveled promptly to Pittsburg Landing, Tennessee, March 14–20. During its service it moved through Tennessee, Mississippi, Louisiana, Georgia, the Carolinas, and Washington D.C. It participated in the battles of Shiloh, Corinth, Jonesboro, Kennesaw Mountain, Atlanta, and Savannah, Sherman's March to the Sea, and the surrender of the Confederate army. On June 7, 1865, the regiment moved to Louisville, Kentucky, where it mustered out on July 12, 1865. The regiment lost 399 men during service. Six officers and 141 enlisted men were killed. Four officers and 248 enlisted men died from disease.

Twentieth Wisconsin Infantry

The Twentieth Wisconsin Infantry Regiment was mentioned in Gilbert's letter of June 8. "Yesterday 4 steamers passed down the river loaded with soldiers. I was told that the 20th Wisconsin was one of the regiments passing." They would have been on their way from St. Louis, Missouri, to the siege of Vicksburg.

The "Roster of Wisconsin Volunteers" gives this short history of the regiment:

> The Twentieth Wisconsin Infantry was organized at Camp Randall in Madison and mustered into service on August 23, 1862. The regiment left Wisconsin for St. Louis, Missouri, on August 30, and quickly traveled to Benton Barracks on September 2 and then to Rolla, Missouri, on September 6. Expeditions and service took the regiment through Missouri, Arkansas, Mississippi, Louisiana, Texas, Mexico, and Alabama over the next three years. It participated in the Battle of Prairie Grove, the Siege of Vicksburg, the protection of the American Consul in Matamoras, Mexico, and the assault and the capture of Fort Blakely, Alabama. The regiment was ordered to Galveston, Texas, and served on duty there until July 14, 1865, when it mustered out. It lost 251 men during service. Five officers and one hundred enlisted men were killed. One officer and 145 enlisted men died from disease.

Twenty-Second Wisconsin Infantry

Esther's cousin Edmund Davis served in the Twenty-Second Wisconsin Infantry Regiment. He is mentioned in letters of March 12, June 24, and July 12.

The "Roster of Wisconsin Volunteers" gives this short history of the regiment:

The 22nd Wisconsin Infantry was organized at Camp Utley in Racine and mustered into service on September 2, 1862. The regiment left Wisconsin for Cincinnati, Ohio, on September 16 and then traveled promptly to Covington, Kentucky. During the war it moved through Kentucky, Tennessee, Missouri, Georgia, the Carolinas, Virginia, and Washington D.C. Nearly 200 men of the regiment were captured at Thompson's Station, Tennessee, on March 5, 1863, and soon thereafter the regiment was surrounded and surrendered after action at Little Harpeth, Tennessee, on March 25. After an exchange of prisoners on May 5, 1863, the regiment reorganized at St. Louis, Missouri. It went on to participate in the battles of Resaca, Lost Mountain, Kennesaw Mountain, the Siege of Atlanta, Sherman's March to the Sea, the campaign of the Carolinas, the Battle of Bentonville, and the surrender of the Confederate army. The regiment mustered out on June 12, 1865, after losing 243 men during service. Two officers and 75 enlisted men were killed. Three officers and 163 enlisted men died from disease.

Twenty-Fourth Wisconsin Infantry

Esther's brother James served in the Twenty-Fourth Wisconsin Infantry Regiment, Company G, from August 11, 1862, until his medical discharge on March 24, 1863. During that time he was mentioned in letters of November 23, November 27, November 30, January 19, February 12, March 2, and March 23.

The "Roster of Wisconsin Volunteers" gives this short history of the regiment:

The 24th Wisconsin Infantry was organized at Milwaukee and mustered into service on August 15, 1862. The regiment left the state for Louisville, Kentucky, on September 5, 1862, and from Kentucky moved through Indiana, Ohio, Tennessee, Georgia, Alabama, and back to Tennessee. It participated in the battles of Perryville, Stones River, Chattanooga, Resaca, Kennesaw Mountain, and Jonesboro, the Siege of Atlanta, and the Battle of Franklin. From Alabama the regiment moved north to Nashville, where it participated in the Battle of Nashville and then remained on duty until being mustered out on June 10, 1865. The regiment lost 201 men during service. Eight officers and 103 enlisted men were killed. Three officers and 87 enlisted men died from disease.

Twenty-Fifth Wisconsin Infantry

On December 18, 1862, one month after Gilbert came to Camp Randall in Madison, the Twenty-Fifth Wisconsin Infantry returned there from their three-hundred-mile march at the end of their engagement with the Indian War in southeastern Minnesota. The Twenty-Fifth's duties during the Sioux Uprising were their first during combat after being mustered in at La Crosse, Wisconsin, on September 14, 1862.

The regiment stayed at Camp Randall until February 17, 1863, when they were sent to Cairo, Illinois, and then to Columbus, Kentucky. Except for brief expeditions, the Twenty-Fifth waited in Columbus until the last day of May when they went down the Mississippi River to join Grant's army advancing on Vicksburg.

For the remainder of the war, the regiment saw plenty of action, taking part in sieges of Vicksburg, Atlanta, and Savannah; in many battles, including Resaca in Georgia where Esther's brother Asa was killed; and in Sherman's "March to the Sea."

Before they were mustered out on June 7, 1865, 49 members of the Twenty-Fifth had died of wounds and 409 of disease.

Twenty-Seventh Wisconsin Infantry

A majority of the Twenty-Seventh enlisted during August 1862. The regiment was organized in Milwaukee and mustered in March 7, 1863.

They were stationed at Columbus, Kentucky, until the end of May 1863 when they went down the Mississippi River along with the Twenty-Fifth Regiment to take part in the siege of Vicksburg. After that the Twenty-Seventh was stationed in Arkansas until February 1865 when they were active in Louisiana, Alabama, and Texas. They mustered out at Brownsville, Texas, August 5, 1865.

They lost 22 men to wounds and 237 to disease.

Twenty-Eighth Wisconsin Infantry

In the letters, most mentions of the Twenty-Eighth Wisconsin Infantry are due to Company C of that regiment being mostly boys from Summit and Oconomowoc. Oconomowoc's postmaster, Thomas Stevens, had helped to recruit the company in 1861 and served as its captain.

The "Roster of Wisconsin Volunteers" gives this short history of the regiment:

> The 28th Wisconsin Infantry was organized at Camp Washburn in Milwaukee and mustered into service on October 14, 1862. It left Wisconsin for Columbus, Kentucky, on December 2, 1862, and then traveled to Helena, Arkansas. The regiment's service took it through Kentucky, Arkansas, Alabama, Louisiana, and Texas. It participated in the campaign against Mobile and its defenses, the sieges of Spanish Fort and Fort Blakely, and the assault and capture of Fort Blakely. The regiment mustered out of active military service August 23, 1865. The regiment lost 240 men during service. One officer and 12 enlisted men were killed. Six officers and 221 enlisted men died from disease.

Thirtieth Wisconsin Infantry

The Thirtieth Wisconsin Infantry was in Camp Randall at the same time as Gilbert and was mentioned in his letters of November 27 and December 17.

The "Roster of Wisconsin Volunteers" gives this short history of the regiment:

The 30th Wisconsin Infantry was organized at Camp Randall in Madison and mustered into service on October 21, 1862. The regiment was detailed to duty at Green Bay and other points in Wisconsin to enforce the draft until March 1863. In that month, the various companies were split on duties ranging from guard boat and supply duty for Sully's Northwestern Indian Expedition up the Missouri River, to draft enforcement across Wisconsin, to fort construction and fort duty. The balance of the regiment eventually came to Kentucky by mid-1864 or early 1865 and was assigned to the 2nd Brigade, 2nd Division, Military District of Kentucky. It primarily served on provost duty there and conducted prisoners to various points. The regiment mustered out on September 20, 1865, after it had lost 69 men. Two enlisted men were killed. Two officers and 65 enlisted men died from disease.

Thirty-First Wisconsin Infantry

The Thirty-First Wisconsin Regiment was mustered in piecemeal between October 1862 and January 1863. The men left Wisconsin for Columbus, Kentucky, on March 1, 1863, and did guard duty there until late September.

They continued mostly on guard duty at various places until they took part in the siege and occupation of Atlanta—Sherman's famous "March to the Sea"—and the siege of Savannah. After that, their duty was in North Carolina until the end of the war.

They were mustered out in two lots in June and July 1865, having lost twenty-three men to wounds and eighty-nine to disease.

Thirty-Fourth Wisconsin Infantry

The Wisconsin Thirty-Fourth was Gilbert's regiment. The regiment was organized at Camp Washburn in Milwaukee and then moved to Camp Randall in Madison. They were mustered in December 31, 1862, and left the state January 31, 1863.

On February 2, the Thirty-Fourth arrived at Columbus, Kentucky, where it was attached to the District of Columbus, Kentucky, Sixth Division, Sixteenth Army Corps, Department of the Tennessee. At Columbus, the regiment performed camp and guard duties at Fort Halleck. On March 3, Company E was ordered to Paducah, Kentucky, and on April 25, Companies I and G were sent to Cairo, Illinois. On April 27, Company A, Gilbert's company, was detached and ordered to duty at Fort Quinby, three-quarters of a mile south of Fort Halleck; and on May 12, Companies B, C, D, F, H, and K were sent to Memphis, Tennessee. On May 11, Brigadier General Asboth, in command of the troops at Columbus, wrote to Major General Stephen A. Hurlbut, commander of the entire Sixteenth Army Corps. He was justifying sending members of Gilbert's regiment, the Thirty-Fourth, to man artillery in four different locations. "The thirty-fourth Regiment Wisconsin Infantry has done heavy artillery duty, and is well drilled in that service." On June 1, Companies I and G returned from Cairo to Columbus; and on August 14, the several detachments of the regiment united at Cairo. On August 16 the entire regiment headed back to Wisconsin.

The regiment was mustered out at Milwaukee, September 8, 1863. Its original strength was 961. Loss by death was somewhere around 20; desertion, 283; discharge, 186. The total mustered out was 472.

REGIMENTAL HISTORIES—OTHER STATES

First Ohio Regiment of Heavy Artillery

On June 29, Esther wrote that her brother John had enlisted in the First Ohio Heavy Artillery. He stayed with that regiment for the rest of the war.

The regiment began as the 117th Ohio Volunteer Infantry on September 15, 1862; however, by the time that John enlisted, it had changed its designation to First Heavy Artillery (on May 2, 1863) and was serving in north central Kentucky. The group constructed fortifications around Covington and Newport, Kentucky, just across the Ohio River from Cincinnati, Ohio, and about 350 miles northeast of Columbus, Kentucky, where Gilbert was stationed.[5]

For most of the remainder of the war, the regiment was on guard duty in Kentucky and Tennessee. It was part of Stoneman's Campaign in southwest Virginia and western North Carolina from February to April 1865 and finally mustered out in July 1865.

Second Tennessee Regiment Heavy Artillery (African Descent)

On July 25, Gilbert wrote that part of the Second Tennessee Negro Regiment was going to man the guns at his fort when they left.

The Second Tennessee Heavy Artillery Regiment (African Descent) was organized at Columbus, Kentucky, in June 1863. In April 1864, they were designated the Fourth United States Colored Heavy Artillery Regiment. Most of their time until June 1865 was spent in garrison duty at Fort Halleck in Columbus. They were then moved to Arkansas where they did garrison duty at Pine Bluff until February 1866 when they were mustered out.

Third Minnesota Infantry Regiment

The Third Minnesota Infantry Regiment was mentioned in Gilbert's letter of March 12. It was part of the force sent to retake Fort Henry and Fort Heiman from the Rebels.

The regiment was mustered in by companies at Fort Snelling, Minnesota, between October 2 and November 14, 1861, and was sent to Kentucky on November 14, 1861. It remained on garrison duty in Kentucky and Tennessee until most of the men were captured by Nathan Bedford Forrest at Murfreesboro, Tennessee, on July 13, 1862. The regiment was formally exchanged on August 27, 1862, and moved home to Minnesota, where it participated in the suppression of the Dakota War of 1862.

The regiment moved to Columbus, Kentucky, February 3, 1863. On March 12, they took part in an expedition to Fort Heiman, and stayed there until June 2. They then returned to Columbus and went on to Vicksburg where they took part in the siege until it ended July 4. They also took part in the capture of Little Rock, Arkansas, on September 10, 1863, and stayed there until April of 1864.

The Third Minnesota Infantry was discharged from service at Fort Snelling on September 16, 1865. Their losses included 17 enlisted men who were killed in action or who later died of their wounds, and 4 officers and 275 enlisted men who died of disease, for a total of 296 fatalities.

Fourth Missouri Cavalry Regiment

On April 25, Gilbert wrote, "I witnessed a battalion drill of the 4th Missouri Regiment of cavalry that was a splendid sight. I wish that the boys could have seen it. It seemed like magic to witness the various evolutions that a thousand horsemen in a body can go through and have every change in harmony throughout the whole." He mentioned the regiment again on July 10 in connection with the skirmish near Lexington, Kentucky, and on July 18 and 26 after two companies of the regiment were captured by some of Forrest's band.

Organized February 1862 by consolidation of the Fremont Hussars and three companies of the Hollan Horse, the Fourth Missouri Cavalry Regiment served mostly in Kentucky, Missouri, and Arkansas until they were mustered out November 13, 1865. They were part of Curtis's campaign in Missouri and Arkansas from January to April 1862. This included battles at Pea Ridge, Arkansas; Fox Creek, Missouri; and Mountain Grove, Missouri. From July until October 1862, they occupied Helena, Arkansas. Company C of the regiment took part in the battles of Iuka and Corinth in Mississippi during this time.

All but Company F moved to Columbus, Kentucky, in April 1863 and had duty there until January 1864. Six companies were then sent against Marmaduke's expedition into Missouri on April 27. Meanwhile, Company F soldiers were in Mississippi and remained there through the siege of Vicksburg, in which they took part from May 18 through July 4, 1863. In addition, a detachment fought in the skirmish near Lexington, Tennessee, on June 29, 1863. That was mentioned in Gilbert's July 10 letter. Companies C and E were at Union City, Tennessee, July 10 of that year. Others were present at the occupation of Hickman, Kentucky, July 15–16, 1863.

During much of 1864, the Fourth Missouri Cavalry Regiment continued operations in Mississippi, Tennessee, and Missouri. From December 21, 1864, until January 15, 1865, they were part of Grierson's expedition to destroy the Mobile & Ohio Railroad. After that they were at Memphis, Tennessee, and along the Memphis & Charleston Railroad until June 1865. In the summer of 1865 the Fourth Missouri Cavalry moved to Louisiana, then to Texas where they finished their service with garrison duty at San Antonio and scouting along the Rio Grande. They were mustered out November 13, 1865.

During service, the regiment lost 4 officers and 56 enlisted men who were killed immediately or mortally wounded, and 6 officers and 177 enlisted men who died from disease.

Ninth Indiana Battery

Gilbert mentioned the Ninth Indiana Battery in his July 18 letter as part of the group that had gone to a newly established post at Clinton, Kentucky.

This battery was organized at Indianapolis, Indiana, in December 1861 and mustered in December 20. Owing to informalities in the original muster, the battery was remustered into service on February 25. On March 27, the group moved to Crump's Landing on the Tennessee River and joined General Lew Wallace's division, with which it reached the battlefield of Shiloh just at the close of the first day's battle. The battery was also part of Grant's Mississippi Campaign, including the siege at Corinth, Mississippi.

The Ninth was at Columbus, Kentucky, from March until July 10, 1863. During that time, the men took part in the expedition to Cape Girardeau from April 29 to May 4. They moved to Clinton, Kentucky. After that they had various duties in Tennessee, Mississippi, Missouri, Arkansas, and Kentucky, and took part in the Battles of Pleasant Hill and Nashville. From Tennessee they were ordered to Indiana on January 25, 1865, but were blown up on the steamer *Eclypse* at Johnsonville on January 27. Out of seventy officers and men, only ten escaped unhurt.

The Ninth Indiana Battery was mustered out June 25, 1865. During their service, sixty-one men died: six enlisted men being killed immediately or mortally wounded and fifty-five dying of disease.

Fifteenth Kentucky Cavalry Regiment

In his letter of July 10, Gilbert mentions that the Fifteenth Kentucky Cavalry wass part of the skirmish near Lexington, Kentucky, which occurred when a scouting expedition was ambushed.

The Fifteenth Kentucky Cavalry Regiment was organized at Owensborough, Kentucky, in October 1862. They served in the Union army for one year, the entire time in the District of Columbus, Kentucky. They took part in scouting expeditions and expeditions in pursuit of Biffle's, Forest's, and Newsome's Confederate cavalry.

The Fifteenth was mustered out beginning on October 6, 1863, and ending on October 29, 1863. During their year of service, the group lost fifty-eight men: one officer and two enlisted men were immediately killed or mortally wounded, and one officer and fifty-four enlisted men died from disease.

Twenty-First Missouri Infantry Regiment

On May 11, Gilbert said that the Twenty-First Illinois Regiment was going to Memphis. He must have meant the Twenty-First Missouri Infantry Regiment. The Twenty-First Illinois Regiment was in Murfreesboro, Tennessee, more than a hundred miles away, but the Twenty-First Missouri was in Columbus, Kentucky, and on their way to Memphis, Tennessee.

The Twenty-First Missouri Infantry Regiment was organized February 1, 1862, from First and Second Northeast Regiments within the Missouri Infantry. They took part in the Battle of Shiloh, the Siege of Corinth, the Battle of Iuka, and the Battle of Corinth in their first eleven months of service. In January 1863, they came to Columbus, where they stayed until they were moved to Memphis on May 11, 1863.

The regiment mustered out April 19, 1866. During their service, the regiment lost 2 officers and 68 enlisted men who were killed immediately or mortally wounded, and 5 officers and 234 enlisted men who died from disease, for a total of 309.

Twenty-Fourth Missouri Infantry Regiment

Gilbert mentioned the Twenty-Fourth Missouri Infantry Regiment in his July 18 letter as part of the group that had gone from New Madrid, Missouri, to a newly established post at Clinton, Kentucky.

The Twenty-Fourth Missouri Infantry Regiment was organized from October through December 1861. In 1862, they were in the Battle of Pea Ridge in Arkansas. They were in the District of Columbus, Kentucky, from June 1863 until January 1864. From March through May 1864 they took part in the Red River Campaign, including the occupation of Alexandria and the Battle of Pleasant Hill. Later in the year they pursued Price through Arkansas and Missouri; and were in the Battles of Franklin and Nashville. Companies E, F, and K were detached early in the war and had different service for much of the war.

The Twenty-Fourth were mustered out beginning in October 1864 and ending on February 1, 1865. During their service, the regiment lost 264 men: 3 officers and 40 enlisted men were killed immediately or mortally wounded, and 1 officer and 220 enlisted men died from disease.

101st Illinois Infantry Regiment

Gilbert mentioned the 101st Illinois Infantry Regiment in his July 18 letter as part of the group that had gone from Columbus, Kentucky, to a newly established post at Clinton, Kentucky. In his letter of July 21, he also said that a cap box he had sent home had been left behind by a member of the 101st Illinois. It was during a time when the separate companies of the 101st were doing different things. Part of the regiment was in Columbus from July 11 until August 21.

The 101st Illinois Infantry Regiment was organized at Jacksonville, Illinois, and mustered into the Union army on September 2, 1862. In December of that year, the men of that regiment were captured at Holly Springs, Mississippi, and were prisoners until June 1863. There followed a time when each company of the 101st had its separate history of scouts, skirmishes, and expeditions, up and down the Mississippi and its tributary streams. In October 1863, the captured companies having been exchanged and the regiment reunited, the 101st marched to the front. In the days and months that followed, the 101st took part in the Battles of Wauhatchie, Chattanooga, Resaca, New Hope Church, and Peachtree Creek. In January 1865, the regiment crossed the Savannah River and went through the great campaign of the Carolinas, participating in the Battles of Averasboro and Bentonville. On June 7, 1865, the 101st was mustered out at Bladensburg, Maryland, and returned to Springfield, Illinois.

During their service, the 101st Illinois Infantry Regiment lost a total of 169 men: 3 officers and 47 enlisted men were killed immediately or mortally wounded, and 1 officer and 118 enlisted men died from disease.

111th Illinois Infantry Regiment

Gilbert first mentioned the 111th Illinois Regiment in his letter of February 7, 1863, just a few days after he arrived in Kentucky. The regiment was also mentioned in his letters of March 12 and March 23.

Columbus, Kentucky, was the first post of the 111th after their two weeks of training at Camp Marshall in Salem, Illinois. They were in Columbus from November 1, 1862, until March 12, 1863, when they moved to nearby Fort Heiman, and May 28 to Paducah, Kentucky. The regiment took part in the Atlanta Campaign from May to September 1864. This included battles at Resaca, Dallas, New Hope Church, Allatoona Hills, Atlanta, and Jonesboro, as well as the siege of Atlanta. They marched with Sherman from Atlanta to the sea, and took part in the Siege of Savannah. Then from January to April 1865, they took part in the Campaign of the Carolinas, including the Battle of Bentonville. They were mustered out June 7 and discharged in Springfield, Illinois, June 27, 1865.

Of the 886 officers and enlisted men they started with, the 111th lost 82 to battle and 168 to disease.

NOTES

1. Information about military recruitment is from the letters of Gilbert and Esther Claflin and "Civil War Draft in Wisconsin." The War Department's General Orders No. 191 is from Ainsworth and Kirkley, *War of the Rebellion*, 414–16.

2. Information about military men is from the letters of Gilbert and Esther Claflin; federal censuses from 1850 to 1880; Scott, *War of the Rebellion*; "Roster of Wisconsin Volunteers"; and Quiner, *Military History of Wisconsin*—these last two sources are easily accessible through the Wisconsin Historical Society's website at http://www.wisconsinhistory.org/civilwar/regiments.asp.

3. Sources for information about the military actions, including the official correspondence, are Scott, *War of the Rebellion*, vols. 7, 22, and 23; Boatner, *Civil War Dictionary*; and Long, *Civil War Day by Day*.

4. Information on regimental histories from Wisconsin is from the letters of Esther and Gilbert Claflin as well as "Roster of Wisconsin Volunteers" and Quiner, *Military History of Wisconsin* (both online at Wisconsin Historical Society's website). Other useful resources include Dyer, *Compendium of the War of the Rebellion*, and Scott, *War of the Rebellion*, vols. 22 and 24.

5. Information on regimental histories from other states is from the letters of Esther and Gilbert Claflin and Dyer, *Compendium of the War of the Rebellion*.

Transcribing and Editing

I did not change any of Gilbert's and Esther's language. Colloquial expressions such as "overhalls" and phrases used repeatedly such as "first rate," "prospects," and "to enjoy each other's society" give a feeling of the way they spoke. I did, however, make some changes to spelling and capitalization and I added paragraph breaks to make their letters more easily accessible to the general reader.

Both Gilbert and Esther sometimes open a letter by writing "Dear" (either at the left or in the middle of the top line) and then starting the body of the letter with the name. Other times they put the salutation as part of the body. I have changed each of these to a salutation of "Dear Gilbert" or "Dear Esther" at the beginning of the line before the body. I have added the comma in most of the salutations. Both Gilbert and Esther sometimes put the addressee's name after the closing. For example, "Yours truly, Esther" would have "Gilbert" written on the following line. I edited these out.

I have standardized the dates to the form of "January 1, 1863." If a letter is undated but I could determine the date from context, I put the date in brackets (e.g., [January 1, 1863] or [probably January 1, 1863]). Gilbert's letters were sometimes dated in variations of the form "J 11/63." If the day of the week is included in the date, I include it, spelling it out if it is abbreviated. Both Esther and Gilbert occasionally added "th" after the date (e.g., Jan 27th 1863). However, they often left it off if a date was given in the letter without the month or year (e.g., "the afternoon of that day, the 25" I changed to "the afternoon of that day, the 25th").

Throughout the letters, I have changed many words ending in "-eing" to "-ing" (such as "making," "taking," "coming," "judging").

Esther occasionally repeats a word or a phrase, which I have edited out. For example, "Last Monday the boys the boys fixed up the stables and made a door to go out of the barn into the shed" becomes "Last Monday the boys fixed up the stables and made a door to go out of the barn into the shed."

In Esther's letters, I have changed "brot" to "brought"; "reg." and "regs" to "regiment" and "regiments"; "Conn" to "Connecticut"; "Tenn" to "Tennessee"; "privaliges" to "privileges"; "com" to "commanded"; "wed" to "weeded."

Though Gilbert rarely capitalized the beginning of a sentence, he did capitalize many words within his sentences. The following words would be capitalized wherever they appeared in the letters: Boys, Camp, His, Headquarters, Gun, Steamer, River, Picket, Fort, Prison, Our, Orchard, Soldier, Officer, Captain, Idea, and many others.

In Gilbert's money notations, I have added the "$," which he rarely included, and I have changed his usual comma to a period. Thus "19,05" becomes "$19.05."

In Gilbert's references to the various regiments, I have spelled out the state and added a suffix after the numeral, which he does only rarely. Thus "25 Ill" becomes "25th Illinois."

In Gilbert's letters, I have added breaks between sentences and paragraphs. I've added punctuation and changed spellings and capitalization to make the letters more readable.

Here is an excerpt from his letter of November 27, 1862, as originally transcribed (two pages from the original letter are reproduced below):

. . . degree of earnestness was manifest I do not spend my evenings in
Barracks but in the tent of the Chaplan or at the Quater-Master department
Liut Certs of the 30th having charge. We are going to start a Prayr meeting
if we can get a room I am sorry I could not be at home to day and have a
Thanksgiving dinner with You But I trust I am thankfull that Gods mercy
and care has been towards us thus far and I can trust Him still I have
been appointed to draw rations For the Waukesha Militia All I have to do is
is to get and present the order and detail the men to get that which I order
in the Provision line I hope you will not shut your self up at home bcause I
am gone but improve every oppertunity you can viseting You must till
Anna not to get the blues because James is sick as it will not help Him a
great deal I should have been very glad to have seen Her So far as a
Substitute is concerned I do not care but little about one on my part
There are pleant of them here in camp and if the draft that is ordered is
made Their will be more substitutes than ther is that want them 200 is the
highest that is offered Thin it is a question if I got a substitute whither I
would not be liable to another draft which will probably be soon Captain
Stone said if I wanted any money He would let me have all I wanted to get
a substitute Perhaps you had better get some money of Mr Eastman or
speek to Him a bout it so as to be sure of it. If I do not get back before the
Taxes are called for get Him to pay them I gues we shall want 15 or 20
dollars The Boys had better take some boards and fix up the shed so that
the cattle can not get under the shed where the sheep go leaving a place for
them to go out

Here is the same excerpt as edited:

. . . degree of earnestness was manifest.

I do not spend my evenings in Barracks, but in the tent of the chaplain or at the quartermaster department Lieutenant Curtice of the 30th having charge. We are going to start a prayer meeting if we can get a room.

I am sorry I could not be at home to day and have a Thanksgiving dinner with you, but I trust I am thankful that God's mercy and care has been towards us thus far and I can trust Him still.

I have been appointed to draw rations for the Waukesha Militia. All I have to do is to get and present the order and detail the men to get that which I order in the provision line

I hope you will not shut yourself up at home because I am gone but improve every opportunity you can visiting.

You must tell Anna not to get the blues because James is sick, as it will not help him a great deal. I should have been very glad to have seen her.

So far as a substitute is concerned I do not care but little about one on my part. There are plenty of them here in camp, and if the draft that is ordered is made there will be more substitutes than there is [those] that want them. $200 is the highest that is offered. Then it is a question, if I got a substitute, whether I would not be liable to another draft, which will probably be soon. Captain Stone said if I wanted any money, he would let me have all I wanted to get a substitute.

Perhaps you had better get some money of Mr. Eastman or speak to him about it so as to be sure of it. If I do not get back before the taxes are called for, get him to pay them. I guess we shall want 15 or 20 dollars.

The boys had better take some boards and fix up the shed so that the cattle cannot get under the shed where the sheep go, leaving a place for them to go out.

degree of earnestness was manifest
I do not spend my evenings in
Barracks but in the tent of the
Chaplain or at the Quarter-Master
department Lieut Curtis of the
30th having charge. We are going
to start a Prayr meeting if
we can get a room I am sorry
I could not be at home to day and
have a Thanksgiving dinner
with you But I trust I am
thankfull that Gods mercy
and care has been towards us
thus far and I can trust Him
still I have been appointed to
draw rations For the Waukesha
Militia All I have to do is
is to get and present the order
and detail the men to get that
which I order in the Provision line
I hope you will not shut yourself
up at home because I am gone but
improve every oppertunity you can

Gilbert's letter, November 27, 1862, pages 3 and 4.

viseting You must tell Anna
not to get the blues because James
is sick as it will not hurt Him a great
deal I should have ban very glad
to have seen Her So far as a
Substitute is conserned I do not
care but little about one on my
part there are pleant of them here
in camp and if the draft that is
ordered is made Then will be more
substetutes than there is that want
them 200 is the highest that is
offered Then it is a yuestion if I
got a substitute whether I would
not be leable to another draft which
will probably be soon Captain Stone
said if I wanted any money He
would let me have all I wanted
to get a substitute Perhaps you had
better get some Money of Mr Eastman
or speck to Him a bout it so as to
be sure of it If I do not get back
before the Taxes are called for get Him
to pay them I gues we shall want
150 or 60 dollars The Boys had better
take some boards and fix up the
shed so that the cattle can not get
under the shed where the sheep go
leaveing a place for them to go out

Although I did not change spellings that give a feeling for the way the Claflins would have spoke, I did make some changes that should make the letters easier to read.

Original spelling:	I changed it to:
ake	ache
allowes	allows
a long	along
ambushcade	ambuscade
an other	another
any thing	anything
antisipations	anticipations
aparant	apparent
apetite	appetite
arriveing	arriving
artilery	artillery
asshure	assure
attact	attack
Col. Attley	Colonel Utley
atacted, attaked	attacked
baithing	bathing
beautifull	beautiful
beuty	beauty
begining	beginning
blew	bloom
bloussems	blossoms
bord	board
bondfires	bonfires
borough	borrow
box cars	boxcars
brest	breast
brestworks	breastworks
brot	brought
Caro	Cairo
camphur	camphor
can not	cannot
cantean	canteen
carefull	careful
cartg(s)	cartridge(s)
caut	caught
selibration	celebration
chainged	changed
chere	cheer

Original spelling:	I changed it to:
cherefull	cheerful
choise	choice
chronick	chronic
citizn	citizen
clere	clear
cloths	clothes
col	cool
commense(d)	commence(d)
comesary, commisary	commissary
complaneing	complaining
conveyence	conveyance
cort	court
cuped	cupped
croud	crowd
deaper	deeper
defeted	defeated
dispare, despare	despair
detatched	detached
devolveing	devolving
diferent	different
digins	diggings
diner	dinner
discorse	discourse
disgrase	disgrace
domesticks	domestics
drest	dressed
driling	drilling
droped	dropped
drownded	drowned
extacies	ecstasies
affect	effect
eliments	elements
immaciated	emaciated
imbrase	embrace
inclosed	enclosed
endereing	endearing
inforced	enforced
engrosed	engrossed
ernest	earnest
evle	evil
expecially	especially
exersise	exercise

Original spelling:	I changed it to:
expens	expense
fartherest	farthest
favorit	favorite
fere	fear
fether	feather
feleing	feeling
fens(es), fensces	fence(s)
firefull	fearful
fetures	features
fiting	fitting
floting	floating
formaly	formerly
foreward	forward
Frederickburg	Fredericksburg
galvanick	galvanic
geather	gather
goosberries	gooseberries
grone(s)	groan(s)
grogeries	groggeries
guard house	guardhouse
growes	grows
gurrilla	guerrilla
gues	guess
happyest	happiest
hapily	happily
head quarters	headquarters
hereing	hearing
hors	horse
hosp, hospit, hospitall	hospital
hurtfull	hurtful
emgination, immagination	imagination
amediate(ly)	immediate(ly)
undefineable	indefinable
indeferible	indivertible
indusing	inducing
inexpressable	inexpressible
insain	insane
intelectual	intellectual
inteligence	intelligence
irens	irons
ishued	issued
interes	interest

Original spelling:	I changed it to:
napsack	knapsack
nee	knee
nocked	knocked
now, no	know
laboured	labored
lattitude	latitude
leasure	leisure
loded	loaded
lope holes	loopholes
lovliest	loveliest
lunges	lungs
magick	magic
Manas	Manassas
mentime, menetime	meantime
midle	middle
mindes	minds
myssails	missiles
morel	moral
musquitoes	mosquitoes
morners	mourners
morter	mortar
narra	narrow
nere(d)	near(ed)
Negrow(es)	Negro(es)
newes	news
oald	old
wonce	once
onely	only
oposite	opposite
aught	ought
out doors	outdoors
pase	pace
peticular	particular
pattent	patent
pay day	payday
pay roles	payrolls
penetance	penitence
permanent, permenant	permanent
pickett	picket
pickeled	pickled
plesent	pleasant
plentifull	plentiful

Original spelling:	I changed it to:
plumbs	plums
popler	poplar
post marked	postmarked
Prattice	practice
prepaired	prepared
prevalege(s)	privilege(s)
proceded	proceeded
proclimation	proclamation
promice	promise
persued	pursued
quarter master	quartermaster
quarie	query
radians	radiance
rapped(ly), rappid(ly)	rapid(ly)
readally	readily
rediness	readiness
rere	rear
reckord	record
redused	reduced
referance	reference
refered	referred
aquired	required
riped	ripped
roaps	ropes
rockey	rocky
ro	rosin
sassafrass	sassafras
Saviour	Savior
scarrify	scarify
sentterny	sedentary
sentinal	sentinel
sergent	sergeant
seperation	separation
shere	shear
sheat	sheet
shiping	shipping
sholder, sholdier	shoulder
shuks	shucks
siting	sitting
small pox	smallpox
sollemn	solemn

Original spelling:	I changed it to:
sope(suds)	soap(suds)
speek(s), speake	speak(s)
speker	speaker
spirt(s)	spirit(s)
spolk	spoke
spred	spread
stand point	standpoint
stm	steam
str, steemer	steamer
stur	stir
stocade	stockade
stoped	stopped
succeded	succeeded
sufferg	suffering
sute	suit
shure	sure
swet	sweat
tal	tallow
terable	terrible
thankfull	thankful
tho	though
thot, thougt	thought
thoughtfull	thoughtful
thretten(s)(ed)	threaten(s)(ed)
through	throw
till	'til
to day	today
tomorrough, to morrough	tomorrow
to night	tonight
trator	traitor
trid	tried
turkies	turkeys
2	twice
cundultivated	uncultivated
verry	very
VicBurge, Vixburge, vicksBurge	Vicksburg
waggon	wagon
wate(d)(ing)	wait(ed)(ing)
waters	waiters
wallnuts	walnuts
weads	weeds

Original spelling:	I changed it to:
were, ware	wear
wareing	wearing
welfair	welfare
wholely	wholly
home	whom
winddow	window
wrks	works
worne	worn
rapper	wrapper
rong	wrong
yeald	yield
yoak	yoke

Gilbert uses homonyms inconsistently in his letters, and I have tried to correct these as follows:

Word in letter:	I changed to:
brake	break
bred	bread
but	butt
by	buy
flower	flour
here	hear
herd	heard
whole	hole
pare, pr	pair
pair	pear
peace	piece
plumb	plum
reel	real
write, wright	right
seam	seem
staid	stayed
there	their
their	there
to	too
week	weak
would	wood
rote	wrote

.

Gilbert uses many abbreviations, which I have spelled out as follows:

Abbreviation:	I changed it to:
adgt	adjutant
bbl, bbb	barrel(s)
be	beeswax
bet	better
cap, capt	captain
cartg(s)	cartridge(s)
cavl, cav.	cavalry
cts	cents
co, com, or comp	company, companies
corp(s)	corporal(s)
co	county
cwt	one hundred pounds
dol	dollar
ft	feet
gov	government
hosp	hospital
Ill, Ino	Illinois
Ioa	Iowa
Inft	infantry
Ky	Kentucky
leut(s), lieut	lieutenant(s)
Lou	Louisiana
Mill	Milwaukee
Miss	Mississippi
ME, MO	Missouri
no	number
oc	o'clock
Oc	Oconomowoc
off	official
ord sergt	orderly sergeant
pr	pair
PA	Pennsylvania
p. office, p.o.	post office
r.berries	raspberries
recd	received
rgt	regiment
regs	regulars
Rev	Reverend
ro	rosin

Abbreviation:	I changed it to:
SS	Sabbath school
sch	school
stm	steam
str	steamer
tal	tallow
Ten, Tenn	Tennessee
3 min	3rd Minnesota
traps	trappings
Va	Virginia
Wm, Wim	William
Wis	Wisconsin
wrks	works

Bibliography

Ainsworth, Fred C., and Joseph W. Kirkley. *The War of the Rebellion: A Compilation of the Official Records of the Union and Confederate Armies.* Correspondence, Orders, etc., from January 1, 1863–December 30, 1863, vol. 3, no. 3. Washington, DC: Government Printing Office, 1899.

Atlas of Waukesha Co., Wisconsin: Drawn from Actual Surveys and the County Records to Which Is Added a Rail Road & Sectional Map of the State of Wisconsin. Madison, WI: Harrison and Warner, 1873.

Barquist, Barbara, and David Barquist. *Oconomowoc: Barons to Bootleggers.* Oconomowoc, WI: Leitzke IV Printing, 1999.

Barquist, Barbara, and David Barquist. *The Summit of Oconomowoc: 150 Years of Summit Town.* Oconomowoc, WI: Summit History Group, 1987.

Basler, Roy P. *The Collected Works of Abraham Lincoln.* Springfield, IL: Abraham Lincoln Association, 1953.

Battle, J. H., William Henry Perrin, and G. C. Kniffin. *Kentucky: A History of the State, Part II; Histories and Biographies of Ballard, Calloway, Fulton, Graves, Hickman, McCracken and Marshall Counties, Kentucky.* Louisville, KY: F. A. Battey Publishing, 1885.

Behling, Ruth W. *The Story of the Founder of Oconomowoc or More Than You Ever Wanted to Know about John S. Rockwell.* Oconomowoc, WI: Oconomowoc Historical Society, 1998.

Boatner, Mark Mayo, III. *The Civil War Dictionary*, revised edition. New York: David McKay, 1959.

Booth, Martin. *Opium: A History.* New York: St. Martin's Press, 1996.

Bragg, Marion. *Historic Names and Places on the Lower Mississippi River.* Vicksburg: Mississippi River Commission, 1977.

"Capt. Thomas N. Stevens." [In the booklet commemorating the 28th Regiment's 11th Reunion on 21–22 June 1893 at Mukwonago, Wisconsin.] Twenty-Eighth

Wisconsin Volunteer Infantry. Last modified March 20, 2013. http://www.28th wisconsin.com/veterans/tstevens.html.

Channick, Herbert. "Boz in Egypt." [First published in *Illinois Heritage*, Illinois State Historical Society, July–August 2007.] David Perdue's Charles Dickens Page. http://charlesdickenspage.com/boz_in_egypt.html.

"Civil War Draft in Wisconsin." Wisconsin Historical Society. http://www.wiscon sinhistory.org/teachers/lessons/civilwar/draft/pdf/draft_final.pdf, accessed May 25, 2013.

"Civil War Pension Index: General Index to Pension Files, 1861–1934." Ancestry .com. http://search.ancestry.com/search/db.aspx?dbid=4654, accessed May 25, 2013.

Denney, Robert E. *The Civil War Years: A Day-by-Day Chronicle of the Life of a Nation*. New York: Sterling Publishing, 1992.

Dictionary of American Regional English. Edited by Frederic G. Cassidy, Joan Hous-ton Hall, and Luanne Von Schneidemesser. 6 vols. Cambridge, MA: Belknap Press of Harvard University Press, 1985–2012.

"Dictionary of Wisconsin History." Wisconsin Historical Society. http://www.wis consinhistory.org/dictionary/, accessed May 26, 2013.

Dyer, Frederick H. *A Compendium of the War of the Rebellion*, vol. 1. Des Moines, IA: Dyer Publishing, 1908.

Ellison, David. "The Civil War Draft in Plover and Stevens Point: A Study in Efforts, Attitudes, Frustrations, and Results." Portage County Historical Society of Wis-consin. http://www.pchswi.org/archives/misc/cwdraft.html, accessed May 26, 2013.

Fortney, Robert M. "The Participation of the Twenty-Fifth Regiment Infantry Wis-consin Volunteers in the Civil War." Seminar Paper, University of Wisconsin–La Crosse, December 1976. http://digital.library.wisc.edu/1793/28941, accessed May 26, 2013.

Hall, B. Clarence, and Clyde Thornton Wood. *Big Muddy: A Journey to America's Heartland*. New York: Dutton-Penguin Books, 1992.

Harrison, Lowell H. *The Civil War in Kentucky*. Lexington: University Press of Ken-tucky, 1975.

Hodgson, Barbara. *In the Arms of Morpheus*. Buffalo, NY: Firefly Books, 2001.

Howard, Benjamin C. "A Report of the Decision of the Supreme Court of the United States, and the Opinions of the Judges Thereof, in the Case of Dred Scott versus John F. A. Sanford." *The North American Review* 85, no. 177 (October 1857): 392–415.

Johnson, Jean Lindsay. *Illustrious Oconomowoc*. Oconomowoc, WI: Franklin Pub-lishers, 1977.

Johnson, Rossiter. *Campfire and Battlefield*. 1894. Reprint, New York: Fairfax Press, 1978.

Long, E. B., with Barbara Long. *The Civil War Day by Day: An Almanac, 1861–1865*. New York: Doubleday, 1971.

Mattern, Carolyn J. *Soldiers When They Go: The Story of Camp Randall, 1861–1865.* Madison: The State Historical Society of Wisconsin, 1981.

McPherson, Edward. *The Political History of the United States of America during the Great Rebellion.* Washington, DC: Philp & Solomons, 1865.

"9th Indiana Light Battery in the American Civil War." Civil War Index. http://www.civilwarindex.com/armyin/9th_in_light_battery.html, accessed May 25, 2013.

"19th-Century Immigration." Wisconsin Historical Society. http://www.wisconsinhistory.org/turningpoints/tp-018/?action=more_essay, accessed May 25, 2013.

Nolan, Libbie. "Oconomowoc Cavalry Guards." *Landmark* 25, no. 1. Waukesha, WI: Waukesha County Historical Society, 1982.

Nosworthy, Brent. *The Bloody Crucible of Courage: Fighting Methods and Combat Experience of the Civil War.* New York: Carroll & Graf, 2003.

Oconomowoc. Oconomowoc, WI: The League of Women Voters of Oconomowoc, 1969.

Potter, Sandra Leitzke, Jane Leitzke Punko, and William H. Leitzke. *Historic Oconomowoc, Wis.* Oconomowoc, WI: Leitzke IV Printing, 1993.

Pritchard, Russ A., Jr. *Civil War Weapons and Equipment.* Guildford, CT: Lyons Press, 2003.

Quiner, E. B. *The Military History of Wisconsin: A Record of the Civil and Military Patriotism of the State, in the War for the Union, with a History of the Campaigns in Which Wisconsin Soldiers Have Been Conspicuous—Regimental Histories—Sketches of Distinguished Officers—the Roll of the Illustrious Dead—Movements of the Legislature and State Officers, Etc.* Chicago: Clarke, 1866.

Reiss, Oscar. *Medicine in Colonial America.* New York: University Press of America, 2000.

Rockwell, John S. *The Questers' Guide to Historic Oconomowoc.* Oconomowoc, WI: The Questers, 1990.

"Roster of Wisconsin Volunteers, War of the Rebellion, 1861–1865." Wisconsin Historical Society. http://www.wisconsinhistory.org/roster, accessed May 25, 2013.

Scott, Robert N. *The War of the Rebellion: A Compilation of the Official Records of the Union and Confederate Armies.* Series 1. Vol. 7, pt. 2, *Correspondence.* Vol. 12, pt. 1, *Reports.* Vol. 22, pt. 1, *Reports,* and pt. 2, *Correspondence.* Vol. 23, pt. 1, *Reports,* and pt. 2, *Correspondence.* Vol. 24, pt. 1, *Reports,* and pt. 3, *Correspondence, Etc.* Vol. 52, pt. 2, *Correspondence.* Washington, DC: Government Printing Office, 1889.

Sifakis, Stewart. *Who Was Who in the Civil War.* New York: Facts on File, 1988.

Thompson, Holland. "The Provost-Marshal and the Citizen (In the American Civil War)." In Francis T. Miller and Robert S. Lanier, eds. *The Photographic History of the Civil War.* Vol. 4, *The Cavalry.* Online at Shotgun's Home of the American Civil War. Last modified February 15, 2002. http://www.civilwarhome.com/ProvostMarshal.htm.

"U.S.–Dakota War of 1862." Minnesota Historical Society. http://www.mnhs.org/library/tips/history_topics/94dakota.html, accessed May 25, 2013.

Vandiver, Frank E. *1001 Things Everyone Should Know about the Civil War*. New York: Doubleday, 1999.

Varhola, Michael J. *Everyday Life during the Civil War*. Cincinnati, OH: Writer's Digest Books, 1999.

Vezzetti, Judy. *Index to Waukesha County, Wisconsin, Marriages, 1846–1907*. Madison: State Historical Society of Wisconsin, 2001.

Washington Past and Present: A History. Edited by John Clagett Proctor. New York: Lewis Historical Publishing Company, 1930.

Waukesha County Land Records from 1839 to 1865. Found in Waukesha Historical Society Archives.

Welcher, Frank J., and Larry G. Ligget. *Coburn's Brigade: The 85th Indiana, 33rd Indiana, 19th Michigan, and 22nd Wisconsin in the Western Civil War*. Carmel: Guild Press of Indiana, 1999.

Wells, Robert W. *Wisconsin in the Civil War*. Milwaukee, WI: Milwaukee Journal, 1962.

Wideman, John C. *Naval Warfare: Courage and Combat on the Water*. New York: Michael Friedman Publishing, 1997.

"Wisconsin in the Civil War, Regiments." Wisconsin Historical Society. http://www.wisconsinhistory.org/civilwar/regiments.asp, accessed May 25, 2013.

"Yazoo Pass Expedition: A Failed Attack on Fort Pemberton, 24 February–5 April 1863." Twenty-Eighth Wisconsin Volunteer Infantry. Last modified March 14, 2013. http://www.28thwisconsin.com/service/yazoo.html.

Index